C000145287

FOREWORD
BY BERNIE ECCLESTONE

 I think you could break this season very comfortably into two halves. That's not January to June and July to now, but the haves and the have nots. We've got Mercedes that has done an incredible job with its power unit and basically dominated. The races it hasn't won it should have won and Red Bull got very lucky with those.

From that point of view, the season has been disappointing. Having said that, there's been good racing down the field.

The reason I was originally campaigning for three races with double points was just in case. If we hadn't been lucky with Nico and Lewis racing each other and one of them had got away and been dominant, the season would have been over by Silverstone.

I thought perhaps Ferrari or Red Bull or one of the other teams would catch up halfway through the season and make up a few points at the end. We've been extremely lucky with what happened, these two guys have been racing each other and it's good that Mercedes has allowed them to do that. If not, we would have had a really lousy championship.

I don't think we could have lived with another Red Bull year, any more than we could have lived with another Schumacher year.

Ricciardo has been a big surprise – I think he was a big surprise for Red Bull. The three races he won, it wasn't a start-to-finish win. If incidents hadn't happened, Red Bull wouldn't have won a race.

I'm a super supporter of Sebastian, but I'm a little bit disappointed with his attitude, which I think has changed. He's acting like a defeated guy and he isn't – that's not his mentality. He's a competitive guy. He doesn't like losing at backgammon. Unfortunately, when he plays me, he does.

Ferrari was very disappointing, getting lost somewhere. Fernando got a little bit like Sebastian halfway through, so I'm a little disappointed in him, too.

The Williams performance was super. I have known Frank for a hundred years and I don't think anybody could wish him more success.

I also have a great respect for Ron Dennis, a lot of time for him. He'll get things sorted out at McLaren. It's good that Honda will be back next year, as it's a good name, and they're racers. Not many manufacturers are what you call racers, and they are.

Finally, I was super-happy with Russia. It did the best job of anybody this year. Unfortunately, it was one of the year's worst races, but what Russia did and the show it put on, was fantastic.

CON

TENTS

TEAM F1

Published in December 2014
A catalogue record for this book is available from the British Library

ISBN 978 0 9575320-6-9

HAYMARKET

Editorial Director, Haymarket Motor Racing
Anthony Rowlinson
Editor Bruce Jones
Chief Contributor Adam Cooper
Contributors Anthony Rowlinson, Edd Straw
Photographs All by LAT (Steven Tee,
Charles Coates, Glenn Dunbar, Alastair Staley,
Steve Etherington, Sam Bloxham, Andrew Ferraro,
Jed Leicester, Will Taylor-Medhurst,
with photograph selection by Zak Mauger).
All imagery © LAT Photographic
Operations Manager LAT Tim Clarke
Illustrations Alan Eldridge
Special Projects Manager Simon Strang
Publishing Manager Sunita Davies
Group Publisher Stuart Williams
Group Director Tim Bulley

F1 Racing Magazine
Haymarket Media Group,
Teddington Studios, Broom Road,
Teddington, Middlesex TW11 9BE, UK
Tel: +44 (0)208 267 5000
Website: www.haymarket.com

ILLUSTRATED LONDON NEWS LTD

Art Director Oliver Campbell
Chief Sub-Editor Samantha Robinson
Sub-Editors Fiona Ferguson, Ian Johns
Client Services Director Tony Long
Group Senior Art Director Grant Turner
Production/Distribution Manager David Gyseman
Production Coordinator Louise Ailish
Partnership Manager David Allard
Finance Director Roger Gallucci
Chief Executive Lisa Barnard

Reprographic: Rhapsody
Printed by: CPI UK,
Croydon, UK

Published in partnership with
Illustrated London News Limited,
46-48 East Smithfield, London EW1 1AW, UK
Tel: +44 (0)20 7426 1010 Fax: +44 (0)20 7426 1020
Website: www.iln.co.uk

haymarket®

THE YEAR

ANTHONY ROWLINSON
EDITORIAL DIRECTOR, HAYMARKET MOTOR RACING

A fter the sound and fury, the laughter, rage, joy and despair, what will we take from the F1 season? A brilliant champion, certainly – one who, after a 19-round head-to-head, prevailed over a rival who forced him to reach higher and dig deeper than ever before.

The wins tally may have favoured Lewis Hamilton post-Abu Dhabi, but the records will also show that Nico Rosberg "did" his vaunted "faster" teammate in qualifying, notching up 11 poles to seven, not to mention five wins, 15 podiums and five fastest laps. So, while Lewis took title spoils on merit and sheer pace, Rosberg delivered an immensely impressive season. It's not always easy to appreciate a classic rivalry unfolding, but the Hamilton versus Rosberg narrative was just that. From Rosberg's immediate 25-point lead in Melbourne as Hamilton retired, to the skulduggery of Monaco, via a nudge too far in Spa, then on to the titanic crescendo in Abu Dhabi, 2014 was a vintage season.

Racing historians will conclude that the right man won, but let's not forget the nervous anticipation felt in the paddock ahead of the decider. For that, huge credit must go to the Mercedes management triumvirate of Niki Lauda, Toto Wolff and Paddy Lowe, who allowed their men to race wheel-to-Advanti-wheel. Going into Abu Dhabi – double points be damned! – either man could have won; more's the pity one of them had to lose.

So, what else from this season to savour? Well, the name "Daniel Ricciardo" was on everyone's lips from the moment he outqualified his quad-champ teammate in Australia and he went on to race like a future champion for the rest of the season. Three brilliant wins, some epic overtakes, combined with a grace and charm outside the cockpit that earned him instant superstar status. A name for next year's season review, without doubt and, who knows, maybe a name for the ages.

Much sadness, too, in a season of extremes. The shocking start, with news that Michael Schumacher had suffered a life-changing accident; then, as we moved towards a conclusion, that terrible afternoon at Suzuka, Jules Bianchi's horror crash and a sport subdued.

These, then, are the abiding memories. Cheers for our heroes. Thoughts, still, with the fallen.

THE
SEASON

THE RULES WERE NEW FOR 2014 AS F1 WELCOMED BACK
TURBOS. ADAM COOPER EXAMINES HOW THE ORDER WAS
SHAKEN UP WITH MERCEDES ADAPTING BEST TO DOMINATE

T he 2014 season represented a brave new world for the FIA F1 World Championship as it entered the turbo power unit era. The hybrid V6s may have been quieter than their predecessors, but there was no ignoring the noise that accompanied them in terms of the ongoing controversy over their introduction.

From the first day of testing to the final race weekend in Abu Dhabi, the debate raged about whether the sport had taken the right direction and, specifically, the fact that one of the three manufacturers had proved so dominant – and that the homologation regulations meant that others could do little about it.

The engineers did their job in creating the new power units, which saw F1 cars running at similar speeds to the previous machinery, while using a third less fuel. The downside was the huge cost associated with their development, and a lack of enthusiasm not just

from a significant element of the public, but also some of the sport's major players, led by Bernie Ecclestone.

Initial testing in Jerez proved so problematic that even the FIA's Charlie Whiting was forced to give serious consideration to what would happen if all cars retired in the opening race. The situation improved quickly, but the noise issue never really went away, and there was a widespread feeling that the power units were far too complex, did little for the show, and that the drivers relied too much on assistance from the pit wall. By the end of the year, Red Bull was calling for a move to a simpler (and louder) twin turbo V6 for 2016 and beyond, with a common ERS system.

The season was saved by the fact that Mercedes employed two hugely talented and immensely competitive drivers and, more importantly, allowed them to race. The fight for the championship between Lewis Hamilton and Nico Rosberg kept fans on their toes all year and was settled only in the closing laps of the Abu Dhabi finale. In the end,

> **"THE BOTTOM LINE WAS THAT MERCEDES WAS BETTER PREPARED THAN ANYONE ELSE FOR THE NEW FORMULA"**

thankfully, double points didn't play a role in the outcome.

The bottom line was that Mercedes was better prepared than anyone else for the new formula. Ross Brawn may have gone from Brackley, but it was the team he had carefully built up that did a superb job to fully embrace the new rules. The key to it was the integration between the chassis and the complex power unit and Mercedes understood earlier than its rivals what was required. Both Ferrari and Renault fumbled the ball.

As a rule, a battle involving rival outfits is always preferable, but an intra-team contest has its own special frisson and Lewis and Nico kept us entertained all year. The only frustration was that technical gremlins cropped up frequently and struck one or the other, spoiling a few races. When they were able to battle hard for a full race distance, we saw some wonderfully intense action. Things came unstuck at Spa, where their collision nearly led to an implosion in the camp, but other than that it was a fair fight between two guys who had known each

Clockwise from far left: Mercedes won the first round, then never looked back, going on to take its first constructors' title; Alonso and Vettel could only give chase; rookie Magnussen was straight into the points for McLaren

other since their karting days, and now found themselves fighting for the highest possible stakes.

In the end, the best man won, a fact that even Rosberg acknowledged – although he was careful to point out that Lewis had an edge only in the races and not qualifying. Indeed, Nico was a revelation in 2014 as he regularly outpaced his teammate when it mattered on Saturdays, and it was Lewis who seemed to feel the pressure. In races, the Briton was often able to turn the tables and he put in some storming performances.

After a crushing run of four World Championships, Red Bull Racing came back to earth in 2014 and its relationship with Renault came under serious strain. Following a disastrous winter of unreliability and little mileage, the team went into Melbourne woefully unprepared. Against the odds, Daniel Ricciardo made the podium, only to be disqualified. Nevertheless the race showed two things: that, once the power unit improved, the RB10 was an excellent car, and that Ricciardo would be a major force.

"AN INTRA-TEAM CONTEST HAS ITS OWN FRISSON AND LEWIS AND NICO KEPT US ENTERTAINED ALL YEAR"

Indeed, the Australian driver's consistently strong form relative to teammate Sebastian Vettel was the biggest surprise of the season, one that even the Red Bull Racing management didn't expect. He hardly put a foot wrong, regularly outqualifying and outracing Vettel, and able to take advantage when Mercedes stumbled. With popular victories in Canada, Hungary and Belgium, he marked himself out as a future title contender.

Vettel hadn't become a chump overnight and, indeed, produced some good performances. However, he struggled to adapt to driving without the extra rear grip he'd enjoyed in previous years, when exhaust-blowing was allowed. He duly decided it was time to move on and in October he told his bosses that he was bound for Ferrari.

The revival of Williams was perhaps the most positive story of the year. After plumbing the depths in 2013, the team underwent a radical transformation. A fresh new look, boosted by a classic Martini livery, was the outward manifestation. However, the

keys were a restructuring of a tired technical organisation by Pat Symonds, and the decision to abandon Renault engines and go with Mercedes.

After a shaky start, Williams quickly usurped McLaren and Force India to become the predominant Mercedes customer team. By the middle of the year, we grew used to seeing the white cars on the second row of the grid – and in Austria Felipe Massa actually beat both Mercedes to pole.

The Brazilian enjoyed a new lease of life at his new home, after his eight-year spell at Ferrari, but he was frequently overshadowed by Valtteri Bottas, who performed superbly all year. A string of podiums confirmed the Finn as the man that all serious players had to add to their long-term wish list. However, in terms of strategy and race weekend operations, the team wasn't always on the ball.

As the only team with both chassis and power unit departments built on one site, Ferrari in theory should have done an even better job than Mercedes of integrating the

two key elements of the package, but that didn't prove to be the case. It was apparent from early in testing that the company lagged behind its main rival in exploiting the new hybrid technology.

Ferrari's performance in the early races was so poor that team principal Stefano Domenicali agreed to walk away, leaving Ferrari president Luca di Montezemolo to call in Ferrari North America boss Marco Mattiacci to take over. Later, engine chief Luca Marmorini was ousted. Then in September it was confirmed that di Montezemolo would be replaced by Fiat chief Sergio Marchionne. There were further changes after the last race of the season when Maurizio Arrivabene arrived from Marlboro to be the team's new boss.

Amid this political chaos, the team endured one of its worst seasons in recent memory. Fernando Alonso did his best, flattering the car with canny drives into finishing positions that it didn't deserve. However, he eventually had enough and found a way out of his contract, leaving his spot to Vettel, who found the lure of the Prancing Horse irresistible. Meanwhile, Kimi Räikkönen stumbled through a difficult year with a car he couldn't come to terms with. A race winner

the previous year, the Finn was often an also-ran.

This was an interim season for McLaren as the team prepared for its reunion with Honda in 2015. Former Lotus boss Eric Boullier was brought in with the title of racing director and team principal Martin Whitmarsh was ousted in what amounted to a coup led by Ron Dennis, who was back in the picture – although careful not to be seen wearing team gear at the circuits.

The team's relationship with Mercedes was a little strained as the Stuttgart manufacturer was wary about protecting its IP, but the real problem was that, once again, the team built a mediocre car and had the difficult task of turning things around as the season went on. There were races where it didn't even make the points, but the package improved and a restructuring of the technical organisation gave hope for the future.

In the short-term, that was of little comfort to Jenson Button and new boy Kevin Magnussen. At opposite ends of their careers, both had to make the best of a difficult situation. Questions over who might be driving in 2015 didn't help as both Alonso and test driver Stoffel Vandoorne waited in the wings. In his 15th season, Button did his usual

solid job and was a superb team player, while rookie Magnussen showed signs of real spark. Never afraid to get involved in a fight, he also picked up a few penalties.

With McLaren now turning to Honda for 2015, Force India strengthened its bonds with Mercedes by taking a full power unit and gearbox package. Previously, the latter had been sourced from the Woking team. That was obviously a great starting point and its VJM07 proved to be quick, especially in the first half the season. The team threw a lifeline to Sergio Pérez, dropped by McLaren at the end of 2013, and the Mexican did much to rebuild his reputation with some feisty performances. After a year at Sauber, Nico Hülkenberg returned to the fold and piled up points without doing enough to land a berth at a top team.

After years with Ferrari power, Scuderia Toro Rosso switched to Renault for 2014, with the aim of forging closer links with the senior Red Bull team. Jean-Éric Vergne upped his game – he had little choice given the impressive form of Daniil Kvyat. The Russian slipped easily into the role of F1 driver and, when Vettel announced he was off, Red Bull wasted little time in confirming that Kvyat would replace him.

"THE HUGE HIKE IN POWER UNIT COSTS TIPPED BOTH CATERHAM AND MARUSSIA OVER THE EDGE FINANCIALLY"

If Williams made the most dramatic improvement in 2014, then Lotus did the opposite. Facing a financial squeeze and having lost several key employees, the team replaced the departed Räikkönen with Pastor Maldonado, who brought precious funding. Unlike fellow customers Red Bull Racing, Lotus never recovered from disastrous winter testing and it was clear that the problems spread far beyond the power unit. A new deal with Mercedes for 2015 is the light at the end of the tunnel.

There is no such boost coming for Sauber. After challenging for podiums in recent years, the Swiss team stumbled badly and matters weren't helped by the poor performance of the Ferrari power unit. At the end of the season, the team signed two well-sponsored drivers for 2015, despite already having two other drivers under contract. It seemed that the financial situation was so desperate that it was worth risking a legal fight.

To no one's great surprise, the huge hike in power unit costs tipped both Caterham and Marussia over the edge financially. Having switched to Ferrari power, Marussia had created a tidy package and a canny race in Monaco saw Jules Bianchi score priceless points with

ninth place. But the debts continued to mount and by October the situation had become untenable. By the end of the season, the management hadn't given up on finding a way to save the team, but its future remained in question.

It was a similar situation at Caterham and at the end of June founder Tony Fernandes walked away and handed the team to a group headed by former Force India and HRT boss Colin Kolles. The team had been on the verge of collapse, but Kolles cut costs, paid bills and even made the car quicker. However, it all ended in a big mess after the Russian GP as it emerged that Fernandes hadn't actually handed over ownership. The team passed into the hands of administrators who, after missing two races, got it to Abu Dhabi.

Sadly, the timing of Marussia's dramas coincided with Bianchi's awful crash at the Japanese GP. It was a wake-up call after two decades of constant safety improvements since the nightmare season of 1994. By the end of the season, the news about the Frenchman was a little more positive and he was flown back to France, but the accident was the lowest point of what was a dramatic and at times turbulent season for the sport.

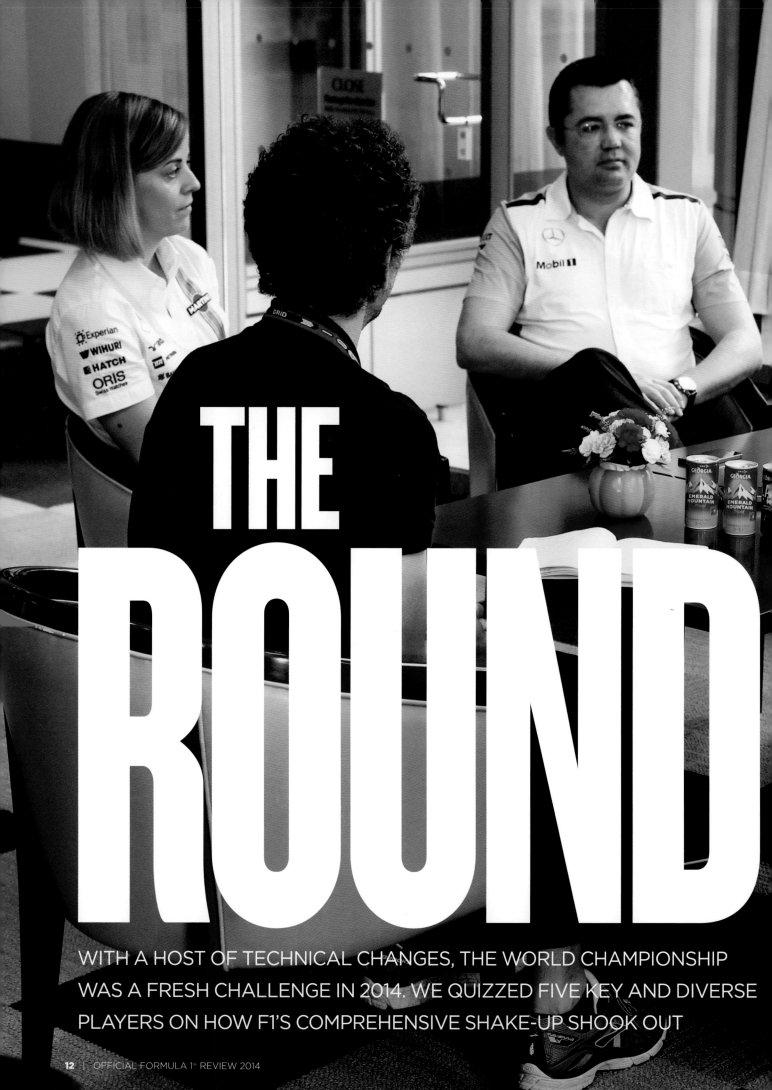

THE ROUND

WITH A HOST OF TECHNICAL CHANGES, THE WORLD CHAMPIONSHIP
WAS A FRESH CHALLENGE IN 2014. WE QUIZZED FIVE KEY AND DIVERSE
PLAYERS ON HOW F1'S COMPREHENSIVE SHAKE-UP SHOOK OUT

TABLE

THE PANEL

ERIC BOULLIER
McLAREN RACING DIRECTOR

MARTIN BRUNDLE
SKY F1 COMMENTATOR

ANDREW COWELL
MD MERCEDES AMG HIGH PERFORMANCE POWERTRAINS

PAUL HEMBERY
PIRELLI MOTORSPORT DIRECTOR

SUSIE WOLFF
WILLIAMS DEVELOPMENT DRIVER

CHAIRED BY

ANTHONY ROWLINSON
GROUP EDITOR F1 RACING

I t might, just, be remembered as a classic year. Mercedes domination, yes, but also Lewis Hamilton versus Nico Rosberg – a rivalry as intense and as closely fought as any F1 head-to-head down the decades.

Speed, skullduggery, echoes of the past, but also glimpses of the future. Also, so sadly, Jules Bianchi and a terrible reminder that F1, for all the advances in safety made year on year, remains a sport in which competitors risk their lives.

The round table panel gathered at the circuit hotel on the Sunday morning of the Japanese GP, just hours before Bianchi's accident, so thoughts about the dangers of the sport were not, then, uppermost in their minds. Talk began, instead, with reflection on F1's root-and-branch technical revamp for 2014…

"I want to look back at the changes to the technical regulations. All-new power units, a cut in downforce, no blown diffusers… it was the biggest technical change for a generation, so could I get your thoughts on whether they've worked and what the particular challenges have been?"

COWELL "The power units were the big change. They're turbocharged, with big energy recovery systems (ERS) rather than tiny kinetic energy recovery systems (KERS). There was a lot of excitement about bringing in a big new technology to a tough deadline. Everybody had to have it for the first race with no option to run one of the old V8s. That meant a battle between Ferrari, Renault and Mercedes to do something for the tests, then turn up in Melbourne.

"We've seen the excitement of that technical challenge and the scare of: 'Are the cars going to finish?' All the nay-sayers were telling us only two or three would finish, but actually a healthy number of cars completed each grand prix. There was also an impressive progression with regard to reliability and performance."

"Susie, you're the only person around this table who has driven a 2014 car with these new power units. What are they like to drive?"
WOLFF "The drivers have had a lot to do this year. I remember the first lap I did in Barcelona last May. It's a different car to drive – less downforce, then there's the torque and the driver management that

Sky commentator
Martin Brundle
had plenty to say
in response to
Anthony Rowlinson's
questions. **Left:**
Susie Wolff and
Andrew Cowell
listen in as McLaren's
Eric Boullier makes a
point at the Suzuka
circuit hotel

goes on. Even doing a test day, the steering wheel commands and the mental capacity necessary to get everything done in the car was high. Then to add on a race situation where the guys are pushing like hell… Also, don't forget tyre management: the degradation means you can't go flat-out every lap like it's the last. It's been a big change, but at Williams it was a chance to start with a clean slate."

"Martin, you tweeted earlier in the year that this has been one of the best seasons you can remember commentating on. Why's that?"
BRUNDLE "The cars have been exciting to watch as they're quite clearly a handful to drive. Yet the reliability has been better than expected and fuel consumption hasn't been an issue.

"We've had racing all the way through the field too. Monza was a classic, where you had Jenson Button and Sergio Pérez fighting side-by-side for the minor points – the kind of action we'd still be talking about if it was Ayrton Senna and Nigel Mansell – and we had it right the way through the field.

"My only complaint would be that I'd like to hear more volume from the engines. At places like Singapore or Monaco, or a circuit

"THE CARS HAVE BEEN EXCITING TO WATCH AS THEY'RE QUITE CLEARLY A HANDFUL TO DRIVE"

Martin Brundle

with canopies on grandstands, they sound good and meaty. But at Silverstone, where the noise dissipates into the sky and the track is a long way away, they don't sound great at all."
WOLFF "The racing has been really entertaining and not just at the front. Even though we've had a dominant team, there's still been a fight between the two, then further down the field there's been fantastic racing and as for some of the moves pulled off, well…"

"For the past couple of seasons we've had a lot of talk about tyres. This year, they've been a non-story. Paul, has that been a relief?"
HEMBERY "Well, there has still been a fair amount of talk about tyres. As Susie said, there has been a dramatic change in the delivery of the power and torque. I remember the first test we did in the simulator and one particular team came back and said: 'Oh my God!' We thought: 'Is it really going to be like that, with wheelspin in every gear? In which direction should we go?'

"Coming into the season we had a lot of unknowns, but the racing has been fantastic. It was right that the focus was on the powertrain and the racing has proved that we got the balance right as a sport."

"So, was 2014 a slightly calmer year for you than 2013 had been?"
HEMBERY "Yes! Every year there has to be a focus. We're in the entertainment business as well as the sporting business, so there will always be a different focus. We'd complain if nobody was talking about us."

"What's the view been like from the pit wall, Eric, even though McLaren hasn't had the best of years?"
BOULLIER "Strategy was very similar to any other year. It's true that we had a lot of fears to start with about fuel consumption. Tyres were also a bit of an unknown, but we soon realised they were more consistent.

"The new powertrain made winter testing very difficult, so I don't think we were as ready as usual, in terms of controlling the tyres – and controlling everything – but the first four races were a learning period for everybody. The racing has been very good; all of us fighting as a grid but, despite that, the focus wasn't in the right place. There was too much talk about engine noise, for example."

"A few of you have mentioned the entertainment aspect of the year. Is F1 selling itself enough? Does that

aspect need to be addressed with better promotion and marketing?"

BRUNDLE "I don't think so. We didn't have big fan numbers in Germany, but it's not due to the sound, as the German fans hadn't heard the engines then. It was more that they swap between Hockenheim and the Nürburgring, so they can't sell tickets.

"Our TV figures are up, so what can you do? The majority of races have been great. In Hungary, I found myself applauding when the cars crossed the line. Then I realised : 'What am I doing, I'm commentating!' I was like a fan as I was so excited by the races and we've had many races like that. Everybody talks about how it used to be better in the old days, but it wasn't. You could come home fourth, two laps down; pole to the back of the grid was 10s, reliability was 50 per cent and these are the days they call the glory days!"

BOULLIER "I'm a huge fan of F1, but it was boring to see those grands prix back then. I'm sorry to say it, but you would see one car, then wait 10s for the next to come around."

BRUNDLE "Those grands prix were boring to drive in, too."

HEMBERY "In motorsport, the rose-tinted spectacles come on. People have a selective memory and we talk ourselves down. Yet, if you look around the teams when the races are on, you can tell that people are excited even if it isn't their driver. They're watching overtaking manoeuvres and going: 'Did you see that!' Some of the moves this season are up there with the best ever and that needs to come through more."

"Do you think that we'll look back on this year as a classic, a vintage season, a great year for F1?"

BRUNDLE "I think so, yes."

"So who has been the standout driver in 2014? Maybe there's more than one, maybe three or four?"

BRUNDLE "Daniel Ricciardo."

WOLFF "Valtteri Bottas."

HEMBERY "Bottas is really good to watch. Daniel, too. It was his big chance. I remember talking to him in Brazil last year and you could tell it was his big moment. He knew that going up against a great champion was his chance to stake his claim, so there was huge pressure. We might have been talking about how he wasn't quite good enough and instead he's

> ## "WE HAVE SEEN THE CAR COME TOGETHER, REALISED IT WAS QUICK AND WOULD GIVE THEM A SHOT AT BEING WORLD CHAMPION"
> Andrew Cowell

seen off Sebastian Vettel. Pressure doesn't come bigger than going against such a great champion."

BOULLIER "These two are very good for the sport. They've also shown that in F1, before you really start to deliver, you need a couple of years at the top level and that's something new. Before, you could break through to F1 straight away from a junior category like, say, Formula Ford 2000, Now, you need to be nurtured for a few years before you can show you're a complete driver and deliver."

"What about the two guys who fought so closely for the title?"

COWELL "It was a great battle. They've both got different strengths. They were driving the best car. Unfortunately, the car gave each of them the odd handicap, but we watched them go into this year, have seen the car come together, realised it was quick and would give them a real shot at being world champion."

"How did you get through the tense moments this year?"

COWELL "Just by talking about them, regardless of what the issues were. If it was the power unit, we'd talk about it; if it was the car, we talked about that; if it was an issue between drivers, we talked with them and moved on."

BRUNDLE "We have to thank Mercedes for this year, for letting the drivers race. That's been a critical part of this year, which is why I've gone to a lot of trouble not to beat up on them, otherwise we'd go back to the days of teams controlling drivers. That's what fans hate. These guys have let the drivers go, taking the flak along the way and I think it's so important we applaud that rather than criticise."

"Is Rosberg/Hamilton an Ayrton Senna/Alain Prost type rivalry?"

WOLFF "From a driving perspective, what those two pulled off this year was outstanding. The pressure they were under – one mistake costs so much – and they're at such a high level, yet there's just hundredths of a second between them at every session. It's been a phenomenal level of racing."

COWELL "If you watch the progression between the first practice session, the second and the third, then qualifying, you'll see either Nico or Lewis get a little advantage, then the other gets a

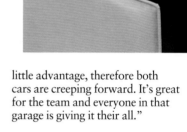

little advantage, therefore both cars are creeping forward. It's great for the team and everyone in that garage is giving it their all."

"Do you think Nico's pace has been surprising this year? Maybe an eye-opener for some people?"

BRUNDLE "He matched Michael Schumacher and then beat him when they were Mercedes teammates, so we now have to re-evaluate how well Michael was doing. I think we've seen it before – like with Damon Hill when he was up for the world championship in the mid-1990s. Some drivers seem to raise their game in a championship battle, which is something quite special. But I'm not surprised at all about Nico."

"What about Fernando Alonso? He's a great presence in the sport, yet he's not really achieving what he deserves. What does the future hold for him?"

BOULLIER "This year we saw so much new technology and change and a new team dominating the championship, plus the rivalry between Nico and Lewis, that Fernando hasn't been attracting so much attention. However, he's still doing a good job when you compare him with his teammate."

"Do we think that because Fernando is in a less competitive car, we're missing out not seeing him winning races and titles?"

BRUNDLE "You're partly responsible for how your team develops, you can't always criticise your car. As the lead driver, you're responsible for the development of that car as well. Fernando is amazing, as he drags the car around and he's made Kimi Räikkönen look pretty second-rate this year. He's spectacular and you could argue that he is the best driver on the grid, but there's more than just being fast. As with all of the great drivers, you get a little bit of baggage. If you think about, say, Prost, Senna, those guys… they're all difficult characters to handle and they're quite extreme people, which is why they achieve extreme things. I love watching Fernando and I'm a huge fan, but quite clearly he has a destructive influence within a team and that's not just this year. On the track, he's very exciting, but he can't keep criticising the teams like that."

"What about some of the other young talent? I'm thinking of Daniil Kvyat, who really caught the eye at Toro Rosso this year, or Max Verstappen, who'll be taking Daniil's seat next year aged just 17?"

"KVYAT HAS DONE A GOOD JOB FOR HIS FIRST YEAR AND I THINK HE DESERVES A TOP JOB"

Eric Boullier

BOULLIER "It's good to have new blood, as I've said before. Kvyat has done a good job for his first year and I think he deserves a top job. That'll be a different pressure to handle driving alongside Ricciardo next year, but he's good."

WOLFF "This year, or in recent years when there's been no testing, the youngsters who have come in have a real battle ahead of them. It's not like when Lewis joined and you could do thousands of kilometres testing to get yourself ready. Now there's very little time in the car before you're expected to go out and perform. It's tough and to rise to the challenge is impressive."

BRUNDLE "I'm amazed how well they did because, OK, they've come through Formula Dallara and karting with loads of grip, but no torque in any car they've driven. I thought they'd struggle like hell as soon as they had an excess of torque over grip, but the kids have just got hold of the cars and driven them. It's just brilliant and so exciting."

BOULLIER "And it's actually very funny as we said the car would be very difficult to drive and we keep hearing that we need to make the cars more difficult to drive and yet they still handle them."

BRUNDLE "I didn't anticipate that. I thought they would struggle to control them. I've driven a GP3 car and, as soon as you get the nose of one of those into the corner, it's like we had in 1993 in F1, with traction control. All it was about then was feeling the torque, then going flat-out. Now the cars have to be almost completely out of the corner before you can apply full power, then they're short-shifting. It's great for F1; the future is secure. We've got such talent coming along."

HEMBERY "I think Red Bull deserves a lot of credit for believing in its young-driver scheme and following it through. Any sport is only as good as the young talent coming through and when you continue to see these young people, who are talented and not just making up the numbers, they'll probably go on to be champions. That's a healthy situation, so it's very exciting to see these youngsters putting the big names under pressure."

"That happened at Red Bull Racing this year? What do we think about Vettel being eclipsed by his teammate? Is it a driving problem, or more of a head problem?"

HEMBERY "Well, there's been a big change in the cars. In previous years, I remember standing in what we thought was the braking zone during testing in Abu Dhabi and

Andrew Cowell,
MD Mercedes AMG
High Performance
Powertrains, asks:
"Are we providing
good value to
the people we're
entertaining?"

the cars were flat-out! They started braking in the middle of the corner and we were saying: 'Hold on! They had already turned in. Did they brake at all?' It's quite a dramatic change in how the cars behave and Sebastian hasn't thrown his toys out of the pram, for which he should get considerable credit. It's tough for such a great driver, but well done Daniel in the end, for really taking his chance. It might only happen once in your career."

BRUNDLE "Obviously, with the blown-exhaust cars of 2011 and 2013, Sebastian was the man of that moment and the car really suited his driving style. Did anyone predict that Ricciardo would thrash him and make him look ordinary?"

ALL "No."

BRUNDLE "It's just extraordinary."

HEMBERY "But isn't that great? With all the expertise and data we have, there wasn't anybody out there saying: 'Watch out for Ricciardo', apart from Daniel himself, of course."

BOULLIER "Thinking about Sebastian, when you have been world champion for four years, you have to consider how much you have to sacrifice to reach that level. When you are a high-level athlete, you have to give so much every year and we just remember the four

years he was world champion.

"We should also remember the eight years before. So, when you give 10 or 12 years of your life at the very high level… you know we are all human and we all go through different stages in our life. Sebastian's wife had a baby last year, so he's going through a different phase of his life as well."

"Switching topics, there's been a lot of concern about the financial difficulties teams on the lower half of the grid are facing. What's your reaction to the demise – or apparent demise – of two teams before the end the season? Should we be worried?"

BRUNDLE "I think it's very significant and underlines the position F1 finds itself in. In some ways I'm amazed Caterham and Marussia lasted as long as they did. They obviously came in with the idea that there was a $40m budget cap – although that was clearly never going to happen. This sort of thing is a great shame for the team members and their families and I hope that if one good thing can come out of this, it's that people can wake up and smell the coffee and make some changes."

HEMBERY "I don't think most people are surprised. Teams have been talking about their financial

concerns since the start of the year and it's more dramatic if they fold during the season – you'd normally expect that they're budgeted to get to the end of a period. It highlights that there are a number of factors in the sport that need to be addressed, but the solutions are very, very complex and tied by a lot of contractual aspects. Maybe F1 needed a watershed to find solutions to its problems."

"Martin, there's so much money in the sport, so why does this sort of thing happen?"

BRUNDLE "There are two reasons: firstly it costs too much money to do this. Gérard Lopez, of Lotus, told me it costs £70m just to show up with the basics, so that's way too much. Then the £900m that comes in isn't distributed in a sensible way.

"So the 'haves' and the 'have-nots' are guaranteed to become further and further apart until the 'have-nots' have dropped off the bottom of the scale and the stretched middle are looking over their shoulders as well."

"How might the troubles be resolved?"

HEMBERY "I think you'll find that there's a list of people who want to come into the sport. There are

> "NO ONE SAID: 'WATCH OUT FOR RICCIARDO', APART FROM DANIEL HIMSELF, OF COURSE"
> Paul Hembery

always people who want to have an F1 team… Haas are coming along, there are indications of others being interested in buying one of the two teams… A lot of teams have come and gone and that's probably going to continue. We've seen a lot of car manufacturers come and go as well – F1 has always been a sport where there's transition of ownership."

"What does F1 need to do about this?"

BOULLIER "If you go back 10 years, there was a lot of disparity as well. And 20 years ago it was the same. The small teams don't have the resources of the top teams, we all know that. So I don't think there is a lot of difference. Actually, at least in financial terms, there might even be less difference than there was 10 years ago in the manufacturer era, or even 20 years ago."

WOLFF "When you enter F1, you know what you're entering, it's not a cheap sport, it's about having the money to go racing or not. You've got to be very clear about that at the beginning of the season."

BRUNDLE "I see great peril, as I'm really concerned about third cars, as eight three-car teams will become five four-car teams and so on. I hear what you say, Eric, but I see more stress further up the field than I've

ever seen. And it can't be addressed because the money distribution is cast in stone.

"I'd like to see a situation where we have teams that seem to have serious business people in them and thus credibility, not that they are only just surviving somehow, hanging on to the greasy pole. We should attract really high-level people to F1, coming in because the sport is financially viable and you can be moderately competitive."

BOULLIER "Top teams were running in the 1990s on a budget of a tenth of what we have today. However, the manufacturers then jumped into F1. When the manufacturers left, they left because of the world economic situation, which doesn't help, but they left regulations where the teams used to spend a lot of money with a lot of people, so we're going through a time of transition.

"When you have been used to running a 500-person team and you're told your new level is 300, there are going to be difficulties to go through and you can't do this in one year. That's why teams are struggling because, over three years, the revenue model that was founded by current manufacturers, went down by 60%, a massive transition.

"McLaren have invested a lot of revenue into our facilities; into making it the institution it is today. Newcomers can come, but we've gone through pain over the decades. So why should they be given in two years what we've built in 40?

"We're in favour of helping, as we don't want to run a three-car team, but we need to address the right points. For 15 years, F1 was clearly going through the roof, in terms of budget and now in three years we have to unstitch what has been done."

COWELL "We all have the responsibility to make sure that we sit down and ask: 'Are we providing good value to the people we're entertaining?' Because, nowadays, you get more information when sitting in your living room than you do sitting in the grandstands. We need to be very careful that we provide value to those people who come to watch."

BRUNDLE "Is that really possible? Teams are hardwired to win, that's all you're interested in and you get blinkers on. I completely understand that, but how can you disadvantage yourself?"

"MASSA WAS KICKED OUT OF FERRARI, THEN CAME TO WILLIAMS AND SHOWED EVERYBODY"

Susie Wolff

HEMBERY "The trouble is that any proposal is always going to have a counter-proposal and you tend to go around in circles and then you convince yourself to do nothing. That's what we tend to see in F1. Some good ideas come out, but by the time that they've gone full circle, people convince themselves: 'Well, actually, we won't do anything'. We have to make some big decisions that will not be universally popular."

BOULLIER "We can agree with most teams, but need to please fans, teams, drivers, media, sponsors, promoters and engine manufacturers, so we have seven groups of different interests to please. Which should we favour?"

HEMBERY "It's such a complex question. We will be driven by fans ultimately. We are in the entertainment business — we're competing against other sports and income will only come from the number of people watching it. That's the number-one driver for sponsors like us – we're a technical partner, but also a sponsor and we evaluate the sport and compare it to other sports where we could invest the same amount of money.

"Ultimately, Martin is right: there's enough money in the sport overall to create a championship. It's just how you decide to spend it."

BOULLIER "We need to bring the competitive level down to a lower figure in terms of money, which will allow more teams to become more competitive in F1. Also, we need to understand what a typical 15-year-old likes and how they use technology. Why spend 100 Euros on a ticket if you can see what you want and what you like when you buy a coffee with your friends?"

"Getting back to the racing, pick a standout moment of 2014."

COWELL "Bahrain, the last few laps. Absolutely awesome."

BRUNDLE "That's what came straight to my mind, too."

HEMBERY "Daniel overtaking Sebastian when he did his dummy at Monza, I thought that was pretty good fun. Something that you looked at and thought: 'That's someone who's right on his game and feeling confident about life'."

WOLFF "Massa's pole in Austria. He was kicked out of Ferrari and had to find his way, then came to Williams and – boom! – showed everybody."

BOULLIER "The podium by McLaren in Melbourne was amazing."

COWELL "Great engine, eh?"

MERCEDES

FORMER TECHNICAL DIRECTOR GARY ANDERSON LOOKS AT HOW
THE 11 TEAMS TACKLED THE LARGEST TECHNICAL CHALLENGE TO HIT
FORMULA ONE IN DECADES – AND HOW MERCEDES CAME OUT AHEAD

RACES TO THE TOP OF THE FORM

A fter one of the most comprehensive rule changes in the history of Formula One, it was inevitable that there would be a major shake-up of the competitive order.

The raft of new regulations were built around the introduction of new 1.6-litre turbocharged V6 engines with potent energy recovery systems technology. There were also new aerodynamic rules, including the narrowing of the front wing by 150mm, the lowering of the nose, the banning of the rear beam wing and the near-total elimination of exhaust-blown downforce, as well as the switch to eight-speed gearboxes with ratios fixed for the season.

Mercedes did everything right to capitalise on the opportunity that this gave them. Ross Brawn, who left Mercedes at the end of last year, deserves a huge amount of credit for turning an underachieving team into a dominant one. The recruitment of key technical leaders such as Bob Bell, Geoff Willis and Aldo Costa in 2011, along with extra investment from Mercedes itself, allowed the Brackley-based team to fulfil its potential.

Also, with work on the new power unit at Mercedes AMG High Performance Powertrains at Brixworth starting significantly earlier than at either Renault or Ferrari, the result was comfortably the strongest package on the grid. Although it occasionally suffered from silly reliability problems, it was a package that was close to unbeatable. Only in unusual circumstances did we end up with victory going to neither Lewis Hamilton or Nico Rosberg.

Success in F1 is never about one particular component or a single design. The performance of the power unit was clearly the key to success in 2014 and Mercedes had what was the all-round strongest engine. The Mercedes-Benz PU106A Hybrid was very well packaged and unique with the turbo compressor mounted low at the front of the engine and the turbine low at the rear, keeping the hot and cold parts of the turbo system separate. The MGU-H was located in the middle of the engine's vee, which helped to keep the centre of gravity low.

These new power units were extremely complex, with management of the use of the power from the V6 itself, along with the energy recovery system, a major challenge.

From early on in testing, it was clear that Mercedes had done its homework better than the rest. Renault had lots of problems; it spent much of winter testing and the early races making major software changes. However, while it did become a very good package in terms of harvesting energy, it was still down on power compared to the Mercedes.

Ferrari also struggled. It seems that rather than building a whole

Clockwise from left: The teams had a challenge in packaging their energy recovery systems; Ferrari's rear end worked well; McLaren's drivers didn't see the lap times they'd have hoped for; Gary Anderson asks Christian Horner about Red Bull Racing's form

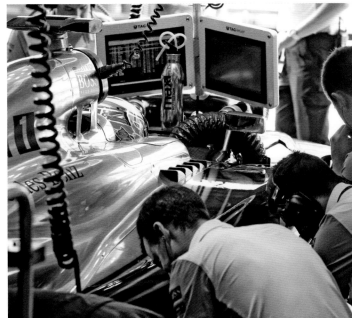

new concept from the ground up, the starting point was Ferrari's old 056 V8 with two cylinders lopped off, which played a major part in it being heavier and less powerful than its rivals. The ERS system was also a problem and it's no surprise that Ferrari, along with Renault, wanted the chance to make changes to the frozen engines during the season.

Mercedes was a long way ahead, but all three engine manufacturers deserve considerable credit for producing powertrain packages that were surprisingly reliable. Finishing rates were far better than expected, particularly early in the season, and the 100kg-per-race fuel limit, meaning that cars had to complete races on two thirds of the fuel used in 2013, proved to be of little problem. As early as the second round, the Malaysian GP, Williams was underfuelled for the race to save weight.

The power unit change also led to the introduction of rear brake-by-wire and this was a system that

"RATHER THAN BUILDING A WHOLE NEW CONCEPT, FERRARI'S STARTING POINT WAS ITS OLD V8 WITH TWO CYLINDERS LOPPED OFF"

some struggled with. While teams like Mercedes and Williams hit the ground running, others struggled for stability. If you don't have a car that's stable and consistent under braking, then the driver has no chance of being able to extract the best from it.

The restrictive aerodynamic regulations meant that the developments seen during the season were in very specific areas. The most visually striking were the new noses, with all sorts of weird and wonderful shapes, including anteaters and twin tusks, on display. This was the result of regulations designed to lower the nose for safety reasons, something that I've always thought was the wrong move.

Some suggested that performance wasn't affected too much by choosing one concept over the other, but I can't believe this, for a very simple reason. The front wing is the first thing that hits the airflow, so the airflow structures that you create with it

define the potential of the whole car. It's not just about how much downforce you can produce there, it's about making all of the car work, all the way back to the diffuser and the rear wing. Consequently, you can't escape the fact that the nose shape will have an influence on the aerodynamic performance of the whole car.

At the front, you want to maximise the airflow between the front wheels, then direct it to the underfloor and around the sidepods to connect the front of the car to the rear diffuser and the coke bottle areas. Teams spent a huge amount of time making small aero changes to achieve this.

With both sides of the front wing being 75mm narrower, every team had a lot of work to do to re-adapt. We saw considerable variation in the front wing endplate turning vanes, with many dropping the idea of having several small winglets to turn the airflow around the front wheels, replacing this with

a single vane with a large turning moment. We also saw a focus on making the front wing work consistently, with endless slot gaps appearing to minimise the risk of airflow separation. While this reduces the size of downforce-producing devices, it makes the wing more consistent. As a driver, you'll always get more pace out of consistent downforce than from potentially higher levels of downforce that is peaky, because confidence is essential.

The championship table doesn't lie and the fact that all four Mercedes-powered teams were in the top six of the constructors' championship tells a story. The works Mercedes team had every opportunity to package its chassis and power unit well, and it capitalised on that: the number of one-two finishes Mercedes achieved this season was impressive.

Red Bull Racing looked all at sea during pre-season testing and barely able to complete a lap

without something burning. But the steps made for the first round in Australia made it possible for Daniel Ricciardo – for me, one of the stars of the season – to finish second before being disqualified for exceeding the fuel-flow limit. From where Red Bull Racing started, finishing as runner-up in the championship was no disgrace and, aerodynamically, the RB10 was the best car in the field.

As has often been the case, Ferrari was disappointing. Aerodynamically, the car wasn't too bad, but I would question the team's understanding of what it wanted to get out of the front wing. The power unit wasn't strong enough and Fernando Alonso seemed to spend most of the year in fifth or sixth position. As for Kimi Räikkönen, they seemed unable to give him a car he was happy with and he was generally too far off Alonso's pace.

The team that really stood out was Williams. In 2013, it was rarely even in the top 10 but,

> **"THE MOST VISUALLY STRIKING DEVELOPMENTS WERE THE NEW NOSES, WITH ALL SORTS OF WEIRD AND WONDERFUL SHAPES"**

thanks to some clever recruiting – with Pat Symonds and Rob Smedley joining over the past 18 months – along with a Mercedes engine deal, it was very often best of the rest.

There were a few too many mistakes, particularly early in the season, but the car had a good drag level so it was always fast on the straights and Valtteri Bottas in particular put it to good use.

McLaren was a disappointment again. Aerodynamically, there still seem to be some problems and, while it had the Mercedes power unit, it wasn't able to make the best use of it. If you look at how hard Force India pushed McLaren through the season, despite being a smaller team, that tells a story.

For the rest of the teams, it was all about troubles with the power unit. The Toro Rosso STR9 was very often quick, but rarely in a position to score at the end of races, while Lotus struggled for most of the season with a car that seemed to change its

handling characteristics by the lap. Watching Pastor Maldonado and Romain Grosjean, it was clear they had no confidence in the car at all. Sauber also struggled, not just because of its Ferrari power unit, but seemingly because it couldn't regain as much of the downforce lost through the rule changes as it wanted to.

At the back of the field, both Caterham and Marussia hit financial troubles, although Marussia at least managed to score its first championship points, thanks to Jules Bianchi in Monaco, and produced a tidy enough car on a small budget.

The 2014 season was all about which team adapted best to the new rules and that was Mercedes. Even in the closing stages of the season, the pace advantage was still very clear. This shows that there will be plenty more developments to come next season. Anyone thinking it will be easy to catch Mercedes next year could end up having a shock.

THE DRIVERS

TWENTY-FOUR DRIVERS WENT OUT TO BATTLE IN 2014, BUT ONLY LEWIS HAMILTON AND NICO ROSBERG HAD A SHOT AT THE TITLE. THEY ALL TALK OF THEIR CHAMPIONSHIP YEAR

1
LEWIS HAMILTON

MERCEDES, 384PTS

This has been an incredible year. I just can't believe how amazing this has all been. A lot of people said that joining Mercedes was the wrong choice when I moved across from McLaren for the 2013 World Championship. However, after the steps that we took last year, followed up by the steps that we made coming into this year, it has been just unbelievable and the fan support has been truly phenomenal. I never in a million years thought I would have that kind of support.

"It has been so intense between Nico and myself all through the season's 19 grands prix. There have been good moments and also bad moments. Without a doubt, we've had a friendship or a relationship that we built a long time ago, so that will always be there. He was a fierce competitor this year and did an exceptional job. Nico is going to be quick for a long time, so I've got to pick up my qualifying pace.

"It could have been either one of us winning this year's title. Obviously, we both wanted it. But I think with our relationship, we'll continue to try to lift the team and we'll work together as we have

done all year. Perhaps things will naturally ease up a little now as he was graceful enough to come up and see me after the race, which I really appreciated. It was really big of him to be able to do that. It's very, very tough. I know what it's like losing a championship so, for sure, we'll keep working at it.

"The Belgian GP was a low moment. It was a very difficult scenario. Years ago, I wouldn't have reacted the way I did this year. I would have chosen another way, which wouldn't have been a positive. I guess with age, as well as maturing and having a different perspective on life, I handled it a different way. I thought about it for the next few days and then turned my focus to a different area.

"I came to the next races with a different approach. I won't explain exactly what I did because I need to bring it to the races next year, but I did tweak some of my approach through a race weekend, which helped me to get those wins. I've still got some improvements to make, as qualifying was good this year but could be better. It would make it much easier if I could get qualifying sorted, because the race pace is very much there.

"I said coming into the Abu Dhabi weekend that I wouldn't

NATIONALITY
British

DATE OF BIRTH
7/1/85

PLACE OF BIRTH
Stevenage
England

HONOURS
2008 & 2014
F1 World
Champion

2006 GP2
Champion

2005 European
F3 Champion

2003 British
Formula Renault
Champion

2000 European
Formula A Kart
Champion

1995 British
Cadet Kart
Champion

change the way the season has gone for anything really, because I've learned a lot. If anything, I felt very, very strong with the way I came out of the good and the bad.

"This really is something incredibly special, what this team has put together, and I think we've got great people in their right positions. Nico and I will continue to push the team forward, as will the boss of Mercedes, which has been so committed to building the best engine. These guys know just as much as I do, so it's been phenomenal this year. The steps we take to move forwards, to continue improving, are really important and I believe the team will do that. I'm looking forward to battling with people for sure, but I do believe that we'll be there fighting with people hopefully for some time.

"I definitely don't feel that I'm looking for a new challenge. As I said when I joined this team, I wanted to be a part of something that was building and growing and knew success like the team hadn't really had before. And so I feel like this is just the beginning. We still have another year to go, so there's no particular rush, but this is my home. I feel very happy here and obviously the team did a mega job, so I'm forever grateful for them."

2
NICO ROSBERG
MERCEDES, 317 PTS

A ll in all, it has been a truly great season for the Mercedes team. I'm proud to be a part of that. The World Championship was extremely close until the very end, the 19th grand prix, and that's why it's tough to take how it finished.

"Lewis deserved to win the drivers' championship today, that's clear. He won it because he won it and whatever happened in Abu Dhabi didn't make any difference to his championship win.

"I still believed in it for a long time through the race because there was still always the possibility that Lewis would pick up a problem and then I would only need to finish in fifth position to become champion. I believed that until the end. I was still pushing on the very last lap of the race because that's what I do. I don't give up, I just push all the way. That's also why I wanted to finish the race.

"Lewis was that little bit better driver this year, a tiny bit, in the races only. So he deserves the title. For me, there's some great things about this year. There are a lot of strong points that I can build on.

"It's been very close between Lewis and I. For the past two years, I've been the better qualifier and that's something I can really build on. I need to find a little bit in racing and I am going to find that little bit. I'm going to work on it and it's going to be a great year next year, for sure. In the latter part of the season, Lewis was ever so slightly better in the racing than me, and that's what I need to work on.

"I know what areas I need to work in, so that's a great challenge and I will find what I need to try and beat Lewis in 2015. I understand what's going on. It's not something that's easy to improve. I need to find that little bit extra, and that's never simple. But I know what the areas are, so I'm going to push for that. I come out every year as a stronger driver. I always try to push myself and I enjoy trying to become a better driver, better person, better everything. This year was an unbelievable year, development wise. It's been such a great experience.

"To be able to fight for wins all the time and to battle it out with Lewis has been great. It was very intense at times. His level is massively high. I was against him – the best on the grid. It was very

NATIONALITY
German

DATE OF BIRTH
27/6/85

PLACE OF BIRTH
Wiesbaden
Germany

HONOURS
2005 GP2
Champion

2002 German
Formula BMW
Champion

close and it was a pity it didn't work out, but I'm proud to be in this moment with the team. It's a very special year and the car has been incredible.

"There were many personal highlights: being on pole position, winning the races that I won, leading the championship for a long time. My home grands prix are mostly my favourite ones. That's Monaco and Germany and maybe Brazil, too.

"It's quite amazing to think that 15 years after Lewis and I met that we're actually in that very position that we used to dream about, to be in the best F1 team, fighting for race wins, fighting for the championship. It's really amazing. Of course, it's much more intense now. There's much more pressure surrounding it.

"It was an intense battle through this year, but a great battle. That's what I race for, the battles like that. Lewis has been the best driver on the grid this year and to be up against him and battling it out, the level was incredibly high. But I also have to find and deliver to be on a level playing field with him, and that's been a great challenge. Most of the time, it's been enjoyable – of course, sometimes it hasn't been – but all in all, a great year."

3
DANIEL RICCIARDO
RED BULL, 238PTS

A lot has happened, definitely. I did have, let's say, a lot of belief and hope that the year would go well, but, when I look back on it, it's definitely gone better than I expected.

"The Australian GP definitely got the first load of pressure off my back. Seb had problems in qualifying and in the race so, even though the grand prix went really well for me, I couldn't quite gauge where I was with him yet – it was still quite early. Then he was just a little bit stronger in Malaysia, so I thought, 'OK, this is probably what I expected to start the season with me a little bit on the back foot compared with him.'

"It was really in Bahrain – and then going back and doing the same in China, in terms of outdoing him in qualifying and also in the race by a decent margin – that I started to realise. And then Spain, Monaco, Canada... But it was probably after China that I realised that I could genuinely fight Seb for the rest of the season.

"I hit the lead in Montreal with only a couple of laps to go. I could feel my heart rate was starting to go up. I was thinking: 'Can I still drive sensibly in the last two laps? Do I have what it takes?' I did and so I thought, 'OK, beauty, I can do that!' Since then, I feel a lot more comfortable about every opportunity that comes up.

"Having already won in Canada, I'm not going to say that Hungary was easy, but once I hit the lead, it was a case of, 'I've been here before. The only thing that's going to stop me is a mechanical failure or that sort of thing.'

"Spa was definitely different – it was less adrenaline, but more pressure, if that makes sense. It was really up to me not to make any mistakes. I knew if I drove clean for the 40-odd laps, as soon as I hit the lead then I had a good chance of winning. At the time, I was thinking that one mistake could cost me the race, so it was more of a concentration race, every corner, hitting the right braking point, getting on the throttle at the right time. Canada and Hungary were just full adrenaline, full attack. That was more intense, but in terms of the concentration, Belgium was more demanding.

"I'm riding a pretty big wave at the moment; I'm sure eventually

that will come down and then back up. It's normal. I think controlling your bad days as best you can is important, controlling those emotions and not getting frustrated with it, figuring out ways to drive around that. Accept that you're not going to win, but a fifth would still be better than a 10th, so try and get fifth.

"It's been a strong point of mine this year, getting the tyres to last longer and still having good pace. It's been the case this year for quite a few races. I don't know if I've found an explanation for that yet. I think generally I'm quite sensitive; if the tyres start to slide a bit too much, then I can adapt to that and maybe back off where I feel I need to.

"At the same time, I feel I've done that in previous years, but it hasn't worked to the same effect as it has this year. I definitely feel at home with the car itself. These new cars are difficult to drive and I think that everyone found it more difficult this year.

"I'm not going to take Daniil lightly next year, but I think I've just got to make sure I'm doing what I'm doing. What I've done this year has worked well, so I'll try and keep this format."

NATIONALITY
Australian

DATE OF BIRTH
1/7/89

PLACE OF BIRTH
Perth
Australia

HONOURS
2009 British F3
Champion

2008 WEC
Formula Renault
Champion

4
VALTTERI BOTTAS
WILLIAMS, 186PTS

It was a positive surprise for everyone in the team in Melbourne when we saw how quick the car was. Of course, we knew that we were going to go better as the year went on. When we saw how things were going with the new regulations and the new engine and also the new developments aero-wise with the car, which was going much better than with the old car, we knew that it was going to be a better season. However, it was nice to see that it's been even better than expected.

"Melbourne was actually quite tough for me. I made a mistake and, as a result, probably lost my first podium. I learned from that, definitely. As a team, we weren't yet at the level of where the pace of the car was with other things. Since then, we've just been getting better and better; we're getting stronger in all areas.

"We've been much more consistent and have been able to turn the pace of the car into good results and that's simply by working hard and analysing the mistakes we've made and always making sure we don't repeat them. I don't think we have repeated any mistakes this year, which is good. It was about a lot of things, setting up the car, getting the most out of the tyres and the strategy. I made some mistakes myself in the early part of the season. We even improved our pit stops a lot from the start of the year.

"Since Pat Symonds arrived, a lot of things have started to move in the right direction and it's not by accident. He's really managed to put the right people in the right positions and also get some new people. It's a big team, 500 people in total, but he has a clear view of the big picture and knows exactly how they need to operate and who is best in which kind of role. He sees the whole team really well and I think getting him last year was really crucial for us, because we were a bit lost.

"My first podium in Austria was really special and I think Germany was really nice when I managed to keep Hamilton behind in the end, defending against him. In Austria, if we'd been more aggressive, we would possibly have made it a bit more difficult for Mercedes. We've got a lot of confidence since then and if we have the pace like that in future, we're a much stronger team than in Austria, so I think we can do better.

"I feel that in most races I got the most out of the car personally, although certainly not in Melbourne. The biggest disappointment was Singapore. It was a really tough race for us, and I was in a reasonable position before the last lap, getting some points in the most difficult race of the rest of the season. It was tough already a few laps before the end of the race and I thought I could just handle it until the end of the last lap, but it was one or two laps too many. I think the problem was that there was a train of cars behind me and when one comes past then normally everyone comes past, because you go a bit off line on worn tyres, you spin the wheels a bit and that's it.

"I'm really happy that we were scoring points regularly, except for Monaco, which was an engine failure, and Singapore. Other than that, I've been scoring good points consistently and that's what I aim to do in the future. Every race, I've been looking at things and at what I can do better and every race I think I've managed to learn something and I've got better during the season. That's the way forward."

NATIONALITY
Finnish

DATE OF BIRTH
28/8/89

PLACE OF BIRTH
Nastola
Finland

HONOURS
2011 GP3 Champion

2009 & 2010 F3 Masters Winner

2008 European & Northern European Formula Renault Champion

2005 Viking Trophy Kart Winner

5
SEBASTIAN VETTEL
RED BULL, 167PTS

I t has been a different kind of year and in the end it probably looks worse on paper than it was.

"On many occasions, we didn't have the chance to show the potential we had because we had other factors slowing us down, but that's how it goes sometimes.

"I think if you look at all the grid, sometimes it hits you a bit more, sometimes a bit less. That's just the way that it goes. But, over the course of a lot of races in the season or a couple of seasons, everyone is in the same boat. In a way, maybe it's good to pack it all in one season and get ready for the next one once again.

"There have been some good moments, but obviously there weren't highlights in terms of wins and stuff. We've been working very hard, though. Obviously, we started the season on the back foot, if you look where we were after the winter testing. However, I think we've done very well and we've ended the year as the second-best team behind Mercedes, who seem to have quite a big gap compared to everyone else. So I think we've

done very well, considering where we started. Personally, there were races where, if things had gone a bit differently, I could have won as well, but it didn't happen. That's just how it goes.

"In a way, it's much easier to learn when you have bad races, or a bad year, simply because it's obvious. Whereas, if you have a good year, people tend not to focus too much on what to improve, because everything is going well.

"I think in both cases you have a chance to learn, so I'm not a big fan of saying only the bad races can teach you a lesson, because there's a lot of stuff that happens to you in good races as well, which helps you to go forward. But, certainly, once you are on the back foot there's more stuff that you need to do right compared with when you have a good race.

"We made a lot of progress through the season working with the car, trying to set it up, trying to understand it. This year it was particularly hard, as it was quite different to drive, since with less downforce the tyres behave differently. So, all in all, it's a completely different lesson. There's less control inside the cockpit, there's a lot of things that

NATIONALITY
German

DATE OF BIRTH
3/7/87

PLACE OF BIRTH
Heppenheim
Germany

HONOURS
2010, 2011, 2012 & 2013
F1 World Champion

2004 German Formula BMW Champion

2001 European Junior Kart Champion

you have to give up simply because it's now more in the hands of the engineers, but you have to get used to that as well and find your way to manage that.

"I think the days when we were only quick in the corners have been over for quite a while. Obviously, historically, we suffered on the straights, for different reasons, mostly in the way that we built our car in the past. Over the years, though, we've got stronger on the straights. This year, though, was a different story, because we knew that we were down a little bit in terms of power, which obviously doesn't help on the straights. Generally, though, we have had a car that works at low speed and at high speed.

"Leaving the team is obviously a tough step after such a long time with Red Bull. I had so many fantastic years and I'm still enjoying my time here. But, at some stage in life, you want to do something else, you want to do something new. It's not the first time that I've been approached over the years – I've had the opportunity before to change. Now, though, I think it felt like the right time, so that's why I decided to do something else."

6

FERNANDO ALONSO

FERRARI, 161PTS

I t has been a difficult and challenging season for us, with a lot of new things coming, new regulations and new technologies. We had to deliver 100% in winter testing and in the first races to understand all of it, but we found ourselves not to be competitive.

"We had high hopes this year with the change of regulations to stop the domination of Red Bull. We did that, but there is another team dominating, so we didn't change our final outcome as we wanted… We were still behind the leaders and still not in a position to take the championship. So, there was some frustration in the team after another difficult season.

"On the personal side, it was probably my best season, though. It's sad to say, because the results are quite poor, with only two podiums in the year. But I had a tough challenge, with a world champion on the other side of the garage, so probably I was performing at my best this year. On this side, I'm half happy.

"The best moment was Hungary, no doubt. I was leading with two laps to the end and finished second. The worst moment was Japan. First, because the race had a terrible feeling because of Jules's accident. Then it was a bad Sunday, too, rainy and I did only three corners before retiring. That weekend in general was the lowest point of my championship.

"The cars are quite complex. We had some issues with the battery and the ERS system at the start of the year in Australia, in Malaysia and in qualifying in Bahrain. We got on top of those and discovered other issues. At Spa, we had the problem with the battery on the grid, when the car didn't start on the formation lap and at Monza it was just an engine blow-up. Overall, it's been a season with mechanical failures for everyone. I was a little bit luckier in the first part of the year, a little less lucky in the second, but I don't think that's any different to our competitors.

"It's now been more than one year without a win for me, but I think there are many others who are in the same position or worse, because they have two years, three years, five years without a win. Especially this year, with the Mercedes domination affecting all the drivers in the paddock, it's more

NATIONALITY
Spanish

DATE OF BIRTH
29/7/81

PLACE OF BIRTH
Oviedo
Spain

HONOURS
2005 & 2006
F1 World
Champion

1999 Formula
Nissan Champion

1997 Italian and
Spanish Kart
Champion

1996 World Kart
Champion

than one year that we don't win… So, it's the same for everyone.

"I didn't pay too much attention to this year's Drivers' Championship; fighting for fourth, fifth or sixth, it's not a great deal. The main target was to help Ferrari in the Constructors' Championship, which I've been doing all season. For the Drivers' Championship, I'm happy where I am. I'm behind some drivers that deserve more than me, as they did a better job and I'm in front of others racing for teams that are in front of us in the Constructors' Championship. I'm proud of that, but the most important thing is the points I managed to collect for the team.

"F1 is a complex sport and you never know how the teams will perform the year after. Mercedes is the team that is dominating now and probably everyone thinks it will dominate next year. We thought the same about Red Bull in 2013. They won the championship and the last nine races and this year they were doing five laps in all of winter testing. You never know how things can change. You need to study the projects, see what are the prospects and follow one direction. If I chose a direction some months ago, it's because I feel it will be better."

7
FELIPE MASSA
WILLIAMS, 134PTS

I t's been a very good year, with the way we started the season, how we were improving, how we were developing, the feelings from the car, how the car was getting better race-by-race, how people were getting better and improving and how the team is growing. I'm so happy to be part of this very famous and important team.

"First of all, when I found out that Williams was interested in me, I tried to study everything they were planning to do for the future. Honestly, I did a very good study. I was very happy to talk to them to understand what they were trying to do and pulling pieces together. I was sure that it was the right thing for me to do, especially because everything was going to start from zero. Every change that Williams was doing was correct to my way of thinking when you put it together and understand what they were doing for this year.

"I don't think it was difficult to start in a new team, I actually think it was nice. It was a fresh start, something that was very empowering for me and I was very motivated to have that. For sure, you don't know before you arrive at another team how it's going to be, you don't really know how the people are, but I think it was very good – a lot better than expected.

"It was really nice to get inside this team. It was unbelievable how much I was welcomed by them and how much people listened to me and tried to understand what I was saying and what I believe we need to do, or I believe we need to change, or whatever. It's really nice to be a part of that.

"It's very nice to work with Valtteri Bottas. He's very fair, very professional and very clever. He's bloody quick too…

"To be honest, the first thing I thought was to do the best for the team. I'm not fighting for the championship, so I don't care about my position at the end. So, to achieve the best, I need to pass everything I can to Valtteri as, in order to have the best position for the team, we both need to be at the front. So, everything I know, everything I understand, I pass to him. I have no problem with that.

It's not the time to lie, it's not the time to not show things, it's the time to be united and the time to do a great job together. So, that's what I'm trying to do with him, but also with all the engineers, with everybody that is working with the team.

"Pole in Austria meant a lot, not just for me, but for the whole team. It was a fantastic lap and a fantastic feeling. We didn't have all the results that we should have had, as we had many races where something happened. They were not even races where you could put the fault on me, but I was there and I lost points, and that wasn't positive.

"The four races where I had accidents were so bad. We had other races, like China, where I had a problem in the pit stop, and Spain where I couldn't have a good pace because I was always in traffic and using the tyres. In Belgium, I took debris in the car and did half of the race going more than 2s slower every lap.

"It wasn't just those four races, as there were another three that were really negative, but I would say in the second part of the season things were going really well. Everything was OK, everything was nice and good.

"We just need to keep working and keep fighting to get better."

NATIONALITY
Brazilian

DATE OF BIRTH
25/4/81

PLACE OF BIRTH
São Paulo
Brazil

HONOURS
2001 Euro
F3000
Champion

2000 European
Formula Renault
Champion

8
JENSON BUTTON
McLAREN, 126PTS

When you look at the results and see one third place, you don't expect that when you're racing for one of the best teams in the world. It's tough, it really is. I think throughout the year we improved as a team in general and I think we also improved the car. Obviously, though, we didn't improve it enough.

"The thing that kept me positive was that last year was a tough year, especially coming off the back of 2012, when we had such a good car. Suddenly we were nowhere. Throughout the whole season, I couldn't really see progress or a direction. So 2013 was a very tough year. This year was a little bit different. It was still difficult, to end up qualifying eighth or so and finishing out of the points in certain races, but at least we've had direction, we've had change in the team. We've employed some very talented people in terms of aerodynamics and engineering and the structure of the team has changed. We've got some true leaders, especially in aerodynamics, which is great to see. So there are lots of positives.

"When I've felt that I've driven my heart out and got the maximum out of the car and finished in eighth, it's tough, but you go through seasons like this. It's about keeping positive and working as hard as you can to pull the team back to the front. The drivers have a big influence in terms of direction with the car and also helping the environment within a team. We're spokesmen for the team and when we're at the factory we spend time with the whole of the staff to try and keep them positive, to uplift them and make sure they know we're giving 100%, so they can't get away with giving 99%.

"I think the reality is that the team has been so close for so many years to winning the World Championship, so you go down the same path every year and think, 'If we just do something a little bit better, we will win the championship.' But suddenly it gets to a point where it starts dropping off, because you haven't gone down new avenues, you haven't really tried anything or moved the personnel around or employed someone from a high-profile team. You can get a little bit lost.

"Sometimes you need a big change to move a team forward.

NATIONALITY
British

DATE OF BIRTH
19/1/80

PLACE OF BIRTH
Frome
England

HONOURS
2009 F1 World Champion

1998 Formula Ford Festival Winner

1997 European Super A Kart Champion

It's difficult, because sometimes when you do that you take a step backward and you've got to fight your way back. It was always going to be a challenge for a team like McLaren and basically it's happened because we haven't made big changes and we haven't realised that we had weaknesses, we've just covered them up with other positives over the last few years. Now we've recognised our weaknesses, big time, with the regulation changes.

"I've felt as though I've really been a team player these last two years, giving it all I have and not being outspoken. I feel like I've done a great job with a car that I don't think I could have scored any more points in. We all have our different skillsets. Some of us are quick on a Saturday, while some of us are quicker on a Sunday. For me, the Sunday is more important. There's the team player aspect, there are so many different areas.

"No driver is perfect, however much some people think so. They all make mistakes and some people aren't team players and think too much about themselves. A team has got to do a lot of work to find the perfect driver and they never will."

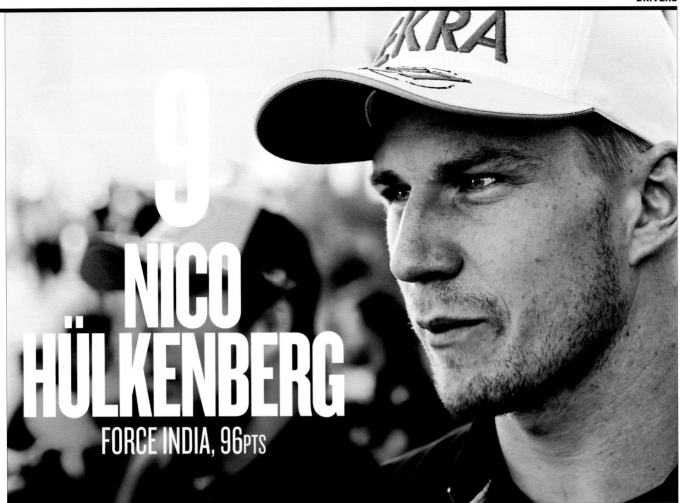

9
NICO HÜLKENBERG
FORCE INDIA, 96PTS

T here's no question that leaving Sauber for Force India was the right decision, but in hindsight it's easy to say, as we had a very good year. Over the course of the season, there's always chances, and you say here and there that it could have been better, but that's the case for every driver and team. We started very strongly, it tailed off a bit towards the end and we weren't as strong as we had been, but we were still able to score points consistently.

"It's a bit strange and unusual to return after a year away, but the welcome was very good. Especially in F1, never say never. It helped a lot that I had been here before and had worked with a lot of the mechanics and my engineer. The settling-in time was next to nothing.

"In some of the later races, we didn't achieve our potential, for whatever reason, and I think some teams out-developed us. Early in the year, in Bahrain, we were racing Ferraris and beating Williams. They clearly overtook us and ended up in front.

"We lost out in development and bringing aero performance to the car. Aero is still king, even with these new cars and new regulations. Other teams just put on more and had a stronger development curve than us. Williams was really good on straightline speed as well as fuel economy.

"One strength of our team is tyre management and tyre understanding and that's quite a valuable asset to have these days. For me to finish fifth in Monaco was pretty nice and also the way we achieved it was cool. Malaysia also stood out. We also achieved that by doing a two-stop. Canada was sort of good, but we couldn't really show the full potential because I qualified outside the top 10. We elected to start on the harder tyre, but that didn't pay off, because the safety car came out right away and compromised my race.

"I managed to score points in every race until the Hungarian GP. That was a shame, because I definitely would have scored some good points there. On that day, I made a mistake and lost the race for it. I had a difficult time in qualifying at Spa-Francorchamps and I was lucky to get a point in the end, but it could have been much better.

"We obviously had to get used to the rule changes at the start of the year. It would be unfair to say that the 2014 cars are not fun. They are still fast, a little slower than the 2013 cars used to be, but it's still fun, still a great challenge and still a great kick to be on the limit.

"We didn't have a race when fuel was critical. We had to do some fuel management, but I think it was better than expected. There were a lot of discussions and rumours out there in the winter about how bad it was going to be, also in terms of reliability. But I think F1 engineers have proved how quickly they can understand and get over things.

"Sometimes it has seemed more difficult to overtake this year and to follow other cars, but overall it's been good. I was always a fan of the driver deciding when to deploy KERS and where and how and so on. That was always a good little challenge in the car, but that has obviously been taken away from the drivers. However, we've seen a lot of good, exciting racing, so it's alright the way it is.

"I'm not frustrated about not being in a winning team. It is what it is, so you just have to hang in there and keep doing your best. Then, one day, your opportunity will come – or not."

NATIONALITY
German

DATE OF BIRTH
19/8/87

PLACE OF BIRTH
Emmerich Germany

HONOURS
2009 GP2 Champion

2008 European F3 Champion

2006/07 A1GP Champion

2005 German Formula BMW Champion

2003 German Kart Champion

10
SERGIO PÉREZ

FORCE INDIA, 59PTS

The team has done a tremendous job this year. If you think that on my car we should have at least 20 points more than we have now, it's really encouraging for the future.

Consider how many issues we had in the early races where, in the first five to seven races, we really struggled to put everything in place. Also, I was adapting after changing teams and it was when the car was at its best. If you consider the DNS that I had in Malaysia, the contacts I had in good races like Canada and Monaco, that really put me a bit behind.

"In a way, I'm surprised what we've achieved this year and how we have achieved it. I'm proud of what we've done. When you land a great result in this team, it's very special.

"When I achieved a good result with McLaren last year, it was probably a fifth or sixth place, which is really nothing for a team like that. For this team, it means a lot, it's something different.

"In the first race, I didn't have my race engineer because his wife

was having their first baby. We had a wet qualifying and in the race I was just out of the points, but Ricciardo had a penalty, so I managed to score a point.

In Malaysia, I couldn't start as I had a hydraulic problem in qualifying. Two races in, Nico had a fifth and a sixth place as the car was at its best then, so we lost big points.

"My season really started in Bahrain. I had a proper weekend, proper qualifying and everything ran smoothly. Basically, I won Bahrain, if you take Mercedes out... That was a great race. Then I had another hydraulic problem in Shanghai, which put me far behind. Whenever I had a clear weekend, I showed very strong pace.

"Canada was the biggest disappointment, as I was so close to winning. I had a brake-by-wire problem and that really prevented me from doing any better. Then I had the hit from Felipe, which spoiled the whole race. Without any issue, I should have finished second, if not first, so it was a huge disappointment.

"I had a penalty from Canada for Austria, so I started very far behind there. I had to make all that progress and I led for a while.

NATIONALITY
Mexican

DATE OF BIRTH
26/1/90

PLACE OF BIRTH
Guadalajara Mexico

HONOURS
2007 British F3 National Class Champion

I think that without the penalty I could have taken another podium, so it wasn't bad at all.

"When you go to McLaren you are aiming to take pole positions, win races and fight for the championship. When I went there, nothing happened, we were basically fighting Force India – we were in front of them, but fighting them.

"If I'm honest, nothing has really changed since I left Sauber. Although McLaren is a very big team, we didn't have any success when I was there.

"The good thing is that I came from a very bad season, with a big impact on my head after getting dropped from McLaren and to come back strongly after that shows good character and good hunger for big things. I'm very hungry to succeed in this sport, and I won't give up in my desire to get to the top.

"The future looks good in this team and I want to try to go forward and make the next step.

"I want to solidify myself in a team, as I've been moving too much in the past two years. I want to establish myself, as I did with Sauber in 2012, and have a very good season."

11 KEVIN MAGNUSSEN
McLAREN, 55PTS

"YOUR FIRST YEAR IN F1 IS going to be pretty spectacular. It's a big thing for any driver to get to F1 and experience it first hand and I think I've had a pretty good season. It's been disappointing in some ways and very exciting in others.

"Obviously, not being able to win was disappointing. I've always been in a position to win, and suddenly you get to F1 and that changes. Still, I've always dreamed of racing for McLaren and to be in F1 and racing for McLaren has been unbelievable.

"It has been quite up and down. F1 is different to other things I've raced. Just because you're at the front in one race doesn't mean you will be at the next race. So, it's tricky and there's so much to learn when you get to F1. One of the things you have to learn is to never know what to expect as there's always something new being thrown at you, a different situation, a different challenge.

"Melbourne was very special. To actually stand on the podium in your first grand prix is such an amazing experience. It also meant that the rest of the season was tougher because having that first result raised expectations and not being able to come back and do the same again is disappointing.

"It's tough out there, definitely. These guys are very talented and it is tough racing with them, but I'm also learning from racing with them. I had some penalties this year, but you can look at them and they were really different situations. I learned from all of them."

NATIONALITY	PLACE OF BIRTH	HONOURS
Danish	Roskilde Denmark	2013 Formula Renault 3.5 Champion
DATE OF BIRTH 5/10/92		2008 Danish Formula Ford Champion

12 KIMI RÄIKKÖNEN
FERRARI, 55PTS

NATIONALITY	PLACE OF BIRTH	HONOURS
Finnish	Espoo Finland	2007 F1 World Champion
DATE OF BIRTH 17/10/79		2000 British Formula Renault Champion
		1998 Finnish & Nordic Kart Champion

"EVERY SEASON THAT YOU don't win the championship you can more or less forget. You are here to try to win championships and, when you don't manage to do that, you've failed. Finishing second or 20th makes little difference. It has been a hard year, but we learned things and it will help us in future.

"It's not much fun when you have a difficult race and then another, but that's how it goes sometimes. We have to believe in what we do. I'm sure we can get back where we should be.

"My driving style is to try to carry the speed in the corners and keep it up mid-corner. You change a little every year and with every car, but I still think it's the fastest way.

"Something has been lacking from the car. If you can't put the car where you want and brake where you want, it's going to be a guessing game. At a few races, it's been OK, but mostly it's been like that, fighting every corner and then the time difference is quite big.

"It's a combination of many things. In 2013, we had very good front tyres at the beginning of the year, then there was a change to not-so-good and I wasn't too happy about it. But we improved a lot... it's a much better car than it was at the beginning of the year.

"Once we get the car on the circuit, then you really know how good it is. There are so many things, even little changes, that can have an effect on that. They started earlier in the year on the design of the new car and they listen to all the things we've been doing this year."

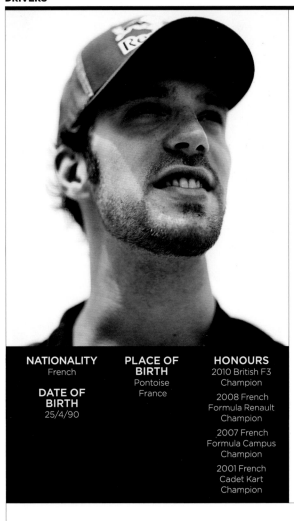

13 JEAN-ÉRIC VERGNE
TORO ROSSO, 22PTS

NATIONALITY
French

DATE OF BIRTH
25/4/90

PLACE OF BIRTH
Pontoise
France

HONOURS
2010 British F3 Champion

2008 French Formula Renault Champion

2007 French Formula Campus Champion

2001 French Cadet Kart Champion

"I'M REALLY HAPPY WITH the job I've done this year, but also with the job the team at Toro Rosso has done.

"In 2013, it was clear that I needed to improve my qualifying and be stronger in my head. The changes I made in the winter were many and I came back this year as a much better driver.

"This season, I've had some great moments, but unfortunately I've had too many reliability problems in the races. It's a bit of a shame. For example, fifth place in Monaco would have been possible and some other good stuff.

"The Hungarian GP was a highlight. I was running second for much of the race and people behind me couldn't overtake. It made me want to have a good car to fight at the front of the field. It felt like this is where I belong.

"It's been really nice that the team was counting on me to set up the car and to develop it. It was good for me to be not the number one driver, because I don't like to use that term, but the experienced driver of the team. It gave me a boost and so it was really good from that point of view.

"Daniel's performance at Red Bull was really encouraging. Last year, it was so tight between him and me to go there. I'm really happy for him, first of all and to see what he was doing gave me a lot of confidence that I can do the same, of course.

"We've always been rivals, but he's someone in the paddock that I respect very highly."

14 ROMAIN GROSJEAN
LOTUS, 8PTS

"IT'S BEEN DISAPPOINTING and frustrating, but, on the other hand, you're still in F1, you're still doing what you love and still enjoying yourself.

"There are days when there are too many problems, there are days when you'd like it to go better. At the end of the story, though, we're all in the same boat, which isn't as quick and as good as it was in 2013.

"There are, however, a lot of positives to get from that situation. For one thing, it has been a character-building year. It's probably not the time to be in such a difficult situation trying to get the whole team back on track. But, if I can do it for 2015, if we can all do better together, then it will make quite a big difference to my career and what I've learned so far.

Unfortunately, after a few laps in testing in the close-season, I knew the E22 wasn't a good car, but I didn't want to admit it to myself. We had a lot of problems with the power unit.

"The first few races were hard, but we could kind of see a positive trend. The Spanish GP was good and we thought, 'Now we're getting there.' In the race, I had a problem with the power unit, otherwise I could have finished in sixth place instead of eighth. After that, though, it got harder again.

"We understood our problems, but it wasn't easy because we didn't have the resources of Red Bull and things take more time. But we know where we need to work and we're going in the right direction for next year."

NATIONALITY
French

DATE OF BIRTH
17/4/86

PLACE OF BIRTH
Geneva
Switzerland

HONOURS
2011 GP2 Champion

2010 Auto GP Champion

2007 European F3 Champion

2005 French Formula Renault Champion

2003 Swiss Formula Renault 1600 Champion

15 DANIIL KVYAT
TORO ROSSO, 8PTS

"THERE'S BEEN A LOT OF action during this season, and everything happened very fast for me, so it's been challenging, but as a driver I like challenges – this is what it's all about.

"The testing was very tough, with almost zero mileage before the Australian GP and no race simulation. Our first race simulation was actually the race itself. The good thing about the low mileage was that I just didn't know and care what was going to happen. I just went there and tried to do what I know how to do.

"It ended up being really good and in the first race I was already fighting both for point-scoring positions and with my teammate. The pace was good, almost better than Jean-Éric, and these were all important things. Of course, I wasn't risking anything in that race as, first of all, we were aiming to finish that race. We finished and I got points. It was a big relief in the end, and a very cool feeling.

"The second half of the season was what I expected and how it should be. I felt more and more comfortable in the car, even though there were a few things that I could work on and adapt for myself.

"There were many races where we did more or less our maximum performance and, of course, some races where we could say that we could have done better, or I was still learning a track which was a bit tough, like the Canadian GP.

"This is a learning process, which has been going very well, so I can't wait for 2015 with Red Bull."

NATIONALITY	PLACE OF BIRTH	HONOURS
Russian	Ufa Russia	2013 GP3 Champion
DATE OF BIRTH 26/4/94		2012 Formula Renault ALPS Champion

16 PASTOR MALDONADO
LOTUS, 2PTS

"IT HAS BEEN A VERY TOUGH season, not only for me but for all of the team, especially after this sequence of very good years that they had at the very top of technology in F1.

"We've not been able to adapt to the new rules. It's not only one problem, I think it's a combination of things. For sure, the car wasn't the greatest, but on the other hand you have the power unit, a very complex one, which was maybe not working well together with our car. Maybe we didn't have the greatest ideas to fix the engine to the car and to get the full performance and on the Renault side we didn't help each other to improve.

"The car was very difficult to drive. It wasn't quick enough on the straights and, because we didn't have the speed in the straights, we had to reduce the amount of downforce and so we were even slow in the corners. On some tracks, where the straights and the power weren't so important, we were able to be closer to the front. Otherwise, we suffered a lot, like at Monza, Spa, these kinds of tracks.

"You can't compare yourself with teams like Ferrari and Red Bull, because they have another structure and have no limit on money. Unfortunately, we were completely limited. We knew what to do immediately, but the decision was taken to wait for next year's car and to invest in that. I understand that. We are a team and we need to be together in the good times and the bad times."

NATIONALITY	PLACE OF BIRTH	HONOURS
Venezuelan	Maracay Venezuela	2010 GP2 Champion
DATE OF BIRTH 9/3/85		2004 Italian Formula Renault Champion
		2003 Italian Formula Renault Winter Champion

17 JULES BIANCHI

MARUSSIA, 2PTS

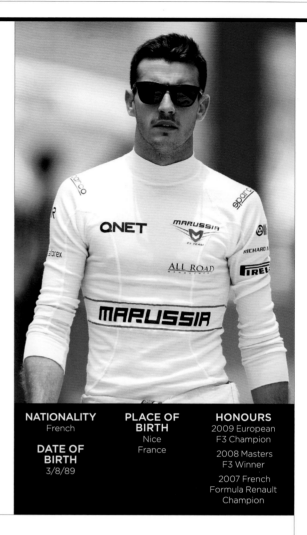

"TESTING WAS REALLY difficult, but that was the case for everybody. It was already a good start that we could be at the first test, even if we missed some days. It was difficult to judge because the car was so different in terms of engine and in terms of grip too, as we lost downforce. I could feel straight away, though, that the car was more balanced, easier to drive and easier to understand, so I felt that it was going to be a better season than 2013.

"I was stronger this year, as I had more confidence with the team and I knew everybody there. However, in terms of driving, I was struggling initially because the car was really different. We had a lot less grip and I didn't really like it in the beginning, so it was a bit difficult. Then I started to feel the limit of the car more and since the Monaco Grand Prix I've felt really good and strong.

"Monaco was just amazing. To finish eighth on track was like a dream and then I was ninth because of the penalty. The result was incredible for us. We had a lot of luck as well and you need that, too, but I think the race we did was perfect and it paid off. After all this work for the team, I was really proud to be the first driver to score points for them. I think we did a really good job together and, for the history books, it was nice for me to be the first one."

Jules was interviewed for the Official Formula 1® Review 2014 at the Singapore GP

NATIONALITY French	PLACE OF BIRTH Nice France	HONOURS 2009 European F3 Champion
DATE OF BIRTH 3/8/89		2008 Masters F3 Winner
		2007 French Formula Renault Champion

18 ADRIAN SUTIL

SAUBER, 0PTS

NATIONALITY German	PLACE OF BIRTH Starnberg Germany	HONOURS 2006 Japanese F3 Champion
DATE OF BIRTH 11/1/83		

"THE SEASON DIDN'T START great and even after the first outing in Jerez I knew it was going to be a lot of work and very difficult. We made some steps and improved in many areas, but it just wasn't enough to go into the points. You can only try to make it better and learn from your mistakes and the lessons that we get every weekend on the engine side and on the new cars in general. They are very complicated to run.

"Reliability was quite a big problem. In many races, we didn't finish due to electrical issues or powertrain issues or other areas, so we had to work on that. I think everyone who didn't have a Mercedes in their car had an issue. They've just done such a good job, so it was very hard to compete. We had a few chances – Singapore was one – but we always struggled with reliability.

"It was difficult, because the balance of the car wasn't predictable. We moved it from one area to another, but it was never giving you 100% confidence.

"Sometimes it was really tricky and we had no choice but to live with a certain problem. For example, we had quite high tyre wear because of that. One problem leads into another and it makes the other thing worse, so you have no confidence.

"I know it from other cars from my years at Force India: the better the car, the easier it is to drive. Then you can do your race, you are deep in the points and everyone is happy."

19 MARCUS ERICSSON
CATERHAM, Opts

"IT'S BEEN A VERY TOUGH year, first of all. It wasn't really what we expected as we thought Caterham was going to take another step and felt during the winter that the whole operation was pushing on hard.

"Quickly, though, we realised that the car was disappointing and we had a lot of work. That made it hard, especially for a rookie, and we also had all these problems with the power unit early on.

"I struggled to get confidence in the car. It was difficult to drive and I didn't get it to my liking. It was very unpredictable, and then we had all these things going on around the team, with Tony Fernandes selling the team, and all this turbulence.

"With the new owners stepping in, we got some fresh momentum. They pushed really hard with the development of the car, especially with weight saving. The problem I had from the start was that I was so much heavier than Kamui. I was 10kg plus heavier, so it was about 0.3 to 0.4s per lap, every circuit, every session, which really doesn't help.

"They got the weight down and the team started to listen to my opinion more and more, and get the car to the way I liked it. The last three races before we stopped were really strong and I started to show a bit of what I was able to do. I didn't show my potential before that.

"Overall, it's been a tough year, but I've learned a lot and I think I've shown what I'm capable of."

NATIONALITY	PLACE OF BIRTH	HONOURS
Swedish	Kumla Sweden	2009 Japanese F3 Champion
DATE OF BIRTH 2/9/90		2007 British Formula BMW Champion

20 ESTEBAN GUTIÉRREZ
SAUBER, Opts

NATIONALITY	PLACE OF BIRTH	HONOURS
Mexican	Monterrey Mexico	2010 GP3 Champion
DATE OF BIRTH 5/8/91		2008 European Formula BMW Champion
		2005 Mexican Rotax Max Kart Champion

"IT'S BEEN A CHALLENGING season, especially coming from a year when I was an F1 rookie. This year, while I made a step as a driver, working on every detail and fighting in every way, I knew I didn't have the same tools as in 2013.

"Naturally, this brings a certain frustration and also pressure. Those two terms have been the challenging things to cope with. On top of that, I feel that I've done a very good – or reasonable – job of trying to cope with them and make some worthwhile achievements, which probably aren't shown very much to the outside world.

"We knew from testing that it was going to be difficult. Things came very late and to get the car ready was pretty tight. As such, we started some steps behind from the first test. You can't point to just one particular thing, but the fundamental problem was the relationship between the power unit, the gearbox and the chassis. You have to make these things synchronised and to synchronise it took time.

"Actually, the team did a really good job in the circumstances and Ferrari has been pushing in every way. Those things were improved, but obviously not as much as we would have liked. We were closing the gap and that was something that was quite evident.

"If I compare the car at the end of the season with the first race and the first test, it was a big step forwards. I think on that side of things we can be sure that we worked in the right direction."

21 MAX CHILTON
MARUSSIA, Opts

"I DON'T KNOW HOW TO PUT into words how truly devastated I am by what has happened to Jules. The support from the F1 family has been incredible and all we can do is be there to support Jules' family.

"I've been giving it my all this year. I kept up my finishing record of completing every grand prix for a long chunk of the year, until the seventh round in Canada. The Italian GP was my first mess-up in 32 races, where I locked up. I should have cut the chicane and didn't. It was a shock, I wasn't expecting to go so high after hitting the kerbs, but I think it was a good thing just to admit it was my fault. Sometimes it's good to be pushing and know you have found the limit.

"I think it's easier in your second year of F1, because last year there were seven or eight tracks I hadn't driven. This year, there were points when I did well and points where I haven't been as good. I think that was part of this year's package. The car was on the edge: sometimes it worked for you, sometimes not. If Jules hadn't got those points in Monaco, it would probably look a bit closer than it was. In Monaco, I was ahead of him and, if I hadn't had the collision with Räikkönen, maybe I could have got the points.

"For most of the year, we were quicker than Caterham in qualifying, although they seemed to match us in the races. I had a good few battles with Marcus Ericsson. Spa was a good one, and we were within 1.5s of each other for the whole race, and I managed to get him at the end."

NATIONALITY	PLACE OF BIRTH	HONOURS
British	Reigate England	None
DATE OF BIRTH 21/4/91		

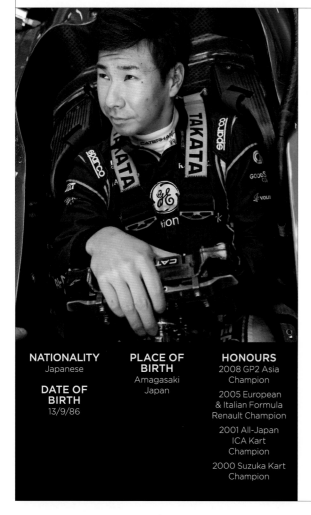

22 KAMUI KOBAYASHI
CATERHAM, Opts

NATIONALITY	PLACE OF BIRTH	HONOURS
Japanese	Amagasaki Japan	2008 GP2 Asia Champion
DATE OF BIRTH 13/9/86		2005 European & Italian Formula Renault Champion
		2001 All-Japan ICA Kart Champion
		2000 Suzuka Kart Champion

"CATERHAM WAS A NEW team for me and the situation was a bit different from where I had been before at Sauber. But this is racing and I knew what to expect. I tried to do my best and focus myself so that I was always doing the best job I could. The situation became ever more difficult from the middle of the season.

"There was a lot to learn with a new package, less downforce, more power. There was a lot of torque from the engine, which was quite difficult. We had a lot of new systems and downshifting was quite difficult at the beginning of the season, although there was a big improvement. I was pretty happy to be part of this game and this learning season was important for me. It's always important to show the car performance and try to help the team.

"Performance-wise, I'm happy with my year – it's just that the car hasn't been fast enough. I enjoyed a lot of the races, but at the same time I often didn't really have a fight with anyone. When I could fight with Marussia it was good, but when we were off the pace it wasn't really exciting for me. We never had any upgrades until late in the season and then we were ahead of them. If we spent a bit of money, there was some potential.

"The financial situation was obviously worse this year. It was not only this team, as Marussia also had quite a confused situation. A lot of F1 teams have had financial problems and I think that's a great shame."

23 WILL STEVENS
CATERHAM, Opts

"I KNEW A WEEK BEFORE THE Abu Dhabi GP that there was a high possibility that I would be in the car. We just needed to get clearance from the FIA for my superlicence.

"I had a good week to look through everything and get to know the car. I'd spent a lot of time in the simulator and, in terms of the steering wheel layout and procedures, I was confident, which helped a lot, so I could then concentrate on the driving side.

"Missing some of the first practice session was a setback, but I just wanted to get through the day, not make any mistakes and build up slowly. That's what I did. On Saturday, I felt good in the car and felt comfortable. The lap time should have been better than it was, but I had a big moment at Turn 17 and lost the rear. I was happy, though, because I knew that the time was in the car and I could get very close to Kamui, but obviously by the same token I'm disappointed because I made a mistake.

"What was good was having Kamui as my teammate, because he's very well respected and has a lot of experience, and everyone knows he can be very quick. I wanted to have a good benchmark to prove myself against. I did it in the right way and built it up slowly.

"I finished the race and that was the first target. I struggled in the first stint as, with the cars coming past, it's quite difficult to keep the temperature in the tyres. After that, my pace compared to Kamui wasn't too bad. Overall, it wasn't a bad day."

NATIONALITY	PLACE OF BIRTH	HONOURS
British	Rochford, England	2007 Asia-Pacific & European KF2 Kart Champion
DATE OF BIRTH 28/6/91		2005 British Junior ICA Kart Champion

24 ANDRÉ LOTTERER
CATERHAM, Opts

"FOR A ONE-OFF, IT WOULD have been great to finish at Spa, no matter where; I could have ticked it off. Now I feel like maybe I should get another go to do a full grand prix.

"I did almost two laps. I had a good start and passed a few guys. Then I went a little bit on the kerb on the exit of Turn 17 and the fuse popped in the battery and everything shut down. I went over the same kerb all weekend and it hadn't happened before.

"It was hard to believe at first: 'Really, it's over already?' At the same time, over my career, I've learned to accept these things and not beat myself up, as there's nothing you can do. I was looking forward to enjoying the car, enjoying the race and getting a rhythm. Unfortunately, it didn't happen. But, at the end of the day, it was a great experience to be an F1 driver for a weekend. I had great feedback from everybody and a warm welcome. Fernando is from the same generation as me, we raced together in karts from 13, while Jenson was one or two categories up.

"It was a great experience and it was just nice to have done it at this stage of my career. I approached it without any pressure and I was totally chilled, which meant I could really enjoy everything. Jacques Villeneuve came up to me and said, 'Man, this is great what you're doing. I love it, jumping in at 32 years old like that!'

"I hope I can have another shot one day."

NATIONALITY	HONOURS	
German	2011, 2012 & 2014 Le Mans 24 Hours Winner	Nippon Champion
DATE OF BIRTH 19/11/81	2012 World Endurance Champion	2006 & 2009 Japanese Super GT Champion
PLACE OF BIRTH Duisburg Germany	2011 Formula	1998 Formula BMW Junior Champion

PHOTOS OF THE YEAR

NINETEEN GRANDS PRIX SPREAD AROUND THE WORLD PROVIDED ACTION, PASSION AND SPECTACLE APLENTY IN 2014. HERE ARE THE PICK OF THE LAT PHOTO AGENCY'S CROP

The 19 grands prix are over and finally the pressure is off for Lewis Hamilton as he celebrates clinching the title at the final round

Clockwise from right: Ferrari fans horse around at Suzuka; sparks fly in the McLaren garage; Felipe Massa is shown his data; Fernando Alonso waves to his fans

Clockwise from top left: Nicole Scherzinger was in Abu Dhabi to watch Lewis Hamilton become champion; Kimi Räikkönen in the pits; an exultant Hamilton in parc fermé; glamour on the grid; an unplanned exit for Sergio Pérez at Monaco; Fernando Alonso deep in thought; a message from the fans; circuit designer Hermann Tilke; Valtteri Bottas guides his FW36 on to Monaco's harbourfront

There can be no mistaking which team gets the most support at Monza, but there was no Ferrari driver for them to cheer on the podium as Lewis Hamilton and Nico Rosberg were joined by Felipe Massa

Clockwise from far left: dedicated numbers arrived in 2014. This is 77, Bottas; Ferrari's prancing horse remains the same; the red, white and blue of Russia; Hamilton and Alonso in parc fermé; Caterham's Kamui Kobayashi; Bernie Ecclestone and wife Fabiana onboard in Monaco

#KeepFightingMichael

Lewis Hamilton had plenty to celebrate through 2014, while the message on the side of his car was one echoed throughout F1 as Michael Schumacher continued his long recovery after his skiing accident

Clockwise from above: Fernando Alonso explains Ferrari's form; Hamiltons father and son embrace after Lewis landed the title in Abu Dhabi; Kevin Magnussen learned a great deal in his rookie year; Felipe Massa goes for a roll at the German GP

Clockwise from right: Nico Rosberg shows his footballing skills; fans in Brazil; no time to lose in the pits; Nicole Scherzinger kisses Hamilton; Bottas prepares to hit the track; Jenson Button hugs his fiancée Jessica Michibata

Clockwise from left: Caterham racer Marcus Ericsson puts things into perspective; one tyre, slightly used...; Lewis Hamilton races past new venue Sochi's unusual backdrop

2014 WAS A YEAR OF HUGE TECHNICAL CHANGE. THIS IS HOW THE 11 TEAMS COPED WITH THE INTRODUCTION OF TURBOCHARGED ENGINES, THROUGH THE EYES OF THEIR TECHNICAL CHIEFS

THE CONSTRU

ICTORS

MERCEDES AMG PETRONA

By Paddy Lowe
EXECUTIVE DIRECTOR (TECHNICAL)

"THE TEAM WAS REASONABLY well advanced with the 2014 car when I joined in June 2013. The engine architecture was set quite early on and the engine project had a much longer lead time than the car itself. There was a lot of work being done on details of packaging and on performance aspects, trying to get things to work as intended. Yet there was still a huge challenge ahead on the engine, mostly making various elements work as well as they should while, in parallel, adding more performance.

"With the main aspect of the car's architecture set, it was a matter of detailing how things fitted in, especially the cooling systems. When I arrived, we were on cooling iteration 27 and by the Japanese GP we had got to 32, which gives an idea of how much development had been done. These are not all systems that actually ran, but the number of concepts we explored.

"When we looked at the 2014 project right at the beginning – when I was at another team – the cooling requirement of this new power unit with the extra ERS, and particularly the intercooler, it looked as though the whole story of the car was going to be how to get

in enough heat-exchange area to get the job done. To produce a car that seemed little different to the year before in terms of radiator area felt pretty amazing and it was a great achievement to get it to that point from what seemed such a challenge a year and a half earlier.

"Incorporating the power unit into the car with the minimum aerodynamic impact is more important than ever. Our long lead time was part of the story of our success, in that we could nibble away at it bit by bit. We pushed up the efficiency of each part of the cooling circuit and that's what brings sizes down. Your first go isn't nearly as good as your 27th.

"We did a lot to clean up the packaging of all the equipment in the car, but concentrated on the sidepods in particular. We tried to make it more modular as well. We had the FRICS that took space, although that was a bit relieved with the loss of FRICS from the German GP.

"It cost us a few tenths of a second in speed but, looking at how everyone else went, we seem to be about on a par. It helped with the balance between the high- and low-speed corners and also stability pre-corner. The biggest penalty is that you get more mid-corner understeer. Without FRICS, the set-up window

was narrowed as it allowed you to make the car better balanced throughout the lap.

"Getting going early was a great help to the programme. We fired the car up in December in the lab, and then went to Silverstone at the end of January. We were also the first car out at 09:00 at the Jerez test and we couldn't have done that without all the dyno work we did over Christmas in the lab. We did much more to the car than you'd normally have done at that point, which meant we'd already worked on the car and its set-up for months.

"We did have a front wing failure at Jerez, which was a shock. Structural failures or suspension or wings are not what you want to present your drivers with and it's not how we'd liked to have ended our first day. However, we were up and running next day with a reinforced structure after flying some parts out.

"A lot of effort went into understanding the tyres last year, particularly in mid-season, and we saw the 2013 car improve a lot in tyre management. It was a big focus this year and we built on all that previous experience. If we'd had this year's car without that learning curve it might have been quite a different story. In the past, we were doing a pit stop more than everyone

> "OUR LONG LEAD TIME WAS PART OF THE STORY OF OUR SUCCESS"

CHASSIS
CHASSIS MODEL
Mercedes F1 W05
FRONT SUSPENSION LAYOUT
Carbon-fibre wishbone and pushrod-activated torsion springs and rockers
REAR SUSPENSION LAYOUT
Carbon-fibre wishbone and pullrod-activated torsion springs and rockers

DAMPERS Penske Racing
TYRES Pirelli
WHEELS Advanti
BRAKE DISCS Not disclosed
BRAKE PADS Not disclosed
BRAKE CALIPERS Brembo
FUEL TANK ATL
INSTRUMENTS
McLaren Electronic Systems

DIMENSIONS
LENGTH 4800mm
WIDTH 1800mm
HEIGHT 950mm
WHEELBASE Not disclosed
TRACK, FRONT Not disclosed
TRACK, REAR Not disclosed
WEIGHT 691kg (including driver and camera)

ENGINE
MAKE/MODEL
Mercedes-Benz PU106A Hybrid
CONFIGURATION 1600cc V6 turbo
SPARK PLUGS Not disclosed
ECU FIA standard issue
FUEL Petronas Primax
OIL Petronas Syntium
BATTERY Not disclosed

1 TEAM

else, so it was an important part of the puzzle to solve.

"We had problems with electrical components overheating in Canada and it was a peripheral aspect of the system. All the main cooling aspects were well-studied, mapped and optimised, but this was related to peripheral aspects of the electronics and caught us by surprise. With the packaging as tight as it is, there isn't a lot of space in which to manoeuvre, but it's well understood now and we will do a better job of it next year.

"The rear electronic brake distribution system has been remarkably easy. We have had problems, such as overheating the rear brakes – to the point that they caught fire in Canada – and we've had boiling brake fluid, so the EBD hasn't worked properly, but that wasn't the fault of the system itself. The first test was difficult, but by the time we got to the first race in Melbourne we were in a spec that we stayed with all year.

"The car improved a lot over the season, but that was more in aerodynamics than the power unit. The idea that aero is no longer a field of competition is wide of the mark. That battle is undiminished: we just have a battle of power units as well, which is great. That's where F1 should be."

THE DRIVERS

ROSBERG   **HAMILTON**

THE TEAM
NON-EXECUTIVE CHAIRMAN
Niki Lauda
MERCEDES MOTORSPORT DIRECTOR
Toto Wolff
EXECUTIVE DIRECTOR (TECHNICAL)
Paddy Lowe
MANAGING DIRECTOR, MERCEDES AMG HIGH PERFORMANCE POWERTRAINS
Andy Cowell
TECHNOLOGY DIRECTOR
Geoff Willis
ENGINEERING DIRECTOR
Aldo Costa
PERFORMANCE DIRECTOR
Mark Ellis
DRIVERS
Lewis Hamilton, Nico Rosberg
SPORTING DIRECTOR
Ron Meadows
CHIEF RACE ENGINEER
Andrew Shovlin
CHIEF TRACK ENGINEER
Simon Cole
SENIOR RACE ENGINEER (HAMILTON)
Peter Bonnington
SENIOR RACE ENGINEER (ROSBERG)
Tony Ross
CHIEF MECHANIC
Matthew Deane
RESERVE DRIVER
Pascal Wehrlein
TOTAL NUMBER OF EMPLOYEES 600
NUMBER IN RACE TEAM 60
TEAM BASE
Brackley, England
TELEPHONE
+44 (0)1280 844000
WEBSITE
www.mercedesamgf1.com

PARTNERS
Petronas, BlackBerry, Swissquote, IWC Schaffhausen, Starwood Preferred Guest, ebmpapst, UBS, Allianz, Monster Energy, Puma, Pirelli, Assos, Spies Hecker, Tata Communications

TEAM STATS
IN F1 SINCE 1999 as BAR, then as Honda Racing 2006-08 and as Brawn GP 2009
FIRST GRAND PRIX Australia 1999
CONSTRUCTORS' TITLES 2
DRIVERS' TITLES 2

TRANSMISSION
GEARBOX Mercedes AMG Petronas
FORWARD GEARS Eight
CLUTCH Not disclosed

MERCEDES AMG PETRONAS FORMULA ONE™ TEAM

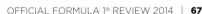

By Rob Marshall
CHIEF DESIGNER

"THE REGULATION CHANGES were significant in 2014, even if you exclude the change of power unit. The narrower front and rear wings meant a lot of work for the aero department to establish what to do with the endplates and the front wing wakes. The loss of exhaust blowing also had a significant effect on aero and the balance of the car, which took a significant amount of resource to sort.

"The power unit had very different requirements in terms of heat rejection and packaging. Most cars have probably 50% more radiator capacity on the car, but we were in reasonably good shape in terms of cooling. The demands of the Renault engine were towards the upper end, but the more you cool it, the more performance you can get out of it. Of course, cooling wasn't a problem in winter testing.

"Pre-season, we had various mechanical failures, which caused the car to set on fire. It's a misconception it happened because it wasn't cooling properly, as the water and oil temperatures were perfectly under control.

"Sometimes, there isn't an overnight fix during a test and some of the bits needed had a long lead time. We knew on the first night that only a long-term fix would nail it. The lead times meant that we got those new bits just in time for the Australian GP. It was a surprise to many at that first race that we managed to get in more than a few laps without setting the car on fire, but it wasn't to us as our fix was a very robust one.

"In terms of packaging, we have always gone as narrow as we can at the rear of the car and did the same in 2014. Mercedes had a much more conventional layout as did the rest of the grid. Our design was very different, because of our design philosophy rather than the packaging of the power unit.

"Early on, some of our software was a bit underdeveloped on the brake-by-wire and there were some issues in getting the systems to talk to each other properly. We soon got on top of that and continued to fine tune it. We became pretty good on the brakes, which is why we did most of our overtaking manoeuvres at the end of the straights rather than down them. So, I'd say that our braking is probably better than most.

"Initially, tyre management was a bit of a struggle. But, as Renault made improvements in driveability, it gave significant performance increase as it stopped the rear tyres being overcooked. Even on a single lap, if you are over-slipping the tyres you can overwork them within a couple of corners. Our tyre usage got better throughout the year in line with those driveability improvements on top of the changes that made the car more stable.

"We introduced a few decent-sized upgrades during the season, mostly just trying new things like you do every year. We did a lot of work to overcome the downforce deficit inherent in the regulation change, but that was mostly iterative. It was a process of chipping away.

"The car's key weakness was that it was underpowered. But we did make some improvements in driveability and power. Total worked very hard and Renault was pushing as much as it could.

"These engines are very knock sensitive and, if you can develop fuels that are less knock sensitive, you can gain performance. If you've got ignition strategies and software to help you detect knock and run closer to the edge, you'll get better performance. Those are the areas where Mercedes excels.

"The car was also sensitive at corner exit when in the traction-limited phase, but I think everyone was the same. With the current generation of F1 cars, even the very good ones have understeer on entry

> **"WE DID A LOT OF WORK TO OVERCOME THE DOWNFORCE DEFICIT"**

CHASSIS
CHASSIS MODEL Red Bull RB10
FRONT AND REAR SUSPENSION LAYOUT
Aluminium alloy uprights, carbon composite double wishbones with torsion springs and anti-roll bars
DAMPERS Multimatic
TYRES Pirelli

WHEELS OZ Racing
BRAKE DISCS Brembo
BRAKE PADS Brembo
BRAKE CALIPERS Brembo
FUEL TANK
Not disclosed
INSTRUMENTS
Not disclosed

DIMENSIONS
LENGTH Not disclosed
WIDTH Not disclosed
HEIGHT Not disclosed
WHEELBASE Not disclosed
TRACK, FRONT Not disclosed
TRACK, REAR Not disclosed
WEIGHT 690kg (including driver and camera)

ENGINE
MAKE/MODEL
Renault Energy F1-2014
CONFIGURATION 1600cc V6 turbo
SPARK PLUGS Not disclosed
ECU FIA standard issue
FUEL Total
OIL Total
BATTERY Not disclosed

RACING

and oversteer on exit. When you had exhaust blowing, you could stop the oversteer on exit.

"A blown diffuser was quite a handy device because it enabled you to fix a lot of ills. If there are some slightly undesirable characteristics designed into the car, you could just dial them out with exhaust blowing. It also allowed you to be more aggressive with some developments in car design. So, with that gone, you have to back off a bit and try to make a car that is more benign.

"Sebastian Vettel was seriously good at driving a car on the very edge with a blown diffuser. I think he was probably the best of all, actually – and our blown diffuser was probably the best, too. So, as a team, we suffered more than most through its loss. Sebastian lost as well, so it was a double whammy.

"You could probably say that Daniel Ricciardo is more used to a car that's not very planted on exit, although the 2013 Toro Rosso wasn't a bad car. He just seemed to really take to our car and was right on the top of his game. Exactly why there was such a big difference is difficult to say. Talk to Sebastian and he will say he doesn't believe in luck, but he did have a bad run of things. When you lose sessions here and there because of problems, you are playing catch-up."

THE DRIVERS

VETTEL   RICCIARDO

THE TEAM
CHAIRMAN
Dietrich Mateschitz
TEAM PRINCIPAL
Christian Horner
CHIEF TECHNICAL OFFICER
Adrian Newey
CHIEF DESIGNER
Rob Marshall
HEAD OF AERODYNAMICS
Dan Fallows
**CHIEF ENGINEER,
CAR ENGINEERING** Paul Monaghan
**CHIEF ENGINEER, PERFORMANCE
ENGINEERING** Pierre Wache
HEAD OF ELECTRONICS
Paul Everington
**TECHNICAL DIRECTOR,
RENAULT ENGINES** Rob White
TEAM MANAGER
Jonathan Wheatley
DRIVERS
Daniel Ricciardo, Sebastian Vettel
RACE ENGINEER (VETTEL)
Guillaume Rocquelin
RACE ENGINEER (RICCIARDO)
Simon Rennie
TEST & RESERVE DRIVER
Sébastien Buemi
TOTAL NUMBER OF EMPLOYEES 550
NUMBER IN RACE TEAM 60
TEAM BASE
Milton Keynes, England
TELEPHONE
+44 (0)1908 279700
WEBSITE
www.infiniti-redbullracing.com

PARTNERS
Infiniti, Total, Renault, Rauch, Geox, Pepe Jeans, Casio, Singha Beer, Pirelli, Alpinestars, AT&T, DMG, Platform Computing, OZ Wheels, Siemens, Hexagon Metrology, Ansys, FLIR, PWR, Sabelt, Sonax, Snap On, Scott, Ultimate Ears, Matrix

TEAM STATS
IN F1 SINCE 1997 as Stewart Grand Prix, then as Jaguar Racing 2000-04
FIRST GRAND PRIX Australia 1997
CONSTRUCTORS' TITLES 4
DRIVERS' TITLES 4

TRANSMISSION
GEARBOX Red Bull Racing
FORWARD GEARS Eight
CLUTCH AP Racing

By Pat Symonds
CHIEF TECHNICAL OFFICER

"THE PROGRESS WILLIAMS made this year can't be attributed to just one cause, but we managed to get a few stars aligned. The 2013 car had very troubled aerodynamics, on top of which it had a blown diffuser that didn't work. But now, the aero department works really well. It's the same people, but they came up with the goods and I'd argue Williams had the best development rate of the year. We weren't bad at the beginning, the car was certainly a bit quicker than results suggested, but we then got ever closer to Mercedes as the season went on.

"The improvement is about engineering integrity, making sure that you understand what you are doing, being honest with yourself and knowing when you don't fully understand something. The whole team's attitude is really good. The group is 95% the same as it was in 2013, but doing things much better.

"Where we needed to be with the 2014 car in terms of drag and downforce was the subject of a lot of debate in the team, but the efficiency targets we set turned out to be rather good. We were a bit light on downforce, but the amount we were down on drag wasn't proportional, so our efficiency was a bit higher than some of the other teams managed. That proved a good way to race and allowed us to be fast on the straights. I'd have loved more downforce, but we established the efficiencies we wanted and are sticking with them.

"We made a choice that was a bit different to others, which was perhaps why we didn't have quite as much downforce. However, it proved to be a success, even though it might have cost us in qualifying. It also improved the fuel efficiency, as the low drag definitely was a help. As a consequence, fuel efficiency wasn't anywhere near as difficult as we thought it might be.

"The fundamental power unit architecture was all there in May last year and we packaged it quite well. We did some things that were maybe not totally necessary. For example, our gearbox has a titanium bellhousing because we weren't certain what the temperatures were going to be around the exhaust.

"Mercedes wasn't worried as long as we achieved our cooling targets and we had a pretty good package from the start. We then retuned it for the Spanish GP and it was very good after that with a nice balance of water/oil and intercooler temperatures, while still keeping quite low drag. It was about refining it. We're not changing very much next year from the basic way we have done it, with the intercooler and ERS heat exchanger for the hydraulics on the right.

"In some ways, we did too much running pre-season because we hadn't expected to be able to do so and thus hadn't got enough parts. By the time we finished the final Bahrain test, though, we really did understand the car. We completed a lot of race distances, understood how to manage the engine and the ERS and it really paid off.

"We did some development work on the wings early on. We were on our fourth front wing iteration by the fourth race and the fifth came in practice at Suzuka. We made a big change to the bodywork and radiator layout for the Spanish GP, which helped us particularly in the hotter races. Early on, we did have tyre difficulties. We had to do three stops in Bahrain to everyone else's two, but later we had slightly better tyre life than our rivals.

"One of the most talked-about changes this season was running without front-to-rear interconnected suspension from the German GP onwards. When I arrived at Williams, I was surprised that it was a bit old-fashioned compared with what we

> **"WE WERE ON OUR FOURTH WING ITERATION BY THE FOURTH RACE"**

CHASSIS
CHASSIS MODEL
Williams FW35
FRONT SUSPENSION LAYOUT
Double wishbones with pushrod-activated springs and anti-roll bar
REAR SUSPENSION LAYOUT
Double wishbones with pullrod-activated springs and anti-roll bar

DAMPERS Williams F1
TYRES Pirelli
WHEELS Rays
BRAKE DISCS Not disclosed
BRAKE PADS Not disclosed
BRAKE CALIPERS AP Racing
FUEL TANK ATL
INSTRUMENTS
McLaren Electronic Systems

DIMENSIONS
LENGTH 5000mm
WIDTH 1800mm
HEIGHT 950mm
WHEELBASE FIA maximum
TRACK, FRONT 1450mm
TRACK, REAR 1400mm
WEIGHT 690kg (including driver and camera)

ENGINE
MAKE/MODEL Mercedes PU106A
CONFIGURATION 1600cc V6 turbo
SPARK PLUGS Not disclosed
ECU FIA standard issue
FUEL Total
OIL Total
BATTERY
Not disclosed

RACING

had had at Marussia. Then, in the Jerez test, we had a problem unrelated to the interconnect but to carry on we had to disconnect it and found the car felt about the same without it. It was worth keeping, but not giving us the advantage I was used to. So, losing FRICS didn't affect us. We had to lift the ride heights and rearrange our skids, but one of the ways that we got closer to Mercedes was because of that change.

"Operationally, we made a lot of progress. Early in the season, we were coming back from every race with 10 points. One of my biggest battles has been to get people to be unhappy with that. Rob Smedley has helped a lot. I didn't want an old-fashioned chief engineer, I wanted a true head of vehicle performance and Rob understood that. It's why we work so well together.

"I'm also really happy with the performance of Felipe Massa and Valtteri Bottas. Valtteri gets better every week and Felipe was the perfect driver for where Williams was in January 2014. We knew he was quick, but he was even quicker than I thought.

"Valtteri's use of tyres was remarkable too and Felipe improved a lot in that respect, particularly in the test after the Spanish GP. They've proved a strong pairing."

TRANSMISSION
GEARBOX Williams F1
FORWARD GEARS Eight
CLUTCH Not disclosed

THE DRIVERS

BOTTAS   MASSA

THE TEAM
TEAM PRINCIPAL Sir Frank Williams
CO-FOUNDER Patrick Head
DEPUTY TEAM PRINCIPAL
Claire Williams
CHIEF EXECUTIVE OFFICER
Mike O'Driscoll
CHIEF TECHNICAL OFFICER
Pat Symonds
CHIEF DESIGNER Ed Wood
HEAD OF AERODYNAMICS
Jason Somerville
HEAD OF AERODYNAMIC
PERFORMANCE Dave Wheater
HEAD OF AERODYNAMIC PROCESS
Shaun Whitehead
HEAD OF VEHICLE DYNAMICS
Craig Wilson
HEAD OF PERFORMANCE
ENGINEERING Rob Smedley
MERCEDES HPP TEAM SUPPORT
Paul Leeming
HEAD OF ENGINEERING OPERATIONS
Jakob Andreasen
DRIVERS Valtteri Bottas, Felipe Massa
TEAM MANAGER
Pete Vale
CHIEF TEST & SUPPORT ENGINEER
Rod Nelson
HEAD OF RACE STRATEGY
Richard Lockwood
RACE ENGINEER (BOTTAS)
Jonathan Eddolls
RACE ENGINEER (MASSA)
Andrew Murdoch
CHIEF MECHANIC Carl Gaden
DEVELOPMENT DRIVER
Susie Wolff
TEST & RESERVE DRIVER
Felipe Nasr
TOTAL NUMBER OF EMPLOYEES
650 (Williams F1)
NUMBER IN RACE TEAM
80 (47 operational, 33 ancillary)
TEAM BASE Grove, England
TELEPHONE
+44 (0)1235 777700
WEBSITE www.williamsf1.com

PARTNERS
Martini, Randstad, Petrobras, Experian, Genworth, Thomson Reuters, Banco do Brasil, Oris, Wihuri, Kemppi, Esquire, Hatch, Pirelli, Dom Reilly Ltd, Shoretel, PPG, Puma, Rays, Michael Caines MBE

TEAM STATS
IN F1 SINCE 1973
FIRST GRAND PRIX Argentina 1973
CONSTRUCTORS' TITLES 9
DRIVERS' TITLES 7

WILLIAMS
MARTINI
RACING

By Pat Fry
ENGINEERING DIRECTOR

"THE CONCEPT OF THE CAR was based on trying to make up for the aerodynamic rule changes, particularly the loss of exhaust blowing. That was something we never really got on top of in previous seasons, so I suspect we lost less there than other teams. We played around with different noses before and after the start of the season, but we stuck with the design we had because we didn't find anything better.

"The main challenge of the chassis was packaging the power unit. There were many trade-offs to be made there. You could have massive radiators and more engine power or smaller radiators and less. We were more towards the aero end of the spectrum on radiator size.

"Our upgraded windtunnel was a reasonable improvement. It was October 2013 when we turned it back on and it has been a definite step forward. It will never be perfect but it became a very sensible tool and a lot of people on the aero side of the team are doing good work. We need to up the development rate from it now that we believe in it.

"We were able to run with some ballast on the car, but it's a massive challenge. It's all part of the trade-offs you have to make technically. It's easy to add an extra 5kg on radiators. We ended up teetering on the brink of where we would have liked to be.

"In terms of power unit learning curve, we made a huge amount of progress in the control systems and getting everything to work better. In the first year of these power units, we learned a huge amount and there is still a long way to go. For the Spanish GP, we found some gains from improving the exhaust system and insulating pipes. To make major steps, though, we needed redesign work. With the engine freeze, there were things we couldn't improve during the season. There's always stuff you can improve beyond that, of course, and we changed a lot of the ancillaries that we were allowed to change. We could have done more, but it comes down to resource.

"However, we made a lot more gains than typically because the power unit was all new. The driveability was improved and the improvements to the car were spread evenly. Normally, it's 80% aerodynamic development, but in 2014 it was 50/50 between aero and the power unit.

"The problems with the car were across all areas, though. Looking at our aero compared with Red Bull, you would say that we had a long way to go. If you compared our engine with Mercedes, you'd say we had a long way to go. Racing a Mercedes was very difficult because of the amount of power they had. Racing a Renault-powered car was hard because of the amount of ERS-H recovery they had. When the car is in clean air, it works very well, but when it's behind another car it loses front end. More power and more downforce will always solve that.

"With all the analysis available, including GPS and sound analysis, you can see where your speed is and how other people could maintain pace while we couldn't. We'll be able to address a lot of these deficiencies from the start of 2015. We need to get everything right.

"As well as saying that we didn't integrate the chassis and the power unit well enough, we should also have started earlier. When you start is crucial. At Mercedes, when the engine freeze came in, it was their engineers who designed KERS and were doing single cylinder research relevant to the 2014 power units four years ago. It's all down to good work and planning on their part, so we need to try harder.

"It's too simplistic to say that the power unit was compromised for the aero. You choose a packaging

> ## "WE DIDN'T INTEGRATE THE CHASSIS AND POWER UNIT WELL ENOUGH"

CHASSIS
CHASSIS MODEL
Ferrari F14 T
FRONT AND REAR SUSPENSION LAYOUT
Independent pullrod-activated torsion springs
DAMPERS Not disclosed
TYRES Pirelli

WHEELS OZ Racing
BRAKE DISCS Brembo
BRAKE PADS
Not disclosed
BRAKE CALIPERS
Not disclosed
FUEL TANK Not disclosed
INSTRUMENTS
Ferrari/Magneti Marelli

DIMENSIONS
LENGTH Not disclosed
WIDTH Not disclosed
HEIGHT Not disclosed
WHEELBASE Not disclosed
TRACK, FRONT Not disclosed
TRACK, REAR Not disclosed
WEIGHT 691kg (including driver and camera)

ENGINE
MAKE/MODEL Ferrari 059/3
CONFIGURATION
1600cc V6 turbo
SPARK PLUGS Not disclosed
ECU FIA Standard issue
FUEL Shell V-Power
OIL Shell Helix Ultra
BATTERY Not disclosed

route and it's always a trade-off. On the aero side, it would be unfair to say that we didn't gain from it because, if we had put bigger radiators on the car or changed the layout, we would have lost out.

"Kimi Räikkönen struggled a lot more with the front end of the car than Fernando Alonso and, by the time you do get that front end into the car, the rear becomes a problem. Fernando's driving style worked well with these tyres and he could drive around and adapt to problems, but Kimi has always been much more sensitive to the feel of the front end.

"It wasn't so bad on the softer-compound tyres. Taking the Singapore GP as an example, when he went on to the super-soft, he found a huge amount of time. It was a challenge getting the front tyres working for him and we had ongoing suspension developments to battle to understand it.

"A change at the top, which Ferrari had during the season, brings new focus and draws a line from which to progress. Team principal Marco Mattiacci is trying to do everything to move forwards and put things in place for the future. There has been a realisation of why we were where we were – which isn't where we wanted to be – and how to make progress in 2015."

THE DRIVERS

ALONSO   **RÄIKKÖNEN**

THE TEAM
PRESIDENT
Sergio Marchionne
CHIEF EXECUTIVE OFFICER
Amadeo Felisa
TEAM PRINCIPAL
Marco Mattiacci
TECHNICAL DIRECTOR
James Allison
ENGINEERING DIRECTOR
Pat Fry
CHIEF OPERATING OFFICER, POWER UNIT Mattia Binotto
HEAD OF TRACKSIDE OPERATIONS & VEHICLE ASSEMBLY
Diego Ioverno
SPORTING DIRECTOR
Massimo Rivola
PRODUCTION DIRECTOR
Corrado Lanzone
CHIEF DESIGNER, POWER UNIT
Lorenzo Sassi
CHIEF DESIGNER, CHASSIS
Nikolas Tombazis
DEPUTY CHIEF DESIGNER
Simone Resta
HEAD OF AERODYNAMICS
Loic Bigois
DRIVERS
Fernando Alonso, Kimi Räikkönen
RACE ENGINEER (ALONSO)
Andrea Stella
RACE ENGINEER (RÄIKKÖNEN)
Antonio Spagnolo
CHIEF MECHANIC
Francesco Uguzzoni
TEST/THIRD DRIVERS
Pedro de la Rosa, Marc Gene
TOTAL NUMBER OF EMPLOYEES
Over 600
NUMBER IN RACE TEAM
Approx 70
TEAM BASE
Maranello, Italy
TELEPHONE
+39 0536 949450
WEBSITE
www.ferrari.com

PARTNERS
Philip Morris International, FIAT, Santander, Shell, Kaspersky Lab, UPS, Weichai Power, Hublot, TNT Energy Drink

TEAM STATS
IN F1 SINCE 1950
FIRST GRAND PRIX Britain 1950
CONSTRUCTORS' TITLES 16
DRIVERS' TITLES 15

TRANSMISSION
GEARBOX Ferrari
FORWARD GEARS Eight
CLUTCH Not disclosed

By Tim Goss
TECHNICAL DIRECTOR

"THE REGULATION CHANGES for 2014 were some of the biggest I've known. Aerodynamically, we had the narrow-span front wing, the lower nose and lower chassis, while at the back of the car we lost exhaust blowing, the beam wing and had a smaller rear wing. There was also a huge change in engine regulations, with the smaller turbocharged V6 and a tenfold increase in energy storage.

"It was a huge challenge to get a car that worked and, secondly, to recover the lost performance. We knew that getting the power unit installation right was an absolute must. In winter testing, we had to make sure that we covered the miles to learn about the car.

"The change in aerodynamic regulations upset the flow structures of the car. Once we made the change to the short-span front wing, it was obvious that the endplates were positioned in the most awkward place possible. The proximity of the front wing endplate to the tyre was a big penalty and the greatest challenge aerodynamically was to recover some sensible flow physics around the car.

"There are some important flow structures that come off the front wing endplate and getting those to negotiate the tyre sensibly and control the front tyre wake was key to getting the car to work well. It wasn't straightforward and it took quite a while to get the flow structures to negotiate the tyre under all conditions of yaw, steer, roll, ride height and so on. Once we were there and had the philosophy, it was a case of just working on it.

"The regulations meant that we were forced down the route of having a low-tipped nose. We looked at the option of going for a low or, within what the regulations allowed, a high nose. Our philosophy was to go with as high a nose as allowed because we wanted to secure a stable rear end to recover the lost downforce. This helped reduce the losses at the mid part of the car and enabled us to get the rear end back to a sensible level of downforce.

"Since the nose and chassis were lower overall, the most sensible arrangement was to go back to pushrod front suspension. If we'd retained the high nose allowed under previous rules, we'd probably have retained the pullrod, but there wasn't much in it. The pullrod was structurally a bit better and lighter.

"Recovering the rear downforce was a challenge and we had a novel rear suspension layout. We realised

"WE'VE LEARNED A LOT ABOUT HOW TO IMPROVE THE FRONT END"

that we could rapidly recover some of that downforce, so we positioned suspension legs along the trailing edge of the diffuser. The regulations limited the shape, but we were able to devise a shape that acted like an aerodynamic wing. They looked quite crude, but worked as a cascade with the diffuser and the trailing-edge gurney flaps. The airflow attaches to the curvature at the back of the legs and that produces a huge amount of upwash in that area, allowing us to work the diffuser much harder and drive the rear wing harder.

"It's clear that we weren't where we wanted to be. McLaren is a team that exists to win races and we didn't do that this season. It was a year of rebuilding the engineering team, with a change of leadership in the aero department. The early part of the season was all about the changes and getting the right leadership, direction and focus in the engineering department.

"The main battleground under these regulations is the front end of the car and so much of that is about detail. It's not about fundamentals like a high or low nose, it's about the design detail of the front wing both inboard and outboard. That's where our challenge lay. We put measurable performance on the car and, over the season, kept pace with

CHASSIS
CHASSIS MODEL McLaren MP4-29
FRONT SUSPENSION LAYOUT
Carbon-fibre wishbone and pushrod suspension operating inboard torsion bar and damper system
REAR SUSPENSION LAYOUT
Carbon-fibre wishbone and pullrod suspension operating inboard torsion

bar and damper system
DAMPERS Not disclosed
TYRES Pirelli
WHEELS Enkei
BRAKE DISCS Not disclosed
BRAKE PADS Not disclosed
BRAKE CALIPERS Akebono
FUEL TANK Not disclosed
INSTRUMENTS McLaren Elec. Sys.

DIMENSIONS
LENGTH Not disclosed
WIDTH Not disclosed
HEIGHT Not disclosed
WHEELBASE Not disclosed
TRACK, FRONT Not disclosed
TRACK, REAR Not disclosed
WEIGHT 690kg (including driver and camera)

ENGINE
MAKE/MODEL
Mercedes-Benz PU106A Hybrid
CONFIGURATION 1600cc V6 turbo
SPARK PLUGS NGK
ECU FIA standard issue
FUEL Mobil
OIL Mobil 1
BATTERY GS Yuasa

the development of Mercedes. We've learned a lot about how to improve the front end and where we need to go now.

"The engines were homologated, but fuel was relatively free in terms of updates. We don't know how the Petronas fuel used by Mercedes compares to our Mobil1 fuel, but we did research with ExxonMobil and Mercedes to develop fantastic fuels. We did ease off, as we have the Honda programme next year so couldn't justify the time and effort going into this engine rather than the future, but we have had significant upgrades. Exxon did a fantastic job and that was a big part of our performance over the season.

"In terms of car updates, we had a huge step for the first race with a new front wing and diffuser. Then there was a nose update at the Malaysian GP. The car didn't change radically over the season, but there was a vast amount of development. In Spain, we had a front wing update and updates to the front corner and diffuser. Austria saw another front wing and diffuser, while in Germany we had our new rear wing for high downforce with a curly trailing edge. In Singapore, we had another front wing and diffuser update. So, over the season, a lot had changed, but it looked much the same."

THE DRIVERS

BUTTON **MAGNUSSEN**

THE TEAM
CHAIRMAN
Ron Dennis
RACING DIRECTOR
Eric Boullier
MANAGING DIRECTOR
Jonathan Neale
TECHNICAL DIRECTOR
Tim Goss
ENGINEERING DIRECTOR
Matt Morris
CHIEF ENGINEER
Doug McKiernan
DRIVERS
Jenson Button, Kevin Magnussen
SPORTING DIRECTOR
Sam Michael
TEAM MANAGER
David Redding
PRINCIPAL RACE ENGINEER
Ciaron Pilbeam
RACE ENGINEERS (BUTTON)
Dave Robson/Tom Stallard
RACE ENGINEER (MAGNUSSEN)
Mark Temple
CHIEF MECHANIC
Jonathan Brookes
TEST & DEVELOPMENT DRIVERS
Oliver Turvey, Stoffel Vandoorne
TOTAL NUMBER OF EMPLOYEES
550 (McLaren Racing)
NUMBER IN RACE TEAM
Not disclosed
TEAM BASE
Woking, England
TELEPHONE
+44 (0)1483 261000
WEBSITE
www.mclaren.com

PARTNERS
Mobil1, Johnnie Walker, SAP, Santander, TAG Heuer, Hugo Boss, Akzo Nobel, Hilton HHonors, Mercedes-Benz, Pirelli, Segafredo Zanetti

TEAM STATS
IN F1 SINCE 1966
FIRST GRAND PRIX Monaco 1966
CONSTRUCTORS' TITLES 8
DRIVERS' TITLES 12

@McLarenF1

TRANSMISSION
GEARBOX McLaren
FORWARD GEARS Eight
CLUTCH Not disclosed

McLAREN MERCEDES

By Andrew Green
TECHNICAL DIRECTOR

"WE STARTED THE 2014 CAR much earlier than the previous cars because of all the new regulations. Teams with our resources are obliged to start that early, otherwise we would never have made it to winter testing and that was critical given all the new systems to be tried out and got up and running. So our strategy was to stop the previous year's car development earlier than normal. Even then, it proved a monumental task.

"We made the first test at Jerez and the strategy of getting on top of the issues early and getting the car out paid off. In the first half of the season we were running and we were relatively competitive. While we weren't that close to Mercedes we didn't think we ever would be, so we maximised the points scored in the early part of the season. To this end, everything went to plan.

"What didn't go to plan were the updates since then. We struggled to address the fundamental issues we have had with the car since the beginning and they have proved difficult to solve given the current restrictions on aerodynamic testing. This makes it extremely hard to sort these problems out in a timely manner and that was

our biggest issue as we became less competitive.

"The car had too narrow a working window and too narrow a set-up window. When it was in that window, it was fine and the drivers were relatively happy with it. But, to get it in that window in the first place was incredibly hard and we only achieved it a few times. We worked to widen that window and had limited success and there were clear directions we realised we needed to adopt that will be carried forward into the 2015 car.

"We took the conservative view in the initial design because we had to hit the ground running and could not have cooling issues. Our target was to maximise the early races and we erred on the side of cooling. The issues we did have came later, once we tried to develop out that excess cooling capacity and turn it into performance. We thought we could trade that for more car performance but we had a few correlation issues.

"Early in the season, we had the upper hand over Williams and McLaren, the two other Mercedes customer teams. The real battle was with McLaren and, with the capability they have, they were able to bring upgrades to the car almost continually and we couldn't compete with that. So they edged ahead of us on out-and-out

> **"WE MAXIMISED THE POINTS SCORED IN THE EARLY PART OF THE SEASON"**

qualifying performance, although we continued to have a good race car on Sunday because our tyre management was superior to most.

"We did make progress with the car during the season, though. At the Spanish GP, we brought an upgrade geared towards the suspension that we subsequently had to take off. Our biggest aerodynamic upgrade was for the Austrian GP in June and that worked well. There was a second aerodynamic upgrade post-Silverstone, which was the one that didn't hit the targets required. Prior to Austria, we had some small upgrades – tweaks to the front and rear wing and diffuser – but the Austrian GP brought the wholesale change to the bodywork. There was another upgrade in Singapore, but it was never going to eliminate all the problems we had.

"We made good progress with brake-by-wire early on and all credit to Mercedes for the integration of that with the power unit, which was about as close to seamless as you could ever get. We did a huge amount of research and due diligence before it ran at the Jerez test, then we switched it on for the second run and that was it – it was as close to an invisible switch-on as you could wish for.

"We had only one issue with it, when we had a sensor fail at a very

CHASSIS
CHASSIS MODEL
Force India VJM07
FRONT SUSPENSION LAYOUT
Aluminium alloy uprights with carbon-fibre composite wishbones, trackrod and pushrod
REAR SUSPENSION LAYOUT
Aluminium alloy uprights with

carbon-fibre composite wishbones, trackrod and pullrod
TYRES Pirelli
WHEELS Motegi Racing
BRAKE DISCS Brembo
BRAKE PADS Brembo
BRAKE CALIPERS AP Racing
FUEL TANK ATL
INSTRUMENTS MES

DIMENSIONS
LENGTH 5100mm
WIDTH 1800mm
HEIGHT 950mm
WHEELBASE Not disclosed
TRACK, FRONT Not disclosed
TRACK, REAR Not disclosed
WEIGHT 691kg (including driver and camera)

ENGINE
MAKE/MODEL
Mercedes-Benz PU106A Hybrid
CONFIGURATION 1600cc V6 turbo
SPARK PLUGS NGK
ECU FIA standard issue
FUEL Petronas
OIL Petronas
BATTERY Not disclosed

F1 TEAM

critical time in the race in Canada. It required Sergio Pérez to reset the system and, unfortunately, during that we got overtaken for second. It was gut-wrenching because it looked as if it was going to be a fantastic result, but we learned from it.

"That race and Bahrain, where Sergio finished third, were races in which more tyre management was required. I don't think there are many drivers who could have done what he did. Sergio and Nico Hülkenberg converged significantly during the season in terms of tyre use. It used to be that Nico would always stop once more, but it soon wasn't so clear-cut. Also, Sergio has definitely learned from Nico on qualifying approach. The two of them have really fed off each other.

"Overall, we're happy with the choices we have made. We had different options with the power unit supplier that we discussed, but we identified Mercedes as the one that was going to be best prepared and it was a strategic decision to stick with them. From what we can see, they are going to deliver even more in the future. We just need to do the power unit justice by bolting it to a chassis that has got a bit more performance in it.

"Our objective is to stick ourselves just behind the works team and we aren't there yet."

TRANSMISSION
GEARBOX Mercedes GP
FORWARD GEARS Eight
CLUTCH AP Racing

THE DRIVERS

HÜLKENBERG   PÉREZ

THE TEAM
TEAM PRINCIPAL & MANAGING DIRECTOR
Vijay Mallya
CHAIRMAN
Subrata Roy Sahara
CO-OWNER
Sahara India Pariwar
SHAREHOLDER
Mol Family
DEPUTY TEAM PRINCIPAL
Robert Fernley
CHIEF OPERATING OFFICER
Otmar Szafnauer
TECHNICAL DIRECTOR
Andrew Green
PRODUCTION DIRECTOR
Bob Halliwell
CHIEF DESIGNERS
Akio Haga, Ian Hall
AERODYNAMICS DIRECTOR
Simon Phillips
DRIVERS
Nico Hülkenberg, Sergio Pérez
SPORTING DIRECTOR
Andy Stevenson
CHIEF RACE ENGINEER
Tom McCullough
RACE ENGINEER (HÜLKENBERG)
Bradley Joyce
RACE ENGINEER (PÉREZ)
Gianpiero Lambiase
RESERVE DRIVER
Daniel Juncadella
RACE TEAM OPERATIONS MANAGER
Mark Gray
NO 1 MECHANICS
Nicholas Howe, Greg Borrill
TOTAL NUMBER OF EMPLOYEES
370
NUMBER IN RACE TEAM
60 operational staff, 75 travelling
TEAM BASE
Silverstone, England
TELEPHONE
+44 (0)1327 850800
WEBSITE
www.saharaforceindiaf1.com

THE PARTNERS
Accelerate, Alpinestars, Astana, Auden McKenzie Group, Chatham, Claro, Condeco, Consorcio Aristos, FICREA, Gatorade, Internap, Kingfisher, Koni, Motegi Racing, Muc-Off, Pirelli, Roshfrans, Royal Challenge, Schroth, Smirnoff, Speedy, STL, STILL, TW Steel, UB Group, Univa, UPS Direct, Varlion, 3D Systems

TEAM STATS
IN F1 SINCE 1991 as Jordan, then as Midland 2005-06 and as Spyker 2007
FIRST GRAND PRIX USA 1991
CONSTRUCTORS' TITLES 0
DRIVERS' TITLES 0

SAHARA Force India
formula one team

By James Key
TECHNICAL DIRECTOR

"WE STARTED THE CAR A BIT late, in October 2012, so we had some catching up to do, but went in a good direction early on from an aerodynamic point of view. It was a very difficult period for a team of our size to effectively run two car programmes in parallel.

"We were very ambitious with our timing. We knew that with the new regulations and the uncertainty over cooling the new power units, we had to do a lot of simulation work. We also knew that 2014 was going to be a development war so we wanted to get on track quickly.

"We were the first Renault team to fire up and the first one to run on a promotional day at Misano before the opening test. That was really important because of our new relationship with Renault, but then winter testing was full of woe.

"Getting the car up and running helped us during testing. We had also been a bit conservative in certain areas for the test car, with an update planned for Australia. This allowed us not to have too many issues on the chassis side, but testing was still tricky for all concerned.

"When you have a rookie driver, as we did with Daniil Kvyat, you want to be doing qualifying simulations, race distances and practice starts, but we didn't do any of that. So that put us on the back foot. We could see the Mercedes runners pounding around gathering both tyre and energy management data.

"We went OK in Melbourne, though, as we were top-10 material and completed our first race distances in the grand prix. That was a very good start considering we were in unknown territory.

"Renault pushed like hell to recover from the tricky start and there was a big improvement. During the early races, there were a few issues that affected our performances, but it was more a knock-on effect from not being able to test as much as our rivals. Unfortunately, the teams who were well-prepared picked up points and that's one of the reasons we didn't score as much as we had hoped to.

"After the Australian GP update, we had more steps in the first part of the season. This started with a small package for the Spanish GP and then we had a good cooling update for Monaco, which made a big difference to how we ran the engine. In Canada, we introduced new rear suspension. We use Red Bull gearbox internals, but the box itself was all-STR, which allowed us to leave our rear

"RENAULT PUSHED TO RECOVER FROM A TRICKY START"

suspension quite late. Then, for Austria, we had a massive aerodynamic package. We probably peaked there because of that, but also the track suited our car.

"Unfortunately, that was at a time when we had some reliability problems. A lot of it was self-inflicted and some of it was bad luck. Monaco was extremely frustrating, as we were looking good for fifth and sixth before we had an exhaust problem. In Austria, we made a stupid mistake with the trackrod design, so that failed. We had a frustrating spell where a lot of random problems hit us.

"In the second half of the season performance was more consistent. We weren't as strong as we were in Austria, but we were still on the edge of the top 10 at Spa and Monza, which are both power circuits. Later in the season, we had a new iteration of the nose at Suzuka and we were reasonably happy with where we ended up.

"The pace was there and, considering where we were coming from, that was quite reasonable. Aerodynamically, the car was OK and we had a strong development programme. You always need more downforce, but I don't think that was much of a weakness.

"With the new regulations and the loss of downforce, it would have

CHASSIS
CHASSIS MODEL
Toro Rosso STR9
FRONT AND REAR SUSPENSION LAYOUT
Upper and lower wishbones, torsion bar springs and anti-roll bars
DAMPERS
Multimatic, Penske Racing

TYRES Pirelli
WHEELS Apptech
BRAKE DISCS Brembo
BRAKE PADS Brembo
BRAKE CALIPERS
Brembo
FUEL TANK ATL
INSTRUMENTS
Scuderia Toro Rosso

DIMENSIONS
LENGTH Not disclosed
WIDTH Not disclosed
HEIGHT Not disclosed
WHEELBASE Not disclosed
TRACK, FRONT Not disclosed
TRACK, REAR Not disclosed
WEIGHT 690kg (including driver and camera)

ENGINE
MAKE/MODEL
Renault Energy F1-2014
CONFIGURATION 1600cc V6 turbo
SPARK PLUGS Not disclosed
ECU FIA standard issue
FUEL Not disclosed
OIL Not disclosed
BATTERY Not disclosed

ROSSO

been easy to make the car go faster early on by putting a lot of 'dirty' high-drag downforce on it. But we were careful not to do that because it creates problems for you later. We had a cap on drag which seemed to be about right for the straights.

"Braking was a big issue to begin with, but as the season went on we turned that into a strength and the drivers could nail it quite well. It was all about getting on top of controlling the brake material temperatures and refining the brake-by-wire strategies. We also improved the mechanical grip.

"Our main weaknesses were the drivability of the car and the platform control. Some of the drivability problems were chassis-related, with work needing to be done on traction, but we weren't behind the other Renault teams. Those, combined with our reliability, were the main issues. However, the car was above average in tyre management, thanks to the suspension we introduced in Canada.

"We had a good balance with the drivers. Jean-Éric Vergne gave us a good reference point to allow us to assess our progress and he definitely stepped up in 2014. Kvyat was fantastic from the outset and learned incredibly quickly. So it was a strong line-up."

THE DRIVERS

VERGNE   KVYAT

THE TEAM
TEAM OWNER
Dietrich Mateschitz
TEAM PRINCIPAL
Franz Tost
TECHNICAL DIRECTOR
James Key
DEPUTY TECHNICAL DIRECTOR
Ben Waterhouse
HEAD OF AERODYNAMICS
Brendan Gilhome
HEAD OF VEHICLE PERFORMANCE
Jody Egginton
SPORTING DIRECTOR
Steve Nielsen
DRIVERS
Daniil Kvyat, Jean-Éric Vergne
TECHNICAL CO-ORDINATOR
Sandro Parrini
LOGISTICS MANAGER
Michela Fabri
CHIEF ENGINEER
Phil Charles
RACE ENGINEER (VERGNE)
Xevi Pujolar
RACE ENGINEER (KVYAT)
Marco Matassa
CHIEF MECHANIC
Domiziano Facchinetti
RESERVE DRIVERS
Sebastien Buemi, Max Verstappen
TOTAL NUMBER OF EMPLOYEES
Around 350
NUMBER IN RACE TEAM
Not disclosed
TEAM BASE
Faenza, Italy
TELEPHONE
+39 (0)546 696111
WEBSITE
www.scuderiatororosso.com

THE PARTNERS
Red Bull, CEPSA, Nova Chemicals, SAPINDA, App Tech, CD Adapco, Del Conca, Duravit, HANGAR-7, hansgrohe, OMP, Pirelli, Red Bulletin, Red Bull Mobile, Renault, Riedel, Servus TV, Siemens, Speedweek, USAG

TEAM STATS
IN F1 SINCE 1985 as Minardi, until 2005
FIRST GRAND PRIX Brazil 1985
CONSTRUCTORS' TITLES 0
DRIVERS' TITLES 0

SAPINDA

TRANSMISSION
GEARBOX Red Bull Technology
FORWARD GEARS Eight
CLUTCH AP Racing

SCUDERIA
Toro Rosso

By Nick Chester
TECHNICAL DIRECTOR

"A COMBINATION OF THINGS went wrong for us this year. We had problems getting the car ready initially and that hurt us in the tests. We also suffered power unit problems at the start of the year.

"We started getting it back on track by the Spanish GP in May, where we gained a fair amount of performance, but we didn't develop enough after that and some of our competitors moved away from us again. We had a few aerodynamic problems that took a while to understand and it takes time to get the performance back after that.

"What happened over the previous 12 months did make it tricky. We lost a lot of staff and didn't have quite the same resources as before. That put us a little bit on the back foot. The new regulations required so much work because everything changed. The chassis was totally different with new side-impact regulations. The nose, front wing, engine installation, the cooling system, ERS, gearbox, brake-by-wire, in fact practically the whole car, was completely different. Nothing carried over from previous cars. The cooling systems were very challenging. With the benefit of hindsight, there were

ways we could have made the cooling system more elegant.

"Aerodynamically, the most important area was the narrower span of the front wing. This was a really big change because it affected flow in front of the car and under the floor to the back. The loss of the lower rear wing and exhaust-blowing was also a big change. In 2013, we developed the exhaust blower well and probably didn't recover enough of that lost downforce. The whole flow around the 'footstep' area of the floor is very different and we had to do a lot of work there. Exhaust-blowing covered up some problems and we saw some sensitivities on the car that we tried very hard to improve. Now we look back on it, there were underlying problems before but with exhaust-blowing you could get away with some of them.

"That late start hurt us badly because we didn't have the mileage. Had we done the first test at Jerez, we'd have found some of the problems earlier and had fixes in place by the time we got to the first races. There were some difficulties with the power unit and sensitivity to the temperatures were different to what we expected, so that forced us into redesigning some things.

"In terms of the way we operated the power unit, we didn't

understand the duty cycles before we started running it, so that pushes all the heat rejection up. In terms of reliability, it achieved a respectable level by mid-season, although there were still problems afterwards, such as an ERS failure in Hungary and, while the power delivery was never ideal, it did get a lot better.

"There was quite a big simulation programme with the power unit, as we struggled so much at the start of the year because everything was late. Renault did have to run it very simply at first, but it did reach a fairly mature state later in the championship. We worked out how to use the energy in the best way and, as Renault developed it, more modes became available to allow us to utilise the power around the lap better.

"There were aerodynamic upgrades for the Spanish GP, including the floor and front wing, and they improved the car a reasonable chunk, which was demonstrated by Romain Grosjean qualifying fifth and finishing eighth. After that, we didn't keep the development going. We went through everything we did post-Barcelona, re-testing to see if we had done something wrong or had a correlation problem, but we didn't find anything. Otherwise, we would have returned to the Barcelona spec.

"THE LATE START HURT US AS WE DIDN'T HAVE THE MILEAGE"

CHASSIS
CHASSIS MODEL Lotus E22
FRONT SUSPENSION LAYOUT
Carbon-fibre top and bottom wishbones with pushrod-operated torsion bar and inboard dampers
REAR SUSPENSION LAYOUT
Carbon-fibre top and bottom wishbones with pullrod-operated

torsion springs and transverse-mounted dampers
TYRES Pirelli
WHEELS OZ Racing
BRAKE DISCS Not disclosed
BRAKE PADS Not disclosed
BRAKE CALIPERS AP Racing
FUEL TANK ATL
INSTRUMENTS MES

DIMENSIONS
LENGTH 5088mm
WIDTH 1800mm
HEIGHT 950mm
WHEELBASE Not disclosed
TRACK, FRONT 1450mm
TRACK, REAR 1400mm
WEIGHT 692kg (including driver and camera)

ENGINE
MAKE/MODEL
Renault Energy F1-2014
CONFIGURATION 1600cc V6 turbo
SPARK PLUGS Not disclosed
ECU FIA standard issue
FUEL Total
OIL Total
BATTERY Not disclosed

"In terms of car balance, we struggled with too much understeer in low-speed corners. That can be hard to rebalance because, if you can't get that right, then you've got to have a car that's nervous elsewhere. We also needed to get more consistency, as the drivers felt that the balance changed too much as they tried to make corrections.

"We did also struggle to get temperature into the tyres sometimes. We still have the same trait as before in that we do more competitive race times than qualifying times. We still look after the tyres well but, as they were harder in 2014, we didn't really get the benefit.

"The ban on FRIC did hurt us quite badly and as a result we had to run the car stiffer. We'd been developing that system for five or six years and all of our aero development was based on controlled ride heights. After that was removed at Hockenheim we did improve, but it took a long time.

"Towards the end of the season, some of the things we did on the car were designed for us to learn for next year, such as trying a different nose at Austin. It was worth switching focus, as it allowed us to try more things in free practice than we would normally do as we looked towards 2015 and the change to the Mercedes power unit."

TRANSMISSION
GEARBOX Lotus F1 team/X-Trac
FORWARD GEARS Eight
CLUTCH Not disclosed

THE DRIVERS

MALDONADO   GROSJEAN

THE TEAM
TEAM PRINCIPAL
Gerard Lopez
CHIEF EXECUTIVE OFFICER
Matthew Carter
CHIEF OPERATING OFFICER
Thomas Mayer
DEPUTY TEAM PRINCIPAL
Federico Gastaldi
TECHNICAL DIRECTOR
Nick Chester
TRACKSIDE OPERATIONS DIRECTOR
Alan Permane
CHIEF DESIGNER
Martin Tolliday
HEAD OF AERODYNAMICS
Nicolas Hennel de Beaupreau
RENAULT SPORT F1 TRACK SUPPORT LEADER
Simon Rebreyend
DRIVERS
Romain Grosjean, Pastor Maldonado
TEAM MANAGER
Paul Seaby
RACE ENGINEER (MALDONADO)
Mark Slade
RACE ENGINEER (GROSJEAN)
Ayao Komatsu
CHIEF MECHANIC
Greg Baker
RESERVE DRIVERS
Esteban Ocon, Charles Pic,
Nicolas Prost, Marco Sorensen
TOTAL NUMBER OF EMPLOYEES
 470
NUMBER IN RACE TEAM
Around 50
TEAM BASE
Enstone, England
TELEPHONE
+44 (0)1608 678000
WEBSITE
www.lotusf1team.com

THE PARTNERS
Group Lotus, PDVSA, Renault, Total, Rexona, Clear, Emaar Properties PJSC, burn, Microsoft Dynamics, Yota Devices, Avanade, Genii, Pirelli, Richard Mille, Peace One Day

TEAM STATS
IN F1 SINCE 1981 as Toleman, then as Benetton 1986-2001 and Renault 2002-11
FIRST GRAND PRIX San Marino 1991
CONSTRUCTORS' TITLES 3
DRIVERS' TITLES 4

LOTUS F1® TEAM

By Dave Greenwood
CHIEF ENGINEER

"OUR 2014 CAR DIDN'T JUST involve a new engine type, we also changed manufacturer from Cosworth to Ferrari. So, a lot of the work was going on in the background from the middle of 2013.

"On the design side, things went pretty well. The guys did a really good job integrating the new powertrain with our new chassis. The reliability we had at the start of the year was good in a mechanical sense, so the real challenge was the integration on the electronics and software side. This pushed the whole team to the limit in testing and we weren't alone in that sense. The big difference is that we were a very small team.

"Not only were we doing new architecture in terms of the electronics boxes and the looms that go with these powertrains, but also all the software that was going on them. The way that we worked with Ferrari on that software was probably the hardest bit that we experienced as a team. That's not because there was an issue with what Ferrari was asking us to do, it was more that everything changed from what we were used to.

"The most frustrating thing for me in testing was having repeat problems. A lot of that came about because we were putting the guys under so much pressure to get the car out of the garage and get some mileage on it so that we knew that the mechanical systems were working. We were rushing and there were fundamental problems in the way that we worked and loaded software on the car or took software off the car.

"We just had to stop and say: 'OK, the car might not go out of the garage for an hour, but we're going to fix this underlying problem.' It's really tough. As an engineer, you want it to be out there, putting laps in. The reality is that you need to say: 'Let's not go out of the garage. Let's sort this problem that keeps coming back every few days.'

"We were slightly conservative with the cooling packaging. There were some areas that were overcooled and some areas that were on the limit. We knew we were overcooled on certain systems and marginal on others by the time that we got to the point of running, but we had to commit to all of those designs several months earlier while we were still getting information through from Ferrari.

"The aero development was pretty constant. The guys were producing stuff and, as soon as it

> **"WE HAD TO DIG DEEP AND FOCUS ON THE JOB IN HAND IN SOCHI"**

made economic sense to make things, that's what we did. Mechanically, the big development was a massively aggressive hydraulically linked suspension. It was unfortunate that we didn't get some parts we needed on the front suspension until the Spanish GP in the middle of May. Once we had those, we fully exploited the potential of the car and it was worth half a second, if not more.

"Before that race, we were compromised by not being able to explore the full envelope of the suspension set-up with that system. We got those in Barcelona but it was in Monaco where we got the best from them and that was the turning point for the season thanks to work done in the post-Spain test.

"That weekend, Jules Bianchi was very quick. He had a differential problem and a grid penalty for a gearbox change, but he finished in ninth place and scored our first top 10 finish despite that penalty. Those two points were key for our championship position and Jules drove superbly.

"Linked suspension was banned in Germany, which hit us hard. We had no time to go back on the seven-post rig and re-optimise the car without it. We could only do that in the August break. We then had new parts for the Belgian GP on

CHASSIS
CHASSIS MODEL Marussia MR03
FRONT SUSPENSION LAYOUT
Carbon-fibre wishbone and pushrod suspension operating inboard torsion bar and damper systems
REAR SUSPENSION LAYOUT
Carbon-fibre wishbone and pullrod suspension operating inboard

torsion bar and damper systems
DAMPERS Penske Racing
TYRES Pirelli
WHEELS BBS
BRAKE DISCS Hitco
BRAKE PADS Hitco
BRAKE CALIPERS AP Racing
FUEL TANK ATL
INSTRUMENTS MES

DIMENSIONS
LENGTH 4900mm
WIDTH 1800mm
HEIGHT 950mm
WHEELBASE 3700mm
TRACK, FRONT Not disclosed
TRACK, REAR Not disclosed
WEIGHT 692kg (including driver and camera)

ENGINE
MAKE/MODEL Ferrari 059/3
CONFIGURATION 1600cc V6 turbo
SPARK PLUGS Champion
ECU FIA standard issue
FUEL Shell
OIL Shell
BATTERY Braille

the rear suspension, although those were actually recycled parts that we had used on the front of the 2012 car. So, we made a step in Belgium and hugely improved the stability of the car under braking.

"We did have issues in 2013 with a car that was a bit more on the edge, but the 2014 car, despite losing the rear beam wing that has a big influence on the underfloor, was much more benign and gave us a much wider set-up window. We did have some more car parts that we wanted to introduce in the final part of the season, but for obvious reasons we were unable to do so.

"We were closer to the front than in previous years. In performance terms, the top guys have moved back, but we stayed roughly where we were. The downforce we came into the year with was about the same as we had in 2013, so we didn't lose out through the regulations. We also managed to get into Q2 on several occasions – the one at Spa was particular good because we all went out on the same tyre and Jules just did a great job.

"After Jules' terrible accident at Suzuka we had to dig deep and just focus on the job in hand in Sochi, but it was a tough weekend because he was such an important and popular part of the team."

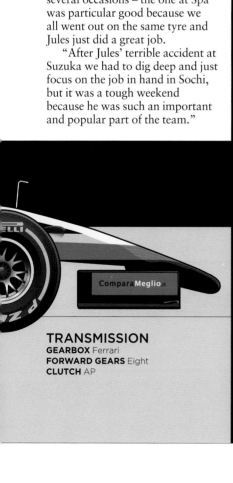

TRANSMISSION
GEARBOX Ferrari
FORWARD GEARS Eight
CLUTCH AP

THE DRIVERS

CHILTON   BIANCHI

THE TEAM
CHAIRMAN
Alex Kasputin
TEAM PRINCIPAL
John Booth
CHIEF EXECUTIVE OFFICER
Andy Webb
PRESIDENT & SPORTING DIRECTOR
Graeme Lowdon
CHIEF DESIGNER
John McQuilliam
DEPUTY DESIGN CHIEF
Rob Taylor
HEAD OF AERODYNAMICS
Richard Taylor
HEAD OF RESEARCH & DEVELOPMENT
Richard Connell
HEAD OF VEHICLE PERFORMANCE
Paul Davison
CHIEF ENGINEER
Dave Greenwood
STRATEGY ENGINEER
Josef Holden
TEAM MANAGER
Dave O'Neill
DRIVERS
Jules Bianchi, Max Chilton
RACE ENGINEER (CHILTON)
Gary Gannon
RACE ENGINEER (BIANCHI)
Francesco Nenci
CHIEF MECHANIC
Richard Wrenn
NO 1 MECHANICS
Kieron Marchant, Ian Staniforth
RESERVE DRIVERS
Rodolfo Gonzalez, Alexander Rossi,
Will Stevens
TOTAL NUMBER OF EMPLOYEES
210
NUMBER IN RACE TEAM
47
TEAM BASE
Banbury, England
TELEPHONE
+44 (0)1295 517270
WEBSITE
www.marussiaf1team.com

PARTNERS
Armin Strom, Instaforex, Marussia,
Pirelli, QNET, RBC, Royals, Sage ERP X3

TEAM STATS
IN F1 SINCE 2010 as Virgin Racing,
until 2011
FIRST GRAND PRIX
Bahrain 2010
CONSTRUCTORS' TITLES 0
DRIVERS' TITLES 0

By Giampaolo Dall'Ara
HEAD OF TRACK ENGINEERING

"THE CHALLENGE OF THIS season was a big one, thanks to the rule changes, and it all started quite late for us for a number of reasons. Some of them were internal, but also the agreement with Ferrari for the power unit supply came late.

"This resulted in us getting to the first test session unprepared. We were aware of this before hitting the track and set up a plan to sort out the reliability and understand the systems as a whole – not just the new power unit but also how to integrate it, how to use it and how to best collect and spend the energy.

"The performance level was nowhere near where it was supposed to be, but we weren't worried because we were sure that we could fix a number of issues in the short term. That didn't prove to be the case. We went through a number of troubles on both the power unit and the chassis. The car was heavy, so we had to allocate time to fix some of the basics. We only got the weight right at the Spanish GP and by the end of the season, while we could run some ballast in Esteban Gutiérrez's car, we couldn't in Adrian Sutil's.

"So, the first four grands prix were a learning exercise. We also had some reliability issues, so we couldn't collect much in the way of results. The Spanish GP was the turning point and we began working as a race team again, with most of the reliability problems understood: performance-wise, it wasn't embarrassing.

"We also had an update package for the Spanish GP that was closer to where the targets were set prior to the season. We lost a lot of downforce through the regulation changes, which even now we couldn't recover all of, but by Barcelona we were back in the fight on the chassis side of things. On the power unit side, though, we only had limited control as that was in Ferrari's hands. Mercedes had done a better job and we couldn't catch up because Ferrari was limited in fixing things because of the homologation regulations. But also we didn't put together a fast car.

"We updated the rear suspension for the Monaco GP, which was an improvement especially in terms of using the Pirelli tyres. When you aren't happy with the aerodynamic performance or are missing downforce, it's always more difficult to make the tyres work well, but the suspension update helped.

"From that point on, the focus was on developing the systems. Early on, we had to sort the braking performance, specifically the trust that the drivers could put in the car. This was in co-operation with Ferrari because, while the brake-by-wire system was Sauber's, it had to interact very closely with the ERS. This is a very important factor and, because every driver reacts differently to the braking feel, it took time.

"During the summer, we were quite happy with the balance of the car. We struggled all year using hard tyres, yet made progress with the super-soft, soft and medium. Apart from the British GP, though, which was affected by this, we felt that we were at least using the potential of the car.

"The updates in the second half of the year, specifically at Singapore, were all in the right direction, but unfortunately the steps weren't big enough. Even forgetting about the power unit limitation, the car didn't have strong points. Looking back over the previous 10 years, we were almost level with the top teams in fast corners every season, but this year we lost momentum.

"Sauber always aims to be a top-10 team. Maybe it isn't possible to fight for podiums, like we did two years ago, but regular points should be possible. It's a matter of record that in 2014 we never really managed to be a top-10 team and failed to race for points regularly.

> ## "SAUBER ALWAYS AIMS TO BE A TOP-10 TEAM"

CHASSIS
CHASSIS MODEL Sauber C33
FRONT SUSPENSION LAYOUT Upper and lower wishbones, inboard springs and dampers actuated by pushrods
REAR SUSPENSION LAYOUT Upper and lower wishbones, inboard springs and dampers actuated by pullrods
DAMPERS Sachs Race Engineering
TYRES Pirelli
WHEELS OZ Racing
BRAKE DISCS Brembo
BRAKE PADS Brembo
BRAKE CALIPERS Brembo
FUEL TANK ATL
INSTRUMENTS Sauber

DIMENSIONS
LENGTH 5300mm
WIDTH 1800mm
HEIGHT 950mm
WHEELBASE Not disclosed
TRACK, FRONT 1460mm
TRACK, REAR 1416mm
WEIGHT 691kg (including driver and camera)

ENGINE
MAKE/MODEL Ferrari 059/3
CONFIGURATION 1600cc V6 turbo
SPARK PLUGS Not disclosed
ECU FIA standard issue
FUEL Not disclosed
OIL Not disclosed
BATTERY Sauber

THE DRIVERS

SUTIL   GUTIÉRREZ

THE TEAM

**TEAM PRINCIPAL &
CHIEF EXECUTIVE OFFICER**
Monisha Kaltenborn
OPERATIONS DIRECTOR
Axel Kruse
CHIEF DESIGNER
Eric Gandelin
HEAD OF AERODYNAMICS
Willem Toet
HEAD OF VEHICLE PERFORMANCE
Elliot Dason-Barber
HEAD OF TRACK ENGINEERING
Giampaolo Dall'Ara
TEAM MANAGER
Beat Zehnder
DRIVERS
Esteban Gutiérrez, Adrian Sutil
RACE ENGINEER (SUTIL)
Marco Schupbach
RACE ENGINEER (GUTIÉRREZ)
Craig Gardiner
HEAD OF TRACK OPERATIONS
Otmar Bartsch
CHIEF MECHANIC
Reto Camenzind
RESERVE DRIVERS
Simona de Silvestro, Adderley Fong,
Sergey Sirotkin, Giedo van der Garde
TOTAL NUMBER OF EMPLOYEES 300
NUMBER IN RACE TEAM 65
TEAM BASE
Hinwil, Switzerland
TELEPHONE
+41 44 937 9000
WEBSITE
www.sauberf1team.com

PARTNERS

Claro, Telmex, NEC, Oerlikon, Chelsea
Football Club, McGregor, Cuervo
Tequila, Interproteccion, Certina,
Pacific Ventures, Unifin

TEAM STATS

IN F1 SINCE 1993, then as BMW Sauber
2006-10
FIRST GRAND PRIX South Africa 1993
CONSTRUCTORS' TITLES 0
DRIVERS' TITLES 0

We kept developing but, while we were able to race regularly with Lotus late in the year, more than that was difficult.

"There were races where we had opportunities. Maybe Singapore was one, but we dropped out too early. However, three grands prix stand out – Monaco, Hungary and Germany. At Monaco, we could have scored but had accidents with both cars. We could have made big points, maybe eighth or ninth place, which might have stopped Marussia and Lotus from scoring. That would have changed the sporting situation a great deal. Hockenheim and Hungary were the other possibilities, but we had problems.

"The troubles we had this year were because of the late beginning of the project. There was a big penalty in the first part of the championship and we just chased race by race, never really catching up. Perhaps the biggest change for us was losing the exhaust-blowing, which was a strength for us in 2012 and 2013.

"We tried hard every race, but ultimately we failed on performance. A number of developments we wanted to bring kept coming fairly late relative to the competition. We did advance through the summer, but some of our competitors just made bigger steps."

TRANSMISSION
GEARBOX Ferrari
FORWARD GEARS Eight
CLUTCH Sauber

By John Iley
TECHNICAL DIRECTOR

"SMALL TEAMS AND MASSIVE rule changes aren't a marriage made in heaven, even though people often see it as an opportunity. We had to focus on powertrain packaging and trying to do the fundamentals right when designing the car. The team actually did a good job of this, because there were people with the same powertrain clearly struggling in testing while we were doing more kilometres. It wasn't perfect, as there were all sorts of issues, but in the first test we were out there and running reasonably reliably. We were assisting Renault with feedback and early development, so perhaps we were a bit overloaded.

"We didn't have packaging and cooling problems, as we couldn't afford to get it wrong. But, equally, there was an opportunity to produce several evolutions after our initial package, which was focused on being solid and reliable. The hope was that we could develop from there but, because of the circumstances of the team, we didn't have the opportunity to do step two, step three or step four from what was a solid, safe initial package.

"The circumstances of the team were documented extensively, although maybe not always completely fairly or accurately, but to make steps you need budget and time. We understood a lot in the early races, so from a technical point of view it was frustrating not to be able to change things because it was very clear what we needed to do. We did do a mild upgrade for the Spanish GP, which was predominantly aerodynamic but, while it gave us what we expected in terms of numbers, it didn't fulfil its potential in terms of laptime. That gave us an indication of other aspects to develop, which we simply weren't able to change.

"The team reached the change of ownership around the British GP at the start of July and, had things not changed, we possibly weren't intending to continue much beyond that race. We highlighted the things that we would do, given budget and resources and at Spa, four races later, we were able to put some of the ideas on to the car. Some changes were mechanical, some were related to the powertrain and some were aerodynamic. The most striking was some rhinoplasty on the nose. The changes to the floor, bodywork and rear wing were things we had wanted to do but didn't previously have the capability.

"Then, there was a second phase in Japan when we finally got the front wing that we'd wanted for a

> "IN JAPAN, WE GOT THE FRONT WING WE'D WANTED FOR A LONG TIME"

long time. What was massively reassuring was that we saw progress, and the competitiveness of the car improved. In Russia, Marcus Ericsson was only 0.1s away from Romain Grosjean and nearly reached Q2, so we gave Sauber and Lotus something to think about.

"The unfortunate thing is that, had the trajectory continued as normal, all of those updates would have come so much earlier in the season and we would have been seeing fifth or sixth iterations rather than what happened in Japan. In F1, if you aren't progressing, you are going backwards and if we had been more competitive at previous races it might have been different, although we would still have needed a strange chain of events to get into a points-scoring position. Sadly, we couldn't instigate that progress until Spa. So we had an eight-race gap during which other teams were bringing updates and changes with almost every race. It's very difficult to be in that position when you are maximising what you have got, but you can't bring new components and parts to it.

"Aerodynamically, we did improve a lot from 2013 to 2014. There was more that we wanted to do, as at the beginning of the season we weren't as strong as we would have liked, but we still made

CHASSIS
CHASSIS MODEL
Caterham CT05
FRONT AND BACK SUSPENSION LAYOUT
Twin non-parallel wishbone, pullrod actuated
DAMPERS Caterham F1 Team, Penske Racing

TYRES Pirelli
WHEELS
OZ Racing
BRAKE DISCS Various
BRAKE PADS Various
BRAKE CALIPERS Brembo
FUEL TANK
Caterham F1 Team & ATL
INSTRUMENTS Various

DIMENSIONS
LENGTH More than 5000mm
WIDTH Not disclosed
HEIGHT 950mm
WHEELBASE More than 3000mm
TRACK, FRONT 1800mm
TRACK, REAR 1800mm
WEIGHT 691kg (including driver and camera)

ENGINE
MAKE/MODEL
Renault Energy F1-2014
CONFIGURATION 1600cc V6 turbo
SPARK PLUGS Not disclosed
ECU FIA standard issue
FUEL Total
OIL Various
BATTERY Caterham F1 Team

significant progress on that. Tyre management and behaviour was an area where we could still have improved, although in terms of mechanical set-up we have understood for a while, what we would like to do. Again, affecting those changes was difficult.

"The current cars are more integrated as a system than ever before, so powertrain behaviour and capability is linked to tyre performance, which is linked to mechanical balance. Because of the complexity of the systems on the car, along with Pirelli arguably going slightly more conservative than in previous years, we had more constraints than before but less aero performance. It took time to get the optimum behaviour from the car. While we created a solid platform, the battle was to get everything working well together.

"It was difficult for the drivers as well. Kamui Kobayashi and Ericsson clearly wanted to be moving forward and challenging for Q2, so it was hard for them to keep their motivation while others were improving. However, they did manage to maintain that even when moving forward was a problem. So, overall, in the circumstances, they did a very good job. The same could be said about everyone working in the team in difficult circumstances."

TRANSMISSION
GEARBOX Red Bull Technology
FORWARD GEARS Eight
CLUTCH AP Racing

THE DRIVERS

ERICSSON   **KOBAYASHI**

THE TEAM
TEAM ADVISOR
Colin Kolles
TEAM PRINCIPAL
Manfredi Ravetto
CHIEF OPERATING OFFICER
Simon Shinkins
TECHNICAL DIRECTOR
John Iley
CHIEF ENGINEER
Gianluca Pisanello
HEAD OF AERODYNAMICS
Hari Roberts
HEAD OF PRODUCTION
Graham Saunders
DRIVERS
Marcus Ericsson, Kamui Kobayashi, André Lotterer
TEAM MANAGER
Miodrag Kotur
CHIEF RACE ENGINEER
Gianluca Pisanello
RACE ENGINEER (ERICSSON)
Angel Baena
RACE ENGINEER (KOBAYASHI & LOTTERER) Tim Wright
CHIEF MECHANIC
Stuart Cramp
RESERVE DRIVERS
Nathanael Berthon, Robin Frijns, Alexander Rossi
TOTAL NUMBER OF EMPLOYEES 320
NUMBER IN RACE TEAM
78 (48 operational, 30 ancillary)
TEAM BASE
Leafield, England
TELEPHONE
+44 (0)1953 851411
WEBSITE
www.caterhamf1.com

THE PARTNERS
Renault, Dell/Intel, Pirelli, CNN, truphone, MODO, DMG MORI, Mimaki, CD-Adapco, Linde, VolPunlimited, FARO, AUTOGLYM, Motorola Solutions, Sparco, RODAC, Usitalia, Takata, Anest Iwata, OZ

TEAM STATS
IN F1 SINCE 2010 as Lotus Racing, then Team Lotus until 2011
FIRST GRAND PRIX Bahrain 2010
CONSTRUCTORS' TITLES 0
DRIVERS' TITLES 0

CATERHAM F1 TEAM

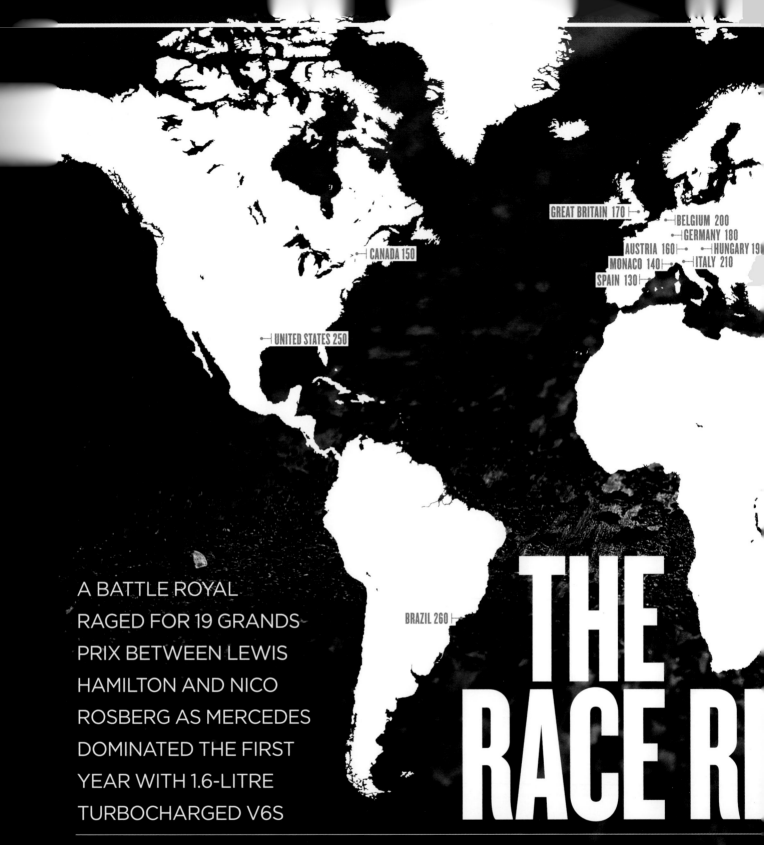

GREAT BRITAIN 170

BELGIUM 200
GERMANY 180
AUSTRIA 160
HUNGARY 19
MONACO 140
ITALY 210
SPAIN 130

CANADA 150

UNITED STATES 250

BRAZIL 260

THE
RACE RI

A BATTLE ROYAL
RAGED FOR 19 GRANDS
PRIX BETWEEN LEWIS
HAMILTON AND NICO
ROSBERG AS MERCEDES
DOMINATED THE FIRST
YEAR WITH 1.6-LITRE
TURBOCHARGED V6S

01 FORMULA 1 ROLEX
AUSTRALIAN GRAND PRIX
MELBOURNE 14-16 March

02 FORMULA 1 PETRONAS
MALAYSIA GRAND PRIX
KUALA LUMPUR 28-30 March

03 FORMULA 1 GULF AIR
BAHRAIN GRAND PRIX
SAKHIR 04-06 April

04 FORMULA 1 UBS
CHINESE GRAND PRIX
SHANGHAI 18-20 April

05 FORMULA 1 GRAN PREMIO
DE ESPAÑA PIRELLI
CATALUNYA 09-11 May

06 FORMULA 1 GRAND PRIX
DE MONACO
MONTE CARLO 22-25 May

07 FORMULA 1 GRAND PRIX
DU CANADA
MONTRÉAL 06-08 June

08 FORMULA 1 GROSSER
PREIS VON ÖSTERREICH
SPIELBERG 20-22 June

09 FORMULA 1 SANTANDER
BRITISH GRAND PRIX
SILVERSTONE 04-06 July

10 FORMULA 1 GROSSER PREIS
SANTANDER VON DEUTSCHLAN
HOCKENHEIM 18-20 July

11 FORMULA 1 PIRELLI
MAGYAR NAGYDÍJ
BUDAPEST 25-27 July

12 FORMULA 1 SHELL
BELGIAN GRAND PRIX
SPA-FRANCORCHAMPS 22-24 Au

RUSSIA 240
JAPAN 230
CHINA 120
RAIN 110
ABU DHABI 270
MALAYSIA 100
SINGAPORE 220
AUSTRALIA 90

PORTS

ROUND 1 ROLEX AUSTRALIAN GRAND PRIX

AUSTR

ALIA

NICO ROSBERG WON EASILY FOR MERCEDES AND, HAD IT NOT BEEN FOR A SPARK PLUG ISSUE FOR LEWIS HAMILTON, THE CLEAR PACESETTERS WOULD HAVE KICKED OFF WITH A ONE-TWO

P re-season predictions of Mercedes' dominance in 2014 were fulfilled as Nico Rosberg scored a comfortable victory after his only realistic rival – teammate and pole man Lewis Hamilton – suffered a frustrating engine issue right at the start. It was a faultless performance by the German in Melbourne.

The real stars of the race were Red Bull's local hero Daniel Ricciardo and McLaren rookie Kevin Magnussen, who joined Rosberg on the podium. However, after the podium ceremonies, Ricciardo was excluded for a fuel-flow irregularity, promoting Magnussen and everyone else by a place. Despite a subsequent appeal by his team, Ricciardo didn't get his result back. Nevertheless, the Aussie had made a big impression,

showing teammate Sebastian Vettel that he meant business.

While it was no great surprise to see a Mercedes on top in qualifying, rain ensured that it was a far from straightforward Saturday. Indeed, Ricciardo turned the form book upside to qualify second.

The first session began in dry conditions, only for the rain to hit with seven minutes to go. Ricciardo topped the times ahead of Magnussen. The track was wet for the second session, and most drivers headed out on intermediates. The top spot see-sawed as conditions changed and Rosberg just edged out Ricciardo.

There was drama right at the end when Ferrari returnee Kimi Räikkönen crashed, ensuring that he didn't go through. The Finn wasn't the only big name not to make it, as Jenson Button – in his first race since the death of his much-missed father John – was

"RICCIARDO WAS BROUGHT DOWN TO EARTH WITH A BUMP WHEN HE WAS EXCLUDED"

bumped out in 11th. However, he still started ahead of Räikkönen and Vettel. It turned out to be a fraught session for the World Champion, who was hampered by a Renault issue.

The rain became heavier before Q3 and full wet tyres were the obvious choice. However, many drivers switched to intermediates in the closing minutes, although both Mercedes drivers stopped for fresh full wets. In the end, it came down to staying out of trouble and who crossed the line last. Rosberg completed his last lap a little too early and was thus bumped by Ricciardo and then Hamilton.

"It made it so much harder for everyone with the conditions," said a delighted Hamilton. "These new cars are so much harder to drive in the wet and it was the first time for me driving in the wet. It was a serious challenge today, but for both me and Nico

Left: A winter's work comes to an end as Lewis Hamilton lines his Mercedes F1 W05 up on pole. Right: Nico Rosberg leads Daniel Ricciardo, Hamilton, Kevin Magnussen, Nico Hülkenberg and Fernando Alonso out of Turn 1 as Felipe Massa is spun around by Kamui Kobayashi in the background. Below: Romain Grosjean spent much of the first two days waiting for problems on his Lotus to be fixed

INSIDE LINE

NICO ROSBERG
MERCEDES

I t's been an amazing day. Everybody has worked so hard over the winter and now to have such an amazing Silver Arrow to drive is unreal. I was very optimistic as we prepared really well for it and from the beginning it went fantastically.

"I was off like a bullet at the start. After that, the car was really quick and the team did such a good job. It's a really good engine, there wasn't much of a problem with fuel consumption and reliability was great.

"I got into a bit of a strange situation in that middle stint because I got graining on the front and then somehow I was losing temperature and it started to get difficult out there. But the team told me to try to stay out and I did and then the graining cleared and I was able to go again.

> **"THE TEAM TOLD ME TO TRY TO STAY OUT AND I DID AND THEN THE GRAINING CLEARED AND I WAS ABLE TO GO AGAIN"**

"It's a fact that we're not 100% sorted. We know that and the team did a great job to get my car working so well in the race, but there's still work to be done. We have two weeks now. We need to identify all the things that we can still do better because even leading up to this weekend there were still a lot of changes on the car and you don't really want to be doing that just going to the first race. Also, in testing, there were still a couple of problems at the end, so it was a great job, but still things need to get sorted.

"I'm just so happy for everybody. They work so hard, I don't think people can really imagine how hard everybody works in my team, so that's the best reward possible — to dominate in such a way the first week, the first race out."

to be up here is a great showing for the team and it's obviously great to see Ricciardo up here for his first race with Red Bull."

Fourth spot went to Magnussen after a superb effort by the Danish rookie who, like Vettel, survived an FIA yellow flag investigation without penalty. Fernando Alonso qualified fifth for Ferrari, while Jean-Éric Vergne did a great job for Toro Rosso to be sixth. Nico Hülkenberg started seventh for Force India, ahead of Toro Rosso rookie Daniil Kvyat, who spun and tapped the wall at the end. Williams' Felipe Massa and Valtteri Bottas took ninth and 10th, but the Finn would drop five places after a gearbox change.

It was dry come Sunday and the most dramatic incident of the race came at Turn 1 when Kamui Kobayashi's Caterham suffered brake system failure and slid helplessly into Massa's Williams, putting both firmly out of the race.

The race was always going to be all about Mercedes and it was decided in Rosberg's favour right at the start. Hamilton got away sluggishly. Then, after he lost positions on the opening lap, he was told by the team to pit to retire at the end of lap 2, with later investigations pinpointing a spark-plug issue.

"My start didn't feel great and I had a lot less power than usual when pulling away," said Hamilton.

TALKING POINT
EXCEEDING EXPECTATIONS

The Australian GP was a big test for F1 and the brave new world of hybrid technology. For the most part, the verdict had to be positive, especially given the poor reliability that most teams had suffered in testing.

It turned out to be a much better weekend than many had anticipated. There were technical gremlins and the ill-prepared Lotus team struggled. Lewis Hamilton and Sebastian Vettel were out of the race within three laps due to engine dramas, while Kamui Kobayashi triggered a first corner accident, but most cars ran reliably, a tribute to how good the F1 teams really are.

The biggest downside was the post-race exclusion of Daniel Ricciardo (above), an own goal for the sport that left a bitter taste in the mouth. It was no coincidence that the controversy was related to a dispute over the complex new regulations and Red Bull expressed its frustration about the accuracy of the FIA mandated fuel-flow meter. However, the appeal confirmed that the FIA was right and the team had tried to be too clever in its interpretation of how fuel flow could be measured.

> "STANDING AT A CORNER AND CHARTING THE CARS' SONIC PROGRESS ON DOWNSHIFTING AND ACCELERATION WASN'T WITHOUT INTRIGUE"

The cars looked good on track and, with less downforce and more torque than their predecessors, they took a lot of driving. The one area criticised by fans and F1 insiders alike was the dull noise they made. However, they were probably better appreciated live than on TV. Standing at a corner and charting their sonic progress on downshifting and acceleration wasn't without intrigue, with the turbo whistle chiming into the mix and the previously masked tyre squeal adding an extra dimension.

The race wasn't without intrigue as drivers managed precious resources – fuel and tyres – but a safety-car period made the former less critical, so the jury was still out on how economy races would unfold. As ever, F1 simply adapted to changing circumstances and got on with it.

There was no escaping the fact that Mercedes had a significant advantage and only the team knew how much Nico Rosberg had in hand.

"So it was obvious that something was wrong. It looks like we only had five cylinders firing and, while I wanted to keep going, we had to play safe and save the engine. It's unfortunate, but we'll recover from this."

Hamilton wasn't the only man in trouble as, from 12th on the grid, Vettel suffered a similar loss of power, the German coming in to retire after just three laps.

Rosberg had got by both Hamilton and second qualifier Ricciardo in the run to Turn 1 and, after that, he never looked back. He made his first stop under yellows when a safety car came out for debris, and retained the lead throughout the race as he managed his tyres and fuel consumption. Clearly keeping a little bit of pace in his pocket, he crossed the line 24.5s ahead of Ricciardo. It all looked very easy and, in truth, it was.

"I had an unbelievably quick car," said Rosberg. "It's such a pleasure to drive. It's such a great feeling and I really look forward to the next races so much now. Of course, it's still going to be tough and reliability isn't 100% sorted, but it's a great start and I'm just excited about the result and sharing it with the whole team."

Local hero Ricciardo did a superb job all weekend and, having started second, he retained that place for the duration. He came under pressure from Magnussen in the closing laps and it looked as though he might lose the spot, but he edged away again to secure it by 2.2s.

"It's a bit surreal still, but I'm sure tomorrow it will all sink in," he said. "I'm really happy with how the whole weekend has gone. In dry and wet conditions, I showed a lot of confidence and some good pace.

Far left: Valtteri Bottas was one of the stars of the race after an early setback.
Left: Marcus Ericsson contemplates his first F1 start.
Below: Fernando Alonso raced to a good points finish, but knew that wins would be a dream for Ferrari in 2014

Obviously, I've got to continue this, but the team has to be pleased with what they're seeing at the moment."

Ricciardo was then brought down to earth with a bump when he was excluded and it became apparent that he'd overstepped the fuel limits when the team attempted to make up for what it deemed to be a faulty flow meter. It wasn't the driver's fault, but he potentially gained a little performance relative to the pursuing McLarens. Nevertheless, it was a good drive.

And it was a fine F1 debut for Magnussen, who had got a bit sideways leaving the grid, but thereafter didn't put a foot wrong.

"It's not a win, but it definitely feels like a bit of a win," he said. "The team is coming off a difficult season. They really wanted to come back and they've worked so hard over the winter. Working with a rookie as well who hasn't got experience, it's been tough for them, for sure. Yet they've done such a good job, made me feel really at home and feel comfortable with everything, so I couldn't have asked for more."

Fourth on the road went to Button in the other McLaren after a good effort by driver and team and if anyone deserved the promotion to third spot, it was the Briton, even if he didn't actually get to step onto it.

Only 10th on the grid, he lost a place to Bottas early on, but when the safety car came out he was able to duck into the pits a lap ahead of those immediately in front of him. That gained Button a couple of places and he gained more with an early second stop that left him in fourth for the balance of the race.

Fernando Alonso had a solid race to fifth on the road for Ferrari, but it was apparent that the Italian car was lacking performance. He

"HAMILTON LOST POSITIONS ON THE OPENING LAP, THEN HE WAS TOLD BY THE TEAM TO RETIRE"

was stuck behind Force India's Hülkenberg for the first part of the race, eventually getting by at the second stops. He finished a demoralising 35s down on the winner and the gift of fourth spot was gratefully received.

Bottas was one of the stars of the race and was responsible for much of the overtaking that took place. Only 15th on the grid after his gearbox grid penalty was imposed, he moved up quickly, but broke a rear wheel when he got sideways and kissed the wall. He somehow managed to get back to the pits and didn't lose much time thanks to the safety car he triggered for debris.

After that, he continued to make passing moves, before ending up in an unrepresentative sixth place on the road. It was clear that he has the potential to be a major player in 2014.

After looking good in fourth early on, Hülkenberg tumbled down to seventh, finishing ahead of Räikkönen, who struggled with tyre graining. He also lost a place when he had to wait behind his teammate Sergio Pérez during the first round of pit stops under the safety car.

It was a good day for Toro Rosso as Vergne and rookie Kvyat took ninth and 10th on the road, the former having been as high as seventh early on. After Ricciardo's exclusion ensured that everyone from Magnussen to Kvyat moved up a place, Pérez inherited the final point for Force India.

Sauber's Esteban Gutiérrez made a good initial start, but was involved in an incident at Turn 3 and spun. After a pit stop, he faced a tough recovery to 12th, one place and 6s behind teammate Adrian Sutil. The German lost performance with an ERS issue early on, while his pit-stop strategy didn't really pay off. Neither Lotus finished, but the black and gold did at least record some race mileage, with Pastor Maldonado making it to lap 30 and Romain Grosjean to lap 44. This new breed of F1 wasn't perhaps as easy as Mercedes made it look.

"IN THE END, IT CAME DOWN TO STAYING OUT OF TROUBLE AND WHO CROSSED THE LINE LAST"

Above: Kevin Magnussen is welcomed back into the pit lane after finishing third on his debut. **Left:** Nico Rosberg couldn't have had a better start, winning for Mercedes by 24s

CLOCKWISE FROM RIGHT: an early first pit stop helped Jenson Button gain two places; brake failure caused Kamui Kobayashi's first corner shunt; Pastor Maldonado joins Williams racers Valtteri Bottas and Felipe Massa; rain during qualifying made conditions tricky for everyone; Daniel Ricciardo was delighted with second place, but he wasn't allowed to keep it; Melbourne's skyline is one of F1's most distinctive backdrops; two ways of welcoming F1 to Melbourne

SNAPSHOT FROM AUSTRALIA

AUSTRALIA
MELBOURNE

ROUND 1

Official Results © [2014]
Formula One World
Championship Limited,
6 Princes Gate, London SW7
1QJ. No reproduction without
permission. All copyright and
database rights reserved.

RACE DATE 16 March

CIRCUIT LENGTH 3.295 miles

NO. OF LAPS 57

RACE DISTANCE 187.815 miles

WEATHER Overcast, 20ºC

TRACK TEMP 27ºC

LAP RECORD Michael Schumacher,
1m24.125s, 141.016mph, 2004

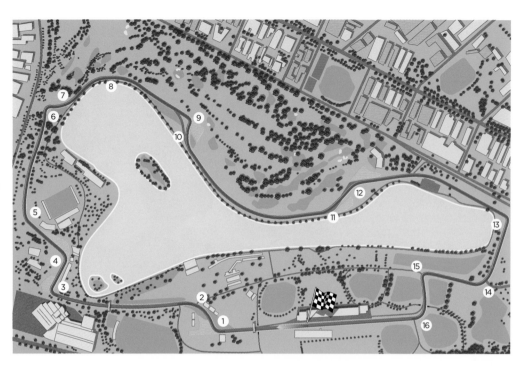

PRACTICE 1				PRACTICE 2				PRACTICE 3				QUALIFYING 1			QUALIFYING 2	
	Driver	Time	Laps		Driver	Time	Laps		Driver	Time	Laps		Driver	Time		Driver	Time
1	F Alonso	1m31.840s	20	1	L Hamilton	1m29.625s	37	1	N Rosberg	1m29.375s	15	1	D Ricciardo	1m30.775s	1	N Rosberg	1m42.264s
2	J Button	1m32.357s	23	2	N Rosberg	1m29.782s	31	2	J Button	1m30.766s	20	2	K Magnussen	1m30.949s	2	D Ricciardo	1m42.295s
3	V Bottas	1m32.403s	27	3	F Alonso	1m30.132s	28	3	F Alonso	1m30.876s	11	3	F Massa	1m31.228s	3	F Alonso	1m42.805s
4	F Massa	1m32.431s	19	4	S Vettel	1m30.381s	41	4	L Hamilton	1m30.919s	13	4	F Alonso	1m31.388s	4	L Hamilton	1m42.890s
5	D Ricciardo	1m32.599s	26	5	J Button	1m30.510s	33	5	D Ricciardo	1m30.970s	13	5	J Button	1m31.396s	5	K Magnussen	1m43.247s
6	N Rosberg	1m32.604s	17	6	D Ricciardo	1m30.538s	38	6	N Hülkenberg	1m30.978s	16	6	V Bottas	1m31.601s	6	N Hülkenberg	1m43.658s
7	S Vettel	1m32.793s	10	7	K Räikkönen	1m30.898s	32	7	K Räikkönen	1m31.156s	12	7	L Hamilton	1m31.699s	7	J-É Vergne	1m43.849s
8	K Magnussen	1m32.847s	28	8	V Bottas	1m30.920s	38	8	K Magnussen	1m31.251s	22	8	S Vettel	1m31.931s	8	V Bottas	1m43.852s
9	K Räikkönen	1m32.977s	19	9	K Magnussen	1m31.031s	34	9	S Pérez	1m31.665s	17	9	K Räikkönen	1m32.439s	9	F Massa	1m44.242s
10	J-É Vergne	1m33.446s	30	10	N Hülkenberg	1m31.054s	33	10	F Massa	1m31.723s	20	10	N Rosberg	1m32.564s	10	D Kvyat	1m44.331s
11	N Hülkenberg	1m33.533s	23	11	J-É Vergne	1m31.060s	35	11	D Kvyat	1m31.925s	17	11	J-É Vergne	1m33.488s	11	J Button	1m44.437s
12	S Pérez	1m33.855s	24	12	F Massa	1m31.119s	31	12	S Vettel	1m32.255s	14	12	A Sutil	1m33.673s	12	K Räikkönen	1m44.494s
13	D Kvyat	1m34.272s	27	13	S Pérez	1m31.283s	36	13	J-É Vergne	1m32.417s	16	13	D Kvyat	1m33.777s	13	S Vettel	1m44.668s
14	E Gutiérrez	1m35.578s	7	14	A Sutil	1m32.355s	36	14	J Bianchi	1m34.184s	15	14	N Hülkenberg	1m33.893s	14	A Sutil	1m45.655s
15	A Sutil	1m36.445s	13	15	E Gutiérrez	1m32.468s	26	15	A Sutil	1m34.188s	16	15	S Pérez	1m34.141s	15	K Kobayashi	1m45.867s
16	J Bianchi	1m40.859s	6	16	D Kvyat	1m32.496s	36	16	K Kobayashi	1m34.413s	19	16	K Kobayashi	1m34.274s	16	S Pérez	1m47.293s
17	M Chilton	1m46.922s	4	17	J Bianchi	1m33.486s	29	17	M Chilton	1m34.717s	15	17	M Chilton	1m34.293s			
18	P Maldonado	no time	2	18	R Grosjean	1m33.646s	12	18	P Maldonado	1m34.754s	15	18	J Bianchi	1m34.794s			
19	M Ericsson	no time	1	19	M Chilton	1m34.757s	29	19	M Ericsson	1m36.159s	21	19	E Gutiérrez	1m35.117s			
20	L Hamilton	no time	1	20	M Ericsson	no time	1	20	R Grosjean	no time	4	20	M Ericsson	1m35.157s			
21	K Kobayashi	no time	1	21	K Kobayashi	no time	0	21	V Bottas	no time	2	21	R Grosjean	1m36.993s			
22	R Grosjean	no time	0	22	P Maldonado	no time	0	22	E Gutiérrez	no time	2	22	P Maldonado	no time			

Best sectors – Practice			Speed trap – Practice			Best sectors – Qualifying			Speed trap – Qualifying		
Sec 1	L Hamilton	29.205s	1	N Rosberg	199.025mph	Sec 1	L Hamilton	29.863s	1	V Bottas	197.285mph
Sec 2	N Rosberg	23.822s	2	L Hamilton	198.652mph	Sec 2	K Magnussen	24.068s	2	S Pérez	195.980mph
Sec 3	L Hamilton	35.838s	3	V Bottas	197.907mph	Sec 3	D Ricciardo	36.344s	3	K Magnussen	195.608mph

Sebastian Vettel

"I lost power on the formation lap. It's disappointing, but that's racing. I thought it was the battery not discharging its power, but it looks as though a cylinder dropped."

Nico Rosberg

"To start with a win is unbelievable. My start was great and I was able to push from there to the end, with our consumption well under control."

Fernando Alonso

"I'd have liked a podium, but I had problems with the electric motor. I had to make changes from the steering wheel. From lap 10 on, though, everything went well."

Pastor Maldonado

"The race was disappointing, but we did more laps than in the pre-season, which is encouraging as we have more data after a negative time in free practice."

Jenson Button

"I had fun chasing Kevin and Daniel, but my tyres were older. I had a good race, but had understeer when I was behind people, though the car worked well in clear air."

Sergio Pérez

"I'm disappointed not to score. My race got difficult on lap 1 when I got hit by Gutiérrez – I got a puncture and had to pit, which dropped me to the back."

Daniel Ricciardo

"Three weeks ago, I'd have bet everything that I wouldn't be on the podium at this race. We don't have the pace of Mercedes, but this is a great result that we can take away."

Lewis Hamilton

"My start wasn't great and I had a lot less power than usual, so something was obviously wrong. I had only five cylinders firing, so we had to save the engine."

Kimi Räikkönen

"I was hit from behind at the first corner. Later, I suffered graining at the front. When it was time for the first stop, we had to do a double stop and that cost me a place."

Romain Grosjean

"I expected to do 15-20 laps in the race after all the issues we've had and managed 45! We've learned a lot today and all the changes made to the car have been positive."

Kevin Magnussen

"This was amazing. My moment at the start was scary – I got on the power too soon and nearly lost it. I had a go at Daniel at the end, but didn't have the speed to get by."

Nico Hülkenberg

"My issue was front graining on the softs, which never cleared, compromising my first two stints. It was a shame to lose places at my second stop [to Button and Alonso]."

POSITIONS LAP BY LAP

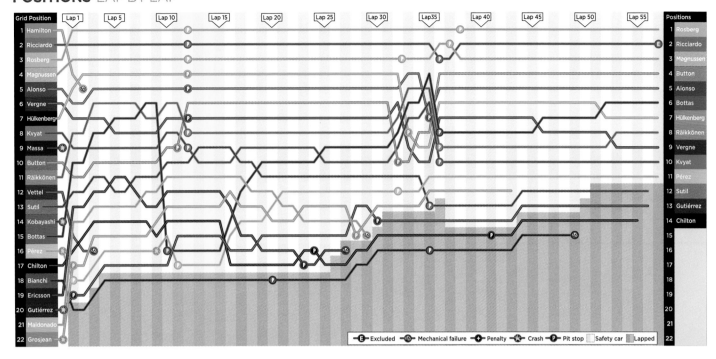

Legend: E = Excluded · Mechanical failure · Penalty · K = Crash · P = Pit stop · Safety car · Lapped

Grid Position: 1 Hamilton, 2 Ricciardo, 3 Rosberg, 4 Magnussen, 5 Alonso, 6 Vergne, 7 Hülkenberg, 8 Kvyat, 9 Massa, 10 Button, 11 Räikkönen, 12 Vettel, 13 Sutil, 14 Kobayashi, 15 Bottas, 16 Pérez, 17 Chilton, 18 Bianchi, 19 Ericsson, 20 Gutiérrez, 21 Maldonado, 22 Grosjean

Positions: 1 Rosberg, 2 Ricciardo, 3 Magnussen, 4 Button, 5 Alonso, 6 Bottas, 7 Hülkenberg, 8 Räikkönen, 9 Vergne, 10 Kvyat, 11 Pérez, 12 Sutil, 13 Gutiérrez, 14 Chilton, 15, 16, 17, 18, 19, 20, 21, 22

Laps marked: Lap 1, Lap 5, Lap 10, Lap 15, Lap 20, Lap 25, Lap 30, Lap 35, Lap 40, Lap 45, Lap 50, Lap 55

QUALIFYING 3

	Driver	Time
1	L Hamilton	1m44.231s
2	D Ricciardo	1m44.548s
3	N Rosberg	1m44.595s
4	K Magnussen	1m45.745s
5	F Alonso	1m45.819s
6	J-É Vergne	1m45.864s
7	N Hülkenberg	1m46.030s
8	D Kvyat	1m47.368s
9	F Massa	1m48.079s
10	V Bottas	1m48.147s

GRID

	Driver	Time
1	L Hamilton	1m44.231s
2	D Ricciardo	1m44.548s
3	N Rosberg	1m44.595s
4	K Magnussen	1m45.745s
5	F Alonso	1m45.819s
6	J-É Vergne	1m45.864s
7	N Hülkenberg	1m46.030s
8	D Kvyat	1m47.368s
9	F Massa	1m48.079s
10	J Button	1m44.437s
11	K Räikkönen	1m44.494s
12	S Vettel	1m44.668s
13	A Sutil	1m45.655s
14	K Kobayashi	1m45.867s
15	V Bottas	1m48.147s
16	S Pérez	1m47.293s
17	M Chilton	1m34.293s
18	J Bianchi	1m34.794s
19	M Ericsson	1m35.157s
20	E Gutiérrez	1m35.117s
21	P Maldonado	no time
22	R Grosjean	1m36.993s

Grid penalties

V Bottas	5-place penalty for changing the gearbox
E Gutiérrez	5-place penalty for changing the gearbox
R Grosjean	Put to back of grid as car modified in parc fermé

RACE

	Driver	Car	Laps	Time	Av mph	Fastest	Stops
1	N Rosberg	Mercedes F1 W05	57	1h32m58.710s	121.209	1m32.478s	2
D	D Ricciardo	Red Bull-Renault RB10	57	1h33m23.235s	120.673	1m33.066s	2
2	K Magnussen	McLaren-Mercedes MP4-29	57	1h33m25.487s	120.624	1m32.917s	2
3	J Button	McLaren-Mercedes MP4-29	57	1h33m28.737s	120.554	1m33.186s	2
4	F Alonso	Ferrari F14 T	57	1h33m33.994s	120.441	1m32.616s	2
5	V Bottas	Williams-Mercedes FW36	57	1h33m46.349s	120.177	1m32.568s	2
6	N Hülkenberg	Force India-Mercedes VJM07	57	1h33m49.428s	120.111	1m33.210s	2
7	K Räikkönen	Ferrari F14 T	57	1h33m56.385s	119.963	1m33.691s	2
8	J-É Vergne	Toro Rosso-Renault STR9	57	1h33m59.151s	119.904	1m33.864s	2
9	D Kvyat	Toro Rosso-Renault STR9	57	1h34m02.295s	119.837	1m32.634s	2
10	S Pérez	Force India-Mercedes VJM07	57	1h34m24.626s	119.365	1m33.366s	3
11	A Sutil	Sauber-Ferrari C33	56	1h33m06.852s	118.903	1m34.564s	1
12	E Gutiérrez	Sauber-Ferrari C33	56	1h33m12.956s	118.774	1m34.202s	2
13	M Chilton	Marussia-Ferrari MR03	55	1h33m21.069s	116.484	1m35.635s	2
NC	J Bianchi	Marussia-Ferrari MR03	49	1h34m32.241s	102.474	1m35.281s	2
R	R Grosjean	Lotus-Renault E22	43	ERS	-	1m34.766s	2
R	P Maldonado	Lotus-Renault E22	29	ERS	-	1m37.332s	2
R	M Ericsson	Caterham-Renault CT05	27	Oil pressure	-	1m37.064s	2
R	S Vettel	Red Bull-Renault RB10	3	Engine	-	1m49.947s	2
R	L Hamilton	Mercedes F1 W05	2	Engine	-	1m40.287s	2
R	F Massa	Williams-Mercedes FW36	0	Accident	-	-	0
R	K Kobayashi	Caterham-Renault CT05	0	Accident	-	-	0

Fastest lap
N Rosberg 1m32.478s
(128.273mph) on lap 19

Fastest speed trap
K Magnussen 196.912mph
Slowest speed trap
F Massa 135.459mph

Fastest pit stop
1 K Räikkönen 21.825s
2 F Alonso 21.978s
3 R Grosjean 22.264s

CHAMPIONSHIP

	Driver	Pts
1	N Rosberg	25
2	K Magnussen	18
3	J Button	15
4	F Alonso	12
5	V Bottas	10
6	N Hülkenberg	8
7	K Räikkönen	6
8	J-É Vergne	4
9	D Kvyat	2
10	S Pérez	1

CONSTRUCTORS

	Team	Pts
1	McLaren-Mercedes	33
2	Mercedes	25
3	Ferrari	18
4	Williams-Mercedes	10
5	Force India-Mercedes	9
6	Toro Rosso-Renault	6

Esteban Gutiérrez
"It was a different kind of racing. We're missing speed on the straights and it's a challenge to compete like this. We need to make sure that we put everything together."

Jean-Éric Vergne
"This is a good result, though the car was tricky to drive as I had brake problems, but we're satisfied to finish with both cars in the points. I'm pleased with my three points, especially."

Felipe Massa
"I'm disappointed as I had a car for a podium, but the incident in the first corner ruined my race. I had tried not to take any risks, but was hit from behind after Kobayashi braked too late."

Max Chilton
"I was preparing for the formation lap when everything cut out, but the team did a great job to push me to the garage. They reset the car and I was able to start from the pit lane."

Marcus Ericsson
"I showed a bit of my potential in the early laps when I passed Sutil and ran in 12th position. My first ever live F1 pit stop went well, but then an oil pressure problem forced me to stop."

Adrian Sutil
"I had a few powertrain issues in the first stint. That improved, but it cost time. I was on a two-stop run, but switched to a one-stop strategy due to the safety car."

Daniil Kvyat
"Finishing my first race with a point is great. The start was messy, but I got into a rhythm. The car seemed competitive and it was close at the end with JEV, but I had to save fuel."

Valtteri Bottas
"The car went well and we can be pleased with that. I'm disappointed with myself as I was pushing too hard and hit the wall, which caused a puncture and put me back a long way."

Jules Bianchi
"The problem at the start was worrying, but the team got me to the garage. I was six laps down when I rejoined and I was never going to recover from that, but that wasn't the point."

Kamui Kobayashi
"I had a good start, but into Turn 1 I made contact with Felipe. From the data, it looked like I had a brake system issue, which meant I couldn't do much about the contact. I'm sorry about that."

A CLASSIC DISPLAY OF DRIVING FROM LEWIS HAMILTON RESULTED IN A COMFORTABLE MERCEDES ONE-TWO, ON A DISASTROUS DAY FOR DANIEL RICCIARDO AND RED BULL

ROUND 2 PETRONAS MALAYSI

MALA

GRAND PRIX

YSIA

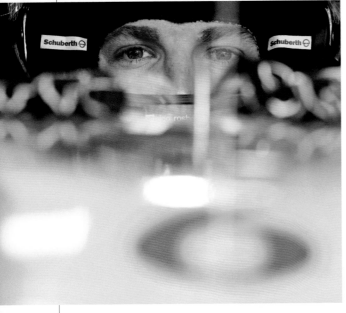

Left: McLaren's Jenson Button gathers his thoughts before starting the race in an unrepresentative 10th place. Below: it was typically close through Turn 1; Lewis Hamilton is shown here leading as Nico Rosberg defends his newly gained second place from Sebastian Vettel. Right: Fernando Alonso started fourth and finished fourth for Ferrari, unable to match the pace of the Mercedes' and Red Bulls

L ewis Hamilton recovered from his early retirement in Australia with a faultless performance in Malaysia, heading home with Nico Rosberg in a comfortable Mercedes one-two. It was an entertaining race that saw some great battles down the field, even if there was only ever going to be one winner.

Not unexpectedly for Sepang, rain added an extra dimension in qualifying and, after a series of delays, the session got under way 50 minutes late. However, the puddles disappeared so quickly that nearly everyone went straight out on intermediates, with only the McLarens trying full wets. That proved to be a wrong decision, and both Jenson Button and Kevin Magnussen were soon back in.

Rosberg and Hamilton set the top two times on their first laps, and thereafter everyone else was left trying to keep up, with Sebastian Vettel – who lost time with a battery issue – getting up to third. The session was red-flagged 35s early after a crash for Caterham rookie Marcus Ericsson, but all the big names made it safely through.

Rain returned before the start of Q2, so most drivers went out on full wets. However, the session was red-flagged almost immediately after Daniil Kvyat collided with Fernando Alonso. The Spaniard suffered broken front suspension, but the team fixed the car and got him out for the restart.

Hamilton topped the Q2 times, although Vettel split the Mercedes drivers. Kevin Magnussen was lucky to escape from the gravel after a spin at the last corner and made it through to Q3. Out of luck were

"THE THIRD AND CRUCIAL SESSION AGAIN SAW FULL WET TYRES AS THE IDEAL CHOICE"

Felipe Massa and Valtteri Bottas, after a frustrating session for Williams saw the team focus initially on intermediates.

The third and crucial session again saw full wets as the ideal choice. Hamilton went top after the first laps and, having improved his time, was still there at the end. He cut it fine, though, as Vettel came close to beating him. Rosberg, consistently edged out by his teammate in the wettest conditions, had to settle for third. Alonso did an impressive job and took fourth, despite his suspension being a little out of kilter. Daniel Ricciardo backed up Vettel with a solid fifth ahead of Kimi Räikkönen in the other Ferrari. Nico Hülkenberg once again showed good wet form for Force India as he took seventh, ahead of Magnussen.

Bottas was then given a three-place penalty for impeding

INSIDE LINE

SEBASTIAN VETTEL
RED BULL RACING

I thought I had a good start, but then I focused on getting in Lewis's tow to attack going into the first corner. Then Nico was there on the right and it was quite tight. Daniel was coming as well as I was trying to get past Nico. So I lost a place, but fortunately I got it back, and then later on I was trying to get as close as I could to Nico.

"At some stage it looked as though we were pretty similar, but then it's like he found another gear. In the end, I was just trying to get the car home. Lewis could probably have gone faster, and we could have gone faster at the end, but our priority was to secure the podium.

"Mercedes looked nearly seamless in winter testing and the package they have is very strong. But, for us, there are mostly positives as our car was competitive at Sepang on a completely different track and in different conditions. It's much better than what we expected during the winter. We know that there's a lot we can do better because it doesn't feel great when we're racing. If you go out on track and observe how the cars behave, on power there's a big difference. It's a question of how soon we manage to catch up.

"We need to make big steps as they are quite far ahead, but I'm quite happy as it's the first race distance I've done this year. Obviously, at some stage during testing, we didn't expect to finish the first couple of races, so well done to all the team on reliability. In terms of driveability, we're not there yet. In terms of power, it's not a big secret, but the guys at Viry are flat out on that."

> **"IF YOU GO OUT ON TRACK AND OBSERVE HOW THE CARS BEHAVE, ON POWER THERE'S A BIG DIFFERENCE BETWEEN US AND MERCEDES"**

Ricciardo. The Finn, who dropped from 15th to 18th, was also given two license penalty points, thus becoming the first driver to accrue points under the new system introduced by the FIA.

Against expectations, the rain stayed away before the start, which was preceded by a minute's silence for the victims of MH370, the missing Malaysian Airlines flight. After the wet qualifying session, everyone had a free choice of tyres, and the whole field went for options.

Unlike in Australia, Hamilton got away cleanly, while Rosberg immediately jumped ahead of Vettel to claim second, although he didn't have much room on the inside line. The World Champion was bundled down to fourth by Ricciardo, who once again demonstrated that he is not to be underestimated.

"I had a really good start, so I was happy about that because it's not so easy this year," said Rosberg. "The rear tyres are harder and we have more torque, so it's very difficult to get it right, but it felt great and I got away well and then with Sebastian it was massively close. I thought he was going to put me right into the wall, but he stopped just before – so thank you for that! My heart skipped a beat, but I kept right on it. Then I had a bit of a moment in Turn 3, a bit of a tankslapper, and that allowed them all to get another run on me, but it all worked out."

Vettel's view was this: "I thought I had a good start but then I focused on getting in Lewis's tow, to maybe attack him going into the first corner. Then Nico was there on the right and it was quite tight. Daniel was coming as well as I was trying to get past Nico, so I lost a place."

For once, the first couple of corners passed without major

TALKING POINT
MERCEDES TO THE FORE

So what were we to make of the start of the season? It was clear in testing that Mercedes had stolen a march, and that was borne out by the way Nico Rosberg and Lewis Hamilton dominated the opening races.

While the power unit was a huge part of the story, it wasn't everything, or the eight Mercedes-equipped cars would have filled the first four rows. But that didn't happen, and both Red Bull and Ferrari were in the mix immediately behind the Mercedes works team.

What was not obvious was how much Mercedes had kept in reserve. Clearly, there was no point in running everything to the limit and winning by a minute, given that the power unit now had to last for five events.

"When they turn everything up and go for a lap, they've proved that they're very fast," said Jenson Button. "They're good in high-speed corners, which is helping them through a run in consistency as well, as they're not overheating the tyres.

"Our strength is low-speed corners. High speed is an area where we need to improve. In the dry, if you don't have enough downforce in the high-speed corners you overheat the tyres, and in the wet you can't get the tyres in a working range, because you can't get them warm enough as you're going too slowly."

Those watching on track suggested that the Red Bull was the most impressive car in the corners, and the numbers told an interesting story – the team was losing out to Mercedes on the straights.

"WHEN MERCEDES TURN EVERYTHING UP AND GO FOR A LAP, THEY'VE PROVED THAT THEY'RE VERY FAST AND THEY'RE GOOD IN HIGH-SPEED CORNERS"

"They've obviously got plenty up their sleeve," said Red Bull boss Christian Horner of his main rivals. "Their advantage is clear in a straight line. Considering where we're at with the engine, to be doing what we're doing is beyond expectation. Renault knows there's a lot more to come once the driveability issues are sorted out. Hopefully with our curve in terms of catching up on straightline speed, we should be able to make steps."

All three manufacturers had to homologate and freeze their power unit specification before the season, and thus the ongoing focus was on areas such as software, where there was still some freedom of movement.

"It's a matter of getting all three elements working in harmony," added Horner. "There's obviously the combustion engine, the turbo and the energy recovery system, which affects your braking as much as it does your acceleration and power delivery."

Clockwise from left: Felipe Massa was asked to let Williams teammate Valtteri Bottas pass by for seventh late in the race but declined; the Red Bull top brass watch as Sebastian Vettel races by to third; Nico Rosberg had no answer to Lewis Hamilton's pace so had to settle for second in the Mercedes one-two; Red Bull team principal Christian Horner watches Daniel Ricciardo's disastrous pit stop; Ricciardo had run ahead of Fernando Alonso until the slip-up in the pits

drama, but then later in the lap backmarkers Pastor Maldonado and Jules Bianchi tangled, earning the latter a 5s penalty. There was more drama at the start of the second lap when Magnussen ran into Räikkönen, giving the Finn a right rear puncture. He made it back to the pits, but his race was ruined, while the Dane picked up a 5s penalty.

Anyone hoping to see a fight between the Mercedes drivers was quickly disappointed. Hamilton was 2s clear at the end of the opening lap and he soon began to build on that, leaving Rosberg in his wake. Ricciardo soon lost his third place to Vettel, who slipped by at the start of lap 4.

Ricciardo was the first of the top four to come in, the Aussie pitting on lap 12. He was followed over succeeding laps by Vettel, Rosberg and Hamilton, whose lead over his teammate had been over 6s. After the stops, Hamilton continued to extend it, and the race turned into a demonstration. He drove faultlessly to win after pitting again on laps 33 and 51. Rosberg remained second for the duration, always stopping a lap before his teammate.

"I don't think any race is ever easy," said Hamilton. "There are opportunities that are presented to you, and obviously you have to take them with both hands, and today that's what I did. But looking after

"ANYONE HOPING TO SEE A FIGHT BETWEEN THE MERCEDES DRIVERS WAS QUICKLY DISAPPOINTED"

the car, looking after fuel, not making any mistakes, it was a massive challenge in that sense.

"I would hear that Nico had stepped up the speed and you have to react to those things without damaging your tyres, so without doubt it was still a great challenge, but one that I was able to do well because the car was spectacular this weekend. So I'm really happy with a great performance by the team. Fortunately, they were spot on with all the pit stops and the timing. Also, the info I was getting was spot on, too."

Rosberg couldn't quite match Hamilton's pace but, despite coming under threat from Vettel in the middle of the race, had plenty in hand. Later, he opened up a gap on Vettel as Mercedes made it look straightforward. However, he wasn't getting too excited about his role as championship leader. "That sounds very good already as it is," said Rosberg, "but there's a long way to go. I'm not thinking about that at the moment. I'm really just taking it race by race, just enjoying the moment, keeping on it. The best example is now Red Bull. The last day of testing was four weeks ago and they were absolutely nowhere, and now he [Vettel] was right in the back of me, pushing me. OK, I had some pace in hand so I could beat him in the end, but still, the way they've ramped up their pace is very impressive, so we need to keep on it to keep our advantage."

Vettel enjoyed an untroubled run to third to log his longest run to date in the Red Bull RB10, after his early retirement in Australia and problems in testing. It turned into a disastrous day for his teammate Ricciardo, though. The Australian was released too early from his second pit stop and a lot of time was lost while his car was pushed back and the front left wheel secured. Later, his front wing broke and caused a puncture and, with the

added burden of a stop-and-go penalty, the team decided to retire the car. In fact, under a new rule, Ricciardo landed both a stop-and-go penalty in the current race and a grid penalty for the next.

"I think the rules are pretty clear," said Red Bull boss Christian Horner. "For an unsafe release, it's a stop-and-go penalty of 10s and a 10-place grid penalty at the next race. The punishment is harsh, but unfortunately it is the rules."

Ricciardo's misfortune left fourth place to Alonso, who had

stayed close to the Red Bulls in the early stages. A bold two-stop strategy left Hülkenberg's Force India in fourth in the closing laps, but on newer tyres Alonso reeled him and reclaimed the position. The German had even led a lap after a late first stop, before Hamilton nipped past on fresh rubber. Teammate Sergio Pérez hadn't even made it to the start after problems when he tried to leave the pits to go to the grid.

Jenson Button enjoyed a solid race to sixth for McLaren, while behind him the Williams duo of Massa and Bottas took seventh and eighth. There was controversy in the closing laps when Massa was told that Bottas was faster, and that he should let the Finn past to attack Button, but the Brazilian chose to ignore the instruction.

Despite losing time with a nose change and a 5s penalty, Magnussen took two points for ninth. The final point went to Daniil Kvyat after another good drive from the Toro Rosso new boy. Lotus finally got some miles on the E22 as Romain Grosjean finished 11th, while Räikkönen took 12th. Räikkönen's return to Ferrari wasn't working out as he'd have hoped.

Left: Nico Hülkenberg qualified well in the mixed conditions for Force India, then took the fight to Alonso in the race.
Below: Lewis Hamilton displays his delight after heading home for his first win of the year and Mercedes' first one-two since 1955

Clockwise from right: conditions were incredibly tricky at the start of qualifying, but Lewis Hamilton was in control in both Q2 and Q3; the tools of the trade for the grid marshals; when it rains in Malaysia, it really rains; snatching a peek from the pit wall; Michael Schumacher was out of sight, but not out of fans' minds; the Petronas Towers dominate Kuala Lumpur's skyline; Lewis Hamilton had every reason to smile as the photographers demanded shots of him and his trophy; Kevin Magnussen keeps cool in the cockpit during a break in practice

SNAPSHOT FROM MALAYSIA

MALAYSIA
SEPANG
ROUND 2

Official Results © [2014]
Formula One World
Championship Limited,
6 Princes Gate, London SW7
1QJ. No reproduction without
permission. All copyright and
database rights reserved.

RACE DATE 30 March

CIRCUIT LENGTH 3.444 miles

NO. OF LAPS 56

RACE DISTANCE 192.864 miles

WEATHER Sunny, 33ºC

TRACK TEMP 46ºC

LAP RECORD Juan Pablo Montoya,
1m34.223s, 131.991mph, 2004

PRACTICE 1				PRACTICE 2				PRACTICE 3				QUALIFYING 1			QUALIFYING 2	
	Driver	Time	Laps		Driver	Time	Laps		Driver	Time	Laps		Driver	Time		Driver	Time
1	L Hamilton	1m40.691s	19	1	N Rosberg	1m39.909s	30	1	N Rosberg	1m39.008s	13	1	N Rosberg	1m57.183s	1	L Hamilton	1m59.041s
2	K Räikkönen	1m40.843s	20	2	K Räikkönen	1m39.944s	30	2	L Hamilton	1m39.240s	13	2	L Hamilton	1m57.202s	2	S Vettel	1m59.399s
3	N Rosberg	1m41.028s	19	3	S Vettel	1m39.970s	30	3	K Räikkönen	1m40.156s	13	3	S Vettel	1m57.654s	3	N Rosberg	1m59.445s
4	J Button	1m41.111s	20	4	L Hamilton	1m40.051s	32	4	S Vettel	1m40.387s	14	4	N Hülkenberg	1m58.883s	4	D Ricciardo	2m00.147s
5	K Magnussen	1m41.274s	18	5	F Alonso	1m40.103s	29	5	N Hülkenberg	1m40.523s	15	5	F Alonso	1m58.889s	5	N Hülkenberg	2m00.839s
6	J-É Vergne	1m41.402s	15	6	F Massa	1m40.112s	34	6	D Ricciardo	1m40.686s	14	6	D Ricciardo	1m58.913s	6	F Alonso	2m01.356s
7	S Vettel	1m41.523s	9	7	D Ricciardo	1m40.276s	29	7	F Alonso	1m40.736s	14	7	K Räikkönen	1m59.257s	7	K Räikkönen	2m01.532s
8	N Hülkenberg	1m41.642s	19	8	J Button	1m40.628s	28	8	F Massa	1m40.781s	20	8	V Bottas	1m59.709s	8	J Button	2m01.810s
9	F Massa	1m41.686s	23	9	V Bottas	1m40.638s	35	9	V Bottas	1m40.891s	20	9	F Massa	2m00.047s	9	K Magnussen	2m02.094s
10	V Bottas	1m41.830s	22	10	N Hülkenberg	1m40.691s	34	10	S Pérez	1m41.029s	15	10	S Pérez	2m00.076s	10	J-É Vergne	2m02.096s
11	F Alonso	1m41.923s	14	11	J-É Vergne	1m40.777s	33	11	D Kvyat	1m41.182s	18	11	R Grosjean	2m00.202s	11	D Kvyat	2m02.351s
12	D Ricciardo	1m42.117s	20	12	K Magnussen	1m41.014s	20	12	J-É Vergne	1m41.441s	18	12	K Magnussen	2m00.358s	12	E Gutiérrez	2m02.369s
13	A Sutil	1m42.365s	21	13	A Sutil	1m41.257s	28	13	A Sutil	1m41.552s	15	13	J Button	2m00.889s	13	F Massa	2m02.460s
14	D Kvyat	1m42.869s	21	14	D Kvyat	1m41.325s	32	14	E Gutiérrez	1m42.041s	17	14	E Gutiérrez	2m01.134s	14	S Pérez	2m02.511s
15	E Gutiérrez	1m42.904s	23	15	E Gutiérrez	1m41.407s	34	15	R Grosjean	1m42.749s	16	15	D Kvyat	2m01.175s	15	V Bottas	2m02.756s
16	J Bianchi	1m43.825s	18	16	S Pérez	1m41.671s	25	16	P Maldonado	1m43.539s	20	16	J-É Vergne	2m01.689s	16	R Grosjean	2m02.885s
17	M Ericsson	1m45.775s	24	17	R Grosjean	1m42.531s	14	17	M Chilton	1m43.977s	16	17	P Maldonado	2m02.074s			
18	M Chilton	1m46.911s	10	18	M Chilton	1m43.638s	20	18	J Bianchi	1m44.170s	18	18	A Sutil	2m02.131s			
19	K Kobayashi	1m51.180s	5	19	J Bianchi	1m43.752s	29	19	M Ericsson	1m44.457s	12	19	J Bianchi	2m02.702s			
20	R Grosjean	No time	4	20	M Ericsson	1m45.703s	31	20	K Kobayashi	1m46.015s	7	20	K Kobayashi	2m03.595s			
21	P Maldonado	No time	2	21	K Kobayashi	no time	0	21	J Button	2m05.555s	4	21	M Chilton	2m04.388s			
22	S Pérez	No time	2	22	P Maldonado	no time	0	22	K Magnussen	no time	5	22	M Ericsson	2m04.407s			

Best sectors – Practice			Speed trap – Practice			Best sectors – Qualifying			Speed trap – Qualifying		
Sec 1	N Rosberg	25.067s	1	V Bottas	200.516mph	Sec 1	N Rosberg	28.537s	1	F Massa	189.518mph
Sec 2	S Vettel	33.658s	2	L Hamilton	199.957mph	Sec 2	L Hamilton	41.280s	2	V Bottas	189.083mph
Sec 3	N Rosberg	40.088s	3	S Pérez	199.895mph	Sec 3	L Hamilton	46.939s	3	S Pérez	188.524mph

Sebastian Vettel
"We've made a good step forwards, but have work to do. It's great to get a podium finish. Considering where we were two months ago, this weekend is a huge step."

Nico Rosberg
"It was tight with Vettel at the start. I closed my eyes, went for the gap and did it. Later, I was able to control the pace and defend my position, but Lewis was out of my reach."

Fernando Alonso
"Today's points are due to a trouble-free weekend in which the changes on the car worked. We need to improve our top speed, as seen from my duel with Hülkenberg."

Pastor Maldonado
"After the start, I lost power, so I had to retire to protect the engine. Despite that, this weekend has been a step forwards as we've been able to run far more with the car."

Jenson Button
"It was hot and, when you've spent all that time watching the Williams' battling behind you, it makes it feel even hotter. Still, it was an enjoyable race."

Sergio Pérez
"I'm disappointed not to race. We're still investigating the cause, but the car kept going into neutral when I was downshifting on the way to the grid."

Daniel Ricciardo
"I made up two places at the start, but later had a problem at the last pit stop and then a puncture. I think we had a front wing failure and then the stop-go penalty."

Lewis Hamilton
"The race was tougher than it looked, but I was able to look after the car, the tyres and the fuel and still keep a bit of pace in hand which made my job that little bit easier."

Kimi Räikkönen
"I'm disappointed with how this race turned out, as I got a good start, but the collision with Kevin damaged my right rear tyre, which meant I had to make an extra stop."

Romain Grosjean
"Eleventh is good for all the guys at Enstone and at the track, and good for me too. Finishing was our objective and then we wanted to see where we were with our car."

Kevin Magnussen
"I'm sorry that I messed things up going into the second corner, with the incident with Kimi. I shouldn't have made a mistake like that so early on."

Nico Hülkenberg
"Today was a team effort and I'm very happy with fifth. We were the only team among the frontrunners to do a two-stop race and we had good pace all afternoon."

POSITIONS LAP BY LAP

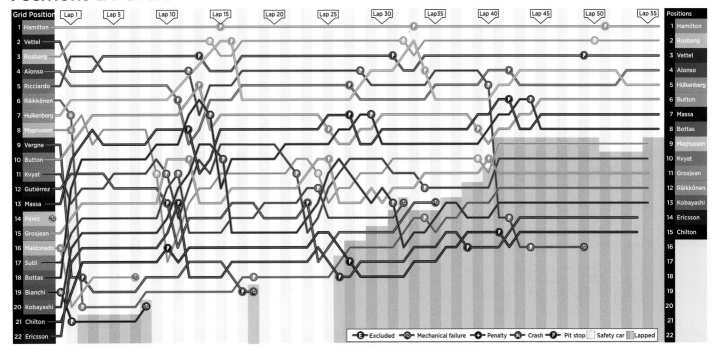

Grid Position													Positions
1 Hamilton	Lap 1	Lap 5	Lap 10	Lap 15	Lap 20	Lap 25	Lap 30	Lap35	Lap 40	Lap 45	Lap 50	Lap 55	1 Hamilton
2 Vettel													2 Rosberg
3 Rosberg													3 Vettel
4 Alonso													4 Alonso
5 Ricciardo													5 Hülkenberg
6 Räikkönen													6 Button
7 Hulkenberg													7 Massa
8 Magnussen													8 Bottas
9 Vergne													9 Magnussen
10 Button													10 Kvyat
11 Kvyat													11 Grosjean
12 Gutiérrez													12 Räikkönen
13 Massa													13 Kobayashi
14 Pérez													14 Ericsson
15 Grosjean													15 Chilton
16 Maldonado													16
17 Sutil													17
18 Bottas													18
19 Bianchi													19
20 Kobayashi													20
21 Chilton													21
22 Ericsson													22

E Excluded   **S** Mechanical failure   **+** Penalty   **X** Crash   **P** Pit stop   ☐ Safety car   ▨ Lapped

QUALIFYING 3

	Driver	Time
1	L Hamilton	1m59.431s
2	S Vettel	1m59.486s
3	N Rosberg	2m00.050s
4	F Alonso	2m00.175s
5	D Ricciardo	2m00.541s
6	K Räikkönen	2m01.218s
7	N Hülkenberg	2m01.712s
8	K Magnussen	2m02.213s
9	J-É Vergne	2m03.078s
10	J Button	2m04.053s

GRID

	Driver	Time
1	L Hamilton	1m59.431s
2	S Vettel	1m59.486s
3	N Rosberg	2m00.050s
4	F Alonso	2m00.175s
5	D Ricciardo	2m00.541s
6	K Räikkönen	2m01.218s
7	N Hülkenberg	2m01.712s
8	K Magnussen	2m02.213s
9	J-É Vergne	2m03.078s
10	J Button	2m04.053s
11	D Kvyat	2m02.351s
12	E Gutiérrez	2m02.369s
13	F Massa	2m02.460s
14	S Pérez	2m02.511s
15	R Grosjean	2m02.885s
16	P Maldonado	2m02.074s
17	A Sutil	2m02.131s
18	V Bottas	2m02.756s
19	J Bianchi	2m02.702s
20	K Kobayashi	2m03.595s
21	M Chilton	2m04.388s
22	M Ericsson	2m04.407s

Grid penalties
V Bottas   3-place penalty for impeding Ricciardo in Q2

RACE

	Driver	Car	Laps	Time	Av mph	Fastest	Stops
1	L Hamilton	Mercedes F1 W05	56	1h40m25.974s	115.233	1m43.066s	3
2	N Rosberg	Mercedes F1 W05	56	1h40m43.287s	114.898	1m43.960s	3
3	S Vettel	Red Bull-Renault RB10	56	1h40m50.508s	114.761	1m44.289s	3
4	F Alonso	Ferrari F14 T	56	1h41m01.966s	114.543	1m44.165s	3
5	N Hülkenberg	Force India-Mercedes VJM07	56	1h41m13.173s	114.332	1m45.982s	2
6	J Button	McLaren-Mercedes MP4-29	56	1h41m49.665s	113.649	1m46.039s	3
7	F Massa	Williams-Mercedes FW36	56	1h41m51.050s	113.624	1m44.897s	3
8	V Bottas	Williams-Mercedes FW36	56	1h41m51.511s	113.615	1m45.475s	3
9	K Magnussen	McLaren-Mercedes MP4-29	55	1h40m28.365s	113.125	1m45.373s	3
10	D Kvyat	Toro Rosso-Renault STR9	55	1h40m55.334s	112.621	1m46.695s	3
11	R Grosjean	Lotus-Renault E22	55	1h40m57.536s	112.580	1m46.224s	3
12	K Räikkönen	Ferrari F14 T	55	1h40m57.674s	112.578	1m45.129s	3
13	K Kobayashi	Caterham-Renault CT05	55	1h41m37.748s	111.838	1m47.753s	2
14	M Ericsson	Caterham-Renault CT05	54	1h40m37.511s	110.900	1m47.500s	3
15	M Chilton	Marussia-Ferrari MR03	54	1h40m37.641s	110.898	1m48.249s	3
R	D Ricciardo	Red Bull-Renault RB10	49	Front wing	-	1m44.675s	5
R	E Gutiérrez	Sauber-Ferrari C33	35	Gearbox	-	1m47.782s	2
R	A Sutil	Sauber-Ferrari C33	32	Power unit	-	1m48.040s	3
R	J-É Vergne	Toro Rosso-Renault STR9	18	Turbocharger	-	1m48.527s	2
R	J Bianchi	Marussia-Ferrari MR03	8	Accident damage	-	1m51.473s	1
R	P Maldonado	Lotus-Renault E22	7	Power unit	-	1m50.929s	0
NS	S Pérez	Force India-Mercedes VJM07	0	Gearbox	-	-	0

Fastest lap
L Hamilton 1m43.066s
(120.310mph) on lap 53

Fastest speed trap
F Massa   201.635mph
Slowest speed trap
P Maldonado   172.554mph

Fastest pit stop
1 F Alonso   24.222s
2 K Räikkönen   24.246s
3 K Magnussen   24.415s

CHAMPIONSHIP

	Driver	Pts
1	N Rosberg	43
2	L Hamilton	25
3	F Alonso	24
4	J Button	23
5	K Magnussen	20
6	N Hülkenberg	18
7	S Vettel	15
8	V Bottas	14
9	K Räikkönen	6
10	F Massa	6
11	J-É Vergne	4
12	D Kvyat	3
13	S Pérez	1

CONSTRUCTORS

	Team	Pts
1	Mercedes	68
2	McLaren-Mercedes	43
3	Ferrari	30
4	Williams-Mercedes	20
5	Force India-Mercedes	19
6	Red Bull-Renault	15
7	Toro Rosso-Renault	7

Esteban Gutiérrez
"After a long stint, I pitted and couldn't engage first. I tried many times, but it didn't work, so there was not much I could do. In the end we made a step forward this weekend."

Jean-Éric Vergne
"I had a great start, but soon lost power and everybody passed me. I found myself between a Caterham and Bianchi and maybe was too ambitious and this resulted in the collision."

Felipe Massa
"I had a good start and made up places on lap 1, but my progress was halted by Magnussen's McLaren, which had good traction out of the last corner, making it hard for me to pass."

Max Chilton
"It was a demanding race. I knew there was going to be trouble in Turn 1, which I avoided. I had a close battle with Ericsson and near the end of the race we were very close."

Marcus Ericsson
"I want to thank the boys for fixing my car after the accident. To finish my first full grand prix in 14th, helping us move up into 10th in the constructors' points, is a great feeling."

Adrian Sutil
"On lap 33, I lost power and suddenly the car switched off. I don't know what happened, so we need to analyse it. It is a shame. Many things don't work well at the moment."

Daniil Kvyat
"The race was very difficult and intense with a lot of fighting. The first two stints were hard when I was fighting the Williams' and McLaren, but they were faster than me on the straight."

Valtteri Bottas
"Going from P18 to P8 is a good result. The car wasn't as competitive as in Melbourne, but I made up six places on lap 1 and then the pace was good and I was able to make up more."

Jules Bianchi
"The situation with Maldonado was due to what happened off the start, when Vergne punctured my left rear. I pitted for new tyres and a front wing but then the car was tricky."

Kamui Kobayashi
"Thirteenth is a great result after such a bad weekend. I had a great start and got up to 16th. After pitting, I was ahead of Chilton on a new set of mediums so went after the Saubers."

MERCEDES DOMINATED THE
SHOW FOR THE SECOND RACE IN
A ROW AS LEWIS HAMILTON AND
NICO ROSBERG PROVIDED AN
ENTHRALLING SPECTACLE, THIS TIME
WITH THE GERMAN FASTER THAN HIS
TEAMMATE BUT UNABLE TO GET PAST

GULF AIR BAHRAIN GRAND PRIX

ROUND 3

BAH

RAIN

A nother superb Mercedes one-two was led by Lewis Hamilton at the end of a Bahrain GP run under floodlights for the first time. The Mercedes drivers were allowed by their team to race and often battled wheel to wheel with no quarter given. With some great racing down the field, an exhilarating event did much to silence critics of the 2014 F1 rules.

Keen to add excitement on the 10th anniversary of their first event, the race organisers had invested in a lighting system, as the night racing experiment begun in Singapore continued. The Sakhir track, not one of the most popular in the schedule, looked spectacular.

Saturday was the first dry qualifying session of the season and so the first time the drivers were able to use the extra set of tyres they've been given to encourage them to run in Q3. Also, the top 10 drivers had to start on the tyre on which they set their best time in Q2, a new rule that didn't come into force at the previous races.

Inevitably, Q3 developed into a battle between the Mercedes drivers. Nico Rosberg had been fastest in Q2 and he again set the pace on the first runs, pipping Hamilton by 0.3s. Hamilton had to dig deep, but his final run was over almost before it started after a lock up at Turn 1. As a consequence, Rosberg was able to abandon his final run, too, his pole secure.

Daniel Ricciardo did a great job to qualify third for Red Bull, but the Australian had a 10-place penalty for the unsafe pit release in Malaysia, so he dropped to 13th. Third was inherited by Valtteri Bottas after his efforts fulfilled

the promise that the Williams had shown in testing. He was joined on row two by Sergio Pérez, Force India having looked good over one lap and, crucially, over longer runs.

Kimi Räikkönen had struggled, but popped up in Q3 with fifth, lining up ahead of Jenson Button, Felipe Massa, Kevin Magnussen and Fernando Alonso. The Spaniard suffered a loss of power, which explained why he lost out to teammate Räikkönen.

There was a huge surprise in Q2 when Sebastian Vettel failed to progress, the German saying he had a problem with downshifts. "There was a little bit more in the car which I couldn't get to," he said. With Ricciardo being demoted, he would at least start 10th.

During Sunday's long build-up to the evening race, Bernie Ecclestone and Ferrari boss Luca di Montezemolo made their thoughts

INSIDE LINE

LEWIS HAMILTON
MERCEDES

This weekend started off well and then I seemed to lose pace while Nico's picked up. I knew I needed to get a good start and things went my way, except when the safety car came out. I've never won here in F1. I won, I think, in F3 back in 2004, so it's been a long time coming.

"The safety car came out and we had different tyres. It was one of the most difficult races. The last time I had a race like that would probably be Indianapolis, 2007. Nico drove fantastically well. When you're with your teammate it's very hard to make the right decisions about where to put your car, when to brake, but it was great.

"We believe the option tyre is worth 0.65s. Keeping Nico out of my slipstream and the DRS was very hard. To be flat-out for 10 laps, it was an exceptional race. Luckily, my tyres didn't go off in those last few laps, so he seemed to lose a little more than me.

> "WHEN YOU'RE WITH YOUR TEAMMATE, IT'S VERY HARD TO MAKE THE RIGHT DECISIONS ABOUT WHERE TO PUT YOUR CAR, WHEN TO BRAKE, BUT IT WAS GREAT"

"Nico was in my blind spot many times, so I tried to leave space. That was very difficult. It feels like a long time since I've been able to have a real racer's race and use whatever skills I've acquired over the years. It's a fantastic feeling to be able to do that.

"I think, ultimately, winning the race is the greatest thing but, deep down inside, I didn't have the pace today and that's always still in the back of my mind. I've got to really go and find out why that is because that wasn't the case in the last race. A lot of the advantages that I had in Malaysia Nico found as we came here, applied them and did even better."

about the 2014 rules clear to the media as the debate continued about improving the show.

At the start, crucially, Hamilton beat pole man Rosberg away on the drag down to Turn 1. Later in the lap, Rosberg had a look around the outside at Turn 4, but Hamilton edged him wide.

Hamilton survived several early attacks by the German, who would sometimes just about get past with the help of DRS, but couldn't make it stick. At the start of lap 19, he hung on for several corners before Lewis barged back

past at Turn 5. It was spectacular. Hamilton then pitted from the lead and in the middle of the race the pair went for alternative strategies, with Hamilton going for the option tyre and Rosberg for the slower prime, meaning that the situation would be reversed in the final stint. Hamilton had opened out a lead of around 10s when the safety car emerged on lap 41 and threatened to change everything. Esteban Gutiérrez had been flipped by contact from a clumsy Pastor Maldonado at Turn 1, fortunately without injury. The Lotus driver,

FERRARI UPSET
WITH FORMULA 1

On Sunday morning, visiting Ferrari president Luca di Montezemolo emphasised his desire for future changes to the F1 rules, but insisted that he didn't want to rein in Mercedes by implementing those changes in 2014. That was an attempt to silence the sceptics who saw his views as a reaction to Ferrari's poor form.

"We want to increase the value, passion and success of F1," he said. "The three problems are we can't have an F1 that is an energy/fuel economy formula, we have to push from the first lap. If an engine drinks less fuel, good, it means that you can do the race with less fuel if you want. The public doesn't like a taxi driver that has to respect the fuel, this is not F1.

"The second problem is the music of the engine, not the noise – that is F1. The third is that the rules are too complicated, particularly for the people on the track. We have to do a formula that's less complicated. Maybe there are some ideas that we can share together to improve the situation, because I don't like to think of the possibility of F1 decline."

When it was suggested that Ferrari and Renault simply had to do a better job, he insisted that his frustration was nothing to do with Maranello's current performance. "What I am saying is nothing to do with today's rules. Ferrari has already said it was against limiting fuel because this isn't F1. We have to consider public opinion to look ahead and to change something without interfering with today's rules. If somebody is in the lead, as is Mercedes, it's absolutely correct not to change something now.

"Ferrari, with today's rules, has to be more competitive, so I'm pushing to be more competitive. It's not a question of changing the rules now."

Di Montezemolo's words seemed a little hollow when just a few hours later the Mercedes drivers – and indeed F1 as a whole – put on a brilliant show. The president also watched a disastrous race for Ferrari and by the next race in China there would be changes at Maranello.

> "WHAT I AM SAYING IS NOTHING TO DO WITH TODAY'S RULES. FERRARI ALREADY SAID IT WAS AGAINST LIMITING FUEL BECAUSE THIS ISN'T F1"

who had been emerging from his second stop, earned himself a stop-and-go penalty plus a five-place grid penalty for China.

Both Mercedes drivers made their final stops straight away and Hamilton instantly lost his hard-earned gap. At the restart, Rosberg had the advantage of the soft tyres for what turned into an 11-lap sprint to the flag. The team didn't issue any orders and a "bring both cars home" radio message from Paddy Lowe meant just that.

"I was aware that the whole world was thinking: 'Huh, here we go, Silver Arrows team orders are here,'" said Rosberg. "But it wasn't that at all, it was just: 'Guys, make sure that you get these cars to the finish. Don't crash.' The message was clear anyway. It wasn't necessary to give such a message because we know that. We drive very hard in the end with the necessary respect, but we're free to race all the way."

At the restart, Rosberg was again squeezed wide at Turn 4. Despite several more attempts to get by, and some more nerve-wracking wheel-to-wheel battling, Hamilton managed to hang on in front.

"It was an exceptional race," said Hamilton. "Nico and I haven't had a race like that since our karting days. I was just saying to him today about our first race together in karting. He was leading the whole way and on the last lap I overtook him and won. I thought today for sure he's going to do the same to me, and get me back. Nico drove fantastically well throughout the race; very fair and it was very hard to keep him behind, particularly at the end. I had built a gap, that was OK, but he was very fast on the option tyre so I was on a knife edge the whole

Left: Felipe Massa finds his Williams between Force India's Nico Hülkenberg and Sergio Pérez as they round Turn 10. **Below:** Daniel Ricciardo puts Kimi Räikkönen under intense pressure as they battle over position. **Bottom:** with both cars hampered by clutch problems, McLaren engineers monitor the situation from the pit wall

time and it was a real relief when I crossed the line."

"I got a bit more overheating on the tyres in the last three laps," said Rosberg. "I was pushing so hard in the slipstream, you know, with less grip, sliding a lot and so the tyres overheated and I couldn't get close enough any more. Also with the hybrid, at times you have more then you have less. It's difficult to be there in the right moment when you do have it. It's not that easy, so there was a period when I didn't have enough boost power either."

Far behind the Mercedes duo there were plenty of other fantastic battles. The man who emerged to join the Silver Arrows pair on the podium was Pérez. Fourth starting spot gave the Mexican a real shot at the podium. He grabbed it with both hands, putting in a superb drive that saw him battling hard with his teammate and both

"CRUCIALLY, HAMILTON BEAT POLE MAN ROSBERG AWAY ON THE DRAG DOWN TO TURN 1"

Williams drivers, getting ahead of Bottas to claim third when the Finn made his final stop, and staying there to the end.

"This is only my third race for the team and it was a really good one," said Pérez. "The strategy was really close for us. It was looking a lot easier until the safety car came out, because when the safety car came out we were going on two stops, so the people behind, the Red Bulls, were on three stops, but we managed to keep it just to the end."

Red Bull's drivers went for different strategies, with Vettel starting on primes and Ricciardo on options. Both men found the inevitable lack of straightline speed a major handicap when fighting rivals. However, they worked their way up, with the Australian eventually outrunning his teammate. He made it as high as fourth, using soft tyres to jump

past Nico Hülkenberg in the closing laps. The Force India driver held on for fifth, moving to an impressive third in the championship after three strong races.

Vettel had to be content with sixth after a frustrating race: "Daniel proved that there was a little bit more to get from the car today, but I couldn't really get to that bit, so I'm not happy with my day. For some reason we seemed to be really slow on the straights, and not just against the Mercedes. They have a stronger package, so there's work ahead of us."

The Williams drivers were in the fight for third place early on, Massa having jumped up to that position with an amazing launch, while in contrast Bottas got away badly and lost two places. They were in the thick of the fight for points throughout, often battling with the Force Indias. Suffering with rear tyre degradation, the team planned three stops, but the safety car came out at a bad time and helped others. They repeated the Malaysian result by finishing seventh and eighth, with Massa ahead.

The final points went to the Ferraris of Alonso and Räikkönen after a lacklustre race for the Italian team. Räikkönen lost ground on the first lap and was hit by Magnussen, while Alonso jumped two places to seventh. They were both involved in fights for most of the race, but suffered on the straights, before making their final stops under the safety car. They finished ninth and 10th, with Alonso ahead.

Daniil Kvyat had another reliable race for Toro Rosso, but the Russian finished out of the points in 11th, lacking the speed to fight his immediate rivals.

It was an awful race for McLaren. Button held on to his sixth place at the start and was in fifth at the restart after the safety car period. However, he lost ground and retired from his 250th GP with clutch problems with two laps to go. The same issue had claimed Magnussen, who lost ground at the start and had a low-key race after early contact with Räikkönen.

"THE FINAL POINTS WENT TO THE FERRARIS OF ALONSO AND RÄIKKÖNEN AFTER A LACKLUSTRE RACE FOR THE ITALIAN TEAM"

Race winner Lewis Hamilton erupts into the arms of his crew after arriving in parc fermé.
Below: Hamilton, Nico Rosberg, Paddy Lowe and the Mercedes team celebrate their second one-two finish in a row

SNAPSHOT FROM BAHRAIN

CLOCKWISE FROM RIGHT:
Kevin Magnussen prepares for round three; Daniel Ricciardo continues to bring a dash of humour to the paddock; Williams' third driver Felipe Nasr also had jokes to share; Esteban Gutiérrez was far from laughing, though, when his Sauber was flipped out of the race by Pastor Maldonado's Lotus; Williams' Head of Performance Engineering Rob Smedley considers the options; cooling fans are ready and waiting for the cars' arrival on the grid before the start of the race; Ricciardo was again Red Bull Racing's pacesetter, rather than Sebastian Vettel

BAHRAIN
SAKHIR

ROUND 3

Official Results © [2014]
Formula One World
Championship Limited,
6 Princes Gate, London SW7
1QJ. No reproduction without
permission. All copyright and
database rights reserved.

RACE DATE 6 April

CIRCUIT LENGTH 3.363 miles

NO. OF LAPS 57

RACE DISTANCE 191.691 miles

WEATHER Sunny, 33ºC

TRACK TEMP 46ºC

LAP RECORD Michael Schumacher,
1m30.252s, 134.262mph, 2004

PRACTICE 1

	Driver	Time	Laps
1	L Hamilton	1m37.502s	14
2	N Rosberg	1m37.733s	13
3	F Alonso	1m37.953s	17
4	N Hülkenberg	1m38.122s	10
5	J Button	1m38.636s	16
6	K Räikkönen	1m38.783s	12
7	K Magnussen	1m38.949s	15
8	D Kvyat	1m39.056s	24
9	S Pérez	1m39.102s	21
10	S Vettel	1m39.389s	16
11	F Massa	1m39.533s	11
12	J-É Vergne	1m39.862s	26
13	F Nasr	1m40.078s	14
14	D Ricciardo	1m40.406s	19
15	A Sutil	1m40.652s	20
16	P Maldonado	1m40.793s	31
17	J Bianchi	1m40.889s	20
18	G van der Garde	1m40.913s	20
19	R Grosjean	1m41.036s	24
20	M Chilton	1m41.794s	20
21	R Frijns	1m42.417s	35
22	M Ericsson	1m42.711s	21

PRACTICE 2

	Driver	Time	Laps
1	L Hamilton	1m34.325s	28
2	N Rosberg	1m34.690s	31
3	F Alonso	1m35.360s	28
4	D Ricciardo	1m35.433s	28
5	F Massa	1m35.442s	13
6	J Button	1m35.528s	21
7	S Vettel	1m35.606s	30
8	D Kvyat	1m35.640s	31
9	K Magnussen	1m35.662s	22
10	S Pérez	1m35.802s	40
11	V Bottas	1m35.920s	9
12	J-É Vergne	1m35.972s	33
13	N Hülkenberg	1m35.998s	18
14	K Räikkönen	1m36.366s	33
15	A Sutil	1m36.962s	13
16	E Gutiérrez	1m36.975s	35
17	P Maldonado	1m37.259s	25
18	R Grosjean	1m37.599s	23
19	J Bianchi	1m37.800s	15
20	M Chilton	1m38.247s	10
21	K Kobayashi	1m38.257s	33
22	M Ericsson	1m39.136s	30

PRACTICE 3

	Driver	Time	Laps
1	L Hamilton	1m35.324s	12
2	N Rosberg	1m35.439s	12
3	S Pérez	1m35.868s	10
4	V Bottas	1m36.116s	10
5	F Massa	1m36.364s	8
6	J Button	1m36.394s	8
7	F Alonso	1m36.454s	12
8	N Hülkenberg	1m36.455s	11
9	D Kvyat	1m36.680s	16
10	K Räikkönen	1m36.772s	13
11	K Magnussen	1m36.822s	8
12	J-É Vergne	1m37.030s	11
13	D Ricciardo	1m37.119s	11
14	E Gutiérrez	1m37.325s	18
15	A Sutil	1m38.089s	24
16	K Kobayashi	1m38.400s	17
17	J Bianchi	1m38.736s	15
18	P Maldonado	1m38.880s	21
19	M Ericsson	1m38.971s	18
20	R Grosjean	1m39.208s	17
21	S Vettel	1m39.225s	8
22	M Chilton	1m39.597s	14

QUALIFYING 1

	Driver	Time
1	N Hülkenberg	1m34.874s
2	V Bottas	1m34.934s
3	S Pérez	1m34.998s
4	F Massa	1m35.085s
5	K Räikkönen	1m35.234s
6	F Alonso	1m35.251s
7	K Magnussen	1m35.288s
8	L Hamilton	1m35.323s
9	D Kvyat	1m35.395s
10	N Rosberg	1m35.439s
11	S Vettel	1m35.549s
12	J Button	1m35.699s
13	J-É Vergne	1m35.815s
14	D Ricciardo	1m36.220s
15	E Gutiérrez	1m36.567s
16	R Grosjean	1m36.654s
17	P Maldonado	1m36.663s
18	A Sutil	1m36.840s
19	K Kobayashi	1m37.085s
20	J Bianchi	1m37.310s
21	M Ericsson	1m37.875s
22	M Chilton	1m37.913s

QUALIFYING 2

	Driver	Time
1	N Rosberg	1m33.708s
2	L Hamilton	1m33.872s
3	D Ricciardo	1m34.592s
4	J Button	1m34.699s
5	F Alonso	1m34.723s
6	S Pérez	1m34.747s
7	V Bottas	1m34.842s
8	F Massa	1m34.842s
9	K Magnussen	1m34.904s
10	K Räikkönen	1m34.925s
11	S Vettel	1m34.985s
12	N Hülkenberg	1m35.116s
13	D Kvyat	1m35.145s
14	J-É Vergne	1m35.286s
15	E Gutiérrez	1m35.891s
16	R Grosjean	1m35.908s

Best sectors – Practice

Sec 1	L Hamilton	29.831s
Sec 2	L Hamilton	40.933s
Sec 3	L Hamilton	23.561s

Speed trap – Practice

1	N Hülkenberg	203.685mph
2	S Pérez	203.188mph
3	L Hamilton	202.629mph

Best sectors – Qualifying

Sec 1	N Rosberg	29.550s
Sec 2	N Rosberg	40.300s
Sec 3	L Hamilton	23.303s

Speed trap – Qualifying

1	S Perez	204.306mph
2	N Hülkenberg	203.747mph
3	J Button	203.312mph

Sebastian Vettel
"It was a busy race, especially at the end after the safety car, but it's a shame we couldn't get further up. Daniel proved there was a little bit more to get from the car today."

Nico Rosberg
"It was a great battle with Lewis and this kind of race is why I'm in F1. Of course, it's disappointing to be second, but I gave it everything and it just didn't quite come off."

Fernando Alonso
"With its long straights, this track shows up our weak points. The safety car helped us make up ground and let us save fuel, but it wasn't enough."

Pastor Maldonado
"I was going well until the incident. We must look at what happened as Esteban seemed to be off his line into Turn 1 and then I was in the corner with nowhere to go."

Jenson Button
"We took a step forward. Our long-run pace was good, and our degradation positive, so we could have raced hard to the finish on the primes, but I was hit by a clutch problem."

Sergio Pérez
"This podium is one of my most special results. The last few laps were hard. I had to keep up the pace as the Red Bulls were coming, but managed to stay ahead."

Daniel Ricciardo
"I got very close to the podium. The car came to me as the race went on and I was happy moving through the pack. It was fun to race Sebastian – hard but fair."

Lewis Hamilton
"Nico had the pace on me but I held on. I knew when the safety car came out he'd be on the options and he'd be quick. To try and stay ahead of him was so difficult."

Kimi Räikkönen
"I was slow away and lost places. Then Magnussen hit me, but trying to move up the order was hard – the lack of aero down the straights made overtaking hard."

Romain Grosjean
"At certain points of the race, I was quite quick, but at others I was struggling for rear grip. Luckily, we now have two days of testing so we'll be able to try lots of set-ups."

Kevin Magnussen
"I lost three places at the start and didn't have enough pace to progress. We'd been hoping the colder conditions might help us, but were less strong than in Malaysia."

Nico Hülkenberg
"I had a good first lap. I was struggling a bit with the hard tyres, but managed to recover some time with the mediums in the next two stints."

POSITIONS LAP BY LAP

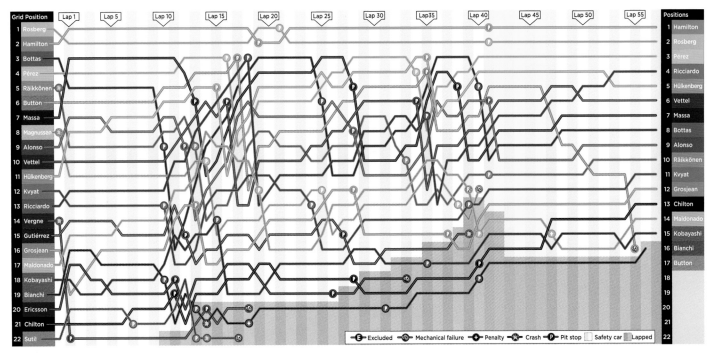

Grid Position		Positions	
1	Rosberg	1	Hamilton
2	Hamilton	2	Rosberg
3	Bottas	3	Pérez
4	Pérez	4	Ricciardo
5	Räikkönen	5	Hülkenberg
6	Button	6	Vettel
7	Massa	7	Massa
8	Magnussen	8	Bottas
9	Alonso	9	Alonso
10	Vettel	10	Räikkönen
11	Hülkenberg	11	Kvyat
12	Kvyat	12	Grosjean
13	Ricciardo	13	Chilton
14	Vergne	14	Maldonado
15	Gutiérrez	15	Kobayashi
16	Grosjean	16	Bianchi
17	Maldonado	17	Button
18	Kobayashi	18	
19	Bianchi	19	
20	Ericsson	20	
21	Chilton	21	
22	Sutil	22	

Legend: **E** Excluded — **S** Mechanical failure — **+** Penalty — **X** Crash — **P** Pit stop — Safety car — Lapped

QUALIFYING 3

	Driver	Time
1	N Rosberg	1m33.185s
2	L Hamilton	1m33.464s
3	D Ricciardo	1m34.051s
4	V Bottas	1m34.247s
5	S Pérez	1m34.346s
6	K Räikkönen	1m34.368s
7	J Button	1m34.387s
8	F Massa	1m34.511s
9	K Magnussen	1m34.712s
10	F Alonso	1m34.992s

GRID

	Driver	Time
1	N Rosberg	1m33.185s
2	L Hamilton	1m33.464s
3	V Bottas	1m34.247s
4	S Pérez	1m34.346s
5	K Räikkönen	1m34.368s
6	J Button	1m34.387s
7	F Massa	1m34.511s
8	K Magnussen	1m34.712s
9	F Alonso	1m34.992s
10	S Vettel	1m34.985s
11	N Hülkenberg	1m35.116s
12	D Kvyat	1m35.145s
13	D Ricciardo	1m34.051s
14	J-É Vergne	1m35.286s
15	E Gutiérrez	1m35.891s
16	R Grosjean	1m35.908s
17	P Maldonado	1m36.663s
18	K Kobayashi	1m37.085s
19	J Bianchi	1m37.310s
20	M Ericsson	1m37.875s
21	M Chilton	1m37.913s
22	A Sutil	1m36.840s

Grid penalties

D Ricciardo	10-place penalty for unsafe release in Malaysian GP
A Sutil	5-place penalty for forcing Grosjean off the track

RACE

	Driver	Car	Laps	Time	Av mph	Fastest	Stops
1	L Hamilton	Mercedes F1 W05	57	1h39m42.743s	115.255	1m37.108s	2
2	N Rosberg	Mercedes F1 W05	57	1h39m43.828s	115.228	1m37.020s	2
3	S Pérez	Force India-Mercedes VJM07	57	1h40m06.810s	114.788	1m39.320s	2
4	D Ricciardo	Red Bull-Renault RB10	57	1h40m07.232s	114.779	1m39.269s	2
5	N Hülkenberg	Force India-Mercedes VJM07	57	1h40m11.397s	114.700	1m38.785s	2
6	S Vettel	Red Bull-Renault RB10	57	1h40m12.622s	114.676	1m39.312s	2
7	F Massa	Williams-Mercedes FW36	57	1h40m14.008s	114.650	1m39.272s	3
8	V Bottas	Williams-Mercedes FW36	57	1h40m14.619s	114.638	1m39.762s	3
9	F Alonso	Ferrari F14 T	57	1h40m15.338s	114.625	1m39.732s	3
10	K Räikkönen	Ferrrari F14 T	57	1h40m16.205s	114.608	1m39.438s	3
11	D Kvyat	Toro Rosso-Renault STR9	57	1h40m24.085s	114.458	1m40.160s	3
12	R Grosjean	Lotus-Renault E22	57	1h40m25.886s	114.424	1m39.443s	3
13	M Chilton	Marussia-Ferrari MR03	57	1h40m42.652s	114.107	1m41.825s	3
14	P Maldonado	Lotus-Renault E22	57	1h40m45.546s	114.052	1m39.666s	4
15	K Kobayashi	Caterham-Renault CT05	57	1h41m10.643s	113.580	1m41.246s	2
16	J Bianchi	Marussia-Ferrari MR03	56	1h40m59.565s	111.790	1m42.175s	5
17	J Button	McLaren-Mercedes MP4-29	55	Clutch	-	1m39.565s	2
R	K Magnussen	McLaren-Mercedes MP4-29	40	Clutch	-	1m40.108s	3
R	E Gutiérrez	Sauber-Ferrari C33	39	Accident	-	1m40.698s	2
R	M Ericsson	Caterham-Renault CT05	33	Oil leak	-	1m41.134s	2
R	J-É Vergne	Toro Rosso-Renault STR9	18	Crash damage	-	1m41.650s	2
R	A Sutil	Sauber-Ferrari C33	17	Accident	-	1m41.791s	2

Fastest lap
N Rosberg 1m37.020s
(124.787mph) on lap 49

Fastest speed trap
F Massa 208.594mph
Slowest speed trap
E Gutiérrez 186.411mph

Fastest pit stop

1	N Hülkenberg	24.440s
2	K Räikkönen	24.453s
3	J Button	24.476s

CHAMPIONSHIP

	Driver	Pts
1	N Rosberg	61
2	L Hamilton	50
3	N Hülkenberg	28
4	F Alonso	26
5	J Button	23
6	S Vettel	23
7	K Magnussen	20
8	V Bottas	18
9	S Pérez	16
10	D Ricciardo	12
11	F Massa	12
12	K Räikkönen	7
13	J-É Vergne	4
14	D Kvyat	3

CONSTRUCTORS

	Team	Pts
1	Mercedes	111
2	Force India-Mercedes	44
3	McLaren-Mercedes	43
4	Red Bull-Renault	35
5	Ferrari	33
6	Williams-Mercedes	30
7	Toro Rosso-Renault	7

Esteban Gutiérrez
"They did the hospital checks and all is fine. I was shocked that Pastor, who came out of the pits, ran into me. I was clearly in front. I turned in and was suddenly hit and rolled."

Jean-Éric Vergne
"It was a mess at Turn 8, but I had a clean exit on the outside. I then found myself next to a Lotus, but got squeezed and when he realised I was about to pass him, just closed the door."

Felipe Massa
"I was in a good position, but the tyre degradation was worse than expected. The safety car didn't help, as we should have been up with the Force Indias rather than the Red Bulls."

Max Chilton
"Qualifying didn't go well but I knew the race would be closer. I didn't get a good start but through the race I managed the tyres well, while still having a good race with the Caterhams."

Marcus Ericsson
"I was 17th by the end of lap 3, fighting with Grosjean. My car didn't feel great on the second set of tyres and I couldn't hold Chilton or Kamui back. Later, my car lost power."

Adrian Sutil
"My race was over soon. Jules braked too late, hit my car at the hairpin and damaged it. He was being aggressive and with his move he destroyed both of our races."

Daniil Kvyat
"I wasn't happy with our pace and it was frustrating to see the other cars just passing. The start was a bit messy and I lost a place. From then on, I tried to push as much as possible."

Valtteri Bottas
"I had wheelspin at the start and lost a few places, so our strategy was compromised. We had issues with the tyres that were worse than expected, but got points from both cars."

Jules Bianchi
"I made up three places on lap 1 and was having a good stint, with the chance to get past Sutil. I was slightly ahead into Turn 1, but he turned into me, which punctured my left rear."

Kamui Kobayashi
"I was fighting with Gutiérrez, but let him go as he was on a different strategy. I was then up with Maldonado and Grosjean as the safety car came in, but had to save fuel so couldn't keep pace."

ROUND 4 UBS CHINESE GRAND PRIX
CHINA

LEWIS HAMILTON SCORED HIS THIRD WIN IN A ROW FOR MERCEDES, WHILE
TEAMMATE NICO ROSBERG HAD TO RACE WITHOUT TELEMETRY AND
FERNANDO ALONSO BEAT DANIEL RICCIARDO TO COMPLETE THE PODIUM

L ewis Hamilton made it three victories in a row after a dominant performance enabled him to lead all way in the Chinese GP. In stark contrast to Bahrain, he was under no threat from Mercedes teammate Nico Rosberg, although the German dropped from fourth to seventh at the start, then had to fight his way through to second, a result that ensured that he remained four points clear.

On a grey and overcast race day, tyres were the dominant factor, as everyone had to deal with front graining. Nevertheless, all the top runners were able to stretch out their mileage sufficiently to manage with two stops and the lack of strategic variation and an absence of on-track battles made for a very different race compared to the thriller in Bahrain.

Rain hit qualifying for the third time in four races. Hamilton was dominant, topping all three sessions, the first of which was run mostly on full wet tyres before intermediates became the norm in the second and third periods.

"It's so slippery out there," said Hamilton, whose 34th pole beat Jim Clark's British record. "You're trying to find the grip while not making mistakes. So it was a tough session. I really enjoyed it as the car was feeling great. We always have stuff we can improve, but the team has done a great job."

The biggest challenge came not from Rosberg, but from the

Far left: as if rain was not enough of a challenge, Force India's Sergio Pérez was slowed by braking problems and failed to make Q3. **Far left below:** Lewis Hamilton leads away at the start. **Left:** Ferrari is the most popular team in China. **Below:** Pastor Maldonado didn't have the best of Fridays, crashing his Lotus while adjusting settings

INSIDE LINE

FERNANDO ALONSO
FERRARI

It was a good weekend. We improved the car a little bit compared with the first three races, so we felt more competitive and being on the podium is a nice surprise for us.

"We had a difficult start of the season with a lack of performance, so it's great to be on the podium despite a weekend of changeable weather conditions. It was a difficult race as well, with this being a unique track that triggers front tyre graining. We managed that quite well and this is hopefully a boost for the team.

"We make very few changes from FP1 to the race. We brought some new parts here, a small step that probably means we are a little bit more competitive and we concentrated on those parts in Friday testing rather than on set-up work.

"We need to catch Mercedes as soon as possible, before the championship is over, so we must keep scoring points and try not to lose too much ground. At the moment, it seems far away as Mercedes have a big advantage. There's nothing special we can do, just not give up. This was only the fourth round, so there's still a long way go but, being realistic, knowing that the gap is very big, it's going to be tough.

"We brought new parts that made the car feel a little bit faster. On the other hand, I've had an extremely good weekend, probably at the level of 2012 in terms of driving and feeling comfortable with the car through Friday, qualifying and today.

"In Bahrain, we were one minute behind the leaders, in ninth and 10th, and today I was on the podium, 7s behind Nico. Hopefully I can keep going like this and we won't give up."

> "THIS WAS ONLY THE FOURTH ROUND, SO THERE'S STILL A LONG WAY GO BUT, BEING REALISTIC, KNOWING THAT THE GAP IS VERY BIG, IT'S GOING TO BE TOUGH"

Red Bulls of Daniel Ricciardo and Sebastian Vettel, further underlining that the RBR10 was a very good chassis. Once again, the Australian made his mark by outpacing his teammate to take second spot, leaving a disappointed Vettel third.

Rosberg had a scrappy session. Fourth in Q1 and third in Q2, the final session culminated in a spin and he had to settle for fourth. Having been quick in the dry on Friday, Fernando Alonso qualified fifth for Ferrari.

Williams hadn't looked strong in the wet thus far in 2014, but Valtteri Bottas did an impressive job to qualify sixth. He just beat Nico Hülkenberg as Force India showed strongly again. Felipe Massa took eighth in the other Williams. Always good in damp conditions, Jean-Éric Vergne took ninth spot for Toro Rosso, while Romain Grosjean earned Lotus a rare Q3 slot in 10th, meaning some big names missed out.

Kimi Räikkönen had a difficult Q2 and ended up 11th, while Jenson Button struggled for grip again and couldn't better 12th.

Hamilton shot into the lead at the start, while Vettel and Alonso both got ahead of Ricciardo. Rosberg lost his telemetry on the formation lap, which contributed to a poor getaway that dropped him to seventh. Meanwhile, there was action at Turn 1 when Alonso tagged Felipe Massa and Rosberg hit Bottas. Remarkably, all four continued unscathed.

All alone out front, Hamilton opened up a gap on Vettel. He then stayed out while everyone else made their first stops in a sequence that allowed Alonso to jump Vettel by pitting early. Hamilton pushed his tyres to the limit to maximise mileage and thus lost ground to those on fresher rubber. When he finally came in on lap 17, he was just 3.7s ahead of Alonso. On new

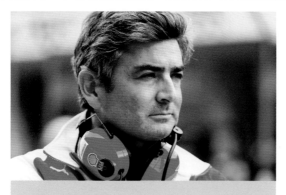

TALKING POINT
FERRARI'S NEW MAN

Ferrari caused a stir when it announced just before the Chinese GP that team principal Stefano Domenicali would be replaced by Marco Mattiacci, a high flier from the road car side. It was easy to assume that Domenicali had been made a scapegoat for the team's poor start, but in truth the popular team veteran had been worn down by the unrelenting pressures of the job and was happy to get a break.

Mattiacci, the erstwhile CEO of Ferrari North America, met his race team and the F1 media for the first time in China. His insistence on wearing sunglasses caused comment, although he blamed it on lack of sleep. He had been in New York when his boss rang. "I received a call at 5.58am on Friday," he said. "It was chairman di Montezemolo and he told me his idea. I thought April Fool was 15 days away. Then I understood that it was serious because there was already a ticket for me to leave New York in three hours for Milan. I arrived at the Fiorano track on Saturday morning."

> "IN THE PAST 20 YEARS, I'VE ASSEMBLED A LOT OF TEAMS AND I'VE BENCHMARKED A LOT OF BUSINESS STRUCTURES. I COME WITH HUMILITY, TO UNDERSTAND AND TO WORK HARD"

Mattiacci said he spent some time talking with Domenicali: "Stefano is a great person, he's a friend. We spent a few hours together on Saturday and all day Monday. He's a person that I have the utmost respect [for], so it was natural for us to discuss the role."

Mattiacci made it clear that his background in business rather than racing was a benefit, not a hindrance. "In the past 20 years, I've assembled a lot of teams and I've benchmarked a lot of business structures. This is a different perspective. Probably not in terms of a sporting team, but definitely assembling teams, working with people, managing people from different nationalities. I'll try to bring, if I have [them], some best practices from there. But I'm aware this is a very specific culture – you need to do things that happened yesterday. I come with humility, to understand and work hard: this is what I can commit to the team, to the drivers. I'm a humble person who will listen and fight to be a facilitator to utilise the best talent within Ferrari."

tyres, he soon began to pull away again. Then, after stopping once more on lap 38, he paced himself to the end without any problems.

An afternoon that produced only two retirements ended in an unusual fashion when a local official threw the chequered flag a lap early. Although Hamilton completed the 56th and final scheduled lap, the FIA declared that the race had finished on lap 55. Then, as per the rules on premature stoppages, the official result then actually went back to lap 54. It was fortunate for all concerned that there were no major changes in the order, although Kamui Kobayashi lost 17th place to Jules Bianchi.

"After P2, I had to make a lot of changes," said Hamilton. "Although yesterday was wet, it worked perfectly and I was able to look after my tyres. After that, I was just racing myself. I lost time after the first stop, but it was still great."

Conversely, Rosberg suffered throughout from the loss of telemetry. "I was completely on my own out there," he said. "The team doesn't see any information from the car, so they have nothing to do. I had to do all the things on my own. It was then telling the team what my fuel level is so they could judge if I was using too much, but I had to do that in Turn 1, a difficult corner, so I didn't enjoy that point."

Rosberg had a lot of work to do in terms of passing as well, but he managed to get by Hülkenberg and Massa in the early laps. He took Ricciardo in the first stops, having switched to mediums on lap 13. He passed Vettel for third at the hairpin on lap 26. After making a second stop on lap 37, his final victim was Alonso and he was able to breeze past, with DRS assistance, on lap

Far left: Nico Rosberg makes his move to pass Sebastian Vettel for second into the Turn 14 hairpin. **Left:** Felipe Massa accelerates out of Turn 4 in a race ruined by a mistake in the pits. **Below** Jenson Button checks the data to try to find McLaren's missing speed

42. Rosberg finished 18s adrift and his easy progress, despite the telemetry issue, showed just what an advantage Mercedes enjoyed.

"Set-up-wise, it was a good team effort," said Rosberg, "because it's a unique track with understeer being the main problem, along with front left tyre wear, so you have to change everything, adapt to the needs of the track. It wasn't perfect in the race, but it was pretty good."

Alonso managed his tyres to perfection to secure a fine third place. He had made a good start, passing Rosberg and Ricciardo to get into third, and then by stopping earlier and getting on to fresh tyres he jumped Vettel at the first stops. He held on to second until the recovering Rosberg breezed past.

The Red Bulls were next. Vettel enjoyed the better start, and immediately jumped up to second, while Ricciardo fell to

fourth. As the race developed, though, the Australian had the advantage through better tyre life. He made his first pit stop three laps later and in the middle stints a struggling and initially reluctant Vettel was told to let his teammate by. They finished fourth and fifth, with Ricciardo just failing to catch Alonso in the closing lap.

Vettel insisted that he had no problem about letting his teammate by once he had been told they were on different strategies, although ultimately they both pitted twice. "Initially, I didn't understand, but once I was told that we were on a different strategy there was no point in blocking him further. Also, if you look at the raw result in the end, it was quite obvious that Daniel was quicker than me today.

"The start was good and in the first stint I was pretty happy with my car. However, I then struggled

"IN THE MIDDLE STINTS, AN INITIALLY RELUCTANT VETTEL WAS TOLD TO LET HIS TEAMMATE BY"

more on the prime tyres than we wished. In the end, the gap to the cars in front was too big."

Hülkenberg had a solid race for Force India to claim sixth place and another useful helping of points. He had got up to sixth at the start, although he was soon overtaken by Rosberg. He then gained a place when Massa had a disastrous first pit stop and held sixth to the end after successfully holding off Bottas.

As noted, both Williams drivers were involved in collisions at Turn 1, with Massa banging wheels with Alonso and Bottas with Rosberg. They survived to run in sixth and eighth places, separated by Hülkenberg. However, at Massa's first pit stop there was a delay of almost a minute when the team initially tried to fit the left rear to the right, and vice versa. That dropped him to last place, from where he recovered to 15th. Despite

Above: Lewis Hamilton was surprised to be shown the chequered flag a lap earlier than he should have been. **Left:** it was all smiles from Hamilton and the Red Bull racers after qualifying, but not quite so much for Vettel after the race

a lack of telemetry, Bottas enjoyed a solid race to seventh.

In contrast with his teammate, Raïkkönen had another difficult grand prix, running 10th in the early laps and then finishing a frustrated eighth.

From 16th on the grid, Sergio Pérez did a good job to move up to ninth, logging more valuable points for Force India.

The fortunes of the Toro Rosso drivers swapped around at the start as Vergne made a bad start from ninth on the grid and dropped to 12th, while his teammate Daniil Kvyat got away well from 13th and moved up to 11th. They then spent the early part of the race in close company, initially separated by Pérez. Kvyat eventually made it into the points in 10th, while Vergne fell away by the flag to finish 12th.

They were split by Button, after another bad Sunday for McLaren. The drivers chose different strategies at the start, with Kevin Magnussen the only driver in the field opting for the medium tyre for the opening stint of the race.

However, both of McLaren's men had frustrating afternoons as they struggled with a car that simply wasn't fast enough. As the last driver to pit, Magnussen briefly rose as high as 10th, but then dropped back down the order to finish 13th, while Button came home an extremely disappointed 11th.

Lotus had even worse luck. Grosjean got up to eighth place at the start but then lost out to Bottas. Later, the Frenchman lost fourth gear and, after the gearbox problems began to get worse, he was forced to retire while running 10th. From 22nd on the grid, Pastor Maldonado had a steady and reliable race to 14th place, gathering valuable data about the still developing E22 along the way.

So, after the first four grands prix of the season, Mercedes had almost three times the points of its closest rival, Red Bull Racing.

CLOCKWISE FROM RIGHT: Jenson Button – winner here in 2010 – had plenty of support; track reconnaissance isn't always conducted in sunshine; Lewis Hamilton smiles as he cycles around the enormous paddock; Valtteri Bottas is becoming a driver in increasing demand from clued-up fans; the Williams pit crew watches the grand prix while waiting to perform its pit-stop duties

SNAPSHOT FROM CHINA

CHINA
SHANGHAI

ROUND 4

Official Results © [2014]
Formula One World
Championship Limited,
6 Princes Gate, London SW7
1QJ. No reproduction without
permission. All copyright and
database rights reserved.

RACE DATE 20 April

CIRCUIT LENGTH 3.390 miles

NO. OF LAPS 54

RACE DISTANCE 183.060 miles

WEATHER Overcast, but dry, 16ºC

TRACK TEMP 21ºC

LAP RECORD Michael Schumacher,
1m32.238s, 132.202mph, 2004

PRACTICE 1				PRACTICE 2				PRACTICE 3				QUALIFYING 1			QUALIFYING 2	
	Driver	Time	Laps		Driver	Time	Laps		Driver	Time	Laps		Driver	Time		Driver	Time
1	F Alonso	1m39.783s	20	1	L Hamilton	1m38.315s	25	1	D Ricciardo	1m53.958s	5	1	L Hamilton	1m55.516s	1	L Hamilton	1m54.029s
2	N Rosberg	1m40.181s	16	2	F Alonso	1m38.456s	28	2	F Massa	1m54.492s	5	2	N Hülkenberg	1m55.913s	2	S Vettel	1m54.499s
3	D Ricciardo	1m40.772s	23	3	N Rosberg	1m38.726s	30	3	R Grosjean	1m54.514s	4	3	S Vettel	1m55.926s	3	N Rosberg	1m55.294s
4	J Button	1m40.970s	23	4	D Ricciardo	1m38.811s	30	4	N Hülkenberg	1m55.032s	6	4	N Rosberg	1m56.058s	4	D Ricciardo	1m55.302s
5	N Hülkenberg	1m41.175s	16	5	S Vettel	1m39.015s	31	5	K Räikkönen	1m55.062s	4	5	V Bottas	1m56.501s	5	F Alonso	1m55.765s
6	K Magnussen	1m41.366s	20	6	F Massa	1m39.118s	25	6	P Maldonado	1m55.228s	12	6	D Ricciardo	1m56.641s	6	V Bottas	1m56.253s
7	J-É Vergne	1m41.505s	26	7	K Räikkönen	1m39.283s	25	7	D Kvyat	1m55.235s	7	7	F Massa	1m56.850s	7	R Grosjean	1m56.407s
8	L Hamilton	1m41.560s	9	8	J Button	1m39.491s	29	8	V Bottas	1m55.381s	5	8	F Alonso	1m56.961s	8	J-É Vergne	1m56.584s
9	S Vettel	1m41.629s	19	9	R Grosjean	1m39.537s	36	9	J Button	1m55.673s	4	9	D Kvyat	1m57.261s	9	F Massa	1m56.757s
10	F Massa	1m41.699s	14	10	D Kvyat	1m39.648s	26	10	S Pérez	1m56.019s	6	10	K Magnussen	1m57.369s	10	N Hülkenberg	1m56.847s
11	D Kvyat	1m41.977s	23	11	N Hülkenberg	1m39.736s	30	11	S Vettel	1m56.233s	8	11	J-É Vergne	1m57.477s	11	K Räikkönen	1m56.860s
12	R Grosjean	1m42.090s	24	12	K Magnussen	1m39.744s	29	12	J-É Vergne	1m56.380s	9	12	J Button	1m57.783s	12	J Button	1m56.963s
13	F Nasr	1m42.265s	13	13	J-É Vergne	1m39.759s	28	13	A Sutil	1m56.760s	8	13	A Sutil	1m58.138s	13	D Kvyat	1m57.289s
14	G van der Garde	1m42.615s	16	14	V Bottas	1m39.830s	25	14	M Chilton	1m56.841s	13	14	K Räikkönen	1m58.279s	14	A Sutil	1m57.393s
15	S Pérez	1m42.733s	13	15	S Pérez	1m40.124s	32	15	E Gutiérrez	1m57.468s	9	15	S Pérez	1m58.362s	15	K Magnussen	1m57.675s
16	P Maldonado	1m43.731s	22	16	E Gutiérrez	1m40.359s	32	16	K Kobayashi	1m57.812s	12	16	R Grosjean	1m58.411s	16	S Pérez	1m58.264s
17	K Kobayashi	1m44.038s	16	17	A Sutil	1m40.395s	30	17	J Bianchi	1m57.976s	14	17	E Gutiérrez	1m58.988s			
18	E Gutiérrez	1m44.162s	7	18	P Maldonado	1m40.455s	12	18	M Ericsson	1m59.507s	6	18	K Kobayashi	1m59.260s			
19	J Bianchi	1m44.270s	17	19	J Bianchi	1m42.327s	27	19	N Rosberg	no time	4	19	J Bianchi	1m59.326s			
20	M Chilton	1m44.782s	20	20	M Chilton	1m43.473s	30	20	L Hamilton	no time	3	20	M Ericsson	2m00.646s			
21	M Ericsson	1m44.835s	22	21	K Kobayashi	1m43.530s	32	21	K Magnussen	no time	3	21	M Chilton	2m00.865s			
22	K Räikkönen	no time	1	22	M Ericsson	1m43.679s	32	22	F Alonso	no time	1	22	P Maldonado	no time			

Best sectors – Practice			Speed trap – Practice			Best sectors – Qualifying			Speed trap – Qualifying		
Sec 1	N Rosberg	25.866s	1	L Hamilton	205.736mph	Sec 1	L Hamilton	28.922s	1	L Hamilton	197.409mph
Sec 2	F Alonso	29.580s	2	N Rosberg	205.673mph	Sec 2	L Hamilton	34.914s	2	N Rosberg	197.036mph
Sec 3	L Hamilton	42.771s	3	S Pérez	203.871mph	Sec 3	L Hamilton	49.653s	3	V Bottas	196.912mph

Sebastian Vettel

"When I was asked to move over for Daniel, I didn't understand as we were on the same tyre, so I checked. When the team said we were on a different strategy, I moved."

Nico Rosberg

"I didn't have telemetry, so my engineers couldn't set up my clutch for the start. I had contact with Bottas and thought that was it. Luckily my car wasn't damaged."

Fernando Alonso

"After a difficult start to the season, this podium is a confidence boost for the team. We've made a step forward because we've partly closed the gap to the leaders."

Pastor Maldonado

"My pace wasn't great, but I pushed hard. We'll look at the data as we seemed to lack pace on the straights, which made it difficult to overtake and also to defend."

Jenson Button

"It was pretty difficult out there: we just couldn't get the front tyres working – they just grained. We've got upgrades for the Spanish GP, but they won't be enough."

Sergio Pérez

"To start 16th and finish ninth is good. I made a fair start then focused on making the two-stop strategy work. I had a few flat spots, but still made it work."

Daniel Ricciardo

"After a poor getaway from the dirty side of the grid, my race was good! With Seb, we were racing and you want to hold your place, but the team radioed and he let me by."

Lewis Hamilton

"All the team's work is paying off – this car is just unbelievable. In the final laps, I was pushing more to keep up the tyre temperatures and it just felt great to drive."

Kimi Räikkönen

"It's been a difficult weekend. I made up two places at the start, but couldn't make up any more ground as I didn't have the pace, nor much grip at either end."

Romain Grosjean

"I started losing fourth gear, then I lost all gears. It's the first time we've had this so we must understand why. I'd been fighting for ninth, which is a clear improvement."

Kevin Magnussen

"It felt like a long race, as there wasn't much I could do. Our car lacks downforce. The way it's set up and how it feels has always been positive; it's just low on grip."

Nico Hülkenberg

"It was a straightforward race after I got in front of Massa: I had to manage my tyres and avoid mistakes and it only got tricky at the end when Bottas was getting closer."

POSITIONS LAP BY LAP

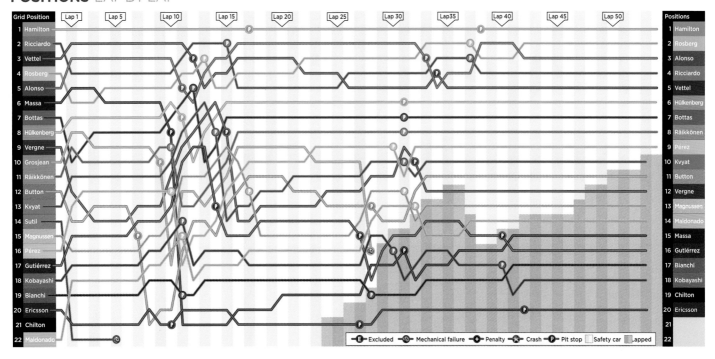

Excluded · Mechanical failure · Penalty · Crash · Pit stop · Safety car · Lapped

QUALIFYING 3

	Driver	Time
1	L Hamilton	1m53.860s
2	D Ricciardo	1m54.455s
3	S Vettel	1m54.960s
4	N Rosberg	1m55.143s
5	F Alonso	1m55.637s
6	F Massa	1m56.147s
7	V Bottas	1m56.282s
8	N Hülkenberg	1m56.366s
9	J-É Vergne	1m56.773s
10	R Grosjean	1m57.079s

GRID

	Driver	Time
1	L Hamilton	1m53.860s
2	D Ricciardo	1m54.455s
3	S Vettel	1m54.960s
4	N Rosberg	1m55.143s
5	F Alonso	1m55.367s
6	F Massa	1m56.147s
7	V Bottas	1m56.282s
8	N Hülkenberg	1m56.366s
9	J-É Vergne	1m56.773s
10	R Grosjean	1m57.079s
11	K Räikkönen	1m56.860s
12	J Button	1m56.963s
13	D Kvyat	1m57.289s
14	A Sutil	1m57.393s
15	K Magnussen	1m57.675s
16	S Pérez	1m58.264s
17	E Gutiérrez	1m58.988s
18	K Kobayashi	1m59.260s
19	J Bianchi	1m59.326s
20	M Ericsson	2m00.646s
21	M Chilton	2m00.865s
22	P Maldonado	no time

Grid penalties
P Maldonado   5-place penalty for causing a collision in Bahrain GP

RACE

	Driver	Car	Laps	Time	Av mph	Fastest	Stops
1	L Hamilton	Mercedes F1 W05	54	1h33m28.338s	117.335	1m41.196s	2
2	N Rosberg	Mercedes F1 W05	54	1h33m46.400s	116.953	1m40.402s	2
3	F Alonso	Ferrari F14 T	54	1h33m51.942s	116.837	1m42.081s	2
4	D Ricciardo	Red Bull-Renault RB10	54	1h33m55.474s	116.765	1m41.473s	2
5	S Vettel	Red Bull-Renault RB10	54	1h34m16.116s	116.338	1m42.169s	2
6	N Hülkenberg	Force India-Mercedes VJM07	54	1h34m22.633s	116.204	1m42.624s	2
7	V Bottas	Williams-Mercedes FW36	54	1h34m24.035s	116.176	1m42.660s	2
8	K Räikkönen	Ferrari F14 T	54	1h34m44.673s	115.754	1m42.300s	2
9	S Pérez	Force India-Mercedes VJM07	54	1h34m50.985s	115.004	1m42.228s	2
10	D Kvyat	Toro Rosso-Renault RB10	53	1h33m31.189s	115.097	1m43.337s	2
11	J Button	McLaren-Mercedes MP4-29	53	1h33m40.256s	114.911	1m43.375s	2
12	J-É Vergne	Toro Rosso-Renault STR9	53	1h33m45.301s	114.808	1m42.896s	2
13	K Magnussen	McLaren-Mercedes MP4-29	53	1h33m49.141s	114.730	1m42.701s	2
14	P Maldonado	Lotus-Renault E22	53	1h33m59.501s	114.519	1m43.067s	2
15	F Massa	Williams-Mercedes FW36	53	1h34m07.633s	114.354	1m42.379s	2
16	E Gutiérrez	Sauber-Ferrari C33	53	1h34m14.186s	114.221	1m42.257s	3
17	J Bianchi	Marussia-Ferrari MR03	53	1h34m54.713s	113.409	1m44.825s	2
18	K Kobayashi	Caterham-Renault CT05	53	1h34m55.939s	113.384	1m43.323s	3
19	M Chilton	Marussia-Ferrari MR03	52	1h33m40.693s	112.733	1m42.875s	3
20	M Ericsson	Caterham-Renault CT05	52	1h33m56.192s	112.423	1m43.620s	3
R	R Grosjean	Lotus-Renault E22	28	Gearbox	-	1m44.366s	1
R	A Sutil	Sauber-Ferrari C33	5	Engine	-	1m58.376s	0

Fastest lap
N Rosberg 1m40.402s
(121.453mph) on lap 39

Fastest speed trap
F Massa   201.635mph
Slowest speed trap
P Maldonado   172.554mph

Fastest pit stop
1 F Alonso   24.222s
2 K Räikkönen   24.246s
3 K Magnussen   24.415s

CHAMPIONSHIP

	Driver	Pts
1	N Rosberg	79
2	L Hamilton	75
3	F Alonso	41
4	N Hülkenberg	36
5	S Vettel	33
6	D Ricciardo	24
7	V Bottas	24
8	J Button	23
9	K Magnussen	20
10	S Pérez	18
11	F Massa	12
12	K Räikkönen	11
13	J-É Vergne	4
14	D Kvyat	4

CONSTRUCTORS

	Team	Pts
1	Mercedes	154
2	Red Bull-Renault	57
3	Force India-Mercedes	54
4	Ferrari	52
5	McLaren-Mercedes	43
6	Williams-Mercedes	36
7	Toro Rosso-Renault	8

Esteban Gutiérrez
"It was a complicated race in terms of tyre management. With these temperatures, the prime tyres weren't working as we'd have liked, so we had to do a three-stop strategy."

Jean-Éric Vergne
"I had a bad start and a bad first lap. After that, I couldn't make the best out of the options as I was stuck behind Button, so it wasn't possible to build a gap and pull away."

Felipe Massa
"I had another great start. I felt some contact with Fernando but the car wasn't damaged. There was a mistake at the first stop and that lost me the race as I came back out in last."

Max Chilton
"I'm pleased to have passed and kept Ericsson behind me. The start went well, but I struggled for balance on the medium tyre and we changed the strategy, before changing back."

Marcus Ericsson
"On every set of tyres the balance just wasn't there and that meant I couldn't push. It's good that we got to the end, but if I hadn't had that understeer I'm sure I'd have been quicker."

Adrian Sutil
"At the start, I had almost no power. Going into Turn 1, I noticed there was a problem with the engine and I lost a lot of positions. I did a few more laps, but then pitted."

Daniil Kvyat
"I had a good start and made up some positions on the first lap. Our pace was very strong and I enjoyed the fight with Jenson. We did a good job with tyre management."

Valtteri Bottas
"It was a good race for me, despite some contact at the start which cost me a few places. I had to drive the whole race without telemetry, which isn't the easiest thing to do."

Jules Bianchi
"I got ahead of Kamui at the start. He regained the place, but I stuck with him. When he stopped for a third time for the option, we saw the opportunity to stay out to get ahead."

Kamui Kobayashi
"After a good battle with Jules I'm pleased with how it went. However, it's a real shame that my move on him on the last lap doesn't count due to the mistake with the chequered flag."

ROUND 5 GRAN PREMIO DE ESPAÑA PIRELLI

SPAIN

LEWIS HAMILTON WAS HANGING ON AS NICO ROSBERG CLOSED IN OVER THE FINAL LAPS OF AN ENTHRALLING SPANISH GP AND IN DOING SO HE TOOK THE CHAMPIONSHIP LEAD BY THREE POINTS

Victory in the Spanish GP gave Lewis Hamilton four wins in a row, but his teammate Nico Rosberg made his life hard and pushed him all the way to the flag. It was Hamilton's first win in Barcelona and, significantly, it put him ahead of Rosberg in the World Championship, by 100 points to 97.

All the drivers struggled for grip on the conservative Pirelli tyres in qualifying and many of the cars looked as though they were a handful to drive on the limit. Hamilton secured another pole position, but it was close. Rosberg was faster by 0.5s in Q1 after Hamilton had an off-track moment and had to try again. The German was again faster in Q2, albeit by a much smaller margin, and it seemed that he was favourite for pole.

In Q3, the first runs of both drivers were compromised by a red flag after Sebastian Vettel parked on track, the German stymied by gearbox problems just after he left the pits at the start of Q3.

The Mercedes drivers had to abandon their laps, then go again on tyres that had already had the edge taken off them. This time Hamilton was fastest. Both men had one final fresh set for their second runs and, when it really counted, the Englishman recorded 1m25.232s, beating Rosberg's 1m25.400s.

With Vettel out of the way, his RBR teammate Daniel Ricciardo seized the advantage to secure third place. Valtteri Bottas did a good job to claim an excellent fourth place for Williams, giving the team a real chance of finally capitalising on the potential that has been evident all season. Romain Grosjean gave the troubled Lotus team a huge boost

by qualifying fifth while teammate Pastor Maldonado had heavy contact with the wall after spinning off early in Q1 before setting a time.

Kimi Räikkönen enjoyed his best session of the season thus far as he earned sixth place, beating local hero Fernando Alonso on home ground, albeit by just 0.036s. Jenson Button and Felipe Massa qualified eighth and ninth ahead of Vettel, who hadn't set a time in Q3 – who then dropped to 15th thanks to a five-place penalty for a gearbox change. Meanwhile, Kevin Magnussen started a lowly 14th after failing to record a time in Q2 after a power-unit problem came to light in the first session.

Hamilton made it to the first corner safely in front and Rosberg slotted into second as Bottas jumped into third ahead of Ricciardo, the Williams again showing a great performance off the line. There was a massive lock-up

Below: Nico Rosberg charged on medium tyres in his final stint and caught but couldn't pass Lewis Hamilton. **Right:** Hamilton leads the way from Rosberg and Bottas in the race down the slope towards the first corner. **Right below:** Romain Grosjean qualified well and held off the Ferraris in the early stages before scoring his first points of 2014

from Grosjean, but he managed to avoid contact with Ricciardo.

"The start unfortunately was poor," said Rosberg. "It's a bit of a weakness that we have at the moment. It's just inconsistent and now I've had a couple of bad starts in a row – actually three bad starts in the races. That's costly, always losing out at the start, so I need to work on that."

By the end of the first lap, Hamilton was already 1.1s clear of his teammate. Inevitably, the two F1 W05s were in a class of their own, and they pulled away from Bottas

at the rate of 1s per lap. The gap from Hamilton to Rosberg settled at around 2s for most of the first stint and Nico's only chance was to try something different.

As in Bahrain, the two drivers were given alternate tyre strategies at the first pit stops. When Hamilton came in on lap 18, he went for another set of the medium tyres and lost almost 1s as the change of the front left was a little slow. When Rosberg pitted three laps later, he was given hards for that crucial middle stint, but by pushing his original tyres that far while

INSIDE LINE

LEWIS HAMILTON
MERCEDES

At the rate the team's going, we're looking strong for at least a few more races. It's by no means easy for me because I've still got a massive challenge with Nico. I could never have imagined winning these four races, but it's still so close and there's a long way to go and I've got a bit more time to find in this car.

"There's no secret really, it's just been hard and constructive work. Often when you're working towards something, you sometimes stumble and fall. Then you have to build it again. Fortunately, the team has just been building, building and building and not having many times when it's falling. It's quite remarkable. The car has very good downforce that I'm sure is very close to Red Bull's, while the engine, is the best engine Mercedes has made.

"It's a lengthy process, though, and last year we found that when you requested

"I GUESS WE'VE CREATED A HYBRID AS NICO HAS COME HALFWAY, I'VE COME HALFWAY AND WE NOW REQUIRE THE SAME THINGS FROM THE CAR"

something to be changed it took time, because you don't want to take their focus away from the most important thing, which is getting downforce. I think Michael had a different driving style to me. He required different things, different seating position, different set-up. I guess Nico and Michael gelled and went in one direction with the balance.

"Then, I've come along and mine is slightly different, so I guess we've created a hybrid as Nico has come halfway, I've come halfway and we now require the same things from the car. Last year, it was a bit different and the engineers spent a while getting to know what I require from a car. Also, it can take a while to really be comfortable with the engineers and to build those relationships and that's probably been a key strength to my second year with the team."

"BOTH MERCEDES DRIVERS WERE COMPROMISED BY A RED FLAG AFTER SEBASTIAN VETTEL PARKED ON TRACK"

MERCEDES IN THE DRIVING SEAT

Mercedes' form in Barcelona was significant because it was clear that, despite the interval since the race in China and the opportunity to bring along updates, nobody had closed the gap to the pacesetters.

In qualifying, the silver cars had an advantage of 1s per lap – huge in F1 terms – and in the race they pulled away at a similar margin. Mercedes had now led every lap of the first five races, a degree of domination previously achieved by McLaren in 1988 and Williams in 1992.

However, this campaign was more akin to 1988, when Ayrton Senna and Alain Prost fought hard all season, than 1992, when Nigel Mansell overwhelmed teammate Riccardo Patrese. One dominant team might not be what fans would like to see, but if two top drivers are given free rein to fight, then we can still have a pretty good show to enjoy. The good news was that the Mercedes management was allowing the drivers to race each other. The only proviso was not to crash into each other.

> MERCEDES MANAGEMENT WAS ALLOWING THE DRIVERS TO RACE EACH OTHER. THE ONLY PROVISO WAS NOT TO CRASH INTO EACH OTHER

"We don't need to manage anything, just let them race," said Niki Lauda. "At the moment, we're on the right track, but things can change."

Mercedes had done its bit, for example, by putting the pair on different strategies. In both Bahrain and Spain, Rosberg used the less favourable harder tyre in the middle of the race and saved the quicker compound for the end, which gave him a better chance of hunting Hamilton down. On both occasions, it added an edge to what might otherwise have looked like a demonstration run.

Hamilton was in brilliant form in Spain. One of the keys was that the F1 W05 had been designed in line with his wishes, whereas the previous year he'd inherited a machine that had been developed around Rosberg and Michael Schumacher. A lot of details related to driving style and cockpit ergonomics had helped to create a car in which he felt supremely comfortable. After four wins in a row, everything was going his way. But would it last?

Left: Both Lewis Hamilton and Daniel Ricciardo had every cause to celebrate on the podium.
Right: Ricciardo's run to third place meant that he got the first podium result that he was allowed to keep.
Below: Valtteri Bottas battles to keep Ricciardo's Red Bull behind his Williams

Hamilton was on fresh rubber, he had dropped back by 3.7s.

It was the long game that mattered, though, and for the third and final stints Hamilton had to switch to the less competitive harder tyres, while Rosberg had the mediums and thus a little more potential pace. Sure enough, after the final pit stops – Hamilton came in on lap 43 and Rosberg two laps later – the gap began to close. From 4.8s, it shrank to 3.0s and then to 0.9s with just seven laps to go.

It looked as though there might be a spectacular battle to the flag. However, passing was another matter, and over those final laps Hamilton did a great job to stay safely ahead, and he eventually crossed the line with an advantage of just 0.6s. The stress he was under was apparent in some terse radio traffic with his engineer, although he was all smiles after the flag.

"Never have I had a car like this and obviously we've never had a gap like this before," said Hamilton. "Nico did a fantastic job, but I'm grateful that I was able to win. I feel that it's a huge blessing, not only for me, but for all the guys in the team because of all the hard work they've done for many years. Now, finally, they're starting to see the fruits of their labour.

"As for degradation, I was very, very fast and I stopped my run with 18 laps or something like that, but if I just brought my pace down a little bit I probably could have eked it out even longer. Those changes just transformed the car and I just wasn't able to attack the corners due to snap oversteer and that's generally where Nico was catching me, through those entries to corners."

Rosberg countered: "I felt comfortable – race pace was good.

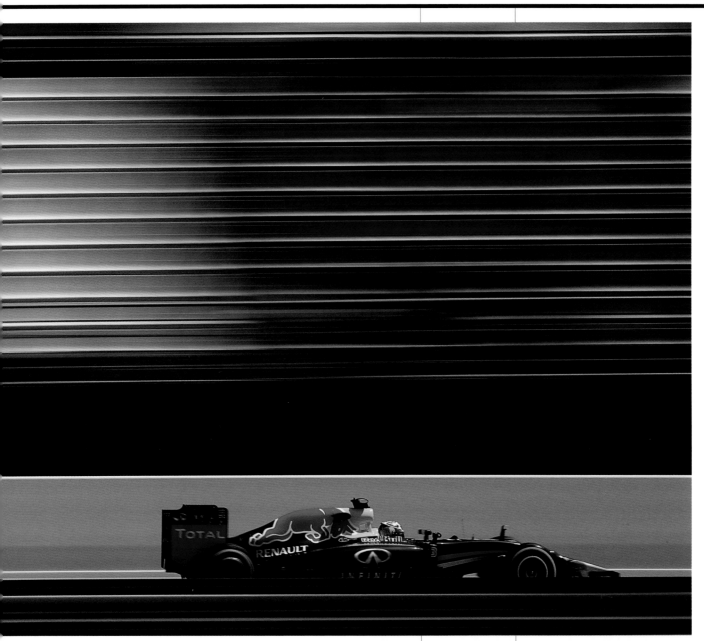

The best thing to do was to switch strategies. That was planned before the race. It worked out perfectly – but this is a really difficult track to get close up to the guy in front. I still got close at Turn 10 on the last lap. I could have gone for a kamikaze move, but it wouldn't have worked. Lewis did a great job all weekend and was just that little bit ahead. However, there are a lot of positives for me to take out of it."

The third podium spot went to Ricciardo, who had lost a lot of time behind Bottas in the first stint. The Australian made an early first pit stop on lap 14 and, when Bottas pitted six laps later, the Red Bull man moved ahead. Once in front, he had a clear track, which meant the Mercedes pair didn't disappear at quite such a fast rate, although he was still a huge 49s behind. It was a solid performance from Red Bull's new boy.

"It wasn't exactly the start I wanted," he said. "I think initially the launch felt OK, but we lost a bit of traction after that and Bottas got past me. In the first stint, I tried to hang in there and had a pseudo-attempt into Turn 1. I got underneath him, but it wasn't deep enough to pull off the move and then it was all about doing an undercut and trying still to make a two-stop work and, from then on, it was a pretty lonely race."

His teammate Vettel put in one of the drives of the race from 15th on the grid. After surviving a first lap tap from Magnussen, he went for an aggressive three-stop strategy, using the hards in his second stint, which allowed him to push hard for most of the race. He was able to do a lot of passing, and that propelled him up the order. Vettel also set the

"LIKE VETTEL, ALONSO ALSO WENT THE THREE-STOP ROUTE AND IT ALSO WORKED OUT FOR HIM"

fastest lap, albeit helped by being on fresher tyres than others in the last stint.

"All in all, it was the maximum we could do," said the World Champion. "I was sort of stuck in the train. I couldn't really feel how far we could go and how quick we were, but once we came in I was able on the harder tyre to stick with the people at the front and even catch them a little bit. We realised that the pace was there. After that, we had the two fresh sets that we didn't use in qualifying and I could go further up the road."

Having run third early on, Bottas slipped back to a creditable fifth place, unable to do anything about the speed of the Red Bulls.

Like Vettel, Alonso also went the three-stop route, and it also worked out for him. He spent most of the race fighting with teammate Räikkönen and fresher tyres finally allowed him to get past the two-stopping Finn in the closing laps, much to the relief of local fans.

Behind Räikkönen, Grosjean took the first points of the season for Lotus with an encouraging eighth, despite a sensor problem costing him performance. The Force Indias of Sergio Pérez and Nico Hülkenberg completed the top 10 as the team struggled to repeat the form shown in earlier races.

Meanwhile, it was another poor weekend for McLaren as Button and Magnussen couldn't better 11th and 12th places, Jenson having edged his young teammate off the track on the opening lap.

A race that was almost totally lacking in incident suffered only two retirements, those of Kamui Kobayashi's Caterham with a braking problem and Jean-Éric Vergne's Toro Rosso with a fractured exhaust, but it wasn't without intrigue.

Heading to Monaco – where action is guaranteed – the title battle was now finely poised, with Hamilton having taken a three-point lead. So, everything was to play for and the other teams knew more than ever that they were going to have to raise their games.

Above: Fernando Alonso hoped for glory on home ground, but had to make do with sixth place after chasing and passing his teammate.
Left: Lewis Hamilton had every reason to celebrate as his fourth win a row put him into the championship lead

SNAPSHOT FROM SPAIN

CLOCKWISE FROM ABOVE: Kevin Magnussen gathers his thoughts; Sergio Pérez finishes off another lap; Lewis Hamilton acknowledges the fans during the drivers' parade; time to head off to the grid; Ferrari past and present as Niki Lauda swaps notes with Luca di Montezemolo; Fernando Alonso – a man in demand; Sebastian Vettel's Red Bull is moved out of the way early in Q3; Jenson Button gets a move on

SPAIN
CATALUNYA
ROUND 5

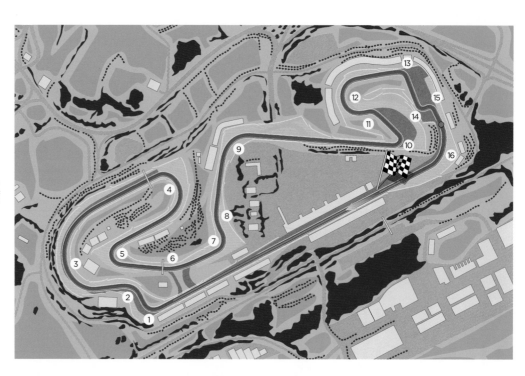

Official Results © [2014] Formula One World Championship Limited, 6 Princes Gate, London SW7 1QJ. No reproduction without permission. All copyright and database rights reserved.

RACE DATE 11 May
CIRCUIT LENGTH 2.893 miles
NO. OF LAPS 66
RACE DISTANCE 190.904 miles
WEATHER Overcast, 23ºC
TRACK TEMP 37ºC
LAP RECORD Kimi Raïkkönen, 1m21.670s, 127.500mph, 2008

	PRACTICE 1				PRACTICE 2				PRACTICE 3				QUALIFYING 1			QUALIFYING 2	
	Driver	Time	Laps		Driver	Time	Laps		Driver	Time	Laps		Driver	Time		Driver	Time
1	L Hamilton	1m27.023s	17	1	L Hamilton	1m25.524s	33	1	N Rosberg	1m25.887s	16	1	N Rosberg	1m26.764s		N Rosberg	1m26.088s
2	J Button	1m27.891s	26	2	N Rosberg	1m25.973s	36	2	L Hamilton	1m26.756s	9	2	L Hamilton	1m27.238s		L Hamilton	1m26.210s
3	D Ricciardo	1m27.973s	21	3	D Ricciardo	1m26.509s	38	3	F Alonso	1m27.188s	15	3	S Vettel	1m27.598s		D Ricciardo	1m26.613s
4	F Alonso	1m28.128s	23	4	F Alonso	1m27.121s	33	4	F Massa	1m27.223s	10	4	D Ricciardo	1m28.053s		F Massa	1m27.016s
5	N Rosberg	1m28.168s	9	5	K Räikkönen	1m27.296s	33	5	R Grosjean	1m27.682s	18	5	F Massa	1m28.061s		S Vettel	1m27.052s
6	K Räikkönen	1m28.337s	19	6	K Magnussen	1m27.788s	37	6	K Magnussen	1m27.806s	16	6	D Kvyat	1m28.074s		R Grosjean	1m27.258s
7	K Magnussen	1m28.423s	27	7	J Button	1m27.811s	29	7	D Ricciardo	1m27.808s	12	7	N Hülkenberg	1m28.155s		K Räikkönen	1m27.335s
8	P Maldonado	1m28.744s	34	8	F Massa	1m27.824s	31	8	J Button	1m28.006s	11	8	J-É Vergne	1m28.194s		V Bottas	1m27.563s
9	S Pérez	1m28.779s	18	9	P Maldonado	1m27.866s	42	9	P Maldonado	1m28.076s	19	9	V Bottas	1m28.198s		J Button	1m27.570s
10	F Massa	1m28.791s	13	10	D Kvyat	1m28.049s	35	10	S Vettel	1m28.085s	20	10	J Button	1m28.279s		F Alonso	1m27.602s
11	D Kvyat	1m28.792s	24	11	N Hülkenberg	1m28.074s	31	11	V Bottas	1m28.101s	12	11	K Räikkönen	1m28.308s		N Hülkenberg	1m27.685s
12	N Hülkenberg	1m28.828s	17	12	J-É Vergne	1m28.246s	30	12	J-É Vergne	1m28.242s	16	12	F Alonso	1m28.329s		S Pérez	1m28.002s
13	J-É Vergne	1m28.859s	24	13	A Sutil	1m28.284s	33	13	D Kvyat	1m28.298s	16	13	E Gutiérrez	1m28.374s		D Kvyat	1m28.039s
14	F Nasr	1m29.272s	15	14	V Bottas	1m28.698s	33	14	K Räikkönen	1m28.419s	16	14	K Magnussen	1m28.389s		E Gutiérrez	1m28.280s
15	A Sutil	1m29.688s	16	15	E Gutiérrez	1m29.105s	24	15	S Pérez	1m28.571s	13	15	S Pérez	1m28.469s		K Magnussen	no time
16	J Bianchi	1m29.820s	22	16	S Pérez	1m29.129s	34	16	N Hülkenberg	1m28.668s	13	16	R Grosjean	1m28.472s		J-É Vergne	no time
17	R Grosjean	1m29.944s	21	17	R Grosjean	1m29.493s	26	17	A Sutilx	1m28.715s	16	17	A Sutil	1m28.563s			
18	G van der Garde	1m30.440s	22	18	J Bianchi	1m29.991s	26	18	E Gutiérrez	1m28.865s	18	18	M Chilton	1m29.586s			
19	M Chilton	1m30.748s	19	19	M Chilton	1m31.148s	28	19	M Chilton	1m30.169s	15	19	J Bianchi	1m30.177s			
20	S Vettel	1m30.942s	4	20	K Kobayashi	1m31.338s	38	20	J Bianchi	1m30.670s	12	20	M Ericsson	1m30.312s			
21	K Kobayashi	1m30.997s	22	21	M Ericsson	1m31.586s	39	21	K Kobayashi	1m30.712s	18	21	K Kobayashi	1m30.375s			
22	M Ericsson	1m31.421s	22	22	S Vettel	no time	0	22	M Ericsson	1m31.559s	19	22	P Maldonado	no time			

Best sectors – Practice			Speed trap – Practice			Best sectors – Qualifying			Speed trap – Qualifying		
Sec 1	L Hamilton	23.391s	1	L Hamilton	208.221mph	Sec 1	L Hamilton	23.156s	1	D Kvyat	209.837mph
Sec 2	L Hamilton	32.369s	2	D Kvyat	207.848mph	Sec 2	L Hamilton	32.152s	2	J-É Vergne	208.656mph
Sec 3	L Hamilton	29.764s	3	N Hülkenberg	207.289mph	Sec 3	N Rosberg	29.783s	3	L Hamilton	207.786mph

Sebastian Vettel
"I lost a place at the start, but got it back. I was then stuck in the train, so couldn't feel how quick we were. Once I got on the harder tyre, I was even able to catch those in front."

Nico Rosberg
"With one more lap, I could have tried to pass Lewis. Once it was clear that I was second, we opted for primes in the middle stint to get a shot at Lewis at the end."

Fernando Alonso
"Our pace was too slow and not making up places at the start didn't help. The decision to go for a three-stop strategy was taken to cover Vettel, but I lost the place at the pitstop."

Pastor Maldonado
"We found some pace, but the lack of top speed meant we weren't able to attack even if we had a quicker car than others around us. We must keep working on that."

Jenson Button
"We gambled on taking the second stop early, thinking we could jump a Force India, but Kvyat's Toro Rosso followed me in, and caused my release to be delayed."

Sergio Pérez
"I had pretty strong pace in the race and my tyre degradation was OK, so I think we probably could have been a bit more aggressive with the strategy."

Daniel Ricciardo
"We knew that we couldn't catch the Mercedes, but we believed we had better pace than the guys behind. It's really nice to stand back up on the podium again."

Lewis Hamilton
"It's fantastic to get my first win here after eight attempts. I had the same problems as in qualifying: I couldn't attack the corners because of snap oversteer."

Kimi Räikkönen
"I had a lack of grip and it was hard to find the right balance. Going for a two-stop strategy proved wrong as tyre degradation meant I couldn't push to the end."

Romain Grosjean
"It's been tough for us to get points and that was one of the hardest races I've contested in a long time as I did all I could to drive around the power unit issues."

Kevin Magnussen
"I went side-by-side with Jenson into Turn 13 and ran wide on to the marbles. As I came back onto the circuit, Vettel hadn't seen me and our cars touched, without damage."

Nico Hülkenberg
"Tyre degradation was high and the car wasn't so easy to drive, but I think everybody was struggling in the final part of the race. I thought we would need to make a third stop."

POSITIONS LAP BY LAP

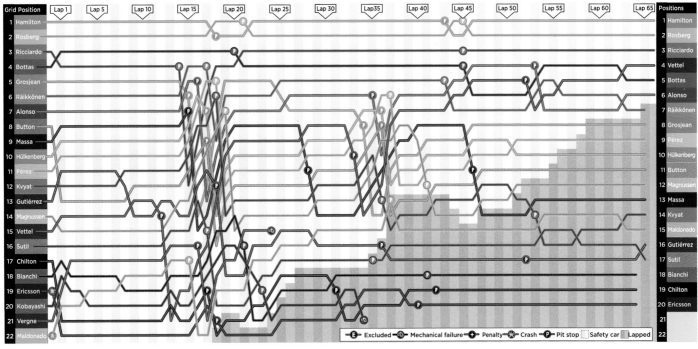

Grid Position		Lap 1	Lap 5	Lap 10	Lap 15	Lap 20	Lap 25	Lap 30	Lap35	Lap 40	Lap 45	Lap 50	Lap 55	Lap 60	Lap 65	Positions	
1	Hamilton															1	Hamilton
2	Rosberg															2	Rosberg
3	Ricciardo															3	Ricciardo
4	Bottas															4	Vettel
5	Grosjean															5	Bottas
6	Räikkönen															6	Alonso
7	Alonso															7	Räikkönen
8	Button															8	Grosjean
9	Massa															9	Pérez
10	Hülkenberg															10	Hülkenberg
11	Pérez															11	Button
12	Kvyat															12	Magnussen
13	Gutiérrez															13	Massa
14	Magnussen															14	Kvyat
15	Vettel															15	Maldonado
16	Sutil															16	Gutiérrez
17	Chilton															17	Sutil
18	Bianchi															18	Bianchi
19	Ericsson															19	Chilton
20	Kobayashi															20	Ericsson
21	Vergne															21	
22	Maldonado															22	

E Excluded — **S** Mechanical failure — **+** Penalty — **X** Crash — **P** Pit stop — Safety car — Lapped

QUALIFYING 3

	Driver	Time
1	L Hamilton	1m25.232s
2	N Rosberg	1m25.400s
3	D Ricciardo	1m26.285s
4	V Bottas	1m26.632s
5	R Grosjean	1m26.960s
6	K Räikkönen	1m27.104s
7	F Alonso	1m27.140s
8	J Button	1m27.335s
9	F Massa	1m27.402s
10	S Vettel	no time

GRID

	Driver	Time
1	L Hamilton	1m25.232s
2	N Rosberg	1m25.400s
3	D Ricciardo	1m26.285s
4	V Bottas	1m26.632s
5	R Grosjean	1m26.960s
6	K Räikkönen	1m27.104s
7	F Alonso	1m27.140s
8	J Button	1m27.335s
9	F Massa	1m27.402s
10	N Hülkenberg	1m27.685s
11	S Pérez	1m28.002s
12	D Kvyat	1m28.039s
13	E Gutiérrez	1m28.280s
14	K Magnussen	no time
15	S Vettel	no time
16	A Sutil	1m28.563s
17	M Chilton	1m29.586s
18	J Bianchi	1m30.177s
19	M Ericsson	1m30.312s
20	K Kobayashi	1m30.375s
21	J-É Vergne	no time
22	P Maldonado	no time

Grid penalties

S Vettel	5-place penalty for changing the gearbox
J-É Vergne	10-place penalty for unsafe realease in FP2

RACE

	Driver	Car	Laps	Time	Av mph	Fastest	Stops
1	L Hamilton	Mercedes F1 W05	66	1h41m05.155s	113.270	1m29.483s	2
2	N Rosberg	Mercedes F1 W05	66	1h41m05.791s	113.252	1m29.236s	2
3	D Ricciardo	Red Bull-Renault RB10	66	1h41m54.169s	112.357	1m30.012s	2
4	S Vettel	Red Bull-Renault RB10	66	1h42m21.857s	111.850	1m28.918s	3
5	V Bottas	Williams-Mercedes FW36	66	1h42m24.448s	111.803	1m30.424s	2
6	F Alonso	Ferrari F14 T	66	1h42m32.898s	111.650	1m29.898s	3
7	K Räikkönen	Ferrari F14 T	65	1h41m08.447s	111.487	1m30.580s	2
8	R Grosjean	Lotus-Renault E22	65	1h41m21.479s	111.249	1m31.068s	2
9	S Pérez	Force India-Mercedes VJM07	65	1h41m22.577s	111.228	1m30.756s	2
10	N Hülkenberg	Force India-Mercedes VJM07	65	1h41m32.981s	111.039	1m31.411s	2
11	J Button	McLaren-Mercedes MP4-29	65	1h41m37.467s	110.957	1m30.563s	2
12	K Magnussen	McLaren-Mercedes MP4-29	65	1h41m38.124s	110.945	1m30.318s	2
13	F Massa	Williams-Mercedes FW36	65	1h41m38.705s	110.934	1m30.468s	3
14	D Kvyat	Toro Rosso-Renault STR9	65	1h41m46.961s	110.785	1m30.269s	3
15	P Maldonado	Lotus-Renault E22	65	1h41m55.021s	110.639	1m31.235s	2
16	E Gutiérrez	Sauber-Ferrari C33	65	1h42m15.363s	110.271	1m30.666s	3
17	A Sutil	Sauber-Ferrari C33	65	1h42m18.487s	110.216	1m31.473s	2
18	J Bianchi	Marussia-Ferrari MR03	64	1h41m29.297s	109.396	1m31.784s	2
19	M Chilton	Marussia-Ferrari MR03	64	1h42m09.988s	108.670	1m31.767s	3
20	M Ericsson	Caterham-Renault CT05	64	1h42m30.846s	108.301	1m33.350s	2
R	K Kobayashi	Caterham-Renault CT05	34	Brakes	-	1m33.064s	1
R	J-É Vergne	Toro Rosso-Renault STR9	24	Exhaust	-	1m31.781s	1

Fastest lap
S Vettel 1m28.918s
(117.112mph) on lap 55

Fastest speed trap
F Massa   212.695mph
Slowest speed trap
K Kobayashi   193.681mph

Fastest pit stop
1 S Vettel   21.599s
2 S Vettel   21.608s
3 F Alonso   21.664s

CHAMPIONSHIP

	Driver	Pts
1	L Hamilton	100
2	N Rosberg	97
3	F Alonso	49
4	S Vettel	45
5	D Ricciardo	39
6	N Hülkenberg	37
7	V Bottas	34
8	J Button	23
9	K Magnussen	20
10	S Pérez	20
11	K Räikkönen	17
12	F Massa	12
13	R Grosjean	4
14	J-É Vergne	4
15	D Kvyat	4

CONSTRUCTORS

	Team	Pts
1	Mercedes	197
2	Red Bull-Renault	84
3	Ferrari	66
4	Force India-Mercedes	57
5	Williams-Mercedes	46
6	McLaren-Mercedes	43
7	Toro Rosso-Renault	8
8	Lotus-Renault	4

Esteban Gutiérrez

"It was a good start and I gained some places. After that I just kept dropping back. It was very challenging to keep the tyres alive and to have good speed on the straights."

Jean-Éric Vergne

"Someone asked me if I feel persecuted by bad luck, but it's part of the game. The first stint was tricky as I had a front left brake problem. Later, an exhaust problem put me out."

Felipe Massa

"I made a good start and could have made more places, but Ricciardo was in front so I couldn't get by. The three-stop strategy would have worked had the first stint been clean."

Max Chilton

"I'm really pleased that we've gained compared to the Caterhams and the Saubers are now in our sights. It's also great to keep my finishing record alive and it's now 24 out of 24."

Marcus Ericsson

"I just couldn't keep Maldonado or Vergne behind me, so I simply focused on my own race. On lap 44, I had a scary moment going into Turn 1 when the left front brake failed."

Adrian Sutil

"The race wasn't exciting as my car's performance wasn't good and I struggled for grip. Both stints with the medium tyres were difficult. The hard tyres worked better."

Daniil Kvyat

"The first stint was positive and it seemed possible to even fight for points. In the end, tyre wear was quite heavy and, together with the lack of pace, it turned out to be a tough race."

Valtteri Bottas

"The strategy was correct and the team did well in the stops, so we made the maximum, but it was a shame Vettel was so quick at the end, I tried to defend, but he had fresher tyres."

Jules Bianchi

"We saw clear signs of improvement. I was able to get ahead of Max at the start, which was my first objective, and to stay ahead of the Caterhams, which was the next."

Kamui Kobayashi

"Maldonado hit me going into Turn 13. His move risked putting both of us out of the race, but my car was alright although its balance wasn't great so I couldn't stay with Chilton."

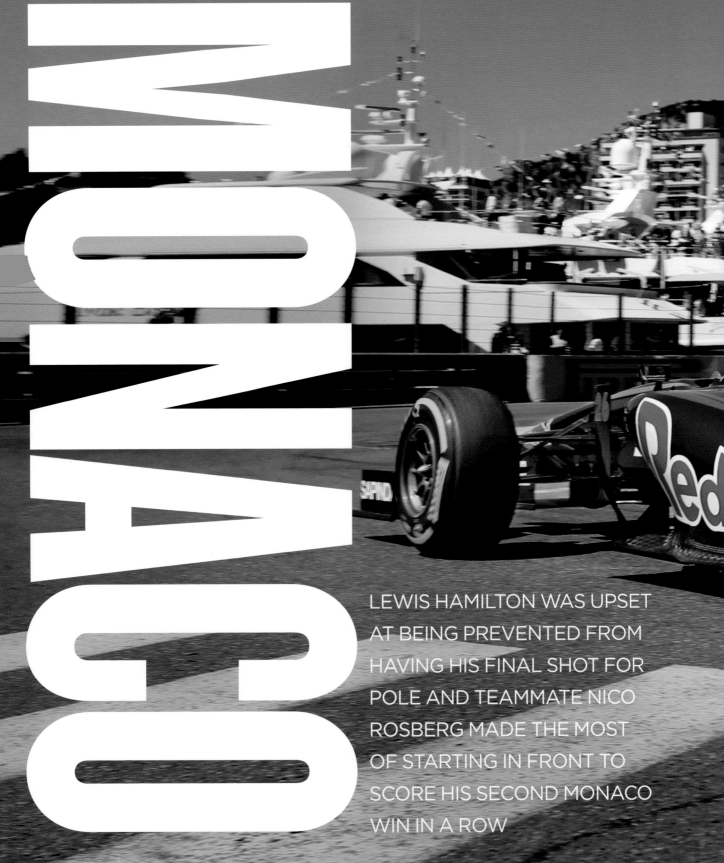

ROUND 6 GRAND PRIX DE MONACO

MONACO

LEWIS HAMILTON WAS UPSET
AT BEING PREVENTED FROM
HAVING HIS FINAL SHOT FOR
POLE AND TEAMMATE NICO
ROSBERG MADE THE MOST
OF STARTING IN FRONT TO
SCORE HIS SECOND MONACO
WIN IN A ROW

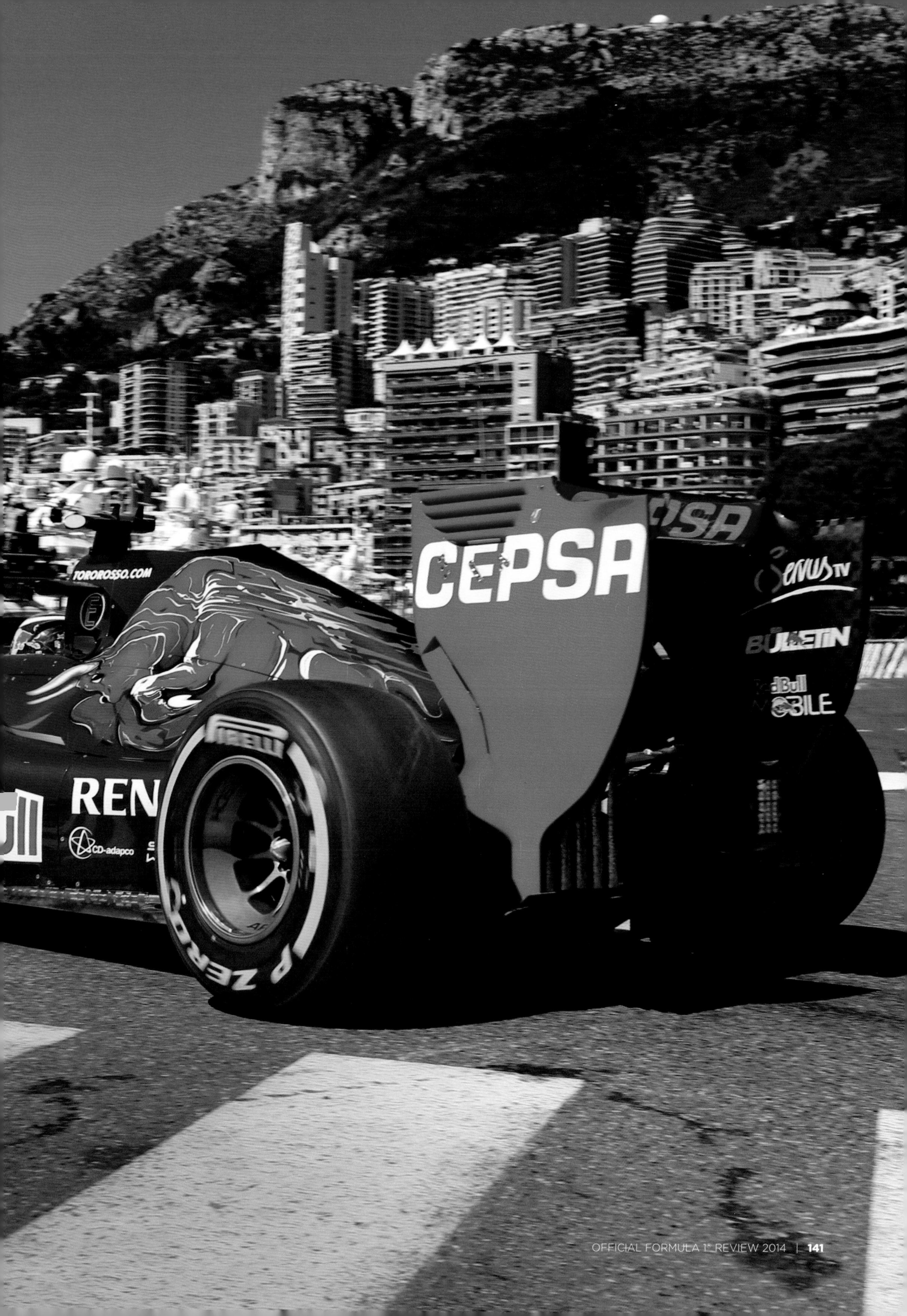
TOROROSSO.COM
CEPSA
CD-adapco
P ZERO

ico Rosberg turned his pole position into a second straight Monaco GP victory after a faultless drive. Hustled by Mercedes teammate Lewis Hamilton for most of the race, he didn't put a foot wrong. The pressure was finally eased when Hamilton dropped away in the closing laps after getting something in his eye that affected his vision.

The result ended Hamilton's streak of victories at four, and also handed the World Championship lead back to Rosberg. It was a perfectly timed success, for Rosberg had been forced to deal with the bitter disappointment of losing out four times in a row and, on a couple of occasions, by the slimmest of margins. Hamilton had been in the ascendancy and, while it was way too early to say that he had one

hand on the title, he certainly had the momentum. Also, people were starting to believe that Rosberg wouldn't be able to turn the tide, so a win at the most prestigious race of them all did just that.

Rosberg beat Hamilton to pole – always so crucial in Monaco – but the German subsequently faced an investigation from the FIA stewards after he was suspected of triggering a yellow flag to prevent Hamilton from going faster.

Rosberg set his time of 1m15.989s on his first run on Q3, while Hamilton managed 1m16.048s. On the second and crucial runs, Rosberg was 0.1s off his previous time when he locked up at Mirabeau and went down the escape road. Although his session was effectively over, he then reversed out and, with the yellow flags waving, Hamilton's lap was ruined.

"I just locked the outside front, I think it was, or the inside – I'm

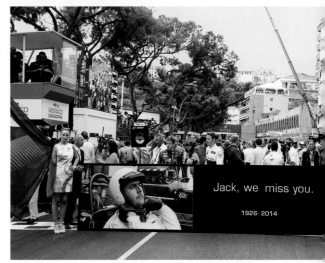

Jack, we miss you.
1926- 2014

Top: contrasting expressions on the podium as Nico Rosberg and Daniel Ricciardo appear delighted and Lewis Hamilton rather less so. **Above:** the

drivers prepare on the grid for a minute's silence in memory of three-time World Champion and 1959 Monaco winner, Sir Jack Brabham.

Top right: Nico Rosberg leads Lewis Hamilton, Sebastian Vettel, Kimi Räikkönen and Daniel Ricciardo through Ste Devote on the opening lap

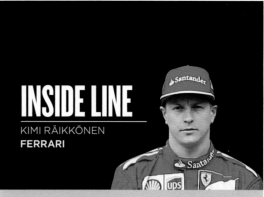

INSIDE LINE

KIMI RÄIKKÖNEN
FERRARI

I was still unhappy with the car in the race, although it was better than in qualifying, but we still have a long way to go to be where we want to be. Obviously, I could take results like we were supposed to get today. At some point at least it will turn around, but it wasn't today.

"It's clear that we need to improve in many areas. We've already done a lot of things with the engine and stuff like that to improve, but we're still lacking speed, and if we have to compare it to Mercedes, they're still quite a way ahead of us. We know what we have to do, but those things will not be easy to fix. It just takes time.

"We're going forward all the time, but other teams are also improving. So we certainly know where the weaknesses are, but if it was easy to solve those then everybody would have a fast car.

"We keep working and I'm sure if we can get the results that we were close to getting today, with the feelings that we have now, I'm sure it's going to be a lot better. But clearly, until we get things fixed and get the results, we have to keep fighting and hopefully just be a bit more lucky in the future.

"I've driven well many times this year, but obviously there's always been something going wrong in the races, punctures from other people hitting me like today, things like that, and it's just never come together really. It's just a shame.

"Again, today, we had a good position and picked up a puncture. It's just bad luck, little things going wrong and making a massive difference. They're just unfortunate things."

> **"IF WE HAVE TO COMPARE OUR ENGINE WITH MERCEDES, THEY'RE STILL QUITE A WAY AHEAD OF US, BUT WE KNOW WHAT WE HAVE TO DO"**

not sure," said Rosberg, "and that put me off line. I was still trying to make it, but at the last moment I had to turn out as I was going to hit the tyre wall. It was close, but I managed to go up the escape road."

"Generally, my lap wasn't too bad," said Hamilton. "Nico's been quick all weekend and I was just working away at it, one step at a time. I remember starting the last lap and thinking: 'This is it, this is going to be the lap.' I was two-and-a-half tenths up and didn't get to finish it."

The incident inevitably drew comparisons with Michael Schumacher's clumsy parking manoeuvre at Rascasse during qualifying in 2006, and the stewards called Rosberg in for an investigation. They eventually decided that "no offence was committed by the driver of car number 6" and, by way of explanation, said that they had examined video and telemetry, and could find no evidence that suggested it was a deliberate attempt to sabotage Hamilton's run.

While Rosberg and the Mercedes team could breathe a sigh of a relief, there was no question that the affair had massively ramped up tension between the two drivers.

Daniel Ricciardo did a great job to qualify third for Red Bull, 0.4s down on the pole lap. Sebastian Vettel had an ERS problem early in the session, but he still took fourth spot on the grid. Meanwhile, Ferrari hogged the third row as Fernando Alonso claimed fifth, a significant 0.7s ahead of teammate Kimi Räikkönen.

Jean-Éric Vergne impressed for Toro Rosso to take seventh, while rookie teammate Daniil Kvyat was two grid positions behind, having been fortunate to recover from a crash at the chicane in Q1. They were split by the McLaren of Kevin Magnussen, who was making his first F1 appearance in Monaco, while Sergio Pérez completed the top 10 for Force India.

Those who failed to make it out of Q2 were led by Nico Hülkenberg in 11th, the German lining up ahead of Jenson Button, Valtteri Bottas, Romain Grosjean and Pastor Maldonado. Felipe Massa made it to Q2, but was involved in a silly collision with Marcus Ericsson late in Q1 and he couldn't get back to the pits from Mirabeau.

TALKING POINT
IN PURSUIT OF MERCEDES

Monaco's tight layout may have given rivals a chance to get closer to Mercedes, but despite Daniel Ricciardo pushing Lewis Hamilton in the closing laps, there was no doubt that the silver cars still had a significant edge.

The key to the 2014 season was the relative performance of the Mercedes, Renault and Ferrari power units. All were subject to pre-season homologation and hardware development was frozen. The only changes were in the name of reliability and they had to be verified by the FIA. To a large degree, that had set the performance pecking order, at least until the winter. However, development in other areas, such as software and fuel, was continuing apace and thus the gap could potentially change race by race.

Despite the focus on Mercedes having the best power unit, we hadn't seen the three customer teams lining up in formation behind. Their form showed it wasn't just about power. Williams, McLaren and Force India all enjoyed strong races, but had been nowhere near the pace of the works team.

Red Bull had led the chase from the first race, having bounced back from a disastrous winter, when problems related both to Renault and Adrian Newey's tight packaging had restricted running. It was clear by now that, allowing for those teething problems, Newey was right to push the limits. The RB10 is a good chassis with a very efficient downforce package. It's generally the most effective in the field in the corners, but loses out on the straights, so the team is relying on Renault and Total to find a little more power.

Ferrari had sometimes been the third force, although often Fernando Alonso had flattered the package. He remained Ferrari's greatest asset, thanks to his ability to seize every opportunity, while Kimi Räikkönen had struggled to get the car to his liking. It was hard to benchmark the performance of the power unit accurately – main customer Sauber had a poor car and was well down the order and Marussia was always destined to be a bit-part player. However, Maranello clearly still had a lot of catching up to do, in all areas.

> "THE RB10 IS A VERY GOOD CHASSIS WITH A VERY EFFICIENT DOWNFORCE PACKAGE. IT'S GENERALLY THE MOST EFFECTIVE IN THE CORNERS, BUT LOSES OUT ON THE STRAIGHTS"

At the start, Rosberg stayed safely in front of Hamilton, while Vettel jumped into third ahead of Räikkönen, Ricciardo and Alonso, the latter having lost ground with a first lap ERS problem.

A collision between Button and Pérez at Mirabeau on the first lap left the Mexican stranded, and triggered a safety-car deployment. While it was circulating, Vettel suffered a turbo problem that led to a pit stop and then an early retirement.

Rosberg and Hamilton pulled away from the field at the restart, and they ran pretty much nose-to-tail. It was clear that everything would depend on the pit stops, which presented Hamilton's only real chance of getting by his German teammate.

However, that became academic when Sauber's Adrian Sutil crashed at the chicane, which eventually triggered a further safety car period.

It was a no-brainer for everyone to pit and Hamilton duly followed Rosberg in and out on lap 26. He now knew that he wasn't going to get the opportunity to use strategy to find a way past and was also frustrated that he hadn't been told to come in a lap earlier, immediately after the Sauber had crashed.

After the restart, Hamilton continued to hound Rosberg until around 10 laps to go, when he told the team via radio he had something in his eye. He dropped back from his teammate at an alarming rate, and even came under threat from Ricciardo in the closing stages.

"I've never really had it before," said Hamilton of his vision problem. "I made sure my visor was as closed as possible but I had quite a bit of wind coming in. I got close to Nico at one stage and all of a sudden I got

Left: with Sergio Pérez's Force India stranded on the track, the safety car had to be scrambled. **Below:** Jules Bianchi's drive to ninth place gave the Marussia team its first ever F1 points. **Bottom** Fernando Alonso was slowed by an ERS problem that hit his Ferrari from the start, but still finished fourth

a bit of debris in my eye, or some dirt, so I was driving with one eye, which is virtually impossible to do. Because of this, I was trying to open my visor through the low-speed corners to clear it up, but it was just making it worse. Fortunately, I think with five laps to go it cleared up, so I was able to stay ahead of Daniel." Indeed, he just managed to remain safely ahead of the Australian as Rosberg cruised home out front, 9.2s clear and under no threat.

"It's a special win, definitely," said the German. "Because Lewis has had the momentum with the results and I really needed to try to break that momentum and somehow I managed to do that this weekend. Of course, taking the lead again in the World Championship and winning here in Monaco makes it really cool."

In the course of the race, though, fuel had become an issue.

> **"HAMILTON NOW KNEW THAT HE WASN'T GOING TO GET THE OPPORTUNITY TO USE STRATEGY TO FIND A WAY PAST"**

"The fuel was very critical and caught me off-guard a little bit," Rosberg continued, "because it was a major change that I had to make, especially with Lewis being so close behind. It was a tough moment, because I had to change my driving style completely, use different gears, different lifting and coasting, different everything. But, again, the team managed that well, and got me to do what I needed to do. And then, once I got into the groove again, it was OK and it was no problem although it was still difficult."

"All the races have been very, very close," said Hamilton, "but this weekend I think I had very good pace. I drove with all my heart and gave it all I could and I feel like I drove fairly all weekend. So I leave today quite happy and I can go into the next race with even more energy and determination."

Ricciardo's run to third place was impressive, especially given his bad start that dropped him to an initial fifth. "Daniel was amazing, considering where he was after the first lap," said RBR principal Christian Horner. "We got a little bit lucky with the puncture for Räikkönen, but his pace was very good. Daniel looked after the tyres well and pushed hard at the end of the race. He was quicker than Lewis, but had no chance to overtake. It's the first time this year that we've been racing a Mercedes, so it's a step in the right direction."

Alonso had a solid race after his poor first lap, eventually finishing fourth – and, remarkably, his Ferrari was the last unlapped car, indicating just how fast Rosberg was going.

Hülkenberg was the best of the rest for Force India in fifth, the German finishing just ahead of

Button and Massa. The latter had gambled by not pitting during the Sutil safety-car period, and thus stopped under green.

An amazing eighth on the road went to Marussia's Jules Bianchi, but the Frenchman lost the place when a 5s time penalty was added, for not lining up in the right place on the grid when several drivers were caught out by Maldonado's absence. He still was classified ninth to claim the priceless first points for the five-year-old team.

Lotus racer Grosjean inherited eighth place, after dropping back with a first lap pit stop, while Magnussen took the final point after an electronic problem dropped him back from what would have been sixth place. He also survived a clash with Räikkönen's Ferrari at the hairpin en route to 10th position.

Räikkönen was the unluckiest driver of all, the Finn picking up a rear puncture under the safety car when hit by Max Chilton at Mirabeau, while the Briton was unlapping himself. This cost him a strong third place, and, after the clash with Magnussen delayed him further, he went on to finish 12th.

> "BIANCHI STILL WAS CLASSIFIED NINTH TO CLAIM THE PRICELESS FIRST POINTS FOR THE FIVE-YEAR-OLD TEAM"

Above: Nico Rosberg is congratulated in parc fermé after victory helped him retake the points lead.
Left: victory in Monaco has special resonance for Rosberg as he grew up here

CLOCKWISE FROM ABOVE: Sebastian Vettel negotiates the Grand Hotel hairpin; Fernando Alonso guides his Ferrari out of Portier; Max Chilton appears a little psyched before a session; Daniel Ricciardo builds his focus; new face, new helmet for Valtteri Bottas; Felipe Massa was frustrated about being hit in qualifying; photographers get the low-down at the chicane; Hamilton and Alonso arrive for the drivers' parade; Vettel appears glad that his mode of transport has four wheels

SNAPSHOT FROM MONACO

46

MONACO
MONTE CARLO

ROUND 6

Official Results © [2014]
Formula One World
Championship Limited,
6 Princes Gate, London SW7
1QJ. No reproduction without
permission. All copyright and
database rights reserved.

RACE DATE 25 May

CIRCUIT LENGTH 2.075 miles

NO. OF LAPS 78

RACE DISTANCE 161.850 miles

WEATHER Sunny, 22ºC

TRACK TEMP 32ºC

LAP RECORD Michael Schumacher,
1m14.439s, 100.373mph, 2004

	PRACTICE 1				PRACTICE 2				PRACTICE 3				QUALIFYING 1			QUALIFYING 2	
	Driver	Time	Laps		Driver	Time	Laps		Driver	Time	Laps		Driver	Time		Driver	Time
1	L Hamilton	1m18.271s	32	1	F Alonso	1m18.482s	15	1	L Hamilton	1m16.758s	27	1	J-É Vergne	1m17.557s	1	L Hamilton	1m16.354s
2	N Rosberg	1m18.303s	31	2	L Hamilton	1m18.901s	12	2	D Ricciardo	1m16.808s	26	2	N Rosberg	1m17.678s	2	N Rosberg	1m16.465s
3	D Ricciardo	1m18.506s	37	3	S Vettel	1m19.017s	15	3	N Rosberg	1m16.874s	24	3	L Hamilton	1m17.823s	3	S Vettel	1m17.074s
4	F Alonso	1m18.930s	31	4	J-É Vergne	1m19.351s	14	4	S Vettel	1m17.184s	23	4	F Alonso	1m17.853s	4	F Alonso	1m17.200s
5	S Vettel	1m19.043s	33	5	V Bottas	1m19.421s	9	5	F Alonso	1m17.428s	22	5	J Button	1m17.890s	5	D Ricciardo	1m17.233s
6	K Räikkönen	1m19.467s	31	6	S Pérez	1m19.668s	9	6	K Räikkönen	1m17.448s	24	6	D Ricciardo	1m17.900s	6	K Räikkönen	1m17.398s
7	V Bottas	1m19.494s	31	7	N Hülkenberg	1m19.712s	10	7	S Pérez	1m17.725s	23	7	K Räikkönen	1m17.902s	7	D Kvyat	1m17.594s
8	S Pérez	1m19.666s	29	8	J Button	1m19.721s	16	8	N Hülkenberg	1m18.074s	21	8	K Magnussen	1m17.978s	8	K Magnussen	1m17.609s
9	K Magnussen	1m19.789s	29	9	D Ricciardo	1m19.779s	11	9	J-É Vergne	1m18.136s	19	9	S Pérez	1m18.108s	9	J-É Vergne	1m17.657s
10	N Hülkenberg	1m19.856s	38	10	K Magnussen	1m20.230s	16	10	D Kvyat	1m18.166s	26	10	F Massa	1m18.209s	10	S Pérez	1m17.755s
11	J Button	1m20.033s	35	11	F Massa	1m20.394s	8	11	K Magnussen	1m18.249s	28	11	R Grosjean	1m18.335s	11	N Hülkenberg	1m17.846s
12	E Gutiérrez	1m20.118s	33	12	D Kvyat	1m20.622s	13	12	J Button	1m18.262s	21	12	S Vettel	1m18.383s	12	J Button	1m17.988s
13	R Grosjean	1m20.207s	33	13	A Sutil	1m20.811s	8	13	V Bottas	1m18.430s	31	13	V Bottas	1m18.407s	13	V Bottas	1m18.082s
14	P Maldonado	1m20.241s	38	14	P Maldonado	1m20.977s	7	14	F Massa	1m18.542s	30	14	N Hülkenberg	1m18.432s	14	R Grosjean	1m18.196s
15	J-É Vergne	1m20.260s	36	15	E Gutiérrez	1m21.467s	8	15	A Sutil	1m18.598s	24	15	P Maldonado	1m18.585s	15	P Maldonado	1m18.356s
16	F Massa	1m20.517s	25	16	R Grosjean	1m21.700s	6	16	R Grosjean	1m18.776s	26	16	D Kvyat	1m18.616s	16	F Massa	no time
17	A Sutil	1m20.736s	18	17	K Kobayashi	1m21.924s	6	17	J Bianchi	1m18.872s	23	17	E Gutiérrez	1m18.741s			
18	D Kvyat	1m20.914s	37	18	J Bianchi	1m21.937s	13	18	P Maldonado	1m19.118s	28	18	A Sutil	1m18.745s			
19	J Bianchi	1m21.310s	27	19	M Chilton	1m22.683s	13	19	E Gutiérrez	1m19.149s	28	19	J Bianchi	1m19.332s			
20	M Ericsson	1m22.063s	40	20	N Rosberg	1m22.862s	11	20	K Kobayashi	1m20.271s	32	20	M Chilton	1m19.928s			
21	K Kobayashi	1m22.492s	38	21	M Ericsson	1m23.164s	6	21	M Chilton	1m20.394s	25	21	K Kobayashi	1m20.133s			
22	M Chilton	1m25.817s	7	22	K Räikkönen	1m45.509s	4	22	M Ericsson	1m20.589s	30	22	M Ericsson	1m21.732s			

Best sectors – Practice			Speed trap – Practice			Best sectors – Qualifying			Speed trap – Qualifying		
Sec 1	N Rosberg	20.056s	1	L Hamilton	180.943mph	Sec 1	N Rosberg	19.826s	1	V Bottas	18.1440mph
Sec 2	S Vettel	35.511s	2	N Rosberg	180.632mph	Sec 2	L Hamilton	35.140s	2	N Rosberg	180.756mph
Sec 3	D Ricciardo	20.902s	3	V Bottas	179.576mph	Sec 3	D Ricciardo	20.875s	3	F Massa	180.259mph

Sebastian Vettel

"I had a good start, then lost boost pressure, so had no power and had to retire. I felt helpless, so I asked what we could do, but there wasn't anything."

Nico Rosberg

"It was a tough race, but it started well. I was comfortable, but then we had to manage my fuel consumption and Lewis was pushing really hard."

Fernando Alonso

"At the start, something in the motor didn't work, but even if I'd had full power, there was no room to pass. The three ahead of me deserved to be there. They were uncatchable."

Pastor Maldonado

"We don't know yet precisely what happened. The engine switched off after 30s. When we did out laps to the grid, the car and the power unit were working well."

Jenson Button

"I paced myself to the end, but couldn't pass Hülkenberg – he was struggling with his tyres, but whenever I pushed, I struggled, too, so I just couldn't make it stick."

Sergio Pérez

"I was in a battle with Nico, who was ahead and I went to take the apex. I was ahead of Jenson when he clipped my rear wheel and spun me around into the barriers."

Daniel Ricciardo

"I got Seb due to his problem and Kimi had a puncture. With 20 laps to go, I thought my tyres would be OK so I pushed and caught Lewis. It was fun, but I couldn't get past him."

Lewis Hamilton

"This was not my weekend. It is such a hard circuit to pass on. I was following Nico as closely as I could, but I couldn't get past. Towards the end, I got dirt in my eye."

Kimi Räikkönen

"I moved up to third and had good pace. Unluckily, in a safety-car period, I was hit by Chilton and I had to make an unscheduled stop as my right rear tyre was damaged."

Romain Grosjean

"It started as a bad day with a puncture on lap 1 after Adrian drove into me. We swapped to the softs, but it was impossible to pass so we changed to supersofts."

Kevin Magnussen

"Despite things going against us – the long hold due to traffic at my stop, the unsafe release in front of me and the engine issue – I can draw a lot from my car feeling really good."

Nico Hülkenberg

"Ten points is a great reward after such a hard race. The last 20 laps were really tricky as my supersofts were at the end of their life and it was hard to hold off the cars behind me."

POSITIONS LAP BY LAP

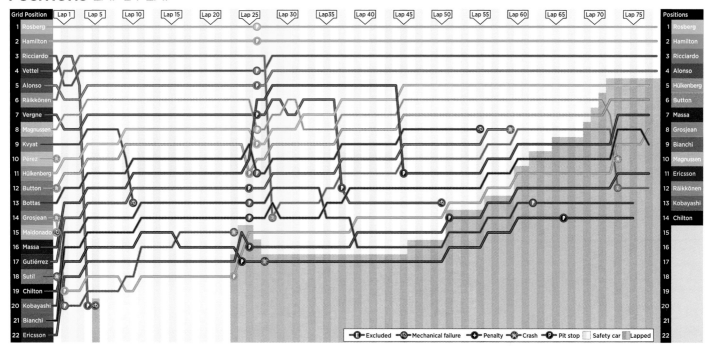

Grid Position | Lap 1 | Lap 5 | Lap 10 | Lap 15 | Lap 20 | Lap 25 | Lap 30 | Lap35 | Lap 40 | Lap 45 | Lap 50 | Lap 55 | Lap 60 | Lap 65 | Lap 70 | Lap 75 | Positions

	Grid		Positions
1	Rosberg		1 Rosberg
2	Hamilton		2 Hamilton
3	Ricciardo		3 Ricciardo
4	Vettel		4 Alonso
5	Alonso		5 Hülkenberg
6	Räikkönen		6 Button
7	Vergne		7 Massa
8	Magnussen		8 Grosjean
9	Kvyat		9 Bianchi
10	Pérez		10 Magnussen
11	Hülkenberg		11 Ericsson
12	Button		12 Räikkönen
13	Bottas		13 Kobayashi
14	Grosjean		14 Chilton
15	Maldonado		15
16	Massa		16
17	Gutiérrez		17
18	Sutil		18
19	Chilton		19
20	Kobayashi		20
21	Bianchi		21
22	Ericsson		22

E= Excluded **M**=Mechanical failure **+**= Penalty **✳**=Crash **P**= Pit stop ☐ Safety car ▨ Lapped

QUALIFYING 3

	Driver	Time
1	N Rosberg	1m15.989s
2	L Hamilton	1m16.048s
3	D Ricciardo	1m16.384s
4	S Vettel	1m16.547s
5	F Alonso	1m16.686s
6	K Räikkönen	1m17.389s
7	J-É Vergne	1m17.540s
8	K Magnussen	1m17.555s
9	D Kvyat	1m18.090s
10	S Pérez	1m18.327s

GRID

	Driver	Time
1	N Rosberg	1m15.989s
2	L Hamilton	1m16.048s
3	D Ricciardo	1m16.384s
4	S Vettel	1m16.547s
5	F Alonso	1m16.686s
6	K Räikkönen	1m17.389s
7	J-É Vergne	1m17.540s
8	K Magnussen	1m17.555s
9	D Kvyat	1m18.090s
10	S Pérez	1m18.327s
11	N Hülkenberg	1m17.846s
12	J Button	1m17.988s
13	V Bottas	1m18.082s
14	R Grosjean	1m18.196s
15	P Maldonado	1m18.356s
16	F Massa	no time
17	E Gutiérrez	1m18.741s
18	A Sutil	1m18.745s
19	M Chilton	1m19.928s
20	K Kobayashi	1m20.133s
21	J Bianchi	1m19.332s
22	M Ericsson	1m21.732s

Grid penalties

J Bianchi	5-place penalty for changing the gearbox
M Ericsson	Made to start from pit lane for causing a collision

RACE

	Driver	Car	Laps	Time	Av mph	Fastest	Stops
1	N Rosberg	Mercedes F1 W05	78	1h49m27.661s	88.736	1m19.425s	1
2	L Hamilton	Mercedes F1 W05	78	1h49m36.871s	88.608	1m19.361s	1
3	D Ricciardo	Red Bull-Renault RB10	78	1h49m37.275s	88.602	1m19.252s	1
4	F Alonso	Ferrari F14 T	78	1h50m00.113s	88.296	1m19.727s	1
5	N Hülkenberg	Force India-Mercedes VJM07	77	1h49m48.580s	87.317	1m20.767s	1
6	J Button	McLaren-Mercedes MP4-29	77	1h49m48.772s	87.314	1m21.047s	1
7	F Massa	Williams-Mercedes FW36	77	1h49m49.482s	87.304	1m20.314s	1
8	R Grosjean	Lotus-Renault E22	77	1h50m06.594s	87.078	1m20.979s	2
9	J Bianchi	Marussia-Ferrari MR03	77	1h50m10.135s*	87.032	1m21.254s	1
10	K Magnussen	McLaren-Mercedes MP4-29	77	1h50m15.783s	86.958	1m20.657s	1
11	M Ericsson	Caterham-Renault CT05	77	1h50m26.405s	86.818	1m20.911s	2
12	K Räikkönen	Ferrari F14 T	77	1h50m27.015s	86.810	1m18.479s	3
13	K Kobayashi	Caterham-Renault CT05	75	1h49m46.283s	85.078	1m22.425s	2
14	M Chilton	Marussia-Ferrari MR03	75	1h50m35.832s	84.443	1m20.579s	3
R	E Gutiérrez	Sauber-Ferrari C33	59	Spun off	-	1m21.146s	1
R	V Bottas	Williams-Mercedes FW36	55	Engine	-	1m21.105s	1
R	J-É Vergne	Toro Rosso-Renault STR9	50	Exhaust	-	1m21.083s	2
R	A Sutil	Sauber-Ferrari C33	23	Spun off	-	1m21.761s	1
R	D Kvyat	Toro Rosso-Renault STR9	10	Exhaust	-	1m22.011s	0
R	S Vettel	Red Bull-Renault RB10	5	Turbocharger	-	1m59.505s	1
R	S Pérez	Force India-Mercedes VJM07	0	Collision	-	-	0
NS	P Maldonado	Lotus-Renault E22	-	Fuel pump	-	-	-

Fastest lap
K Räikkönen 1m18.479s
(95.206mph) on lap 75

Fastest speed trap
L Hamilton 180.197mph

Slowest speed trap
S Vettel 171.125mph

Fastest pit stop
1	F Massa	24.264s
2	N Rosberg	24.672s
3	R Grosjean	25.029s

CHAMPIONSHIP

	Driver	Pts
1	N Rosberg	122
2	L Hamilton	118
3	F Alonso	61
4	D Ricciardo	54
5	N Hülkenberg	47
6	S Vettel	45
7	V Bottas	34
8	J Button	31
9	K Magnussen	21
10	S Pérez	20
11	F Massa	18
12	K Räikkönen	17
13	R Grosjean	8
14	J-É Vergne	4
15	D Kvyat	4
16	J Bianchi	2

CONSTRUCTORS

	Team	Pts
1	Mercedes	240
2	Red Bull-Renault	99
3	Ferrari	78
4	Force India-Mercedes	67
5	McLaren-Mercedes	52
6	Williams-Mercedes	52
7	Lotus-Renault	8
8	Toro Rosso-Renault	8
9	Marussia-Ferrari	2

Esteban Gutiérrez

"Unfortunately, I couldn't finish. It was the most painful mistake in my career. I touched the guardrail at the entry to Rascasse, spun and that was the end of the race."

Jean-Éric Vergne

"I was saving the tyres and the strategy looked good. Then, my engineer told me about the drive-through penalty for 'unsafe release' and, finally, I had the exhaust problem."

Felipe Massa

"I'm very happy with seventh after starting 16th. I took risks when I changed strategy at the safety car and had to make my tyres last, so I made the most of the opportunities I had."

Max Chilton

"I'm very proud to be part of something so special, but I have mixed emotions as everything that could have gone wrong for me today did, but that's racing and I'll have my chance one day."

Marcus Ericsson

"Finishing my first Monaco GP was an amazing experience and the fact we've equalled the team's best-ever finish is great. The balance was OK and I was able to push to the flag."

Adrian Sutil

"As I came around Turn 5, many cars ahead of me stopped and I got front wing damage. Later, coming out of the tunnel, I made a mistake and hit the guardrail."

Daniil Kvyat

"It's disappointing to retire as I had a good chance of finishing in the points. I was able to hold my position and even move up to eighth before I had to retire with an exhaust problem."

Valtteri Bottas

"I had an issue with the power unit, which is frustrating. There are some investigations to do to find out what happened. I was quickly in the points, so it could have been a good weekend."

Jules Bianchi

"It wasn't an easy race: there were some highs along the way, but a couple of concerning moments. What matters at the end is that we got there and can savour the highlights."

Kamui Kobayashi

"Even though I finished 13th, I'm not happy as I'm sure I'd have finished in the points if Bianchi hadn't hit me when he forced his way past. The car was basically undriveable after that."

CANAD

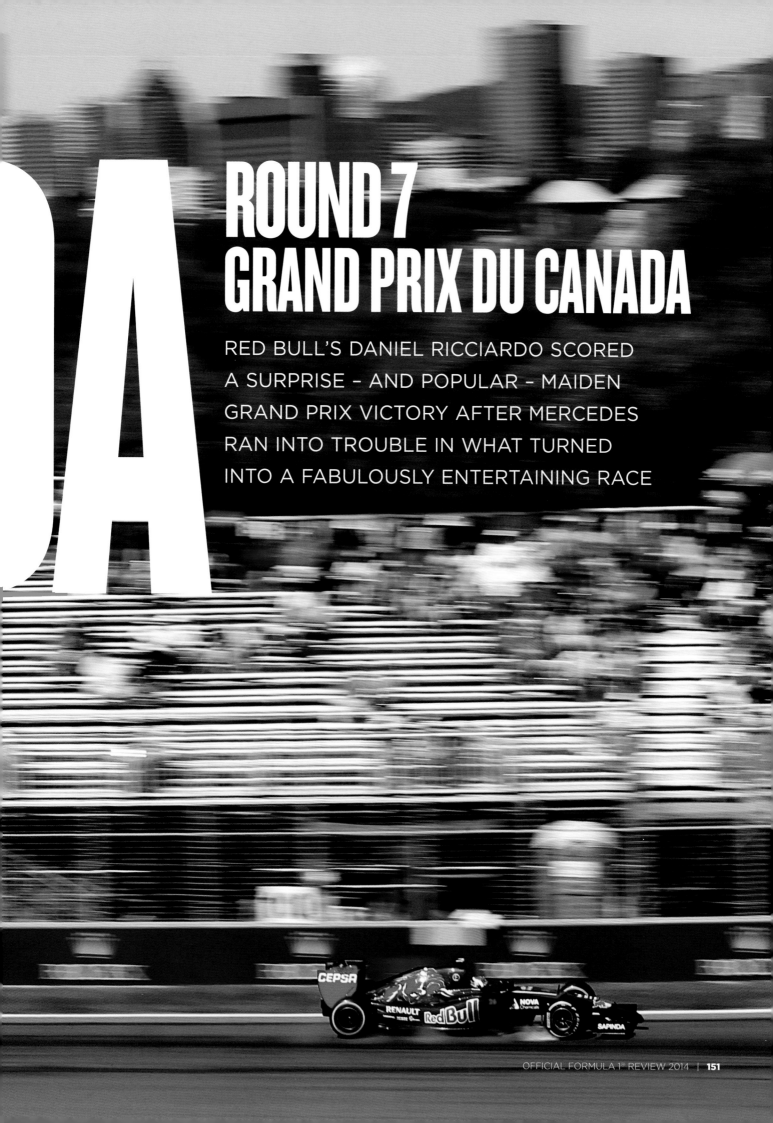

ROUND 7
GRAND PRIX DU CANADA

RED BULL'S DANIEL RICCIARDO SCORED
A SURPRISE – AND POPULAR – MAIDEN
GRAND PRIX VICTORY AFTER MERCEDES
RAN INTO TROUBLE IN WHAT TURNED
INTO A FABULOUSLY ENTERTAINING RACE

1996
DAMON HILL

1999
MIKA HAKKINEN

2002
HAEL SCHUMACHER

2005
RNANDO ALONSO

2008
S HAMILTON

The usual fight for supremacy between Mercedes' title rivals ended when both Nico Rosberg and Lewis Hamilton suffered overheating issues with their MGU-K units, which convert power recovered from braking energy. While Hamilton was forced to retire, Rosberg was able to continue and, importantly, collect points towards his championship tally. Despite a loss of power, he was somehow able to hang on in front until the closing laps, when Daniel Ricciardo finally found a way past. It was the first win for anyone other than Rosberg or Hamilton in a season hitherto dominated by the Silver Arrows.

As in Monaco, Rosberg gave Hamilton something to think about by qualifying on pole, but this time there was no controversy;

the German simply outpaced his teammate. Hamilton had won three times in Canada and the track was widely regarded as one that would favour him, so pole was a psychological boost for Rosberg.

Hamilton had been fastest in Saturday morning's FP3 session, in Q1 and in Q2, but Rosberg pipped him by 0.068s on the first runs in Q3. Hamilton still had the final run in which to claim top spot, but Rosberg improved with a 1m14.874s and Hamilton failed to respond, his scrappy lap including moments at both Turns 6 and 8.

"It wasn't a great lap, to be honest," said the British driver. "I should have got the banker lap in before, a bit like in Monaco, and I didn't. Ultimately, I know I have good pace here, I just didn't do it. I was behind traffic at the last corner on the first lap and then I was behind people and had to back off, so it wasn't the best preparation."

"SEBASTIAN VETTEL DID A SUPERB JOB TO BEAT ALL THE MERCEDES CUSTOMERS AND QUALIFY THIRD"

The rest were far behind, but the battle for third was close, with the Red Bull and Williams drivers setting times in the 1m15.5s bracket. High-speed Montreal wasn't supposed to suit the RB10, but Sebastian Vettel did a superb job to beat the Mercedes customers and qualify third; he just sneaked ahead of the Williams duo, Valtteri Bottas and Felipe Massa. Ricciardo had to settle for sixth in the other Red Bull, despite being just 0.041s off his teammate; the Australian admitted that an adjustment for his final run hadn't worked.

Ferrari seemed to have found some pace thanks to updates on Friday and Fernando Alonso was actually fastest in FP1, but most of the bits were removed on Saturday for reliability purposes The team paid the price when Alonso was unable to qualify higher than seventh, while Kimi Räikkönen lined up 10th on the starting grid.

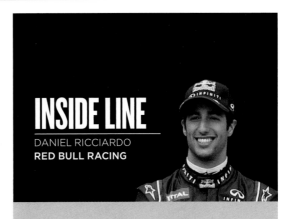

Far left: Daniel Ricciardo didn't have long to savour the arrival of his first F1 win – he took the lead only three laps from the finish, then the yellow flags were flown. **Left:** Nico Rosberg leads Mercedes teammate Lewis Hamilton in the early stages of the race. **Below:** Ricciardo leads the chasing pack of Sergio Pérez, Sebastian Vettel and Felipe Massa as the race enters its fabulous final few laps

INSIDE LINE

DANIEL RICCIARDO
RED BULL RACING

The race came to life in the last 15 to 20 laps. Hamilton had a problem, and then we saw Rosberg was slow on the straights. I was struggling to get past Pérez, as they had a pretty good car on the straights and he was holding me off well in the corners. I finally got a run out of the last chicane and made a nice move.

"I knew I was strong braking into Turn 1 – I was really quick into there – so once I had the outside line I went in and made it work. That was the place I wanted to do it. I had been trying all the time and it was only then that the opportunity came, but I hadn't been holding back.

"Then I set my sights on Rosberg and, with only a couple of laps to go, I found myself in the right spot to get the DRS.

> "I KNEW I WAS STRONG BRAKING INTO TURN 1 – I WAS REALLY QUICK INTO THERE – SO ONCE I HAD THE OUTSIDE LINE I WENT IN AND MADE IT WORK"

"I think it surprised us, because of the pace Mercedes had all year. Obviously, I'm still going to take the victory, don't get me wrong, but they had their issues on the day, which allowed us to attack. It's nice that we capitalised on that. I think it would have been disappointing if they had had issues and were still able to get the best of us. At least we capitalised when we could.

"The key is confidence, and the more time I spend here – here being F1 – the more comfortable I feel. In any sport, a lot of it comes down to belief. If you truly believe in something, then you tend to make it work.

"I knew I'd have a great team behind me and I believed with that I'd be able to get some great results. It's really nice to have the first victory."

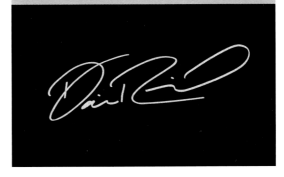

Jean-Éric Vergne did a great job to qualify eighth for Toro Rosso, while Jenson Button was ninth for McLaren. Nico Hülkenberg was the fastest driver to fail to make it out of Q2 and thus started 11th. His Force India teammate, Sergio Pérez, qualified 13th, with the pair separated by Kevin Magnussen.

Rosberg eased Hamilton wide at the start, allowing Vettel to get between the pair. A first-lap clash involving the two Marussia drivers led to a seven-lap safety car period and, after the green flag flew, it took less than three laps for Hamilton to get back into second, where he set his sights on his teammate.

Rosberg pitted for the first time on lap 19, with Hamilton following a lap later, and the status quo was maintained until the second round of stops, with Rosberg pitting on lap 44. He suffered a little delay and Hamilton jumped ahead when he came in next time around.

It had all looked routine for Mercedes, but suddenly everything went awry. Both drivers suffered from MGU-K overheating issues and Hamilton's rear brakes quickly became critical. After less than a lap in front, he was forced to retire.

Rosberg was more fortunate. Not only was he able to keep going, but, with advice from the pits, the German driver was also able to manage the situation. Despite losing some 160bhp – without the kinetic boost around which the power unit

TALKING POINT
MANAGING
THE SITUATION

Nico Rosberg's drive to second place in Montreal was an extraordinary feat, given the problems that struck his Mercedes F1 W05. It also said much about the team's advantage that, despite a significant power loss, he managed to stay in the lead until the closing laps and ultimately only fall back to second.

"When you lose the energy recovery system, it makes it extremely difficult with rear brakes," he explained. "Considering that Montreal was critical for rear brakes anyway, to lose the recovery system on top pushed it into a zone where it was really on a knife edge. It's always going to be a challenge if it does happen.

"It was an extremely difficult race, having pressure from behind the whole race, and having to manage brakes and fuel all the time – that was unusual and demanding. Then the KERS failed...

"All the braking forces were completely different. Arriving with 30kph less down the straight, you brake in a completely different place and the Montreal braking points are difficult to get right anyway. The second point was just using the front brakes a lot more, so there was more risk of locking up."

Rosberg admitted that, in retrospect, he rued losing the win. "Shortly after the race, I was pleased with second place, considering everything," he said. "In hindsight, a lot of things went wrong and our ambition is really to have a perfect weekend and win the race. But, taking everything into consideration, I was definitely pleased with second. It was really damage limitation because the team didn't expect better than eighth place at some points in the race."

Meanwhile, one of the big questions was why Rosberg was able to continue in the race, but teammate Hamilton wasn't.

"I think it was more to do with the fact that Nico was in clear air in front of me," said Lewis. "He's constantly got cool, free, clean air coming in and I was very close behind all the time, so I was having dirty warm air. You can see a slight difference in the temperatures. They were both on the limit and mine went over."

> **"ARRIVING WITH 30KPH LESS DOWN THE STRAIGHT, YOU BRAKE IN A WHOLLY DIFFERENT PLACE AND THE MONTREAL BRAKING POINTS ARE DIFFICULT ANYWAY"**

Left: Jenson Button worked his way forward from ninth, then gained four places in the final two laps to finish fourth. **Below left:** Kamui Kobayashi's

Caterham and Jules Bianchi's Marussia sit abandoned behind the barriers after they both departed from the race. **Below:** Felipe Massa's

Williams slides to a halt after its last-lap collision with Sergio Pérez's Force India. Sebastian Vettel, in the foreground, managed to keep out of the way

was designed – he was soon lapping once more at a respectable pace.

Nevertheless, he fell back into the chasing pack, which was led by Pérez. Both Force India drivers went for one-stop strategies, with the Mexican starting on supersoft tyres and Hülkenberg faring a little less successfully on softs. Their late single pit stops duly propelled both men up the race order.

Rosberg and Pérez were trailed by Vettel and Ricciardo, who had got ahead of his teammate at the second round of stops, helped by a great in-lap. These four cars circulated together, just in front of a second group of Hülkenberg, Bottas, Massa and Alonso.

The Williams drivers had retained their positions in the first stint, but Massa lost some crucial time with a stuck wheel at his first pit stop. In an attempt to recover, he made a very late second stop and even led the race briefly after the Mercedes came in. That left the Brazilian with fresher tyres than all of his rivals for the run to the flag, although he lost some momentum when stuck behind his teammate for many laps.

With eight cars now running in two lead groups, it was fabulous stuff. Rosberg's struggles had been transmitted to the rest of the pit lane by his radio messages, so those behind needed no more motivation.

With five laps to go, Ricciardo finally managed to force his way past Pérez to claim second, the Mexican having lost momentum briefly as a result of ERS and brake-by-wire issues, although these were quickly corrected. Clear of Pérez at last, Ricciardo was soon on the tail of Rosberg's Mercedes and, with a little over two laps remaining, he dragged past the helpless Mercedes driver to take the lead.

There was still plenty going on behind, with Pérez trying to hold off his pursuers on uncomfortably worn tyres. Vettel got past to claim third at the end of the penultimate lap and, a few seconds later, as the group headed into the first corner for the final time, there was heavy contact between Pérez and Massa as the Brazilian tried to find a way through. Both cars spun heavily into the tyre wall, with the Williams just missing Vettel, who was minding his own business after overtaking Pérez.

"IT HAD ALL LOOKED ROUTINE FOR MERCEDES, BUT SUDDENLY EVERYTHING WENT AWRY"

"I got past him and then into Turn 1 I saw they were very close to each other," said Vettel. "I saw something white coming in the mirror. At the last second, I reacted and opened the car, basically turned right, and Felipe was in the air flying past. It was kind of surreal, but I was quite fortunate that he didn't hit me in that instance and I saw him just in time."

Inevitably, race control called for a safety car. Out front and unaware of what had happened, Ricciardo thus saw yellow flags for the remainder of his final lap and it was a bit of an anticlimax when he led Rosberg and Vettel over the line. "It's not that we were leading the whole race," said Ricciardo, his famous smile wider than ever, "so it's not that I had time to understand that I was going to win. It all happened in the last few laps, so I think that's why it's still taking a while to comprehend. But it's really nice, a really good feeling. The race came to life at the end."

Rosberg was happy to claim 18 points on a day when Hamilton failed to score. "It was a big battle all the way," he said. "I didn't have

Left: Fernando Alonso finished sixth after a last lap stumble with Nico Hülkenberg.
Below: Ricciardo was delighted to become Australia's fourth grand prix winner

on the penultimate lap. The McLaren man, no doubt smiling, steered his way past both of them.

Hülkenberg finished in fifth place, while Alonso claimed sixth and Bottas slipped to seventh after being hampered by high brake and engine temperatures. Vergne had passed Alonso at the start to run in seventh place, but he dropped back after the first round of pit stops. Helped by some attrition ahead, he eventually finished eighth.

Magnussen, meanwhile, moved up from 12th place to ninth after, like teammate Button, spending much of the time stuck behind other cars.

The final point went to Räikkönen, who had a spin himself and spent a lot of the race stuck behind slower cars, notably Daniil Kvyat's Toro Rosso.

Pérez and Massa were classified 11th and 12th, a lap down, and both teams were well aware of the opportunity they had wasted. The stewards punished the Mexican with a five-place grid penalty for the Austrian GP, although he insisted he hadn't been at fault. The case would be revisited a fortnight later by the stewards at the Red Bull Ring, although there would be no change to the original decision.

the best getaway at the start, but I got through Turn 1 better, so I managed to keep the lead through Turn 2 and from then on it was a big battle all the way through. I managed to stay ahead until the second pit stop and then we had a problem in that stop and I dropped behind as a result.

"From then on, I didn't really know what was going on, because I lost a lot of power and was very slow down the straights. I was just trying to hang on, trying to put in the equivalent of qualifying laps all the time, but it didn't quite work out against Ricciardo."

From nowhere, Button jumped up to fourth place at the end of the race, taking advantage of the Pérez/Massa accident and also the fact that Alonso and Hülkenberg stumbled over each other at the hairpin while fighting for position

> "AS THE GROUP HEADED INTO THE FIRST CORNER FOR THE FINAL TIME, THERE WAS HEAVY CONTACT BETWEEN PÉREZ AND MASSA"

CLOCKWISE FROM RIGHT: Jenson Button shares a joke with Max Chilton, Nico Rosberg, Daniel Ricciardo and Nico Hülkenberg; Sir Frank Williams and Rob Smedley are all smiles in the Williams garage; Rosberg helps Ricciardo to the bubbly; the marshals bring welcome experience to the event; the final chicane on the finish straight, with the Olympic rowing lake in the background; Montreal's distinctive skyline under a stormy sky; a spectator's well-travelled – and well-worn – cap

SNAPSHOT FROM CANADA

CANADA
MONTREAL

ROUND 7

Official Results © [2014]
Formula One World
Championship Limited,
6 Princes Gate, London SW7
1QJ. No reproduction without
permission. All copyright and
database rights reserved.

RACE DATE 8 June
CIRCUIT LENGTH 2.710 miles
NO. OF LAPS 70
RACE DISTANCE 189.686 miles
WEATHER Sunny, 28°C
TRACK TEMP 45°C
LAP RECORD Rubens Barrichello,
1m13.622s, 132.511mph, 2004

	PRACTICE 1				PRACTICE 2				PRACTICE 3				QUALIFYING 1			QUALIFYING 2	
	Driver	Time	Laps		Driver	Time	Laps		Driver	Time	Laps		Driver	Time		Driver	Time
1	F Alonso	1m17.238s	21	1	L Hamilton	1m16.118s	42	1	L Hamilton	1m15.610s	18	1	L Hamilton	1m15.750s	1	L Hamilton	1m15.054s
2	L Hamilton	1m17.254s	25	2	N Rosberg	1m16.293s	39	2	F Massa	1m16.086s	16	2	K Magnussen	1m16.446s	2	N Rosberg	1m15.289s
3	N Rosberg	1m17.384s	32	3	S Vettel	1m16.573s	26	3	N Rosberg	1m16.120s	20	3	N Rosberg	1m16.471s	3	F Massa	1m15.773s
4	S Vettel	1m18.131s	28	4	K Räikkönen	1m16.648s	31	4	F Alonso	1m16.488s	15	4	J Button	1m16.631s	4	V Bottas	1m15.806s
5	V Bottas	1m18.361s	20	5	F Alonso	1m16.701s	27	5	D Ricciardo	1m16.504s	15	5	F Massa	1m16.666s	5	D Ricciardo	1m15.897s
6	D Ricciardo	1m18.435s	26	6	F Massa	1m16.774s	37	6	K Räikkönen	1m16.528s	22	6	V Bottas	1m16.772s	6	S Vettel	1m16.109s
7	J Button	1m18.446s	33	7	V Bottas	1m16.893s	37	7	V Bottas	1m16.684s	20	7	N Hülkenberg	1m16.897s	7	F Alonso	1m16.131s
8	K Magnussen	1m18.514s	31	8	K Magnussen	1m17.052s	42	8	D Kvyat	1m16.820s	21	8	D Kvyat	1m16.938s	8	J Button	1m16.214s
9	K Räikkönen	1m18.578s	15	9	J Button	1m17.059s	38	9	J-É Vergne	1m16.824s	19	9	F Alonso	1m17.010s	9	K Räikkönen	1m16.245s
10	J-É Vergne	1m18.643s	14	10	J-É Vergne	1m17.180s	40	10	S Vettel	1m16.884s	15	10	K Räikkönen	1m17.013s	10	J-É Vergne	1m16.255s
11	N Hülkenberg	1m18.733s	30	11	R Grosjean	1m17.626s	28	11	N Hülkenberg	1m16.944s	17	11	D Ricciardo	1m17.113s	11	N Hülkenberg	1m16.300s
12	S Pérez	1m18.959s	22	12	D Ricciardo	1m17.644s	36	12	K Magnussen	1m16.993s	19	12	J-É Vergne	1m17.178s	12	K Magnussen	1m16.310s
13	A Sutil	1m19.108s	24	13	N Hülkenberg	1m17.712s	35	13	R Grosjean	1m17.121s	21	13	S Vettel	1m17.470s	13	S Pérez	1m16.472s
14	R Grosjean	1m19.142s	32	14	S Pérez	1m17.819s	33	14	S Pérez	1m17.188s	19	14	A Sutil	1m17.519s	14	R Grosjean	1m16.687s
15	D Kvyat	1m19.177s	21	15	P Maldonado	1m17.868s	27	15	P Maldonado	1m17.224s	21	15	R Grosjean	1m17.732s	15	D Kvyat	1m16.713s
16	P Maldonado	1m19.340s	37	16	A Sutil	1m17.964s	47	16	J Button	1m17.360s	23	16	S Pérez	1m18.235s	16	A Sutil	1m17.314s
17	F Massa	1m19.575s	7	17	E Gutiérrez	1m18.340s	43	17	A Sutil	1m17.900s	23	17	P Maldonado	1m18.328s			
18	E Gutiérrez	1m19.804s	15	18	M Chilton	1m18.693s	34	18	J Bianchi	1m18.518s	25	18	M Chilton	1m18.348s			
19	J Bianchi	1m20.200s	15	19	D Kvyat	1m18.732s	9	19	M Chilton	1m18.525s	19	19	J Bianchi	1m18.359s			
20	M Chilton	1m20.844s	26	20	K Kobayashi	1m20.244s	38	20	M Ericsson	1m19.865s	23	20	K Kobayashi	1m19.278s			
21	M Ericsson	1m21.404s	33	21	M Ericsson	1m22.418s	13	21	K Kobayashi	1m20.227s	14	21	M Ericsson	1m19.820s			
22	A Rossi	1m21.757s	27	22	J Bianchi	1m32.127s	3	22	E Gutiérrez	1m22.388s	6	22	E Gutiérrez	no time			

Best sectors – Practice			Speed trap – Practice			Best sectors – Qualifying			Speed trap – Qualifying		
Sec 1	L Hamilton	21.074s	1	F Massa	207.413mph	Sec 1	L Hamilton	20.894s	1	S Pérez	209.837mph
Sec 2	L Hamilton	24.437s	2	N Rosberg	206.978mph	Sec 2	N Rosberg	24.177s	2	F Massa	209.712mph
Sec 3	L Hamilton	30.038s	3	V Bottas	206.108mph	Sec 3	N Rosberg	29.723s	3	V Bottas	208.532mph

Sebastian Vettel
"We could have taken more risk with strategy, but it's hard to know what's going on around me when I'm not on the pit wall. We must develop the car more for the straights."

Nico Rosberg
"Both cars lost the MGU-K system and a lot of power. I lost time in the second stop which let Lewis jump me. Towards the end, Daniel was too fast on the straights."

Fernando Alonso
"Looking at the wild finish, I picked up some 'lucky' points, but we can't be happy with where we finished. My pace wasn't good and I wasn't happy with my balance."

Pastor Maldonado
"I had a similar problem to yesterday where I lost power. It's a shame, as it was going well, I had strong pace, the strategy was good and I was looking good for a one-stop."

Jenson Button
"The first stint on the option was tough, so I moved to the prime early. I kept coming up on traffic, but I fought my way through and got down inside Fernando and Nico."

Sergio Pérez
"On the final lap, I was defending my position into Turn 1 when I got hit from behind. I'm OK, but I'm sad for the team, as the one-stop strategy was working well."

Daniel Ricciardo
"I was third, then it all happened in an exciting fashion. Once I got past Pérez, I knew I had to drive clean and get in Rosberg's DRS zone. From then on, it was awesome."

Lewis Hamilton
"I did the best that I could. We were managing the loss of power, but as soon as I made the jump on Nico in the second pit stop, my brakes failed going into Turn 10."

Kimi Räikkönen
"Early on, I had some brake problems. Then, after a few laps, the tyres behaved better, but still with highs and lows. For a lot of laps, I was stuck behind Kvyat."

Romain Grosjean
"Today wasn't great in terms of pace, but there are some positives looking forwards. We can see that a Renault Sport F1 team can win a race, so we have a target there."

Kevin Magnussen
"This race was a bit of a challenging and frustrating one. I was racing Vergne for a long time towards the end of the race, but I just didn't have the pace to get past."

Nico Hülkenberg
"I gained places at the end due to the crash between Sergio and Massa, but I lost one to Jenson when I was battling with Alonso. I was always going to score."

POSITIONS LAP BY LAP

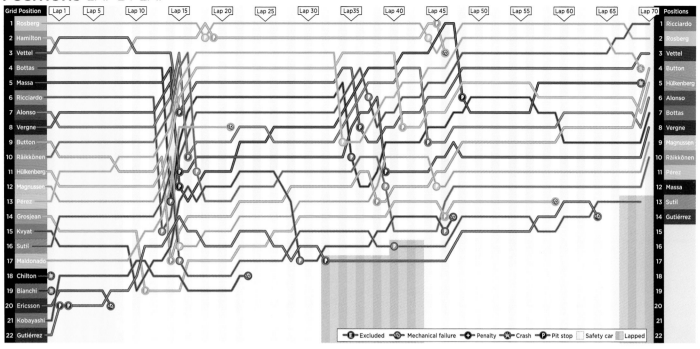

Grid Position															Positions
	Lap 1	Lap 5	Lap 10	Lap 15	Lap 20	Lap 25	Lap 30	Lap35	Lap 40	Lap 45	Lap 50	Lap 55	Lap 60	Lap 65	Lap 70	
1 Rosberg																1 Ricciardo
2 Hamilton																2 Rosberg
3 Vettel																3 Vettel
4 Bottas																4 Button
5 Massa																5 Hülkenberg
6 Ricciardo																6 Alonso
7 Alonso																7 Bottas
8 Vergne																8 Vergne
9 Button																9 Magnussen
10 Räikkönen																10 Räikkönen
11 Hülkenberg																11 Pérez
12 Magnussen																12 Massa
13 Pérez																13 Sutil
14 Grosjean																14 Gutiérrez
15 Kvyat																15
16 Sutil																16
17 Maldonado																17
18 Chilton																18
19 Bianchi																19
20 Ericsson																20
21 Kobayashi																21
22 Gutiérrez																22

Legend: **E** Excluded · Mechanical failure · Penalty · **K** Crash · **P** Pit stop · Safety car · Lapped

QUALIFYING 3

	Driver	Time
1	N Rosberg	1m14.874s
2	L Hamilton	1m14.953s
3	S Vettel	1m15.548s
4	V Bottas	1m15.550s
5	F Massa	1m15.578s
6	D Ricciardo	1m15.589s
7	F Alonso	1m15.814s
8	J-É Vergne	1m16.162s
9	J Button	1m16.182s
10	K Räikkönen	1m16.214s

GRID

	Driver	Time
1	N Rosberg	1m14.874s
2	L Hamilton	1m14.953s
3	S Vettel	1m15.548s
4	V Bottas	1m15.550s
5	F Massa	1m15.578s
6	D Ricciardo	1m15.589s
7	F Alonso	1m15.814s
8	J-É Vergne	1m16.162s
9	J Button	1m16.182s
10	K Räikkönen	1m16.214s
11	N Hülkenberg	1m16.300s
12	K Magnussen	1m16.310s
13	S Pérez	1m16.472s
14	R Grosjean	1m16.687s
15	D Kvyat	1m16.713s
16	A Sutil	1m17.314s
17	P Maldonado	1m18.328s
18	M Chilton	1m18.348s
19	J Bianchi	1m18.359s
20	M Ericsson	1m19.820s
21	K Kobayashi	1m19.278s
22	E Gutiérrez	no time

Grid penalties

K Kobayashi	5-place penalty for changing the gearbox
E Gutiérrez	Made to start from pits as car modified in parc fermé

RACE

	Driver	Car	Laps	Time	Av mph	Fastest	Stops
1	D Ricciardo	Red Bull-Renault RB10	70	1h39m12.830s	114.718	1m18.640s	2
2	N Rosberg	Mercedes F1 W05	70	1h39m17.066s	114.632	1m18.881s	2
3	S Vettel	Red Bull-Renault RB10	70	1h39m18.077s	114.612	1m19.171s	2
4	J Button	McLaren-Mercedes MP4-29	70	1h39m24.585s	114.487	1m18.759s	2
5	N Hülkenberg	Force India-Mercedes VJM07	70	1h39m25.673s	114.466	1m18.936s	1
6	F Alonso	Ferrari F14 T	70	1h39m27.699s	114.427	1m18.614s	2
7	V Bottas	Williams-Mercedes FW36	70	1h39m36.408s	114.261	1m19.321s	2
8	J-É Vergne	Toro Rosso-Renault ST9	70	1h39m40.856s	114.175	1m19.399s	2
9	K Magnussen	McLaren-Mercedes MP4-29	70	1h39m42.084s	114.152	1m18.819s	2
10	K Räikkönen	Ferrari F14 T	70	1h40m06.508s	113.688	1m18.529s	2
11	S Pérez	Force India-Mercedes VJM07	69	Collision	-	1m19.491s	1
12	F Massa	Williams-Mercedes FW36	69	Collision	-	1m18.504s	2
13	A Sutil	Sauber-Ferrari C33	69	1h39m29.355s	112.761	1m20.226s	2
14	E Gutiérrez	Sauber-Ferrari C33	64	Power unit	-	1m20.112s	3
R	R Grosjean	Lotus-Renault E22	59	Rear wing	-	1m19.650s	2
R	D Kvyat	Toro Rosso-Renault STR9	47	Transmission	-	1m19.978s	2
R	L Hamilton	Mercedes F1 W05	46	Brakes	-	1m18.942s	2
R	K Kobayashi	Caterham-Renault CT05	23	Suspension	-	1m23.130s	0
R	P Maldonado	Lotus-Renault E22	21	Power unit	-	1m21.514s	0
R	M Ericsson	Caterham-Renault CT05	7	Power unit	-	1m51.041s	0
R	M Chilton	Marussia-Ferrari MR03	0	Collision	-	-	0
R	J Bianchi	Marussia-Ferrari MR03	0	Collision	-	-	0

Fastest lap
F Massa 1m18.504s, 124.270mph, lap 58

Fastest speed trap
F Massa 215.678mph

Slowest speed trap
M Ericsson 161.121mph

Fastest pit stop
1 D Ricciardo 23.274s
2 S Vettel 23.340s
3 V Bottas 23.448s

CHAMPIONSHIP

	Driver	Pts
1	N Rosberg	140
2	L Hamilton	118
3	D Ricciardo	79
4	F Alonso	69
5	S Vettel	60
6	N Hülkenberg	57
7	J Button	43
8	V Bottas	40
9	K Magnussen	23
10	S Pérez	20
11	F Massa	18
12	K Räikkönen	18
13	R Grosjean	8
14	J-É Vergne	8
15	D Kvyat	4
16	J Bianchi	2

CONSTRUCTORS

	Team	Pts
1	Mercedes	258
2	Red Bull-Renault	139
3	Ferrari	87
4	Force India-Mercedes	77
5	McLaren-Mercedes	66
6	Williams-Mercedes	58
7	Toro Rosso-Renault	12
8	Lotus-Renault	8
9	Marussia-Ferrari	2

Esteban Gutiérrez

"It was very challenging early on, as I was struggling with my tyres. When I pitted, I got a fresh set of softs, which felt way better, but then I lost power and had to retire."

Jean-Éric Vergne

"It was maybe the best race of my F1 career, as everything went perfectly and I scored again. I was able to gain a place on Alonso after a good start and later kept Magnussen behind."

Felipe Massa

"I'm happy that I'm here with no problems, but I'm disappointed for what happened with Pérez on the last lap and also for the pit stop, as I think we could even have fought for victory."

Max Chilton

"I had a good start, pulled away from the cars behind into Turn 1, queued into Turn 2, then Jules and I had a coming together into Turn 3. The resulting accident was unfortunate."

Marcus Ericsson

"As soon as the formation lap started, I could feel that the power unit wasn't pulling hard in any of the gears. The team tried to fix it, but there wasn't anything that we could do."

Adrian Sutil

"It was a long race with many incidents. I was able to keep out of all the trouble from start to finish. Hence, I'm satisfied with my own performance, but all this led only to 13th."

Daniil Kvyat

"At the start, I lost a position and later on made a mistake in Turn 1 when my tyres were cold. At this point, my race was compromised and then I had to stop when I lost drive."

Valtteri Bottas

"Red Bull was a little bit stronger than expected, so we were looking to fight for fourth. After my second stop, I didn't come back out where I should have and was then in traffic."

Jules Bianchi

"At the start, I kept everyone behind me. Max and I were racing each other through Turns 2 and 3. I braked into Turn 3 and there was an impact, then I ended up in the wall."

Kamui Kobayashi

"I managed to avoid the debris from the Marussia crash. Later, I felt a problem with the rear coming out of Turn 2 and had to stop the car. It turned out to be a rear suspension problem."

AUSTR

ROUND 8 GROSSER PREIS VON ÖSTERREICH

A

NICO ROSBERG PIPPED
LEWIS HAMILTON AS
MERCEDES SCORED
A ONE-TWO ON RED
BULL'S HOME PATCH IN
AUSTRIA. HOWEVER,
IT WAS FAR FROM
STRAIGHTFORWARD FOR
THE SILVER ARROWS

T he reason that Mercedes had to push so hard was that customer team Williams kept the championship leaders on their toes. Indeed, in a race unfettered by safety cars, third-placed Valtteri Bottas finished just 8.1s behind the winner.

Both Mercedes drivers had to keep an eye on brake and power unit temperatures in the hot conditions which, following their ERS problems in the Canadian GP, was another sign that the W05 wasn't infallible.

Everyone was delighted to be back in Austria and it was perhaps appropriate that pole position went to one of the few drivers who had raced in the previous incarnation of the event. Felipe Massa earned the top spot as Williams swept the front row and the usually dominant Mercedes faltered.

Two key factors had an impact on the session. First, it was important to get the tyres up to temperature and working well from the start of the lap, which Williams had worked on hard. Second, the FIA clamped down on drivers running wide at Turn 8, the penultimate corner. Anyone who put all four wheels beyond the white line had that time cancelled.

That's exactly what happened to Hamilton, who lost his time from the first run in Q3 and had to rely on his second attempt. Alas, he spun at Turn 2 – and the yellow flags he triggered forced teammate Nico Rosberg to back off and abandon his second attempt. Rosberg now knew how Hamilton felt when he had his crucial run ruined in Monaco, although in that case the man who brought out the flags had pole in his pocket already...

Williams thus secured a popular front row. A delighted Massa would start alongside teammate Valtteri Bottas, who was quickest on the first runs in Q3 but made a mistake on the crucial final run.

Behind Rosberg, Fernando Alonso claimed fourth spot, the Ferrari driver having survived a trip across the grass at the exit of the last corner early in Q3. Montreal winner Daniel Ricciardo qualified fifth after another solid performance. Once again, he humbled teammate Sebastian Vettel, who didn't make Q3.

Kevin Magnussen bounced back from recent disappointments to qualify sixth for McLaren, lining up ahead of STR's Daniil Kvyat. Kimi Räikkönen was eighth, while Hamilton moved up to ninth despite not setting a time, as Nico Hülkenberg had his lap disallowed for going wide at Turn 8. The Force India driver thus dropped to 10th.

Hülkenberg's teammate Sergio Pérez just missed out on Q3 when he took 11th place. However, thanks to the five-place grid penalty he incurred in Montreal, which was upheld after being revisited by the FIA stewards in Austria, he dropped down to 16th. The 11th grid slot instead went to Jenson Button, who was unable to match his teammate's pace, while Vettel was back in lowly 12th.

Massa led Bottas and Rosberg at the start, while there was a little confusion behind as Ricciardo was forced wide. The big question was how long Hamilton would take to make his way up from ninth. We soon got the answer.

> "HAMILTON SPUN AT TURN 2 AND THE FLAGS HE TRIGGERED FORCED ROSBERG TO BACK OFF"

A good getaway off the line and an aggressive first lap saw him charge through and by the end of the first circuit he was in a remarkable fourth. Rosberg must have been stunned to see a familiar silver car in his mirrors so early, given the six-place gap between them on the grid. It was clear we had an intriguing contest on our hands.

Meanwhile, the race quickly turned into a disaster for Vettel and Red Bull. Having made no progress from 12th on the second lap, the German slowed and coasted to a halt on track. He eventually got going again after some frantic re-setting on the steering wheel, but he was already a lap down.

The Williams drivers were able to stay ahead until the first stops, which shuffled the pack. Rosberg came in early on lap 11; he was followed by Hamilton on lap 13 and Massa on lap 14. After leading briefly, Bottas came in on lap 15.

Massa leads into the first corner, with Nico Rosberg having made the most of a great start to get past Valtteri Bottas. **Right:** Massa celebrates his pole position with Sir Frank Williams. **Middle right:** Rosberg holds off Lewis Hamilton. **Bottom right:** Pit stop time for Kevin Magnussen

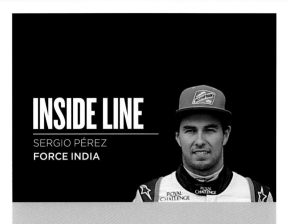

INSIDE LINE

SERGIO PÉREZ
FORCE INDIA

This was a good, solid race for us, really strong. I'm just a bit disappointed about the grid penalty from Montreal. Without it, who knows what could have happened?

"We went to show all the evidence we had – the data, the line, the pictures we couldn't show in Montreal. For that reason, we felt very confident that we had the proof. The stewards looked to be quite sensible and agreed to an extent with everything I said, but in the end the situation didn't change at all.

"I think we had the pace to fight for a podium, so it's a bit unfortunate on that side, but I'm happy we did a good job. I'm satisfied with the job the team did, I just feel a bit sorry for my guys that we got a penalty. We also had a problem with the engine mode in qualifying, so we didn't have the qualifying mode on my quickest laps. It's always those little details. We had the pace to qualify in the top 10, but we didn't.

"IT WAS KEY TO GET BUTTON AT THE START. I ENJOYED LEADING, BUT I KNEW THAT WASN'T OUR POSITION AT THAT TIME"

"We deserved more points, but, considering where we started, I think we made the most of the race. Starting on the prime tyre, it was key to get Jenson Button at the start of the race. I enjoyed leading, but I knew that wasn't our position at that time. In the end, I'm just happy that we got the points.

"In the past couple of races, we've done really well, apart from Monaco, where we didn't have the opportunity. It's just unfortunate that we've been unlucky, for example in Montreal where we were close to winning. We're getting there, that's the positive thing. We just have to keep doing what we do, but we don't have quite the downforce levels of Williams."

TALKING POINT
A RETURN FULL OF CHARACTER

F1's return to Austria after 11 years provided a boost at a time when there were concerns over the sport's connection with its fanbase. We were back at an old-school European venue, one with an F1 history that stretches back to 1970 – or 1964, if you count the grand prix held at the nearby Zeltweg Air Base.

The circuit formerly called the Österreichring and the A1-Ring is now named after owner Red Bull. The drinks company was the force behind the return of the race, and a giant bull statue located in the infield provided a reminder.

Good promotion ensured a full house and fans enjoyed extras such as air displays and demo runs by past Austrian heroes. The sight of Niki Lauda lapping in a Ferrari 312T2 was a highlight.

Apart from details such as kerbs, the track hadn't changed at all since it last hosted a grand prix in 2003, but the pit buildings and main grandstand structure were new and state of the art. The upgrades helped make the Red Bull Ring a top-class facility for the 21st century.

The good news was that the venue's overall character was similar to that in 1970, with trees and grassy hillsides still surrounding the track. The views were superb, and many spectators opted to stay in the busy campsites, where the partying continued into the night.

Given the good vibes generated by Red Bull, it was ironic that its team suffered its worst race in some time. Sebastian Vettel posted his third retirement of the year after losing a lap due to an electronic glitch, while Daniel Ricciardo could manage only eighth place. Team boss Christian Horner made clear his frustration at Renault's ongoing unreliability and poor performance.

"There needs to be change at Renault because it can't continue like this," he said. "We need to work together as partners, as there won't be another engine in the back of the car next year. We want to be competitive, we want to run at the front and these kinds of issues can't and shouldn't happen. It's not our business, it's not our responsibility, we're the end user. It's just frustrating that the product isn't working."

> "FANS ENJOYED EXTRAS SUCH AS AIR DISPLAYS AND DEMO RUNS BY PAST AUSTRIAN HEROES. NIKI LAUDA LAPPING IN A FERRARI WAS A HIGHLIGHT"

Massa was the big loser in all this and Rosberg the winner. He was now in front of Bottas, Hamilton and a frustrated Massa, with the erstwhile race leader at a loss to understand how he had tumbled down to fourth place in this group. However, he was in fact only fifth, as all four drivers found themselves stuck behind Pérez's Force India, which had, as mentioned, started a penalised 16th and had yet to stop.

One of several drivers to have started on the soft rather than supersoft tyre, the Mexican was able to run an extra long first stint and he stayed out resolutely as the supersoft runners came in. Indeed, he remained ahead for a good 11 laps before the performance of his tyres finally dropped off.

Rosberg overtook him for the lead on lap 27 and was quickly followed by Bottas and, a lap after that, Hamilton. After Massa passed him, Pérez finally came in on lap 29.

At the second round of pit stops, Mercedes again did a better job than Williams. Hamilton was the first to come in, on lap 39, and he was followed in by Rosberg on lap 40 and then Bottas – who again led briefly – on lap 41. Thanks to a charge on fresh rubber, Hamilton was able to jump the Finn.

Massa was the last of the top four to pit, staying out until lap 43, so he enjoyed a brief return to the lead. As at the first pit stops, the lead now passed to someone operating a different strategy – in this case Alonso, who had been running in fifth. The Ferrari ace

Far left: Valtteri Bottas was able to keep Lewis Hamilton behind him until the second round of pit stops. **Above left:** Jenson Button in a rare moment when he wasn't caught in traffic. **Left:** Daniel Ricciardo was Red Bull's only finisher, in eighth place

stayed out front for some five laps before he finally came in on lap 47.

Now we had a familiar scenario, with the two Mercedes drivers running together on track. For 30 laps after their final stops, Hamilton chased Rosberg, albeit without ever really being in a position to pull off a pass. The gap stabilised at 1.5-2s, before Hamilton closed up over the last few laps and it looked as though things might get interesting.

Both drivers had to keep an eye on their equipment and it was a far from easy race for either of them or for the team to manage from the pit wall. Despite a big lock up on the last lap, Rosberg crossed the line safely in front to register his third win of the year and further extend his championship lead.

"ROSBERG MUST HAVE BEEN STUNNED TO SEE A FAMILIAR SILVER CAR IN HIS MIRRORS SO EARLY"

"I knew pre-race that even if I am third after the start, the chances are still very good to make it and win," said Rosberg. "We have just a little bit more pace and less tyre degradation than the Williams – we expected to have less, at least – so we could go aggressive on the stops, and that's what we did and it worked out really well."

Hamilton admitted his brakes had been marginal. "I was following people all the time, so that's not always the best, but unfortunately I was being told to back off quite a lot," he said. "I tried to eke it up a little bit more in the last couple of laps, but I still had to be cautious. I'm just grateful I finished, as I didn't finish the last race, and that's got to be the goal for the next few races – trying to actually finish."

Bottas did well to bring his car home third and stay respectably close to Hamilton to earn the first podium of his career. Massa fell away in the latter part of the race, but still claimed fourth.

"I think that from all the data we had from practice, we knew the race was going to be difficult," said Bottas. "Overall, Mercedes have still got the quickest car. We really nailed it yesterday, so we knew that maybe today could be difficult. Actually, it was a bit better than I expected, as we were really close to them on pace."

Once again, Alonso flattered the Ferrari F14 T with a strong drive to fifth place, even leading for four laps when he made his second pit stop later than those ahead. However, on a track where power was key, he had no chance of doing any better.

Pérez's strategy played out with sixth place, after a late charge on the option tyres helped him to take the position from McLaren's Magnussen. Ricciardo lost a lot of ground when he ran wide at the start, but he recovered to eighth place, overtaking Hülkenberg on the final lap, the German being hampered by an energy-store issue.

Räikkönen struggled with brake and handling problems, and his first stop came too late in the race, as his tyres were done. He eventually finished a lowly 10th. Like Pérez, Button started on the soft tyres and ran a long first stint, but he lost several positions by being pushed wide on the race's opening lap, which cost him dearly: he finished just out of the points in 11th.

Kvyat also lost several positions at the start, but the Russian still looked set to bring home some points before a rear suspension problem and tyre failure led to a spectacular retirement on lap 25.

Meanwhile, it was a disastrous day for Vettel. While trying to make up ground after his early delay, the World Champion crunched his nose on Esteban Gutiérrez's rear wheel. Having lost so much time, the team decided to retire the car just before half distance. It could not have happened at a worse venue.

"BOTTAS DID WELL TO BRING HIS CAR HOME THIRD AND STAY RESPECTABLY CLOSE TO HAMILTON"

Nico Rosberg shows his delight at having held off teammate Hamilton for his third win of 2014. **Below:** the Williams team celebrates Valtteri Bottas' first podium

19 FELIPE MASSA

77 VALTTERI BOTTAS

CLOCKWISE FROM RIGHT: Sebastian Vettel poses with Austrian F1 veterans Niki Lauda, Gerhard Berger and Helmut Marko; Jenson Button listens in with race engineer Dave Robson; Red Bull lines up a great show; Caterham's Kamui Kobayashi in his "office"; rubber pick-up; girls in traditional Austrian dress add to the scene; Felipe Massa climbs out of his pole-placed Williams FW36 on the grid; a giant bull overlooks the Red Bull Ring

SNAPSHOT FROM AUSTRIA

AUSTRIA
RED BULL RING

ROUND 8

RACE DATE 22 June

CIRCUIT LENGTH 2.688 miles

NO. OF LAPS 71

RACE DISTANCE 190.848 miles

WEATHER Sunny, 22°C

TRACK TEMP 44°C

LAP RECORD Michael Schumacher, 1m08.337s, 141.606mph, 2003

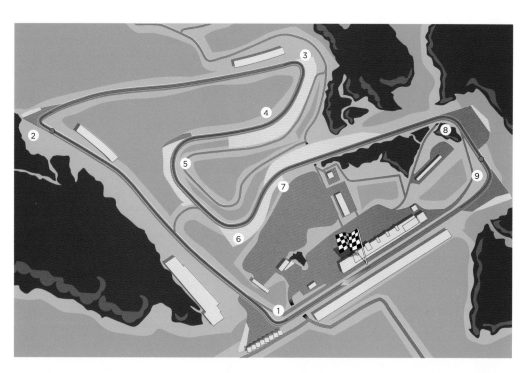

	PRACTICE 1				PRACTICE 2				PRACTICE 3				QUALIFYING 1			QUALIFYING 2	
	Driver	Time	Laps		Driver	Time	Laps		Driver	Time	Laps		Driver	Time		Driver	Time
1	N Rosberg	1m11.295s	19	1	L Hamilton	1m09.542s	37	1	V Bottas	1m09.848s	22	1	L Hamilton	1m09.514s	1	N Rosberg	1m08.974s
2	L Hamilton	1m11.435s	32	2	N Rosberg	1m09.919s	50	2	L Hamilton	1m09.898s	25	2	D Kvyat	1m09.678s	2	L Hamilton	1m09.092s
3	F Alonso	1m11.606s	23	3	F Alonso	1m10.470s	40	3	F Massa	1m09.901s	21	3	N Rosberg	1m09.695s	3	V Bottas	1m09.096s
4	F Massa	1m11.756s	27	4	V Bottas	1m10.519s	44	4	D Kvyat	1m09.927s	25	4	K Magnussen	1m10.081s	4	F Massa	1m09.239s
5	J Button	1m11.839s	33	5	F Massa	1m10.521s	39	5	N Rosberg	1m09.999s	31	5	S Pérez	1m10.124s	5	K Magnussen	1m09.473s
6	S Pérez	1m12.009s	33	6	S Vettel	1m10.807s	39	6	F Alonso	1m10.054s	17	6	J-É Vergne	1m10.161s	6	F Alonso	1m09.479s
7	N Hülkenberg	1m12.072s	20	7	J Button	1m10.813s	44	7	D Ricciardo	1m10.392s	19	7	J Button	1m10.252s	7	D Kvyat	1m09.490s
8	V Bottas	1m12.114s	21	8	D Ricciardo	1m10.920s	36	8	K Magnussen	1m10.449s	23	8	K Räikkönen	1m10.285s	8	N Hülkenberg	1m09.624s
9	K Magnussen	1m12.313s	36	9	K Magnussen	1m10.936s	45	9	K Räikkönen	1m10.488s	22	9	F Massa	1m10.292s	9	D Ricciardo	1m09.638s
10	J-É Vergne	1m12.364s	30	10	J-É Vergne	1m10.972s	39	10	S Vettel	1m10.562s	21	10	N Rosberg	1m10.356s	10	K Räikkönen	1m09.657s
11	K Räikkönen	1m12.365s	21	11	K Räikkönen	1m10.974s	45	11	N Hülkenberg	1m10.683s	22	11	N Hülkenberg	1m10.389s	11	S Pérez	1m09.754s
12	D Kvyat	1m12.372s	35	12	D Kvyat	1m11.261s	45	12	P Maldonado	1m10.776s	26	12	D Ricciardo	1m10.395s	12	J Button	1m09.780s
13	D Ricciardo	1m12.570s	28	13	S Pérez	1m11.296s	36	13	J-É Vergne	1m11.043s	22	13	F Alonso	1m10.405s	13	S Vettel	1m09.801s
14	E Gutiérrez	1m12.984s	29	14	E Gutiérrez	1m11.491s	42	14	R Grosjean	1m11.103s	22	14	R Grosjean	1m10.461s	14	P Maldonado	1m09.939s
15	S Vettel	1m12.988s	25	15	P Maldonado	1m11.765s	30	15	S Pérez	1m11.235s	18	15	S Vettel	1m10.630s	15	J-É Vergne	1m10.073s
16	R Grosjean	1m13.168s	28	16	A Sutil	1m11.806s	42	16	A Sutil	1m11.294s	24	16	P Maldonado	1m10.821s	16	R Grosjean	1m10.642s
17	P Maldonado	1m13.642s	27	17	N Hülkenberg	1m11.935s	39	17	E Gutiérrez	1m11.558s	23	17	A Sutil	1m10.825s			
18	J Bianchi	1m13.738s	26	18	M Chilton	1m12.229s	43	18	J Bianchi	1m11.848s	21	18	E Gutiérrez	1m11.349s			
19	M Chilton	1m13.857s	28	19	R Grosjean	1m12.262s	46	19	K Kobayashi	1m12.320s	23	19	J Bianchi	1m11.412s			
20	K Kobayashi	1m14.611s	24	20	J Bianchi	1m12.279s	36	20	M Ericsson	1m12.892s	27	20	K Kobayashi	1m11.673s			
21	A Sutil	1m14.691s	9	21	K Kobayashi	1m12.937s	24	21	M Chilton	1m12.915s	14	21	M Chilton	1m11.775s			
22	M Ericsson	1m17.501s	8	22	M Ericsson	1m13.596s	48	22	J Button	1m14.237s	4	22	M Ericsson	1m12.673s			

Best sectors – Practice				Speed trap – Practice				Best sectors – Qualifying				Speed trap – Qualifying		
Sec 1	N Rosberg	17.182s	1	N Rosberg	198.652mph		Sec 1	L Hamilton	16.957s	1	F Massa	203.499mph		
Sec 2	L Hamilton	30.647s	2	N Hülkenberg	198.031mph		Sec 2	L Hamilton	30.113s	2	V Bottas	200.765mph		
Sec 3	L Hamilton	21.490s	3	F Massa	197.782mph		Sec 3	N Rosberg	21.296s	3	S Pérez	220.516mph		

 **Sebastian Vettel**

"I retired as we wanted to save engine mileage. Obviously, it has been a bad first half of the season, with a few retirements and other problems, but I guess it's part of the game."

 Nico Rosberg

"We chose the aggressive way, to pit earlier and to pass the Williams that way, and that worked well. I had to look after my brakes, which was a big job all race."

Fernando Alonso

"I can consider this to be my best race of the season, as finishing 18s off the Mercedes in a race without a safety car or any particular incidents is a good result."

 **Pastor Maldonado**

"We're losing time in the low-speed corners. Annoyingly, I had brake issues from very early on, so I wasn't able to fight, even though it was nice to be running in the top 10."

Jenson Button

"Nico pushed me wide out of Turn 1, so I lost two places. From then on, my race was all about waiting for people ahead to pit and trying to make my strategy work."

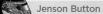 **Sergio Pérez**

"My only regret is that, without the penalty, I'd have been further up the grid, which would have made a big difference, as we had the pace to fight for a podium."

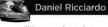 Daniel Ricciardo

"It's never nice going backwards on lap one. From then on, I tried to catch up, but just didn't have much pace. It wasn't until the last bit that I was able to pass Hülkenberg."

Lewis Hamilton

"After qualifying, this was all about damage limitation, so I'm as happy as I can be with a P2 finish. I had the pace in the car but wasn't able to capitalise on that."

Kimi Räikkönen

"On lap 2, I began to have a brake overheating problem. This meant I had to slow. At the time of my first stop, my tyres were dead. On my in-lap alone, I lost two places."

 Romain Grosjean

"I had various issues during the race to add to our struggle for performance, so it was a challenge. I stopped early for soft tyres, but soon experienced graining."

Kevin Magnussen

"I really thought I was going to finish sixth, but Checo [Pérez] had too much pace at the end. That wasn't great, but it's positive that we're making improvements."

  Nico Hülkenberg

"I struggled for balance, but had some good battles, especially with Ricciardo on the final lap. I was fighting hard to keep him behind, but he had a tyre advantage."

POSITIONS LAP BY LAP

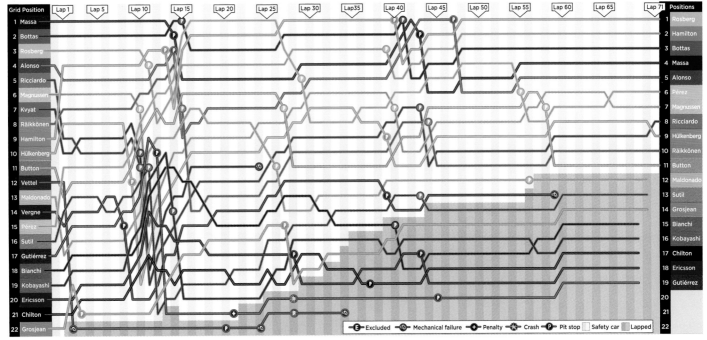

Grid Position	Lap 1	Lap 5	Lap 10	Lap 15	Lap 20	Lap 25	Lap 30	Lap 35	Lap 40	Lap 45	Lap 50	Lap 55	Lap 60	Lap 65	Lap 71	Positions
1 Massa																1 Rosberg
2 Bottas																2 Hamilton
3 Rosberg																3 Bottas
4 Alonso																4 Massa
5 Ricciardo																5 Alonso
6 Magnussen																6 Pérez
7 Kvyat																7 Magnussen
8 Räikkönen																8 Ricciardo
9 Hamilton																9 Hülkenberg
10 Hülkenberg																10 Räikkönen
11 Button																11 Button
12 Vettel																12 Maldonado
13 Maldonado																13 Sutil
14 Vergne																14 Grosjean
15 Pérez																15 Bianchi
16 Sutil																16 Kobayashi
17 Gutiérrez																17 Chilton
18 Bianchi																18 Ericsson
19 Kobayashi																19 Gutiérrez
20 Ericsson																20
21 Chilton																21
22 Grosjean																22

E- Excluded Mechanical failure Penalty Crash P- Pit stop Safety car Lapped

QUALIFYING 3

	Driver	Time
1	F Massa	1m08.759s
2	V Bottas	1m08.846s
3	N Rosberg	1m08.944s
4	F Alonso	1m09.285s
5	D Ricciardo	1m09.466s
6	K Magnussen	1m09.515s
7	D Kvyat	1m09.619s
8	K Räikkönen	1m10.795s
9	L Hamilton	no time
10	N Hülkenberg	no time

GRID

	Driver	Time
1	F Massa	1m08.759s
2	V Bottas	1m08.846s
3	N Rosberg	1m08.944s
4	F Alonso	1m09.285s
5	D Ricciardo	1m09.466s
6	K Magnussen	1m09.515s
7	D Kvyat	1m09.619s
8	K Räikkönen	1m10.795s
9	L Hamilton	no time
10	N Hülkenberg	no time
11	J Button	1m09.780s
12	S Vettel	1m09.801s
13	P Maldonado	1m09.939s
14	J-É Vergne	1m10.073s
15	S Pérez	1m09.754s
16	A Sutil	1m10.825s
17	E Gutiérrez	1m11.349s
18	J Bianchi	1m11.412s
19	K Kobayashi	1m11.673s
20	M Ericsson	1m12.673s
21	M Chilton	1m11.775s
22	R Grosjean	1m10.642s

Grid penalties

M Chilton	3-place penalty for collision in Canadian GP
S Pérez	5-place penalty for collision in Canadian GP
R Grosjean	Made to start from pit lane for changing gearbox

RACE

	Driver	Car	Laps	Time	Av mph	Fastest	Stops
1	N Rosberg	Mercedes F1 W05	71	1h27m54.976s	130.197	1m12.598s	2
2	L Hamilton	Mercedes F1 W05	71	1h27m56.908s	130.148	1m12.217s	2
3	V Bottas	Williams-Mercedes FW36	71	1h28m03.148s	129.995	1m12.581s	2
4	F Massa	Williams-Mercedes FW36	71	1h28m12.334s	129.769	1m12.586s	2
5	F Alonso	Ferrari F14 T	71	1h28m13.529s	129.740	1m12.595s	2
6	S Pérez	Force India-Mercedes VJM07	71	1h28m23.522s	129.495	1m12.142s	2
7	K Magnussen	McLaren-Mercedes MP4-29	71	1h28m27.007s	129.410	1m12.746s	2
8	D Ricciardo	Red Bull-Renault RB10	71	1h28m38.498s	129.131	1m13.060s	2
9	N Hülkenberg	Force India-Mercedes VJM07	71	1h28m39.113s	129.116	1m13.156s	2
10	K Räikkönen	Ferrari F14 T	71	1h28m42.753s	129.027	1m12.884s	2
11	J Button	McLaren-Mercedes MP4-29	71	1h28m45.942s	128.950	1m12.858s	2
12	P Maldonado	Lotus-Renault E22	70	1h28m08.413s	128.035	1m13.187s	2
13	A Sutil	Sauber-Ferrari C33	70	1h28m34.751s	127.401	1m13.709s	2
14	R Grosjean	Lotus-Renault E22	70	1h29m09.548s	126.572	1m13.953s	2
15	J Bianchi	Marussia-Ferrari MR03	69	1h27m59.668s	126.415	1m14.476s	1
16	K Kobayashi	Caterham-Renault CT05	69	1h28m31.645s	125.653	1m15.274s	1
17	M Chilton	Marussia-Ferrari MR03	69	1h28m33.756s	125.604	1m14.847s	1
18	M Ericsson	Caterham-Renault CT05	69	1h28m41.191s	125.428	1m14.672s	2
19	E Gutiérrez	Sauber-Ferrari C33	69	1h28m41.483s	125.421	1m14.036s	3
R	J-É Vergne	Toro Rosso-Renault STR9	59	Brakes	-	1m13.317s	2
R	S Vettel	Red Bull-Renault RB10	34	Pulled out	-	1m14.254s	2
R	D Kvyat	Toro Rosso-Renault STR9	24	Suspension	-	1m14.332s	1

Fastest lap
S Pérez 1m12.142s, 134.138mph, lap 59

Fastest speed trap
F Massa 199.708mph

Slowest speed trap
J Bianchi 180.782mph

Fastest pit stop
1	V Bottas	21.133s
2	F Alonso	21.234s
3	J Button	21.242s

CHAMPIONSHIP

	Driver	Pts
1	N Rosberg	165
2	L Hamilton	136
3	D Ricciardo	83
4	F Alonso	79
5	S Vettel	60
6	N Hülkenberg	59
7	V Bottas	55
8	J Button	43
9	F Massa	30
10	K Magnussen	29
11	S Pérez	28
12	K Räikkönen	19
13	R Grosjean	8
14	J-É Vergne	8
15	D Kvyat	4
16	J Bianchi	2

CONSTRUCTORS

	Team	Pts
1	Mercedes	301
2	Red Bull-Renault	143
3	Ferrari	98
4	Force India-Mercedes	87
5	Williams-Mercedes	85
6	McLaren-Mercedes	72
7	Toro Rosso-Renault	12
8	Lotus-Renault	8
9	Marussia-Ferrari	2

Esteban Gutiérrez
"We made a mistake during the first stop, as the wheel nut on the right rear wheel wasn't secured, so my mechanics had to pull me back. Afterwards, I got a 10s stop-and-go penalty."

Jean-Éric Vergne
"I struggled with the brakes from the start. It's hard to drive the car with such a considerable rear locking. It's not good for tyre life or for the balance, so it was really a tricky race."

Felipe Massa
"We had a good fight with the Mercedes, but it was clear we were never going to win. To stop first and come out fourth is a bit disappointing, but that's racing."

Max Chilton
"I had a very good strategy that enabled me to keep Ericsson behind in the latter stages of the race, but unfortunately I just ran out of laps as the gap came down to only 2s."

Marcus Ericsson
"I had passed a couple of cars at the start, but we planned to stretch the first stint to lap 28 so I didn't defend. Sadly, I had to extend the second stop by 4s due to a Ferrari in the fast lane."

Adrian Sutil
"Up to lap 15, it all went to plan. Suddenly, I got the instruction to stop straight away. However, the message wasn't for me but for Esteban, and this cost me time."

Daniil Kvyat
"I lost a few places at the start, but I managed to get one back. From then on, I was able to push hard, but around lap 26 I saw my rear right tyre blow up and I was forced to stop."

Valtteri Bottas
"I had one pit stop that really put in me in the fight and changed my race. I had put in a good lap before that, so I got in front of Felipe and from there I could manage my pace."

Jules Bianchi
"It wasn't easy trying to make our one-stop strategy work, but I kept everyone behind me until it wasn't possible to keep pace with the supersoft tyre and Kobayashi was able to get by."

Kamui Kobayashi
"As soon as it became clear Bianchi was stopping once, I switched strategy during the second stint, which meant I had to manage that set of softs for the final 55 laps."

ROUND 9
GREAT BRITAIN

SANTANDER BRITISH GRAND PRIX

LEWIS HAMILTON GOT HIS TITLE CHALLENGE BACK ON TRACK WITH
A POPULAR VICTORY TO END A RECENT RUN OF DISAPPOINTMENT
THAT HAD EXTENDED TO A FRUSTRATING QUALIFYING SESSION

Top: Nico Rosberg leads the way into Luffield for Mercedes on the opening lap, ahead of McLaren's Jenson Button and Kevin Magnussen, with Hamilton fourth. **Top right:** Nico Hülkenberg keeps Fernando Alonso and Daniel Ricciardo at bay early in the race. **Middle right:** Valtteri Bottas was eliminated in Q1, along with Williams teammate Felipe Massa and both Ferrari drivers. **Above:** Ricciardo made it through Q1 but only scraped into Q3, in which he ended up only eighth after not going out for a final run and losing four positions by doing so

A lthough Lewis Hamilton managed to turn recent trials into triumph, it was a bad day for his teammate Nico Rosberg, the German retiring from the lead with a gearbox problem – and seeing his championship lead cut to just four points.

Rosberg took pole, but that familiar outcome was the only thing that was straightforward about a rain-affected qualifying session. An hour of high drama saw Hamilton tumble from first place to sixth in the dying seconds and the Ferrari drivers left stranded in 19th and 20th on the timesheets.

The first session started in wet conditions but, in the closing minutes, the track dried sufficiently for slicks, with the Marussia drivers, Jenson Button and Kamui Kobayashi the first to venture out.

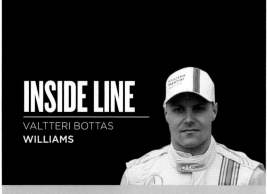

INSIDE LINE

VALTTERI BOTTAS
WILLIAMS

We knew that this race could be good fun. We knew that we had a quick car. Maybe it was a bit surprisingly quick today but, since the pace was good from the first stint and from the first lap, I was able to cut through the field. Of course, it sometimes needed a bit of risk because it's really important to get through quickly and not get stuck behind people.

"I managed to get to where the pace of the car was. I'm just really happy with what we've been doing as a team and my race pace shows we're doing the right things.

"Our prediction was that Mercedes was going to be strong. We also thought that Red Bull would be a bit quicker than us in the race and that Ferrari would be close to our pace. So, we knew that it wasn't going to be that easy to score good points. We weren't really thinking about the podium, we were just thinking about scoring some points, and it was a positive surprise in the early laps of the race.

"WE'RE DEFINITELY A STRONGER TEAM THAN WE WERE IN MELBOURNE. IT'S DIFFICULT TO COMPARE TO TWO YEARS AGO OR EVEN TO LAST YEAR"

"Tyre life wasn't really a limitation, so we could do our strategy. I have to say the strategy guys did a really good job and we switched the strategy during the running, as we saw the tyre wear was so low.

"We're definitely a stronger team than we were in Melbourne. It's difficult to compare to two years ago or even to last year. I think we're really getting stronger all the time. It's not going to be easy to be on the podium in every race as I think this season is going to be quite race-by-race in nature, but we're definitely going in the right direction."

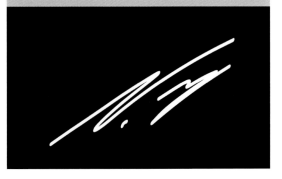

It was soon obvious that they had made the right call and a mad dash into the pit lane followed.

Many drivers were left with only one lap, which was then ruined by a return of the rain and yellow flags after Fernando Alonso spun and Adrian Sutil went into the gravel. That left us with a mixed-up order led by Rosberg, with Jules Bianchi and Max Chilton in fourth and sixth for Marussia.

But the real news was at the bottom of the timing screens. The Red Bulls of Daniel Ricciardo and Sebastian Vettel just sneaked through in 15th and 16th, but both Williams drivers and both Ferrari drivers were out, with Valtteri Bottas ahead of Felipe Massa, Alonso and Kimi Räikkönen.

After the second shower, Q2 began on intermediate tyres before once again the track dried and everyone switched to slicks. Hamilton and Rosberg topped the times, while the first driver to miss out on Q3, in 11th, was Romain Grosjean. Bianchi and Chilton did superbly to qualify 12th and 13th, but the Englishman had to add a five-place grid penalty for a gearbox change.

The third session proved just as dramatic. It was dry at the start, wet in the middle and then it began to dry again at the end. However, it wasn't obvious that the track was going to be any better on the crucial final lap and, indeed, neither Ricciardo nor the Toro Rosso drivers bothered to go out again as they sat in a provisional fourth, fifth and sixth.

Feeling that he had secured pole, Hamilton decided to abort early in his final lap, but others decided to go for it – which proved to be a wise decision as the final sector of the lap was dry. So, in the closing seconds, the order was scrambled and the now helpless Hamilton slipped

TALKING POINT
RÄIKKÖNEN HITS A NEW LOW

Kimi Räikkönen's crash at Silverstone seemed to sum up the Finn's disappointing season on his return to Ferrari after two superb years at Lotus.

Starting well down the grid after both he and teammate Fernando Alonso were caught out in a rain-hit session, Kimi ran wide out of Aintree on lap 1 and lost control on the grass as he tried to regain the track. He then had a spectacular impact with the barrier, from which he was fortunate to emerge with just bruising.

Kimi is famous for his refusal to do the track walks that other drivers undertake on Thursdays with their engineers and cynics were quick to point out that, had he made the effort. he might have spotted the bumpy run-off. It was a little unfair, but it reflected the widespread perception that Kimi wasn't getting the job done as we approached the halfway mark of the season.

> "KIMI RAN WIDE OUT OF AINTREE AND LOST CONTROL AS HE TRIED TO REGAIN THE TRACK. HE THEN HAD A SPECTACULAR IMPACT WITH THE BARRIER"

All year, Kimi had struggled to come to terms with the F14 T, a car that simply didn't suit his driving style, and which even the more adaptable Alonso didn't enjoy driving. Nevertheless, the irrepressible Spaniard had, as always, extracted the maximum potential out of it on any given day. It said a lot that he left Silverstone with 87 points, while Kimi had just 19.

Ferrari brought Kimi back because they saw him as a ruthless points-gathering machine, but things simply hadn't gelled. The Finn has a two-year contract, but when he intimated at Silverstone that he might not race beyond that, it led to speculation about whether that mindset – what appeared to be a countdown to retirement – was what Ferrari needed.

As a result of the shunt, Kimi missed the following week's Silverstone test, where he could have run useful mileage. He was replaced by Marussia's Jules Bianchi, a reminder that Ferrari had a talented protegé waiting in the wings.

By now, Stefano Domenicali, the man who got Kimi back to Ferrari, was long gone, but new team boss Marco Mattiacci insisted that the team was fully behind its man and that both drivers would stay on in 2015.

down to sixth as Rosberg, Sebastian Vettel, Button, Nico Hülkenberg and Kevin Magnussen claimed the top five places on the grid.

Sergio Pérez caught the chequered flag at the start of his final lap and thus had to settle for seventh, while Ricciardo, Daniil Kvyat and Jean-Éric Vergne were left frustrated by their decision to stand on their earlier times as they fell to eighth, ninth and 10th.

At the start, Rosberg got away well in front while second qualifier Vettel bogged down, allowing McLaren's Button and Kevin Magnussen to get through. From sixth, Hamilton jumped up to fifth and then muscled his way past Vettel for fourth a few corners into the lap.

Further down the field, there was drama as Kimi Räikkönen ran wide off the track out of Aintree and then lost control when he tried to regain it after the car hit a bump and bounced. He slammed hard into the barrier and spun across the track. Massa tried to spin in avoidance but still hit the Ferrari, while other cars had to take to the grass or were hit by debris.

A red flag came out so the debris could be cleaned up and there was an unexpectedly long delay of a full hour while a damaged section of barrier was replaced. Räikkönen escaped with bruises, while Massa, making his 200th GP start, was also out for the day.

The race eventually restarted with one lap behind the safety car and the field in the order at the end of the opening lap, which meant Rosberg was ahead of Button, Magnussen, Hamilton, Vettel and Hülkenberg. Vettel had lost three places and, for the restart, both Red Bull drivers switched to hard tyres on the grid.

It took Hamilton just two flying laps to barrel his way past Magnussen and Button to reach second. Rosberg was already some 5s up the road, but now we had a race on between the two World Championship protagonists.

Hamilton had cut the gap to around 2.5s when Rosberg made his first pit stop on lap 18.

Hamilton took the lead and then stayed out for another six laps. He lost around 1.5s in the pits due to a slow left rear wheel change and emerged 5s down on his teammate.

The key factor was that while Rosberg had stuck with another set of medium tyres, Hamilton now went for the hards. In theory, he could get to the end having used both types, although the initial intention was for him to pit again.

A great battle was in prospect, and Hamilton began to bring the gap down once more, reducing it to 4s by lap 27. Rosberg had been nursing a gearbox issue and, after suffering some downshifting glitches, he lost 2s of his advantage. On the very next lap the problem became terminal and he had no choice but to pull off and park on the grass.

"I had a small issue on the installation lap," said Rosberg, "but the car felt great in the early laps. By lap 20, though, the gearbox started to become a serious problem and from then it got worse. I tried to get it into some safety settings, let Lewis through and just keep going until the end of the race. But there was nothing we could do, so I had to stop the car. All I can do is accept that these things happen and work with the team to find out what went wrong."

To the delight of the huge crowd, Hamilton swept into the lead. Now under no threat from behind, he had plenty of time to make a second stop for fresh tyres on lap 41, although the set of hards he was using would have carried him home.

"It was 2008 when I had my win [at home]," said Hamilton, "and I just feel very, very grateful for the opportunity to do it again.

"I honestly feel that I had the pace today. I was catching Nico in the first stint. I was able to extend my first stint longer than ever before. I was feeling pretty comfortable. Of course, you never want a teammate to fall away, to win like that. I was looking forward to a wheel-to-wheel battle, but I'm sure we'll get many in the future."

Bottas was one of the real stars of the race. From 14th on the grid, the Williams man jumped up to ninth place before the red flag, and at the restart he charged through the order. Most drivers opted for a single pit stop, but no one pitted later than the Finn, who stayed out until lap 31. His great first stint established him firmly in second place.

Third place went to Ricciardo after a solid race for the Red Bull Racing driver, who just managed to hold off a charging Button on much fresher tyres in the closing laps. After switching to the hard tyre on the grid before the restart, the Australian pitted on lap 15 and then managed to do an extra-long second stint on the medium tyres, which wasn't easy.

"We chose to restart on the prime," said Ricciardo. "It didn't seem like the best thing to do at first because we were really slow at the restart. Valtteri and Fernando got past me pretty easily and pulled away and I was coming on the radio basically saying 'let's see if we can try something a little bit different', as we didn't really have the pace

> **"RÄIKKÖNEN ESCAPED WITH BRUISES, WHILE MASSA, MAKING HIS 200TH GP START, WAS ALSO OUT FOR THE DAY"**

that we had hoped for. Once we came in for the option, we just ran and pushed pretty much for the whole stint."

In contrast, his teammate Vettel stopped twice, on laps 10 and 33, on his way to fifth. The World Champion spent much of the race stuck behind Alonso, and the two put on a great battle that had them both complaining on the radio that their rival was exceeding track limits. Alonso, who also served a 5s penalty at his pit stop after parking his car ahead of its grid slot at the start, had to settle for sixth.

Magnussen couldn't match the pace of his McLaren teammate on his way to seventh. Hülkenberg lost places at the start and didn't have the pace with which to compete with the cars around him. He slipped back to finish eighth.

Vergne lost ground at the start after contact with Pérez and he used a one-stop strategy to catch up, while teammate Kvyat was one of only four drivers in the field to go for two stops. The outcomes proved to be similar, as they finished where they started in ninth and 10th. Pérez dropped to the back after the first-lap incident with Vergne, which meant he had to fight his way through after the restart. He crossed the line just outside the points in 11th.

Pastor Maldonado was catapulted into the air by contact from Esteban Gutiérrez and eventually retired with an exhaust problem, while the Sauber driver earned himself a three-place grid penalty for Hockenheim.

"MOST DRIVERS OPTED FOR A SINGLE STOP, BUT NO ONE PITTED LATER THAN BOTTAS"

Vettel, Alonso and Magnussen fight over the minor placings. **Below:** Lewis Hamilton punches the air in delight as he takes the chequered flag for his second home win. **Bottom:** Hamilton laps up the home support

CLOCKWISE FROM LEFT: The Red Arrows put on their usual spectacular show; Sir Jackie Stewart was as immaculate as ever; Prince Harry shares a joke with Red Bull team principal Christian Horner; family support for Felipe Massa at the marking of his 200th grand prix; Lewis Hamilton savours the British GP trophy; special pink T-shirts were brought out in memory of Jenson Button's father, John; Sebastian Vettel shelters from the sun on this occasion, not the rain; Susie Wolff was all smiles before her frustratingly short run for Williams in FP1

SNAPSHOT FROM GREAT BRITAIN

GREAT BRITAIN
SILVERSTONE
ROUND 9

RACE DATE 6 July
CIRCUIT LENGTH 3.659 miles
NO. OF LAPS 52
RACE DISTANCE 190.262 miles
WEATHER Sunny, 22ºC
TRACK TEMP 40ºC
LAP RECORD Fernando Alonso,
1m30.874s, 145.011mph, 2011

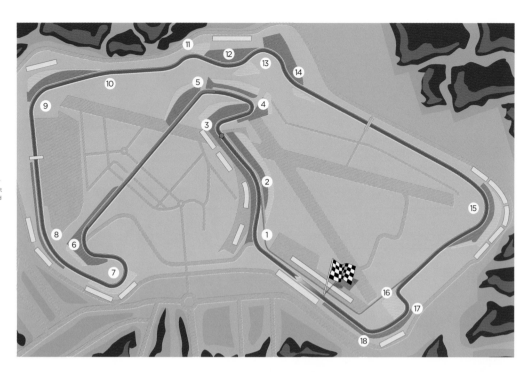

	PRACTICE 1				PRACTICE 2				PRACTICE 3				QUALIFYING 1			QUALIFYING 2	
	Driver	Time	Laps		Driver	Time	Laps		Driver	Time	Laps		Driver	Time		Driver	Time
1	N Rosberg	1m35.424s	25	1	L Hamilton	1m34.508s	14	1	S Vettel	1m52.522s	6	1	N Rosberg	1m40.380s	1	L Hamilton	1m34.870s
2	L Hamilton	1m36.155s	22	2	N Rosberg	1m34.736s	35	2	D Ricciardo	1m52.631s	6	2	D Kvyat	1m41.032s	2	N Rosberg	1m35.179s
3	F Alonso	1m36.263s	23	3	F Alonso	1m35.244s	32	3	P Maldonado	1m53.044s	10	3	L Hamilton	1m41.058s	3	S Vettel	1m36.410s
4	D Ricciardo	1m36.623s	21	4	D Ricciardo	1m35.511s	11	4	R Grosjean	1m53.566s	6	4	J Bianchi	1m41.169s	4	J Button	1m36.579s
5	K Räikkönen	1m36.703s	23	5	S Vettel	1m35.627s	27	5	A Sutil	1m53.585s	12	5	N Hülkenberg	1m41.271s	5	D Kvyat	1m36.813s
6	S Vettel	1m36.921s	20	6	V Bottas	1m36.016s	33	6	D Kvyat	1m53.654s	15	6	M Chilton	1m42.082s	6	N Hülkenberg	1m37.112s
7	J Button	1m36.963s	25	7	J Button	1m36.228s	34	7	K Magnussen	1m53.911s	5	7	S Pérez	1m42.146s	7	S Pérez	1m37.350s
8	D Kvyat	1m37.175s	29	8	K Magnussen	1m36.299s	35	8	J Button	1m54.041s	6	8	K Magnussen	1m42.507s	8	K Magnussen	1m37.370s
9	J-É Vergne	1m37.227s	25	9	K Räikkönen	1m36.554s	29	9	V Bottas	1m54.217s	4	9	A Sutil	1m42.603s	9	J-É Vergne	1m37.800s
10	K Magnussen	1m37.231s	30	10	J-É Vergne	1m36.583s	26	10	K Räikkönen	1m54.558s	5	10	J-É Vergne	1m43.040s	10	D Ricciardo	1m38.166s
11	S Pérez	1m37.720s	22	11	F Massa	1m36.671s	29	11	J-É Vergne	1m54.602s	6	11	R Grosjean	1m43.121s	11	R Grosjean	1m38.496s
12	R Grosjean	1m37.910s	21	12	D Kvyat	1m36.778s	31	12	E Gutiérrez	1m54.761s	13	12	E Gutiérrez	1m43.285s	12	J Bianchi	1m38.709s
13	E Gutiérrez	1m38.056s	18	13	E Gutiérrez	1m36.951s	35	13	F Massa	1m55.003s	4	13	P Maldonado	1m43.892s	13	M Chilton	1m39.800s
14	D Juncadella	1m38.083s	23	14	P Maldonado	1m37.064s	35	14	N Hülkenberg	1m55.688s	6	14	J Button	1m44.425s	14	E Gutiérrez	1m40.912s
15	G van der Garde	1m38.328s	19	15	R Grosjean	1m37.097s	33	15	S Pérez	1m56.918s	7	15	D Ricciardo	1m44.710s	15	P Maldonado	1m44.018s
16	J Bianchi	1m38.917s	12	16	S Pérez	1m37.236s	37	16	M Ericsson	1m57.091s	10	16	S Vettel	1m45.086s	16	A Sutil	no time
17	F Massa	1m39.461s	7	17	N Hülkenberg	1m37.449s	27	17	J Bianchi	1m57.566s	6	17	V Bottas	1m45.318s			
18	M Chilton	1m39.814s	24	18	A Sutil	1m37.520s	25	18	K Kobayashi	1m57.914s	10	18	F Massa	1m45.695s			
19	M Ericsson	1m40.597s	19	19	J Bianchi	1m38.658s	11	19	L Hamilton	no time	5	19	F Alonso	1m45.935s			
20	R Frijns	1m42.261s	11	20	K Kobayashi	1m39.068s	31	20	F Alonso	no time	4	20	K Räikkönen	1m46.684s			
21	S Wolff	1m44.212s	4	21	M Chilton	1m39.224s	28	21	N Rosberg	no time	4	21	M Ericsson	1m49.421s			
22	P Maldonado	no time	2	22	M Ericsson	1m39.762s	21	22	M Chilton	no time	1	22	K Kobayashi	1m49.625s			

Best sectors – Practice			Speed trap – Practice			Best sectors – Qualifying			Speed trap – Qualifying		
Sec 1	L Hamilton	29.780s	1	K Magnussen	200.268mph	Sec 1	N Rosberg	29.304s	1	N Rosberg	202.132mph
Sec 2	L Hamilton	38.522s	2	V Bottas	199.273mph	Sec 2	L Hamilton	38.740s	2	S Pérez	201.262mph
Sec 3	L Hamilton	26.122s	3	S Pérez	198.590mph	Sec 3	L Hamilton	26.008s	3	L Hamilton	200.951mph

Sebastian Vettel
"It got a bit silly when both Fernando and I complained about the other going off track; I don't think people care too much if the car is a little bit to the left or the right."

Nico Rosberg
"By lap 20, the gearbox began to become a problem and from then it got worse. I tried to get it into some safety settings, let Lewis past and just keep going."

Fernando Alonso
"I had a 5s penalty for being out of position. Then I had duels with Button and Vettel. When Seb caught me, I was saving fuel and battery power, so knew he'd overtake me."

Pastor Maldonado
"There was contact from Gutiérrez, the result of which I'm told looked spectacular, but we're not sure if this added to the cause of me having to retire."

Jenson Button
"Circuits with high-speed changes of direction aren't our forte. At the end, I crossed the line 0.9s behind Daniel; if there'd been just one more lap, I think I could've got by."

Sergio Pérez
"We can't judge what our real pace was as the contact with Vergne at the start compromised it. I fell to last and from there it was very difficult to salvage anything."

Daniel Ricciardo
"I'm not normally ecstatic with a third, but I really am today, obviously to redeem myself from yesterday and also the fact that I don't think we had an awesome race car today."

Lewis Hamilton
"After extending my first stint, I switched to the primes and couldn't believe the pace I had and was catching Nico. Of course, he then had a problem and pulled off."

Kimi Räikkönen
"Sadly, my race ended on lap 1, after I had made up enough ground to be fighting for 11th. At Turn 5, I went off and, while trying to get back on, I must have hit a kerb."

Romain Grosjean
"I avoided the incident with Kimi, but my visor got damaged by debris. Near the end, my pace was better. I came close to the points, but had started too far back."

Kevin Magnussen
"I made a really good start to be third initially and after that I struggled to keep the Ferrari and Red Bull behind. So, I think we should be reasonably satisfied with seventh."

Nico Hülkenberg
"I lost two positions at the start and then was struggling with my car's balance, which may have been related to the wind because it was very gusty out there."

POSITIONS LAP BY LAP

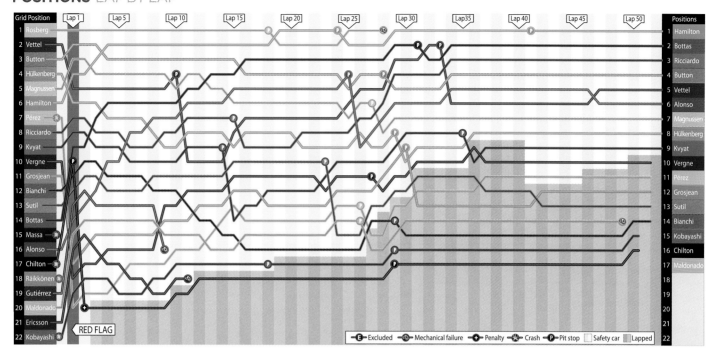

Legend: –E– Excluded –S– Mechanical failure –●– Penalty –✖– Crash –P– Pit stop ▢ Safety car ▧ Lapped

RED FLAG

Grid Position: 1 Rosberg, 2 Vettel, 3 Button, 4 Hülkenberg, 5 Magnussen, 6 Hamilton, 7 Pérez, 8 Ricciardo, 9 Kvyat, 10 Vergne, 11 Grosjean, 12 Bianchi, 13 Sutil, 14 Bottas, 15 Massa, 16 Alonso, 17 Chilton, 18 Räikkönen, 19 Gutiérrez, 20 Maldonado, 21 Ericsson, 22 Kobayashi

Positions (finish): 1 Hamilton, 2 Bottas, 3 Ricciardo, 4 Button, 5 Vettel, 6 Alonso, 7 Magnussen, 8 Hülkenberg, 9 Kvyat, 10 Vergne, 11 Pérez, 12 Grosjean, 13 Sutil, 14 Bianchi, 15 Kobayashi, 16 Chilton, 17 Maldonado

QUALIFYING 3

	Driver	Time
1	N Rosberg	1m35.766s
2	S Vettel	1m37.386s
3	J Button	1m38.200s
4	N Hülkenberg	1m38.329s
5	K Magnussen	1m38.417s
6	L Hamilton	1m39.232s
7	S Pérez	1m40.457s
8	D Ricciardo	1m40.606s
9	D Kvyat	1m40.707s
10	J-É Vergne	1m40.855s

GRID

	Driver	Time
1	N Rosberg	1m35.766s
2	S Vettel	1m37.386s
3	J Button	1m38.200s
4	N Hülkenberg	1m38.329s
5	K Magnussen	1m38.417s
6	L Hamilton	1m39.232s
7	S Pérez	1m40.457s
8	D Ricciardo	1m40.606s
9	D Kvyat	1m40.707s
10	J-É Vergne	1m40.855s
11	R Grosjean	1m38.496s
12	J Bianchi	1m38.709s
13	A Sutil	no time
14	V Bottas	1m45.318s
15	F Massa	1m45.695s
16	F Alonso	1m45.935s
17	M Chilton	1m39.800s
18	K Räikkönen	1m46.684s
19	E Gutiérrez	1m40.912s
20	P Maldonado	no time
21	M Ericsson	1m49.421s
22	K Kobayashi	1m49.625s

Grid penalties

M Chilton	5-place penalty for changing the gearbox
E Gutiérrrez	Excluded from qualifying for a technical infringement
P Maldonado	5-place penalty for changing the gearbox

RACE

	Driver	Car	Laps	Time	Av mph	Fastest	Stops
1	L Hamilton	Mercedes F1 W05	52	2h26m52.094s	77.731	1m37.176s	2
2	V Bottas	Williams-Mercedes FW36	52	2h27m22.229s	77.462	1m38.264s	1
3	D Ricciardo	Red Bull-Renault RB10	52	2h27m38.589s	77.320	1m38.459s	1
4	J Button	McLaren-Mercedes MP4-29	52	2h27m39.484s	77.311	1m38.284s	1
5	S Vettel	Red Bull-Renault RB10	52	2h27m45.958s	77.255	1m37.481s	2
6	F Alonso	Ferrari F14 T	52	2h27m52.040s	77.202	1m38.587s	1
7	K Magnussen	McLaren-Mercedes MP4-29	52	2h27m54.657s	77.180	1m38.677s	1
8	N Hülkenberg	Force India-Mercedes VJM07	52	2h28m20.786s	76.953	1m38.625s	1
9	D Kvyat	Toro Rosso-Renault STR9	52	2h28m21.434s	76.947	1m38.407s	2
10	J-É Vergne	Toro Rosso-Renault STR9	51	2h26m55.203s	76.205	1m39.261s	1
11	S Pérez	Force India-Mercedes VJM07	51	2h27m03.051s	76.137	1m38.716s	1
12	R Grosjean	Lotus-Renault E22	51	2h27m05.820s	76.113	1m38.919s	1
13	A Sutil	Sauber-Ferrari C33	51	2h27m24.590s	75.952	1m40.041s	1
14	J Bianchi	Marussia-Ferrari MR03	51	2h27m58.536s	75.662	1m39.961s	1
15	K Kobayashi	Caterham-Renault CT05	50	2h27m56.295s	74.196	1m41.462s	2
16	M Chilton	Marussia-Ferrari MR03	50	2h28m27.554s	73.936	1m40.399s	3
17	P Maldonado	Lotus-Renault E22	49	Exhaust	-	1m40.314s	1
R	N Rosberg	Mercedes F1 W05	28	Gearbox	-	1m38.091s	1
R	M Ericsson	Caterham-Renault CT05	11	Suspension	-	1m44.319s	0
R	E Gutiérrez	Sauber-Ferrari C33	9	Accident	-	1m42.566s	0
R	F Massa	Williams-Mercedes FW36	0	Accident	-	-	0
R	K Räikkönen	Ferrari F14 T	0	Accident	-	-	0

Fastest lap
L Hamilton 1m37.176s
(135.614mph) on lap 26

Fastest speed trap
V Bottas 204.741mph

Slowest speed trap
M Chilton 190.574mph

Fastest pit stop
1 N Rosberg 28.329s
2 D Ricciardo 28.483s
3 D Kvyat 28.575s

CHAMPIONSHIP

	Driver	Pts
1	N Rosberg	165
2	L Hamilton	161
3	D Ricciardo	98
4	F Alonso	87
5	V Bottas	73
6	S Vettel	70
7	N Hülkenberg	63
8	J Button	55
9	K Magnussen	35
10	F Massa	30
11	S Pérez	28
12	K Räikkönen	19
13	J-É Vergne	9
14	R Grosjean	8
15	D Kvyat	6
16	J Bianchi	2

CONSTRUCTORS

	Team	Pts
1	Mercedes	326
2	Red Bull-Renault	168
3	Ferrari	106
4	Williams-Mercedes	103
5	Force India-Mercedes	91
6	McLaren-Mercedes	90
7	Toro Rosso-Renault	15
8	Lotus-Renault	8
9	Marussia-Ferrari	2

Esteban Gutiérrez
"I had a good start. After the restart I was fighting Pastor. When I tried to pass him in Turn 16 he didn't leave me enough space and I couldn't avoid a collision with him."

Jean-Éric Vergne
"Starting from the back of the grid after the red flag and overtaking the cars in front of me was actually fun. I think I have found again the aggressiveness I knew I had."

Felipe Massa
"Kimi came across the track and I never had a chance to miss him, and sadly the damage was too much to continue. Luckily I turned, as it could otherwise have been a worse accident."

Max Chilton
"It was scary when I was hit by the flying tyre. I pitted as I needed a new front wing and for the team to check the car, but of course by then the race had been red-flagged."

Marcus Ericsson
"I had a fantastic start. Then, after we restarted under the safety car I was ahead of Kamui but, going into Turn 6, I hit something in the kerbs that smashed my suspension."

Adrian Sutil
"It took a few laps to pass Jules, but I was then able to improve my lap times. We decided to go for a one-stop run, but after my stop I could not get the hard tyres to work."

Daniil Kvyat
"This was an intense race, especially near the end when I was catching Hülkenberg. I was quicker than him and was definitely getting very close, but wasn't able to pass him."

Valtteri Bottas
"We knew we had a quick car and maybe it even surprised us. I went through the field fast in the first stint and am so happy for the team, as they've worked on race pace and it shows."

Jules Bianchi
"From 10th place at the restart, I had a very enjoyable opening stint. I knew that I wouldn't be able to hold off the faster cars behind me, but it proved to be a good test of our pace."

Kamui Kobayashi
"I saw Kimi's impact and had to go way off to avoid him, slightly damaging my car's nose. We restarted under the safety car. I'd lost downforce, but kept going as hard as I could."

ROUND 10

GERMA

GROSSER PREIS SANTANDER VON DEUTSCHLAND

INY

THIS WAS A STRAIGHTFORWARD HOME
WIN FOR NICO ROSBERG, BUT THERE
WAS PLENTY OF ACTION BEHIND HIM AS
HOCKENHEIM PRODUCED SOME TYPICALLY
ENTERTAINING RACING DOWN THE ORDER

Rosberg leads the charge towards the first corner from the Williams duo, with Lewis Hamilton out of sight at the back. **Top right:** Felipe Massa is clipped by Kevin Magnussen into the first corner and tipped over (bottom right). **Middle right:** the giant grandstands make the arena section feel like an auditorium

ith perfect timing, Nico Rosberg celebrated his recent marriage and the extension of his contract with Mercedes by winning an entertaining race at Hockenheim. In so doing, he consolidated his World Championship lead over teammate Lewis Hamilton, who put in a strong performance to salvage third, after a disastrous time in qualifying left him 20th on the grid.

Having set the second-best time of Q2 up to that point, Hamilton had a heavy crash at the lefthander in the stadium, striking the tyre wall hard. Replays indicated that something was amiss and the team confirmed that the right front Brembo disc had failed.

The session was red-flagged with 7m21s still to run. Rosberg hadn't set a time at that point, after locking up and going off the track on his first run. After the restart, he quickly went fastest to ensure his safe passage through to Q2.

The second qualifying session passed without major incident, but some big names simply didn't have the pace to make it through to Q3. Jenson Button thought he had done so, but the McLaren driver was bumped down to 11th right at the end, while fellow former World Champion Kimi Räikkönen also missed out, ending up only 12th.

Williams had looked strong throughout, especially Valtteri Bottas, and it was clear that Rosberg couldn't afford any slip-ups. He went top after the first runs in Q3 with a lap of 1m16.540s and on the second runs Bottas came close to toppling him with a 1m16.759s. Rosberg wasn't able to improve after he pressed the DRS button a fraction too early, but it didn't matter as his pole position was secure. Behind

"HAMILTON HAD A HEAVY CRASH AT THE LEFTHANDER IN THE STADIUM, STRIKING THE TYRE WALL HARD"

Bottas, his teammate Felipe Massa qualified third, emphasising the pace of the FW36.

Kevin Magnussen showed that recent updates at McLaren had paid off by qualifying a strong fourth, ahead of the Red Bulls of Daniel Ricciardo and Sebastian Vettel, the Australian once again coming out on top. The top 10 was completed by Fernando Alonso, Daniil Kvyat, Nico Hülkenberg and Sergio Pérez.

Come Sunday, the major topic of conversation was the fact that Mercedes had switched Hamilton from Brembo front discs to the products of Carbone Industrie. Rivals were surprised when the FIA deemed that this was not a "change of specification" in parc fermé, which would have led to Hamilton starting from the pit lane.

The expected rain didn't arrive, but temperatures were much lower than they had been earlier in the weekend. That had the effect of

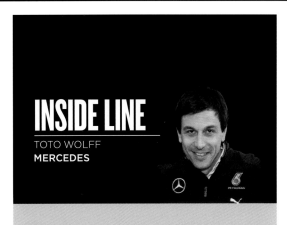

INSIDE LINE

TOTO WOLFF
MERCEDES

It feels great. I have so many friends over here, and we're so near to Stuttgart and our board, with many of our colleagues and employees here. The pressure was on because we won the British GP with Lewis, Austria was good, Malaysia was good. This was the pinnacle of the home grands prix.

"I know it doesn't for Lewis because he's very competitive, but for me it feels like a one-two. Because he was coming from P20 and recovering to where he did, considering there were difficult early laps – it wasn't like making up five or six or seven places on lap 1, he was working really hard to get back to the front.

"How close was it? I think the misunderstanding with Jenson probably cost him some lap time. He was down on downforce on the front wing and then at the end, with the strategy going back to the option tyre, we knew that the window was very narrow. Valtteri kept his cool and defended well.

> **"BECAUSE LEWIS WAS COMING FROM P20, IT WASN'T LIKE MAKING UP FIVE OR SIX, PLACES ON LAP 1. HE WAS WORKING REALLY HARD"**

"We had precise data on what the nose was looking like and how it was performing. We were very much aware, though, that there wasn't structural damage on the front wing, just the front wing endplate and some of the fins. We decided that the front wing wasn't deteriorating any further, so we kept it on. The car could have had much more performance with the wing not damaged. He lost many points of downforce from the front wing.

"Williams has been rising from the ashes and I'm obviously very happy for them. Their car looked to be very competitive on the last three tracks and they did 346kph on the straight today, which is a spectacular number."

FRIC COMES UNDER THE SPOTLIGHT

The FIA caused a stir before the German GP when it announced a clampdown on FRIC, or front-to-rear interconnected suspension systems, which have been in use since 2008 as a tool for controlling constant ride height.

In essence, Technical Delegate Charlie Whiting had decided that some teams had been pushing the limits – and concluded that the systems they planned for 2015 would be a step too far.

As had happened in the past with contentious technical items, Whiting's initial view was that FRIC systems could remain in use until the end of the season. However, in order to give a green light to that approach, all 11 teams had to agree.

The technical directive from Whiting read: "Having now seen and studied nearly every current design of front-to-rear linked suspension system, as well as reviewing future developments some teams have shared with us, we are firmly of the view that the legality of all such systems could be called into question, particularly with respect to Article 3.15 of the F1 Technical Regulations.

"As these systems, in one form or another, have been in use for some time, we are inclined to permit their continued use for the remainder of the current season. However, we feel we would need the agreement of all participating teams to take this approach. We would therefore be very grateful if you could indicate whether you may be in a position to agree with such an approach.

"Failing this, we would have to consider making a report to the stewards about the non-compliance of any car fitted with a system that appears to allow the response of the suspension at either or both of the rear corners to drive the response of the suspension at either or both of the front corners (or vice versa)."

Of course, unanimous agreement was never going to be reached. In fact, in the build-up to Hockenheim, one by one the teams revealed that they had decided to remove FRIC in order to avoid any possible sanctions and thus all were forced to follow suit. In the end, the consensus was that its absence made little or no difference to the performance of the cars at Hockenheim.

> "IN THE BUILD-UP TO HOCKENHEIM, TEAMS QUIETLY REVEALED THAT THEY HAD DECIDED TO REMOVE FRIC IN ORDER TO AVOID ANY SANCTIONS"

making the cars more front limited than rear limited – in other words, the emphasis went from the rear tyres going off first, to the front left. Everyone had to take that fact into account as they juggled their race strategies.

Not that Rosberg had too much to worry about. With Hamilton down in 20th – a gearbox change penalty had dropped him down from the 16th he was left in after his qualifying crash – his main opposition came from the Williams pair. Their number was reduced by one at the first corner when Massa turned in and was clipped by fourth qualifier Magnussen.

In an instant, the Brazilian flipped over and skated along the track upside down, before the car righted itself again. He was unhurt, and the stewards would subsequently deem it a racing incident. Ricciardo also suffered in the incident, as he fell to 15th after running wide in avoidance.

When the race went green again after a two-lap safety car period, Rosberg soon edged away from Bottas, as Vettel, Alonso, Hülkenberg and Button led the chase. Rosberg was 2.5s clear of the Williams after five laps, and by 10 laps the gap was out to 6.2s.

It was obvious that, unless something went drastically wrong, there wasn't going to be a fight for the lead. All the excitement was down the field, and much of it focused on Hamilton's progress – after 10 laps he had risen to 10th. He had started on the soft tyres and was thus programmed to do a long opening stint and gain as much ground as he possibly could.

Alonso was the first of the frontrunners to stop, the Spaniard coming in from fourth place on lap 12. Vettel came in from third on lap 14 and then leaders Rosberg and Bottas – by now separated by 10s – came in together on lap 15.

Hamilton, who had no intention of stopping any time soon, was third at this point, some 23s behind his teammate. When Rosberg and Bottas emerged from their pit stops, Hamilton was between them in second place. However, his tyres were now getting old and on lap 20 Bottas, on brand new softs, pushed him down to third.

Hamilton was still able to stay comfortably ahead of Vettel until finally coming in and taking a new set of softs on lap 26. He dropped to eighth and from there soon began picking off rivals again. However, on lap 30 he damaged his front left endplate against Button's McLaren. The subsequent loss of downforce proved crucial and cost Hamilton

There was some great racing between Sebastian Vettel, Kimi Räikkönen and Fernando Alonso. **Top right:** Räikkönen locks up as he holds off Hamilton. **Middle right:** the Lotus duo raced hard but still failed to score. **Bottom right:** Daniil Kvyat's race came to an end when ignition failure let unburnt fuel reach the exhausts

valuable speed, causing him to use up his front tyres faster than he had anticipated.

While Hamilton was in attack mode, it was all too easy for Rosberg out front. He was around 16s clear when Bottas made his second pit stop on lap 40 and Rosberg responded by coming in on the following lap. Thereafter, he just had to manage the car to the chequered flag, his only worry coming when Adrian Sutil spun at the exit of the final corner on lap 47 and a safety car deployment looked inevitable. Surprisingly, it never came.

Behind him, things got more interesting. Hamilton's original plan had been for him to make it home on two stops, but the wing damage and the fact that he had to push hard made that difficult. He finally came in for new supersofts on lap 42, with 25 laps to run. At that stage, he was third and close behind Bottas, but the team knew that he wouldn't be able to get up to second place as the tyres wouldn't last and the Finn could make it home on his softs.

Hamilton thus made a third stop after just eight laps, on lap 50, giving himself another new set of options for the final part of the race. He dropped back to fourth, behind Alonso and nearly 17s shy of Bottas. The Ferrari driver then made a

> ## "ALL THE EXCITEMENT WAS DOWN THE FIELD, MUCH OF IT FOCUSSED ON HAMILTON'S PROGRESS"

third pit stop of his own, leaving Hamilton free to hunt down the Williams. By lap 60, he was right on his rival's gearbox but, despite strenuous efforts, he couldn't quite find a way past.

Almost unnoticed out front, Rosberg crossed the finish line over 20s clear of Bottas. "I'm a bit surprised because in qualifying the Williams were quite close, so I didn't really expect to have such a big advantage in the race," he said. "I'm very, very thankful to Mercedes for the car that they've built us, as it's really a pleasure at the moment. The Hungarian GP will be good."

After his podiums in the previous two races, Bottas put in another superb performance and he did well to ultimately outrun Hamilton. "We always aim for more, but for now we

need to be happy with these points," said the Finn. "Of course we were unlucky with Felipe again, we didn't get both cars in a good position, but I think today's was the maximum result. We did everything perfectly and managed to keep Lewis behind in the end which got us an extra few points, but in the future, we are definitely aiming for more and this is not the maximum."

While Rosberg and Bottas made it on two pit stops, everyone else in the top 10, bar Hülkenberg, stopped three times. Second place would have been ideal, but nevertheless Hamilton had to be satisfied to reach third from 20th on the grid. It was another reminder of just how strong Mercedes' F1 W05 was.

"I did as well as I could today," said Hamilton. "It was very hard to get through the pack safely. I had a little bit of a collision with Jenson. I honestly thought he was opening the door to let me past. It's very hard to overtake at the end, they were so fast on the straights, but I'm very happy I got some points."

Vettel ultimately took fourth, having spent a chunk of the race fighting with Alonso. It was one of many battles down the field that provided some great entertainment. Alonso's later third stop ultimately cost him relative to the World Champion. The Spaniard also had an eye on fuel consumption and he performed miracles to get around the last lap and cross the line safely ahead of Ricciardo, after some great battling between the pair. The Australian drove a strong race to recover to sixth after being delayed avoiding the upturned Massa.

The change in emphasis to the front rather than rear tyres helped Hülkenberg more than his Force India teammate Pérez. After gaining places at the start, the German was able to run two stops on his way to a solid seventh place.

Button had jumped up to sixth at the start, but he felt that the team didn't get his strategy right as he survived the bump from Hamilton to finish in eighth place. Magnussen was able to recover from his first corner clash with Massa to come home ninth, while Pérez had contact with Kvyat en route to 10th place. Räikkönen, slowed by wing damage after an eventful afternoon, finished just outside the points in 11th.

"IN AN INSTANT, MASSA FLIPPED AND SKATED ALONG THE TRACK UPSIDE DOWN, BEFORE THE CAR RIGHTED ITSELF"

Above: Rosberg shows his delight in parc fermé.
Right: Adrian Sutil walks in after his Sauber's engine cut out and he spun.
Below: it was smiles all around in the Mercedes camp

SNAPSHOT
FROM GERMANY

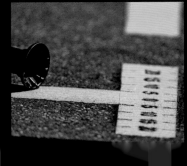

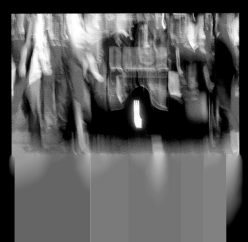

GERMANY
HOCKENHEIM
ROUND 10

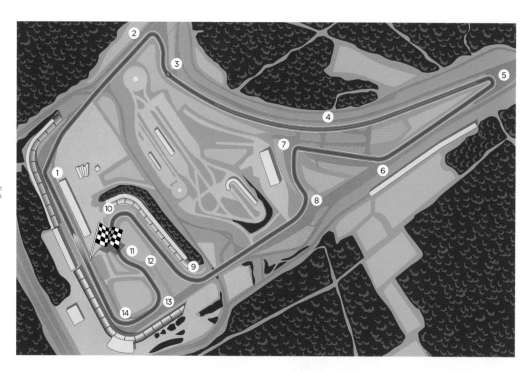

Official Results © [2014]
Formula One World
Championship Limited,
6 Princes Gate, London SW7
1QJ. No reproduction without
permission. All copyright and
database rights reserved.

RACE DATE 20 July

CIRCUIT LENGTH 2.842 miles

NO. OF LAPS 67

RACE DISTANCE 190.414 miles

WEATHER Overcast, 26ºC

TRACK TEMP 33ºC

LAP RECORD Kimi Räikkönen,
1m14.917s, 138.685mph, 2004

PRACTICE 1				PRACTICE 2				PRACTICE 3				QUALIFYING 1			QUALIFYING 2	
	Driver	Time	Laps		Driver	Time	Laps		Driver	Time	Laps		Driver	Time		Driver	Time
1	N Rosberg	1m19.131s	29	1	L Hamilton	1m18.341s	38	1	N Rosberg	1m17.779s	24	1	N Rosberg	1m17.631s	1	N Rosberg	1m17.109s
2	L Hamilton	1m19.196s	25	2	N Rosberg	1m18.365s	39	2	L Hamilton	1m18.380s	20	2	D Ricciardo	1m18.117s	2	V Bottas	1m17.353s
3	F Alonso	1m19.423s	21	3	D Ricciardo	1m18.443s	35	3	F Alonso	1m18.384s	11	3	S Vettel	1m18.194s	3	F Massa	1m17.370s
4	D Ricciardo	1m19.697s	27	4	K Räikkönen	1m18.887s	38	4	F Massa	1m18.575s	18	4	V Bottas	1m18.215s	4	S Vettel	1m17.646s
5	J Button	1m19.833s	24	5	K Magnussen	1m18.960s	40	5	V Bottas	1m18.611s	19	5	K Magnussen	1m18.260s	5	K Magnussen	1m17.788s
6	S Vettel	1m20.097s	28	6	F Massa	1m19.024s	36	6	K Magnussen	1m18.756s	16	6	F Massa	1m18.381s	6	D Ricciardo	1m17.855s
7	K Magnussen	1m20.105s	32	7	J Button	1m19.221s	40	7	D Ricciardo	1m18.769s	13	7	F Alonso	1m18.389s	7	F Alonso	1m17.866s
8	K Räikkönen	1m20.210s	21	8	S Vettel	1m19.248s	35	8	K Räikkönen	1m18.842s	8	8	J Button	1m18.425s	8	N Hülkenberg	1m18.017s
9	D Kvyat	1m20.337s	28	9	F Alonso	1m19.329s	32	9	S Vettel	1m18.890s	17	9	J-É Vergne	1m18.496s	9	D Kvyat	1m18.103s
10	A Sutil	1m20.505s	18	10	V Bottas	1m19.385s	34	10	N Hülkenberg	1m19.127s	19	10	D Kvyat	1m18.530s	10	S Pérez	1m18.161s
11	F Massa	1m20.542s	19	11	A Sutil	1m19.417s	41	11	D Kvyat	1m19.131s	19	11	K Räikkönen	1m18.534s	11	J Button	1m18.193s
12	J-É Vergne	1m20.586s	23	12	D Kvyat	1m19.452s	27	12	J-É Vergne	1m19.470s	20	12	L Hamilton	1m18.683s	12	K Räikkönen	1m18.273s
13	N Hülkenberg	1m20.592s	22	13	S Pérez	1m19.581s	28	13	J Button	1m19.489s	15	13	E Gutiérrez	1m18.739s	13	J-É Vergne	1m18.285s
14	S Pérez	1m20.598s	24	14	N Hülkenberg	1m19.593s	32	14	S Pérez	1m19.505s	21	14	R Grosjean	1m18.894s	14	E Gutiérrez	1m18.787s
15	S Wolff	1m20.769s	22	15	J-É Vergne	1m19.760s	32	15	E Gutiérrez	1m19.601s	23	15	S Pérez	1m18.916s	15	R Grosjean	1m18.983s
16	G van der Garde	1m20.782s	23	16	P Maldonado	1m20.158s	35	16	R Grosjean	1m20.078s	23	16	N Hülkenberg	1m18.927s	16	L Hamilton	no time
17	R Grosjean	1m21.603s	20	17	R Grosjean	1m20.358s	35	17	J Bianchi	1m20.198s	21	17	A Sutil	1m19.142s			
18	P Maldonado	1m21.854s	30	18	E Gutiérrez	1m20.504s	40	18	P Maldonado	1m20.466s	19	18	J Bianchi	1m19.676s			
19	K Kobayashi	1m22.572s	31	19	J Bianchi	1m21.328s	31	19	A Sutil	1m20.844s	6	19	P Maldonado	1m20.195s			
20	J Bianchi	1m22.982s	24	20	M Ericsson	1m21.870s	21	20	K Kobayashi	1m21.018s	21	20	K Kobayashi	1m20.408s			
21	M Ericsson	1m23.256s	35	21	M Chilton	1m21.898s	28	21	M Ericsson	1m23.077s	14	21	M Chilton	1m20.489s			
22	M Chilton	1m23.299s	22	22	K Kobayashi	1m23.728s	12	22	M Chilton	1m23.449s	7	22	M Ericsson	no time			

Best sectors – Practice			Speed trap – Practice			Best sectors – Qualifying			Speed trap – Qualifying		
Sec 1	N Rosberg	16.925s	1	F Massa	206.419mph	Sec 1	N Rosberg	16.680s	1	N Rosberg	206.606mph
Sec 2	N Rosberg	36.085s	2	V Bottas	204.928mph	Sec 2	N Rosberg	36.545s	2	V Bottas	205.984mph
Sec 3	N Rosberg	24.748s	3	N Rosberg	204.679mph	Sec 3	N Rosberg	24.100s	3	F Massa	205.425mph

Sebastian Vettel
"The second stop was a bit too close and Fernando was able to pass, which put us on the back foot, but we decided to be more aggressive and make sure I got the undercut."

Nico Rosberg
"I came here hoping for a win and it worked out perfectly. My Silver Arrow was so dominant, I was worried later that without the FRIC system the gap would be smaller."

Fernando Alonso
"We changed from a two- to a three-stop strategy. It wasn't easy fighting while keeping an eye on consumption. But, with the help of newer tyres, I got ahead of Ricciardo."

Pastor Maldonado
"The incident in Turn 1 was hard to avoid but then my pace was consistent. I did my best to manage degradation, which was high, and we were able to do only two stops."

Jenson Button
"I ran as high as sixth, but we got the strategy wrong at my second stop. I'm not sure why we stopped so early, but it made it extremely difficult for me to keep my tyres alive."

Sergio Pérez
"I couldn't make my tyres last like usual, so I struggled with the balance. It was a strange race and it was the front tyres that were suffering from degradation, not the rears."

Daniel Ricciardo
"I had to avoid Massa's collision and went way down the field. From then, I got on to the radio and said let's make an amazing recovery and make ourselves proud today."

Lewis Hamilton
"When you start at the back, it's hard to imagine that you could be on the podium. It was pretty straightforward, but it was difficult following what was going on."

Kimi Räikkönen
"It's a shame the way my race went as I twice found myself squeezed between two cars and my front wing got damaged both times and that compromised my race."

Romain Grosjean
"I didn't have an easy start on the softs, but my pace was good, though I suffered from a loss of power due to an issue with our cooling system so was asked to switch off."

Kevin Magnussen
"I could've had a decent race if I hadn't had the accident at Turn 1. I did my best to avoid it, but there wasn't much else I could do. I spun after that, and had to pit for tyres and a nose."

Nico Hülkenberg
"It was a difficult race, mainly due to the track being 20 degrees cooler. I also had to overcome some engine issues in the middle of the race as there were some hesitations."

POSITIONS LAP BY LAP

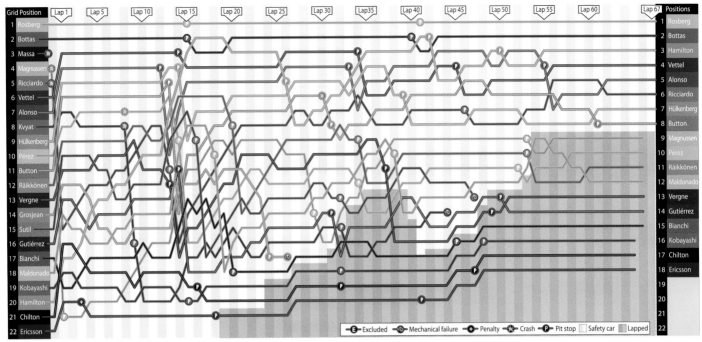

Grid Position	Lap 1	Lap 5	Lap 10	Lap 15	Lap 20	Lap 25	Lap 30	Lap 35	Lap 40	Lap 45	Lap 50	Lap 55	Lap 60	Lap 67	Positions
1 Rosberg															1 Rosberg
2 Bottas															2 Bottas
3 Massa															3 Hamilton
4 Magnussen															4 Vettel
5 Ricciardo															5 Alonso
6 Vettel															6 Ricciardo
7 Alonso															7 Hülkenberg
8 Kvyat															8 Button
9 Hülkenberg															9 Magnussen
10 Pérez															10 Pérez
11 Button															11 Räikkönen
12 Räikkönen															12 Maldonado
13 Vergne															13 Vergne
14 Grosjean															14 Gutiérrez
15 Sutil															15 Bianchi
16 Gutiérrez															16 Kobayashi
17 Bianchi															17 Chilton
18 Maldonado															18 Ericsson
19 Kobayashi															19
20 Hamilton															20
21 Chilton															21
22 Ericsson															22

Legend: —E— Excluded —S— Mechanical failure —+— Penalty —X— Crash —P— Pit stop ☐ Safety car ▨ Lapped

QUALIFYING 3

	Driver	Time
1	N Rosberg	1m16.540s
2	V Bottas	1m16.759s
3	F Massa	1m17.078s
4	K Magnussen	1m17.214s
5	D Ricciardo	1m17.273s
6	S Vettel	1m17.577s
7	F Alonso	1m17.649s
8	D Kvyat	1m17.965s
9	N Hülkenberg	1m18.014s
10	S Pérez	1m18.035s

GRID

	Driver	Time
1	N Rosberg	1m16.540s
2	V Bottas	1m16.759s
3	F Massa	1m17.078s
4	K Magnussen	1m17.214s
5	D Ricciardo	1m17.273s
6	S Vettel	1m17.577s
7	F Alonso	1m17.649s
8	D Kvyat	1m17.965s
9	N Hülkenberg	1m18.014s
10	S Pérez	1m18.035s
11	J Button	1m18.193s
12	K Räikkönen	1m18.273s
13	J-É Vergne	1m18.285s
14	R Grosjean	1m18.983s
15	A Sutil	1m19.142s
16	E Gutiérrez	1m19.787s
17	J Bianchi	1m19.676s
18	P Maldonado	1m20.195s
19	K Kobayashi	1m20.408s
20	L Hamilton	no time
21	M Chilton	1m20.489s
22	M Ericsson	no time

Grid penalties

E Gutiérrez	3-place penalty for causing collision at British GP
L Hamilton	5-place penalty for changing the gearbox
M Ericsson	Put to back of grid as car modified in parc fermé

RACE

	Driver	Car	Laps	Time	Av mph	Fastest	Stops
1	N Rosberg	Mercedes F1 W05	67	1h33m42.914s	121.922	1m21.298s	2
2	V Bottas	Williams-Mercedes FW36	67	1h34m03.703s	121.467	1m21.494s	2
3	L Hamilton	Mercedes F1 W05	67	1h34m05.444s	121.429	1m19.908s	3
4	S Vettel	Red Bull-Renault RB10	67	1h34m26.928s	120.969	1m21.545s	3
5	F Alonso	Ferrari F14 T	67	1h34m35.381s	120.789	1m20.548s	3
6	D Ricciardo	Red Bull-Renault RB10	67	1h34m35.463s	120.787	1m20.846s	3
7	N Hülkenberg	Force India-Mercedes VJM07	67	1h34m47.092s	120.540	1m22.098s	2
8	J Button	McLaren-Mercedes MP4-29	67	1h35m07.625s	120.106	1m21.346s	3
9	K Magnussen	McLaren-Mercedes MP4-29	66	1h33m45.841s	120.098	1m20.224s	3
10	S Perez	Force India-Mercedes VJM07	66	1h33m53.317s	119.875	1m20.752s	3
11	K Räikkönen	Ferrari F14 T	66	1h34m01.664s	119.698	1m21.338s	3
12	P Maldonado	Lotus-Renault E22	66	1h34m11.018s	119.499	1m22.305s	2
13	J-É Vergne	Toro Rosso-Renault STR9	66	1h34m11.755s	119.484	1m21.876s	3
14	E Gutiérrez	Sauber-Ferrari C33	66	1h34m18.091s	119.350	1m22.008s	3
15	J Bianchi	Marussia-Ferrari MR03	66	1h34m52.992s	118.618	1m22.522s	2
16	K Kobayashi	Caterham-Renault CT05	65	1h34m09.390s	117.722	1m22.866s	3
17	M Chilton	Marussia-Ferrari MR03	65	1h34m21.470s	117.471	1m23.035s	3
18	M Ericsson	Caterham-Renault CT05	65	1h34m50.325s	116.875	1m23.230s	3
R	A Sutil	Sauber-Ferrari C33	47	Spun off	-	1m22.529s	3
R	D Kvyat	Toro Rosso-Renault STR9	44	Ignition	-	1m22.179s	2
R	R Grosjean	Lotus-Renault E22	26	Cooling	-	1m24.137s	1
R	F Massa	Williams-Mercedes FW36	0	Accident	-		0

Fastest lap
L Hamilton 1m19.908s
(128.049mph) on lap 53

Fastest speed trap
L Hamilton 214.497mph
Slowest speed trap
R Grosjean 196.539mph

Fastest pit stop
1 D Ricciardo 18.868s
2 S Vettel 18.879s
3 J Button 18.916s

CHAMPIONSHIP

	Driver	Pts
1	N Rosberg	190
2	L Hamilton	176
3	D Ricciardo	106
4	F Alonso	97
5	V Bottas	91
6	S Vettel	82
7	N Hülkenberg	69
8	J Button	59
9	K Magnussen	37
10	F Massa	30
11	S Pérez	29
12	K Räikkönen	19
13	J-É Vergne	9
14	R Grosjean	8
15	D Kvyat	6
16	J Bianchi	2

CONSTRUCTORS

	Team	Pts
1	Mercedes	366
2	Red Bull-Renault	188
3	Williams-Mercedes	121
4	Ferrari	116
5	Force India-Mercedes	98
6	McLaren-Mercedes	96
7	Toro Rosso-Renault	15
8	Lotus-Renault	8
9	Marussia-Ferrari	2

Esteban Gutiérrez
"From Friday on, we developed the car as best we could, but 14th isn't satisfying. I was fighting the entire race, trying to gain positions and keep cars behind me."

Jean-Éric Vergne
"I was having a good race until the moment in which I had to make a 5s stop-and-go penalty during my second pit stop, which compromised any possibility of scoring points."

Felipe Massa
"Going into Turn 1, I was near to Valtteri but had to back off to stop an accident; sadly some others didn't do the same. To have another race ended by another driver isn't easy."

Max Chilton
"I avoided the Turn 1 incident on the opening lap, but after that my race wasn't so good. We changed the strategy to try to get ahead of Kobayashi but it didn't work out for us."

Marcus Ericsson
"I had to serve a 10s stop-go penalty for breaking parc fermé rules after the issue with the power unit straight after the safety car came in. From then on, I had to try and play catch up."

Adrian Sutil
"After my last pit stop, I lost power and thought the engine would switch off. In the last corner I had a similar problem, then I spun and this time the engine did switch off."

Daniil Kvyat
"My first stint was OK until contact with Pérez, which lost me time. I didn't look after my tyres well enough in the second stint, but the final stint was looking good until I lost drive."

Valtteri Bottas
"To keep a Mercedes behind at the end showed that it's possible, and the car is very strong. The engineers shared information with me about the tyres and where Lewis was."

Jules Bianchi
"I had an issue at the start and fell to the back but got back ahead of Kobayashi and Max. Then the race went pretty well as I could keep everyone behind but couldn't catch the Saubers."

Kamui Kobayashi
"Bianchi got ahead so I pushed to the first pit stop where the crew helped me jump Chilton. After that, the balance was OK, but I didn't have the pace to catch the cars ahead."

ROUND 11

FORMULA 1 PIRELLI MAGYAR NAGYDÍJ

HUNGARY

AS IN THE CANADIAN GP, DANIEL RICCIARDO AND RED BULL RACING WERE IN THE RIGHT PLACE AT THE RIGHT TIME WHEN THINGS DIDN'T GO ACCORDING TO PLAN FOR MERCEDES

D aniel Ricciardo scored a popular victory in a dramatic Hungarian GP that had four cars battling for the lead in the closing laps. At a time when there was much talk about improving the show, F1 put on a fabulous display as rain and safety cars contributed to the action.

Just a week after his brake failure in qualifying for the German GP, Lewis Hamilton again found his weekend compromised by a mechanical failure that was beyond his control. Q1 started with the astonishing sight of the British Mercedes driver coasting into the pit lane entry with the rear of his car alight. It took some time to get the fire under control.

"I had bailed out of that timed lap," explained Hamilton, "and I was thinking of doing another lap when something happened to the brakes. Something failed on the brake system, so I had to engage some settings to try and correct it, and then the engine just died. I thought 'I'm right next to the pit entry, so I'll roll back and at least get them to fix it'. Then I looked in my mirrors and it was on fire. I was hoping to get it into neutral, so I could push it back or something, but no luck. Then they said 'stop, stop, stop'. I tried to stop and the brakes weren't working, the car's rolling forward, the engine's sometimes working, sometimes not working, so it's all pretty bad..."

With this problem for Hamilton and an energy store issue for Pastor Maldonado, it appeared to make getting into Q2 a formality. Alas, Ferrari relaxed too much and Kimi Räikkönen was sitting in the garage when he was bumped to 17th by Jules Bianchi.

The drama continued into Q3 as a shower affected some of the track,

and especially Turn 1. Nico Rosberg ran wide as he started his first lap and immediately behind him Kevin Magnussen spun into the tyre wall, bringing out a red flag.

At the resumption of the session, the track, although still tricky in places, soon dried out. Sebastian Vettel emerged as a pole contender and went top with his last lap, but Rosberg grabbed it back when he crossed the line a few seconds later.

Behind Vettel, Valtteri Bottas put in another good performance to claim third, ahead of the other Red Bull of Daniel Ricciardo. Fernando Alonso gave Ferrari a boost by qualifying fifth, ahead of Felipe Massa, Jenson Button, Jean-Éric Vergne and Nico Hülkenberg. Both Hamilton and Magnussen required a change of chassis, so they were demoted to pit lane starts.

Come Sunday, rain just before the start left the track soaking and the field started on intermediate tyres with the forecast suggesting that there would be more rain to come. In fact, there wasn't, but those early wet laps were a key element in how the race played out.

Rosberg led the 22 cars away on the downhill dash to the first corner, while, from his pit lane start, Hamilton spun and clipped the barrier at Turn 2. Through sheer good luck his car suffered no ill effects and he was able to continue on his way and catch up with the tail of the pack.

As Hamilton began to make up ground, Rosberg led from Bottas, Vettel, Alonso, Button and Ricciardo. The complexion of the race changed, though, when Marcus Ericsson crashed his Caterham heavily on lap 8, triggering a safety car period. The top four drivers all missed the pit exit, but Button and everyone behind him, bar Bianchi and Magnussen, came rushing in.

Button took on more intermediate tyres, as McLaren was expecting

"VETTEL EMERGED AS A POLE CONTENDER AND WENT TOP WITH HIS LAST LAP, BUT ROSBERG GRABBED IT BACK"

INSIDE LINE

DANIEL RICCIARDO
RED BULL RACING

I knew that the first safety car deployment played right into our hands. I inherited the lead there, pitting for slick tyres and then was looking alright.

"Then we had the second safety car period, and I pitted again for another set of tyres, but I obviously lost the lead. I then wasn't really sure what was going to happen next.

"I stayed out pretty long that stint and was leading a fair chunk of the mid-race laps, but then I knew I wasn't going to get to the end of the grand prix on that set of tyres.

"So I had to pit for a third time and that put me out of position. Then we knew that I had to overtake if I wanted to win.

"I then had a scare in the middle of the race as I had some issues. I was down on power and had to get a bit crazy on the switches, so I thought the race could have ended early, but we got through that.

"I ATTEMPTED LEWIS INTO TURN 2, I THINK THE LAP OR MAYBE TWO BEFORE I EVENTUALLY GOT HIM, BUT I LOCKED UP AND WENT WIDE"

"There was only one way to win it and that was to get around Hamilton and Alonso. Obviously I had the advantage of the fresher tyres, but I knew that they wouldn't make it easy. I attempted Lewis into Turn 2, I think the lap or maybe two before I eventually got him, but I locked up and went wide. I had a second crack at it and still locked up, but I managed to hang on and just had a bit more grip around the outside there. So that was that.

"Then, once I got close enough to Fernando, I knew I just had to go for it. Being in that sandwich, Lewis was still in the DRS zone, so basically I couldn't waste too much time and that's what I did. Then, once I got the lead, I knew that it was just a couple of laps to go."

TALKING POINT
HAMILTON REBUTS TEAM ORDERS

I t was unfortunate that Daniel Ricciardo's brilliant performance in Hungary was largely overshadowed after the race by the debate over Lewis Hamilton's controversial decision to ignore team orders.

The Mercedes drivers were running different strategies when Nico Rosberg came up behind and Lewis was asked to let him by. He chose not to because he was racing his teammate and because Rosberg never got that close and letting him by would have meant Lewis lost time.

"You know, I was in the same race as him," said Hamilton. "Just because he had one more stop than me doesn't mean I wasn't in the same race as him. Naturally, if I'd have let him past, he would have had the opportunity to pull away and when he does pit, he's going to come back and overtake me. So I was very, very shocked that the team would ask me to do that, to be able to improve his position. But, to be honest, he didn't get close enough to overtake me and I was never going to lift off and lose ground to Fernando or Daniel to enable him to have a better race. So, that was a bit strange."

> "THE MERCEDES DRIVERS WERE ON DIFFERENT STRATEGIES WHEN NICO CAME UP BEHIND AND LEWIS WAS ASKED TO LET HIM BY"

Mercedes bosses Toto Wolff and Niki Lauda were quick to claim after the race that they supported Hamilton's choice. Lauda admitted that the call had resulted from "panic" on the pit wall and agreed that Rosberg was never really close enough to justify any help from Hamilton.

"Mercedes was used to being in the lead and racing against each other," said Lauda. "This race, because of the safety car in the beginning and the wet conditions, was a completely different race, so every minute you had to decide something different. In this stress, the team told Lewis he should let Nico by, as he's on softer tyres and has to come in anyway.

"In Lewis's position, it was clear that if he had been in the DRS position, with Nico one second behind, for sure he would have let him by. But Nico never got that close, so therefore I do understand that Lewis asked 'Why should I stop now in the middle of the circuit to let my team colleague by?'"

further rain, while everyone else went for slicks. The top four were able to pit next time around, but when they blended back into the queue they had all lost places. The order was now Ricciardo, Button, Massa, Rosberg, Magnussen on his original intermediates, Vergne, Vettel, Alonso, Hüllkenberg, Pérez and, in a disastrous 11th place, Bottas. Hamilton was only two positions behind in the queue.

As the cars circulated behind the safety car and no more rain came, McLaren realised that both of its drivers were in trouble. At the restart at the end of lap 13, Button soon overtook Ricciardo for the lead as the track was still a little damp, but after just a couple of laps he had to pit for dry tyres, his race now ruined.

Ricciardo was left in the lead, and he gradually pulled away from Massa, to the tune of some 6s. Rosberg actually dropped away at

the restart, so Alonso was third, from Vergne. Rosberg ran fifth, just ahead of Vettel and Hamilton.

The safety car emerged for a second time on lap 23 after Sergio Pérez's Force India ran wide on to the wet artificial grass at the final corner and spun hard into the pit wall. Leaders Ricciardo and Massa both dived into the pits, as did Bottas a little further down the order. The majority of drivers opted to stay out this time, though.

The queue thus settled down with Alonso leading from Vergne, Rosberg, Vettel and Hamilton, with Ricciardo having slotted into sixth place after his pit stop.

The field was unleashed again at the end of lap 26 and Alonso soon pulled out a gap over Vergne, who was doing a great job keeping Rosberg, Vettel and Hamilton behind him. Rosberg then pitted on lap 32, to be followed a lap

Left: Vettel harries Rosberg through Turn 7, but neither would end up on the podium Above: Romain Grosjean's race came to an ignominious end when he spun out during the first safety car period Below: Daniil Kvyt leads a train of cars, but he only had the Marussias behind him by the end of the race

later by Vettel and then Vergne a lap after that.

However, Alonso stayed resolutely out front, now with none other than Hamilton sitting behind him, both men pushing their tyre life to the limit. Hamilton closed the gap to around 3s before Alonso came in on lap 39, the Mercedes driver then stopping a lap after that.

All of that activity put Ricciardo back in the lead. However, crucially the Australian planned to make one more stop, ensuring that he was on fresh rubber for the duration, while Alonso and Hamilton now wanted to go to the end of the 70-lap race.

Rosberg was following a similar strategy to Ricciardo and there was drama when he came up behind Hamilton. Mercedes told Hamilton to move over, given that his teammate was on a different strategy, had a pit stop to come and was potentially faster. An angry

"THE SAFETY CAR EMERGED FOR A SECOND TIME ON LAP 23 AFTER SERGIO PÉREZ SPUN HARD INTO THE PIT WALL"

Hamilton refused to comply. Rosberg was, in any case, never quite close enough to make a move and Hamilton didn't want to lose any track time by going out of his way to let his teammate by.

Ricciardo dropped out of the lead when he pitted for a third time on lap 54 and then Rosberg did the same on lap 56. We now had Alonso and Hamilton at the front trying to make it home on old tyres, while Ricciardo quickly caught them. Rosberg was in turn closing in in fourth, albeit from some way back. Ricciardo then pulled off two great passing moves to shoot past first Hamilton and then Alonso to claim the lead with just two laps to go.

By now, Alonso's tyres were completely shot, but somehow he held off Hamilton over the remaining few miles while Hamilton in turn managed to stay ahead of Rosberg to claim the final spot on

the podium. The top four were covered by just 6.361s as they swept past the flag. It had been quite a race. Red Bull's strategy had played out to perfection and Ricciardo had put in a faultless performance.

"This is even more satisfying than Montreal because we actually beat them without problems," said Red Bull Racing's Christian Horner. "We got the strategy right, it was a great performance by Daniel, the pit stops were good, the overtaking moves were excellent and we beat two Mercedes that didn't have any mechanical problems."

Alonso put in a brilliant drive with the unloved F14 T, making his soft tyres last for the final 32 laps – while pursuer Hamilton did 31 on the more durable mediums. The Spaniard compared it to a victory, given the usual form of the car.

"This circuit didn't change our performance much," he said, "but today we had a little bit of a chaotic race and took every opportunity we had in front of us. I think cars from behind also had some issues, with Rosberg, with Hamilton yesterday, with the issues in qualifying, so we got this position for free."

Hamilton's great drive from the pit lane to third was inevitably overshadowed by the team order saga and neither driver was happy afterwards. The team bosses didn't blame Hamilton for not ceding his position, despite suggestions that Rosberg could have won the race had he been given clean air.

Both Williams drivers had pitted for medium tyres when the second safety car came out on lap 23, with the intention of running to the end. It proved to be a mistake, as they lacked speed and both had to make a second stop anyway, with Bottas finally giving in with 11 laps to go. Massa finished fifth, but his teammate could salvage only eighth.

From 17th on the grid, Räikkönen lost a lot of time in traffic, but he worked his way up to sixth by the finish. Vettel could only recover to seventh after losing out under that first safety car, and later surviving a spectacular spin on the pit straight.

On a fully dry track, Vergne slipped back to ninth, behind Bottas. A frustrated Button salvaged a point for 10th, finishing just ahead of Magnussen, with McLaren blaming its quirky strategy choice on a weather forecasting software problem. It was truly an afternoon to forget for the Woking team.

"RICCIARDO THEN PULLED OFF TWO GREAT PASSING MOVES TO SHOOT PAST FIRST HAMILTON AND THEN ALONSO"

Above: Alonso's tyre management was remarkable en route to second. **Right:** Ricciardo flashes across the finish line and his delight at winning was clear to all in parc fermé (below)

CLOCKWISE FROM RIGHT:
The crowds were, as always, huge in Hungary; Felipe Massa splashes out of the pits; sunset splendour; another new helmet livery for Romain Grosjean; Jenson Button and fiancée Jessica Michibata; Nico Hülkenberg runs back to the pits; Mercedes tech chief Paddy Lowe checks to see what weather is arriving

SNAPSHOT FROM HUNGARY

HUNGARY
HUNGARORING
ROUND 11

Official Results © [2014]
Formula One World
Championship Limited,
6 Princes Gate, London SW7
1QJ. No reproduction without
permission. All copyright and
database rights reserved.

RACE DATE 27 July
CIRCUIT LENGTH 2.719 miles
NO. OF LAPS 70
RACE DISTANCE 190.300 miles
WEATHER Wet but drying, 22ºC
TRACK TEMP 28ºC
LAP RECORD Michael Schumacher,
1m19.071s, 123.828mph, 2004

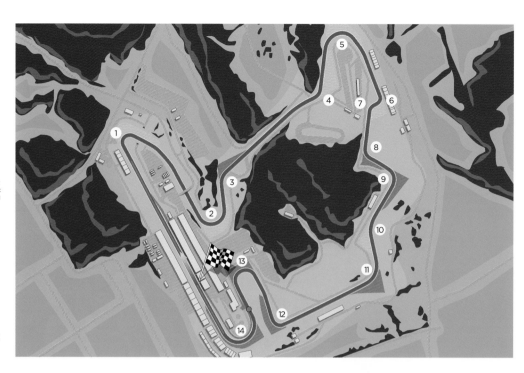

PRACTICE 1				PRACTICE 2				PRACTICE 3				QUALIFYING 1			QUALIFYING 2	
	Driver	Time	Laps		Driver	Time	Laps		Driver	Time	Laps		Driver	Time		Driver	Time
1	L Hamilton	1m25.814s	27	1	L Hamilton	1m24.482s	38	1	L Hamilton	1m24.048s	21	1	J-É Vergne	1m24.941s	1	N Rosberg	1m23.310s
2	F Alonso	1m25.997s	31	2	N Rosberg	1m24.720s	38	2	N Rosberg	1m24.095s	24	2	N Rosberg	1m25.227s	2	S Vettel	1m23.606s
3	K Räikkönen	1m26.421s	29	3	S Vettel	1m25.111s	33	3	S Vettel	1m24.455s	16	3	D Kvyat	1m25.361s	3	D Ricciardo	1m23.676s
4	F Alonso	1m26.872s	23	4	F Alonso	1m25.437s	26	4	D Ricciardo	1m24.678s	15	4	D Ricciardo	1m25.495s	4	V Bottas	1m23.776s
5	S Vettel	1m27.220s	28	5	K Magnussen	1m25.580s	34	5	V Bottas	1m24.685s	21	5	S Vettel	1m25.662s	5	F Massa	1m24.030s
6	K Magnussen	1m27.357s	28	6	K Räikkönen	1m25.730s	30	6	F Alonso	1m24.769s	11	6	V Bottas	1m25.690s	6	F Alonso	1m24.249s
7	J-É Vergne	1m27.683s	30	7	D Ricciardo	1m25.983s	29	7	K Räikkönen	1m24.818s	19	7	E Gutiérrez	1m25.709s	7	J Button	1m24.502s
8	D Ricciardo	1m27.782s	16	8	V Bottas	1m25.999s	37	8	K Magnussen	1m24.867s	21	8	S Pérez	1m25.910s	8	K Magnussen	1m24.585s
9	J Button	1m27.804s	27	9	J Button	1m26.234s	33	9	J-É Vergne	1m25.162s	17	9	A Sutil	1m26.027s	9	J-É Vergne	1m24.637s
10	F Massa	1m27.960s	24	10	F Massa	1m26.402s	18	10	D Kvyat	1m25.170s	19	10	F Alonso	1m26.087s	10	N Hülkenberg	1m24.647s
11	E Gutiérrez	1m27.967s	25	11	D Kvyat	1m26.689s	42	11	F Massa	1m25.231s	18	11	R Grosjean	1m26.136s	11	D Kvyat	1m24.706s
12	N Hülkenberg	1m28.101s	28	12	J-É Vergne	1m26.703s	37	12	J Button	1m25.468s	14	12	N Hülkenberg	1m26.149s	12	A Sutil	1m25.136s
13	D Kvyat	1m28.208s	32	13	N Hülkenberg	1m26.789s	39	13	P Maldonado	1m25.829s	22	13	K Magnussen	1m26.578s	13	S Pérez	1m25.211s
14	P Maldonado	1m28.266s	28	14	A Sutil	1m26.919s	41	14	R Grosjean	1m25.859s	19	14	F Massa	1m26.592s	14	E Gutiérrez	1m25.260s
15	V Bottas	1m28.330s	21	15	S Pérez	1m27.013s	39	15	A Sutil	1m25.934s	21	15	J Button	1m26.612s	15	R Grosjean	1m25.337s
16	S Pérez	1m28.376s	24	16	P Maldonado	1m27.019s	40	16	E Gutiérrez	1m26.023s	23	16	J Bianchi	1m26.728s	16	J Bianchi	1m27.419s
17	R Grosjean	1m28.593s	24	17	R Grosjean	1m27.021s	14	17	N Hülkenberg	1m26.035s	19	17	K Räikkönen	1m26.792s			
18	A Sutil	1m29.025s	23	18	E Gutiérrez	1m27.480s	32	18	S Pérez	1m26.142s	17	18	K Kobayashi	1m27.139s			
19	K Kobayashi	1m30.363s	30	19	K Kobayashi	1m28.370s	35	19	K Kobayashi	1m27.560s	23	19	M Chilton	1m27.819s			
20	M Ericsson	1m30.892s	24	20	J Bianchi	1m28.469s	26	20	M Chilton	1m28.083s	17	20	M Ericsson	1m28.643s			
21	M Chilton	1m31.004s	5	21	M Chilton	1m28.586s	35	21	M Ericsson	1m28.605s	22	21	L Hamilton	no time			
22	J Bianchi	1m31.248s	20	22	M Ericsson	1m29.036s	34	22	J Bianchi	1m28.821s	14	22	P Maldonado	no time			

Best sectors – Practice			Speed trap – Practice			Best sectors – Qualifying			Speed trap – Qualifying		
Sec 1	L Hamilton	29.615s	1	L Hamilton	196.167mph	Sec 1	N Rosberg	29.197s	1	F Massa	196.229mph
Sec 2	L Hamilton	30.407s	2	F Massa	194.924mph	Sec 2	N Rosberg	30.036s	2	V Bottas	195.607mph
Sec 3	L Hamilton	23.729s	3	N Rosberg	194.302mph	Sec 3	N Rosberg	23.482s	3	N Rosberg	193.619mph

Sebastian Vettel

"It wasn't a great race. I spun and before that was unlucky with the safety car in the first stint. Unluckily, I was then in the wrong mode for the restart and I lost two places."

Nico Rosberg

"A few things didn't work out. The safety car cost me the lead as I just missed the pit entry. I also had braking issues after it went in. Then I was able to push a lot."

Fernando Alonso

"This podium means a lot to me as, after so many difficult races, we managed to get the most out of everything, also taking a few risks and so second seems like a win."

Pastor Maldonado

"It was a tough race as it was a struggle to find enough grip and the track was very slippery. I didn't always have full power, which certainly added to the challenge."

Jenson Button

"It was a tough afternoon as we didn't make the right decisions. The opening laps in the rain were great: I got up into fifth place, but it all went downhill from there."

Sergio Pérez

"Just when it looked like I could score some big points. I went wide on the exit kerb of the final corner, lost the rear and that was it. I was in the wall. It was very unlucky."

Daniel Ricciardo

"To have to pass guys again to win, as I did in Canada, makes it a lot more satisfying. In this environment I feel I am a different driver and in a way now a different sportsman."

Lewis Hamilton

"I was just pushing as hard as possible to get as high as I could. I can't express the pain I feel when we have issues such as in the last couple of races; it's hard to swallow."

Kimi Räikkönen

"After qualifying, sixth place was the most I could hope for. I got away well at the start but lost time behind a Sauber and when I caught Massa, couldn't get by."

Romain Grosjean

"The conditions were tricky and I couldn't get the best out of the tyres. We made the right call to move to slicks when the safety car came out but I made a slight mistake."

Kevin Magnussen

"Having started from the pit lane, I don't think that I lost too much by choosing to stay on the inters. I know we took a risk to wait for more rain, but we had to take that risk."

Nico Hülkenberg

"The track was drying when I made contact with Checo at the final corner. He'd taken a wider line on the previous lap so I tried to pass on the inside, but he took a tighter line."

POSITIONS LAP BY LAP

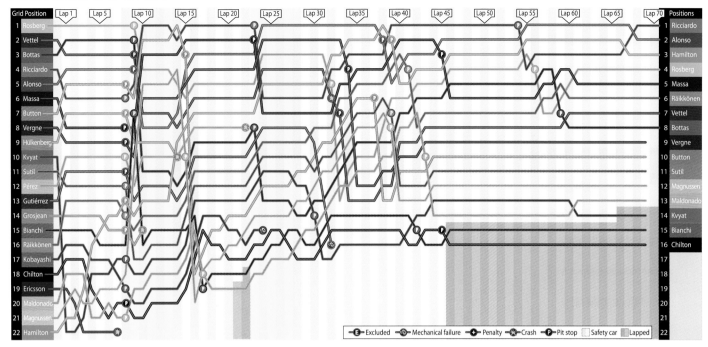

Grid Position		Positions	
1	Rosberg	1	Ricciardo
2	Vettel	2	Alonso
3	Bottas	3	Hamilton
4	Ricciardo	4	Rosberg
5	Alonso	5	Massa
6	Massa	6	Räikkönen
7	Button	7	Vettel
8	Vergne	8	Bottas
9	Hülkenberg	9	Vergne
10	Kvyat	10	Button
11	Sutil	11	Sutil
12	Pérez	12	Magnussen
13	Gutiérrez	13	Maldonado
14	Grosjean	14	Kvyat
15	Bianchi	15	Bianchi
16	Räikkönen	16	Chilton
17	Kobayashi	17	
18	Chilton	18	
19	Ericsson	19	
20	Maldonado	20	
21	Magnussen	21	
22	Hamilton	22	

Legend: E- Excluded · M- Mechanical failure · P- Penalty · K- Crash · P- Pit stop · Safety car · Lapped

QUALIFYING 3

	Driver	Time
1	N Rosberg	1m22.715s
2	S Vettel	1m23.201s
3	V Bottas	1m23.354s
4	D Ricciardo	1m23.391s
5	F Alonso	1m23.909s
6	F Massa	1m24.223s
7	J Button	1m24.294s
8	J-É Vergne	1m24.720s
9	N Hülkenberg	1m24.775s
10	K Magnussen	no time

GRID

	Driver	Time
1	N Rosberg	1m22.715s
2	S Vettel	1m23.201s
3	V Bottas	1m23.354s
4	D Ricciardo	1m23.391s
5	F Alonso	1m23.909s
6	F Massa	1m24.223s
7	J Button	1m24.294s
8	J-É Vergne	1m24.720s
9	N Hülkenberg	1m24.775s
10	D Kvyat	1m24.706s
11	A Sutil	1m25.136s
12	S Pérez	1m25.211s
13	E Gutiérrez	1m25.260s
14	R Grosjean	1m25.337s
15	J Bianchi	1m27.419s
16	K Räikkönen	1m26.792s
17	K Kobayashi	1m27.139s
18	M Chilton	1m27.819s
19	M Ericsson	1m28.643s
20	P Maldonado	no time
21	K Magnussen	no time
22	L Hamilton	no time

Grid penalties

P Maldonado 5-place penalty for gearbox change
K Magnussen Put to back of grid as car modified in parc fermé
L Hamilton Put to back of grid as car modified in parc fermé

RACE

	Driver	Car	Laps	Time	Av mph	Fastest	Stops
1	D Ricciardo	Red Bull-Renault RB10	70	1h53m05.058s	101.096	1m26.608s	3
2	F Alonso	Ferrari F14 T	70	1h53m10.283s	101.013	1m27.419s	2
3	L Hamilton	Mercedes F1 W05	70	1h53m10.915s	101.004	1m27.380s	2
4	N Rosberg	Mercedes F1 W05	70	1h53m11.419s	100.996	1m25.724s	3
5	F Massa	Williams-Mercedes FW36	70	1h53m34.899s	100.648	1m28.229s	3
6	K Räikkönen	Ferrari F14 T	70	1h53m36.549s	100.624	1m27.983s	2
7	S Vettel	Red Bull-Renault RB10	70	1h53m46.022s	100.484	1m28.746s	2
8	V Bottas	Williams-Mercedes FW36	70	1h53m46.402s	100.479	1m26.850s	3
9	J-É Vergne	Toro Rosso-Renault STR9	70	1h54m03.585s	100.226	1m29.120s	2
10	J Button	McLaren-Mercedes MP4-29	70	1h54m12.338s	100.098	1m29.156s	3
11	A Sutil	Sauber-Ferrari C33	70	1h54m13.227s	100.085	1m28.704s	2
12	K Magnussen	McLaren-Mercedes MP4-29	70	1h54m23.523s	99.936	1m28.883s	2
13	P Maldonado	Lotus-Renault E22	70	1h54m29.082s	99.854	1m29.128s	3
14	D Kvyat	Toro Rosso-Renault STR9	69	1h53m23.731s	99.373	1m29.401s	2
15	J Bianchi	Marussia-Ferrari MR03	69	1h53m53.390s	98.942	1m29.883s	3
16	M Chilton	Marussia-Ferrari MR03	69	1h53m53.894s	98.935	1m29.499s	2
R	E Gutiérrez	Sauber-Ferrari C33	32	Power unit	-	1m30.485s	1
R	K Kobayashi	Caterham-Renault CT05	24	Fuel system	-	1m32.888s	1
R	S Pérez	Force India-Mercedes VJM07	22	Spun off	-	1m30.280s	1
R	N Hülkenberg	Force India-Mercedes VJM07	14	Accident	-	1m41.151s	1
R	R Grosjean	Lotus-Renault E22	10	Spun off	-	1m46.312s	1
R	M Ericsson	Caterham-Renault CT05	7	Spun off	-	1m48.459s	0

Fastest lap
N Rosberg 1m25.724s
(114.326mph) on lap 64

Fastest speed trap
V Bottas 196.104mph

Slowest speed trap
R Grosjean 181.316mph

Fastest pit stop
1 S Vettel 21.608s
2 F Alonso 21.634s
3 K Magnussen 21.812s

CHAMPIONSHIP

	Driver	Pts
1	N Rosberg	202
2	L Hamilton	191
3	D Ricciardo	131
4	F Alonso	115
5	V Bottas	95
6	S Vettel	88
7	N Hülkenberg	69
8	J Button	60
9	F Massa	40
10	K Magnussen	37
11	S Pérez	29
12	K Räikkönen	27
13	J-É Vergne	11
14	R Grosjean	8
15	D Kvyat	6
16	J Bianchi	2

CONSTRUCTORS

	Team	Pts
1	Mercedes	393
2	Red Bull-Renault	219
3	Ferrari	142
4	Williams-Mercedes	135
5	Force India-Mercedes	98
6	McLaren-Mercedes	97
7	Toro Rosso-Renault	17
8	Lotus-Renault	8
9	Marussia-Ferrari	2

Esteban Gutiérrez
"The race started well, as I gained places. I pitted during the safety car period then, after the restart, was fighting with Kimi, but then my car developed an ERS problem."

Jean-Éric Vergne
"The team did a fantastic job to call me in straight after the safety car. I knew that I didn't have the pace to keep up with the others around me, but it was a great fun race."

Felipe Massa
"It was a very difficult race. We had many fights and it was difficult to stay on the track. We took some risks with the tyres in the pit stops and in the end it was a good result."

Max Chilton
"I got a good start. Then, with Kobayashi and Ericsson out of the picture and Jules having to make an unscheduled pit stop, it was good to be able to move up through the field."

Marcus Ericsson
"It was quite a good race until I crashed on lap 7. I was having a good fight with Chilton and Maldonado, trying to line them up through Turn 3 and I was a bit too eager on the throttle."

Adrian Sutil
"I pitted during the first safety car period, but had to wait as Esteban was there. I was faster than Jenson in the corners, but I just couldn't overtake him and so I finished 11th."

Daniil Kvyat
"I'm not sure what happened at the start, as it's never happened before. The engine just stalled and so I was forced to start from the pit lane. I tried to catch up but overtaking was difficult."

Valtteri Bottas
"After three podiums in a row, eighth place isn't satisfying. There was more to come today but we were unlucky with the safety car when I went from second to out of the top 10."

Jules Bianchi
"That was a tough race as I had to drive for more than 50 laps with a damaged car. Maldonado came from nowhere and hit me in the side. I was really fearful it would put me out of the race."

Kamui Kobayashi
"I had a big moment with Maldonado when he spun. That's the third race in a row I've had a near miss. Later, my car had an issue with the fuel system and I had to stop as I had no power."

BELGI

SHELL BELGIAN GRAND PRIX

A DRAMATIC AFTERNOON ENDED IN A
THIRD VICTORY FOR DANIEL RICCIARDO,
BUT THE MAJOR TALKING POINT WAS
THE SECOND LAP COLLISION BETWEEN
NICO ROSBERG AND LEWIS HAMILTON

T he clash between Lewis Hamilton and Nico Rosberg that occurred on lap 2 resulted in a puncture for Lewis and his eventual retirement in the closing laps when it became clear that he wouldn't score any points. Delayed by front wing damage, Rosberg at least salvaged second after just failing to chase down Ricciardo. He was booed by fans when he walked out on to the podium and, sadly, the internal strife at Mercedes unfairly took attention away from another superb drive by Ricciardo, who outperformed teammate Sebastian Vettel again.

Rosberg outpaced Hamilton to take his fourth consecutive pole in a tricky, wet qualifying session, although it was also only the fifth time in 12 races that Mercedes had locked out the front row, an indication that things hadn't always gone to plan in 2014. A rainstorm that included hail ensured that the track was soaking for qualifying, and further showers meant that it remained wet for the duration. However, despite the conditions, qualifying proved to be relatively uneventful, with Mercedes dominating all three sessions.

Rosberg was fastest in Q1, but the tables were turned in Q2 as Hamilton pipped him. However, when it mattered in Q3, Hamilton had some brake issues and struggled to get a clean lap in. After a couple of moments, he ended up 0.228s behind Rosberg.

"I had a glazed front left brake, so the car was pulling to the right," said an obviously disappointed Hamilton. "This is a circuit where, like all circuits, you need to have confidence in the brakes."

There was a 2.126s margin from Rosberg on pole to Vettel in third.

Red Bull had anticipated a tough weekend at a track where straightline speed is so vital, so the weather obviously helped the RB10 to beat the rest. Ferrari's Fernando Alonso jumped up to fourth at the end, ensuring that there were two World Champions on the second row, waiting to pounce should the Mercedes hit any trouble.

Ricciardo qualified fifth, while Valtteri Bottas was only sixth at a track where Williams was expected to push Mercedes hard. Kevin Magnussen earned seventh for McLaren ahead of Kimi Räikkönen, Felipe Massa and Jenson Button.

Sunday turned out dry and there was excitement at the start of the formation lap when Alonso had a problem and the Ferrari mechanics were late stepping away from the car. The stewards gave the Spaniard a 5s stop-and-go penalty, which rivals thought was a lucky escape.

Rosberg got away poorly from

With Nico Rosberg having a poor start, Lewis Hamilton and Sebastian Vettel were ahead by La Source. **Right:** Hamilton leads Vettel and Rosberg through Eau Rouge. **Below right:** it was wet in qualifying and Valtteri Bottas was disappointed to qualify only sixth

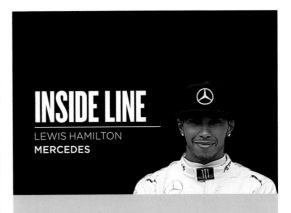

INSIDE LINE
LEWIS HAMILTON
MERCEDES

I thought that today was going to be a good day. When I started second, I knew I was on a different strategy to Nico. I knew that I would be on the prime tyre in the middle stint of the race, so I knew that I had a chance even if I didn't get him at the start. I knew that it would be a long race, a hard race, and I thought that we would have a good one.

"The team has allowed us to race and we've been good at racing wheel-to-wheel. I heard someone say that it was inevitable that we were going to crash one day, I don't feel that today was that inevitability. I took the inside line, I had the corner, we braked very deep, because if I'd braked early he would have come down the outside. I made the corner on my normal line. He was in my blind spot. I can see actually quite far behind me, and I knew that he was behind, so I continued along my line.

"I TOOK THE INSIDE LINE, I HAD THE CORNER, WE BRAKED VERY DEEP, BECAUSE IF I'D BRAKED EARLY HE WOULD HAVE COME DOWN THE OUTSIDE"

"When a car is less than half a car length alongside you and you're in the inside, it's your racing line. It's not your job to go massively out of your way to leave extra room. And it wasn't one of those corners where there's a wall there or anything.

"I thought for sure there would be an investigation. I'm mostly disappointed for the team, but also for myself because I lose points, and that makes my championship challenge a lot harder. Coming into this weekend the team – I don't know why because we were already racing hard with each other – said we want you to be able to race. I don't know how Nico took that differently, because for me the priority was still for the team to finish."

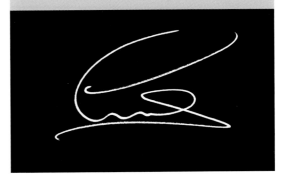

pole and both Hamilton and Vettel went around the outside of him.

The Red Bull driver then tried to overtake Hamilton for the lead on the outside line at the top of the hill. It was a cheeky move, but he thought better of it and ran wide over the Les Combes chicane, dropping back to third. Right behind him, Ricciardo briefly got past Alonso, but he too ran wide, although he didn't cut the corner as dramatically as his teammate had.

It was in the same place on the second lap that Rosberg had a look down the outside of Hamilton. When the British driver stuck to the racing line, the German kept his nose there and, as he turned in, he clipped his teammate's left rear wheel. In an instant, the tyre deflated but Hamilton managed to keep control of the car. However, he was left with an agonisingly long drive back to the pits and by the time he emerged with a new set of

tyres he was a minute behind leader Rosberg. Inevitably, the flailing tyre had also caused some aero damage.

Rosberg himself had lost a chunk of his front wing endplate, which cost him some front-end grip. The team told him to stay out and wait until the pit stop window opened. The result was that, unlike in other races in 2014, he couldn't open up a gap. Meanwhile, from fifth on the grid, Ricciardo passed Alonso and then took Vettel when the World Champion ran wide and had a tankslapper on a kerb. Now in second place, Ricciardo really kept Rosberg on his toes.

"I actually had the inside of Alonso at Turn 5 on the opening lap," said the Australian, "but then I locked up and went off, so he got me back and then I was able to get in front a few laps later. And then Seb looked like he just dropped a wheel on the Astroturf exit of the first part of Pouhon and with the

TALKING POINT
RACE CLASH LEADS TO MEETINGS

The summer break had allowed tensions to relax in the Mercedes camp after the Hungarian GP team-orders saga, but following the second lap collision at Spa things quickly reached boiling point once again and team boss Toto Wolff found himself dealing with another crisis.

After the race, both Wolff and Niki Lauda were quick to blame Nico Rosberg for breaking the golden rule by making contact with his teammate, and things ramped up when Lewis Hamilton spoke to British journalists after what must have been a fairly heated debrief.

"We just had a meeting about it and he basically said he did it on purpose," said the British driver. "He said he did it on purpose – he said he could have avoided it. He said 'I did it to prove a point'. You don't have to just rely on me, go and ask Toto about it and those guys, who were not happy with him either.

> **"AFTER THE RACE, BOTH WOLFF AND NIKI LAUDA WERE QUICK TO BLAME NICO ROSBERG FOR BREAKING THE GOLDEN RULE BY MAKING CONTACT"**

"What we're told to do is that we have to finish for the team. The team has priority, always. Even if they say we can race, the team has priority, so it doesn't mean that we can go out there and crash into each other."

This was manna from heaven for the media, especially given that the FIA had not even formally investigated the collision, after quickly deeming it a racing incident. However, Wolff immediately responded by saying that Rosberg's words had been misinterpreted. As for the FIA, Hamilton's allegation was a matter of hearsay resulting from a behind-closed-doors discussion and there was no point in pursuing it further.

The following Friday, the drivers met Wolff and Paddy Lowe again back at the team's base in Brackley. A team statement said that Rosberg had acknowledged responsibility and that "suitable disciplinary measures have been taken for the incident", although details of what that entailed were never officially confirmed.

The team noted: "Lewis and Nico understand and accept the team's number one rule – there must be no contact between the team's cars on track. It has been made clear that another such incident will not be tolerated."

rain overnight and this morning it was still a bit slippery, so I was able to get past him."

Mercedes opted to bring Rosberg in very early, on lap 8. He changed to the prime tyre and lost seven extra seconds relative to a normal pit stop while the nose was replaced. Ricciardo thus assumed the advantage that would put him into the lead after his pit stop.

"I think Nico came in for a front wing change," said Ricciardo, "and so we were able to get into the lead and then the pace was pretty good. We were happy with what we were doing and the consistency was there. We were making the tyres last too."

Red Bull knew that Spa would be a tough circuit for the Renault power unit and had set the cars up with low downforce, and that proved just the ticket as Ricciardo was able to pull away from Vettel, Bottas and Alonso while keeping his tyres in good shape.

After his long pit stop dropped him down the order, Rosberg had a lot of overtaking to do. With his new nose, he was lapping at a representative pace once more and was gaining ground, although he was distracted for a while by a piece of debris that became caught on an antenna on top of the cockpit.

Vettel pitted from second on lap 11 and leader Ricciardo came in a lap after that, leaving Bottas in front until he pitted, along with Alonso. The Ferrari driver then lost some ground thanks to his 5s penalty.

When they were all back on track, Ricciardo led again from

Far left: Ricciardo harried Rosberg and the pressure paid off. Above: This sweep through Eau Rouge continues to epitomise the attraction of Spa-Francorchamps. Left: Jean-Éric Vergne ended up just outside the points in 11th

Räikkönen (who had gained from an early pit stop), Vettel, Rosberg and Bottas. Rosberg now found himself stuck behind Vettel and was told on the radio that he had to pass the Red Bull. Yet, given that he was on the prime and Vettel on the quicker option, it wasn't that easy. At the end of lap 16, Rosberg had a big lock-up at the chicane in his efforts to get past. That allowed Bottas to close up and, with the help of DRS, the Finn drafted past.

Rosberg now had even more work to do and, having flat-spotted a front tyre, he made an early second pit stop on lap 19, again taking the harder compound tyre and dropping as low as 10th. Once again, he had some passing to do.

Ricciardo was doing a superb job out front and he was able to

"WHEN THE BRITISH DRIVER STUCK TO THE RACING LINE, THE GERMAN KEPT HIS NOSE THERE"

stay out longer than most of his pursuers at the second round of pit stops, finally coming in on lap 27. Bottas would have taken the lead, but came in a lap after that.

When it all settled down, Ricciardo still led, from Rosberg, Räikkönen, Vettel and Bottas. Now it was a question of who could get to the chequered flag without another stop. Mercedes took a gamble by bringing Rosberg in for a third pit stop with 10 laps to go and putting him on the faster soft tyres, while Ricciardo was trying to get to the flag with a 17-lap final stint on the medium.

Following Rosberg's pit stop, Ricciardo had a margin of 22s to play with, but the Mercedes driver immediately began to bring it down. At one stage, it seemed certain that he would catch the Red Bull by the

last lap, but in the end Ricciardo hung on to win by just 3.3s.

Regarding his clash with Hamilton, Rosberg said: "It is always going to be an intense battle, that's clear. It was clear from the onset and there will always be difficult moments. Then, just as we did after Hungary, we had a discussion and moved on. I'm sure we're going to have to discuss today again and we'll review it and then we'll move on."

Bottas had another strong race for Williams to take third place, passing countryman Räikkönen with four laps to go. Fourth place still represented the Ferrari driver's best result of the year so far. Like Rosberg, Vettel also made a third pit stop to give himself fresh tyres for the run to the flag and in the closing laps he was able to recover to fifth place after fighting his way through a gaggle of cars.

Magnussen took sixth place on the road after being embroiled in a dramatic fight with Vettel, Button and Alonso in the closing laps. However, the stewards deemed that he had leaned too hard on the Spanish driver and he dropped down to 12th after being docked 20s. Button thus moved up to sixth, ahead of Alonso, who had crunched his nose on Vettel at the start of the last lap and had to crawl around to the flag. The top 10 was completed by Daniil Kvyat, Sergio Pérez, and Nico Hülkenberg.

Hamilton had asked several times about continuing, as he was making little progress and was just putting unnecessary miles on his power unit. Late in the race, the team let him park, a move that also allowed the management to talk to him before he met the media. Nevertheless, in the hours after the race it was clear that this story wouldn't go away.

"MERCEDES TOOK A GAMBLE BY BRINGING ROSBERG IN FOR A THIRD STOP WITH 10 LAPS TO GO"

Top: Ricciardo had every reason to celebrate after winning a race that his team was sure would go to Mercedes. Right: Ricciardo wins with Rosberg in the background

CLOCKWISE FROM RIGHT: Red Bull Racing team principal Christian Horner does the ice-bucket challenge; Eau Rouge in the wet; Ferrari's lack of horsepower clearly didn't delight Fernando Alonso; Daniil Kvyat puts up spray as he heads out to qualify; André Lotterer was to have the briefest of F1 debut runs for Caterham; Ferrari F1 boss Marco Mattiacci; Valtteri Bottas enters the Williams pit garage; tree-framed shots continue to be a staple at Spa-Francorchamps

SNAPSHOT FROM BELGIUM

BELGIUM
SPA-FRANCORCHAMPS
ROUND 12

Official Results © [2014]
Formula One World
Championship Limited, 6
Princes Gate, London, SW7
1QJ. No reproduction without
permission. All copyright and
database rights reserved.

RACE DATE 24 August

CIRCUIT LENGTH 4.352 miles

NO. OF LAPS 44

RACE DISTANCE 191.488 miles

WEATHER Overcast, 16ºC

TRACK TEMP 31ºC

LAP RECORD Sebastian Vettel,
1m47.263s, 146.065mph, 2009

PRACTICE 1

	Driver	Time	Laps
1	N Rosberg	1m51.577s	25
2	L Hamilton	1m51.674s	24
3	F Alonso	1m51.805s	16
4	J Button	1m52.404s	21
5	K Räikkönen	1m52.818s	17
6	S Pérez	1m52.903s	24
7	K Magnussen	1m52.922s	23
8	N Hülkenberg	1m52.937s	22
9	D Ricciardo	1m52.972s	19
10	V Bottas	1m53.172s	20
11	S Vettel	1m53.369s	11
12	D Kvyat	1m53.594s	21
13	R Grosjean	1m53.597s	20
14	A Sutil	1m53.703s	14
15	F Massa	1m53.968s	20
16	J-É Vergne	1m54.189s	20
17	G van der Garde	1m54.335s	16
18	P Maldonado	1m55.336s	21
19	J Bianchi	1m55.782s	19
20	A Rossi	1m57.232s	20
21	A Lotterer	1m57.886s	24
22	M Ericsson	1m57.977s	24

PRACTICE 2

	Driver	Time	Laps
1	L Hamilton	1m49.189s	26
2	N Rosberg	1m49.793s	28
3	F Alonso	1m49.930s	19
4	F Massa	1m50.327s	24
5	J Button	1m50.659s	31
6	V Bottas	1m50.677s	26
7	D Kvyat	1m50.725s	25
8	D Ricciardo	1m50.977s	16
9	K Magnussen	1m51.074s	31
10	N Hülkenberg	1m51.077s	26
11	J-É Vergne	1m51.383s	26
12	A Sutil	1m51.450s	29
13	S Pérez	1m51.573s	28
14	R Grosjean	1m52.196s	25
15	K Räikkönen	1m52.234s	18
16	J Bianchi	1m52.776s	23
17	E Gutiérrez	1m53.955s	7
18	M Chilton	1m54.040s	18
19	M Ericsson	1m54.050s	30
20	A Lotterer	1m54.093s	24
21	P Maldonado	no time	2
22	S Vettel	no time	0

PRACTICE 3

	Driver	Time	Laps
1	V Bottas	1m49.465s	12
2	D Ricciardo	1m49.733s	9
3	N Rosberg	1m49.739s	13
4	K Räikkönen	1m49.817s	9
5	L Hamilton	1m49.817s	13
6	F Alonso	1m49.890s	9
7	D Kvyat	1m49.893s	11
8	J Button	1m50.203s	11
9	F Massa	1m50.423s	11
10	J-É Vergne	1m50.535s	10
11	S Pérez	1m50.592s	12
12	K Magnussen	1m50.748s	11
13	S Vettel	1m50.814s	10
14	N Hülkenberg	1m50.866s	11
15	A Sutil	1m50.962s	12
16	R Grosjean	1m51.509s	9
17	P Maldonado	1m51.610s	10
18	E Gutiérrez	1m51.898s	15
19	J Bianchi	1m52.457s	14
20	M Chilton	1m52.984s	14
21	M Ericsson	1m54.294s	11
22	A Lotterer	1m55.008s	13

QUALIFYING 1

	Driver	Time
1	N Rosberg	2m07.130s
2	L Hamilton	2m07.280s
3	F Massa	2m08.403s
4	V Bottas	2m09.250s
5	J-É Vergne	2m09.811s
6	K Räikkönen	2m09.885s
7	D Ricciardo	2m10.089s
8	S Vettel	2m10.105s
9	F Alonso	2m10.197s
10	D Kvyat	2m10.445s
11	J Button	2m10.529s
12	S Pérez	2m10.666s
13	R Grosjean	2m10.898s
14	J Bianchi	2m11.051s
15	A Sutil	2m11.051s
16	K Magnussen	2m11.081s
17	P Maldonado	2m11.261s
18	N Hülkenberg	2m11.267s
19	M Chilton	2m12.566s
20	E Gutiérrez	2m13.414s
21	A Lotterer	2m13.469s
22	M Ericsson	2m14.438s

QUALIFYING 2

	Driver	Time
1	L Hamilton	2m06.609s
2	N Rosberg	2m06.723s
3	F Alonso	2m08.450s
4	V Bottas	2m08.451s
5	K Räikkönen	2m08.646s
6	F Massa	2m08.833s
7	S Vettel	2m08.868s
8	K Magnussen	2m08.901s
9	D Ricciardo	2m08.989s
10	J Button	2m09.272s
11	D Kvyat	2m09.377s
12	J-É Vergne	2m09.805s
13	S Pérez	2m10.084s
14	A Sutil	2m10.238s
15	R Grosjean	2m11.087s
16	J Bianchi	2m12.470s

Best sectors – Practice

Sec 1	F Alonso	31.024s
Sec 2	L Hamilton	48.600s
Sec 3	F Alonso	29.200s

Speed trap – Practice

1	F Alonso	194.365mph
2	D Ricciardo	194.302mph
3	L Hamilton	193.495mph

Best sectors – Qualifying

Sec 1	N Rosberg	33.678s
Sec 2	N Rosberg	59.395s
Sec 3	N Rosberg	32.486s

Speed trap – Qualifying

1	L Hamilton	172.865mph
2	V Bottas	170.131mph
3	D Ricciardo	168.267mph

Sebastian Vettel
"I was in a rush near the end to get through as the laps were going down and Alonso and Magnussen didn't have fresh tyres, so Jenson and I caught them fairly quickly."

Nico Rosberg
"I had the pace to win, but the incident cost us a top result. As drivers, we're here to entertain, so our duels are always on the limit. I regret that Lewis and I touched."

Fernando Alonso
"My race started on the back foot as the car didn't fire up. It's a shame as we had strong pace all weekend and, if I'd started fourth, I could have finished on the podium."

Pastor Maldonado
"It might have been possible to fight with Sauber and Force India, but I felt a loss of power at the end of lap 1 and saw in the mirrors that the engine was smoking a lot."

Jenson Button
"We played the long game and I felt I kept the tyres in good condition. I also had a lot of fun out there, especially racing Kevin, Sebastian and Fernando at the end."

Sergio Pérez
"Somehow I avoided all the battles and my race was straightforward. I lost time in the second stint, having to pass the McLarens and took too much out of the tyres."

Daniel Ricciardo
"Everyone was saying we didn't have a chance here, but I think we had really good pace today and surprised ourselves. It feels a bit surreal, but another win is very, very cool."

Lewis Hamilton
"I didn't fully understand what had happened until I saw the replay, but I gave Nico space, took the corner like I usually do and suddenly felt a big hit from behind."

Kimi Räikkönen
"We had decided to tackle this race aggressively, making an early stop. When Bottas began to close on me, I knew I didn't have the speed to defend on the straight."

Romain Grosjean
"The car was pretty good. Unfortunately, my race was compromised as we had to change the nose on the first lap and picked up damage later on from debris."

Kevin Magnussen
"Despite being penalised, I had great fun, being involved in exciting racing on an awesome circuit. It was a tough challenge, as everyone around me had fresher tyres."

Nico Hülkenberg
"I paid the price for mistakes yesterday that gave me so much ground to recover. Early on, I had good pace, but it was hard to show it because I was stuck in heavy traffic."

POSITIONS LAP BY LAP

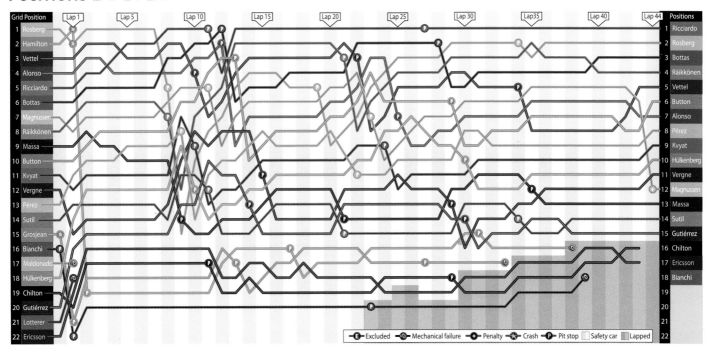

Grid Position		Positions	
1	Rosberg	1	Ricciardo
2	Hamilton	2	Rosberg
3	Vettel	3	Bottas
4	Alonso	4	Räikkönen
5	Ricciardo	5	Vettel
6	Bottas	6	Button
7	Magnussen	7	Alonso
8	Räikkönen	8	Pérez
9	Massa	9	Kvyat
10	Button	10	Hülkenberg
11	Kvyat	11	Vergne
12	Vergne	12	Magnussen
13	Pérez	13	Massa
14	Sutil	14	Sutil
15	Grosjean	15	Gutiérrez
16	Bianchi	16	Chilton
17	Maldonado	17	Ericsson
18	Hülkenberg	18	Bianchi
19	Chilton	19	
20	Gutiérrez	20	
21	Lotterer	21	
22	Ericsson	22	

Legend: —E— Excluded —N— Mechanical failure —+— Penalty —X— Crash —P— Pit stop ☐ Safety car ▨ Lapped

QUALIFYING 3

	Driver	Time
1	N Rosberg	2m05.591s
2	L Hamilton	2m05.819s
3	S Vettel	2m07.717s
4	F Alonso	2m07.786s
5	D Ricciardo	2m07.911s
6	V Bottas	2m08.049s
7	K Magnussen	2m08.679s
8	K Räikkönen	2m08.780s
9	F Massa	2m09.178s
10	J Button	2m09.776s

Grid penalties

GRID

	Driver	Time
1	N Rosberg	2m05.591s
2	L Hamilton	2m05.819s
3	S Vettel	2m07.717s
4	F Alonso	2m07.786s
5	D Ricciardo	2m07.911s
6	V Bottas	2m08.049s
7	K Magnussen	2m08.679s
8	K Räikkönen	2m08.780s
9	F Massa	2m09.178s
10	J Button	2m09.776s
11	D Kvyat	2m09.377s
12	J-É Vergne	2m09.805s
13	S Pérez	2m10.084s
14	A Sutil	2m10.238s
15	R Grosjean	2m11.087s
16	J Bianchi	2m12.470s
17	P Maldonado	2m11.261s
18	N Hülkenberg	2m11.267s
19	M Chilton	2m12.566s
20	E Gutiérrez	2m13.414s
21	A Lotterer	2m13.469s
22	M Ericsson	2m14.438s

RACE

	Driver	Car	Laps	Time	Av mph	Fastest	Stops
1	D Ricciardo	Red Bull-Renault RB10	44	1h24m36.556s	135.740	1m52.974s	2
2	N Rosberg	Mercedes F1 W05	44	1h24m39.939s	135.649	1m50.511s	3
3	V Bottas	Williams-Mercedes FW36	44	1h25m04.588s	134.994	1m52.716s	2
4	K Räikkönen	Ferrari F14 T	44	1h25m13.371s	134.762	1m54.090s	2
5	S Vettel	Red Bull-Renault RB10	44	1h25m28.752s	134.358	1m52.953s	3
6	J Button	McLaren-Mercedes MP4-29	44	1h25m31.136s	134.295	1m53.483s	2
7	F Alonso	Ferrari F14 T	44	1h25m37.718s	134.124	1m53.879s	2
8	S Pérez	Force India-Mercedes VJM07	44	1h25m40.849s	134.042	1m54.532s	2
9	D Kvyat	Toro Rosso-Renault STR9	44	1h25m41.903s	134.015	1m54.159s	2
10	N Hülkenberg	Force India-Mercedes VJM07	44	1h25m42.253s	134.005	1m53.612s	2
11	J-É Vergne	Toro Rosso-Renault STR9	44	1h25m48.476s	133.844	1m53.276s	2
12	K Magnussen	McLaren-Mercedes MP4-29	44	1h25m50.818s	133.783	1m54.203s	2
13	F Massa	Williams-Mercedes FW36	44	1h25m52.531s	133.738	1m52.512s	3
14	A Sutil	Sauber-Ferrari C33	44	1h25m59.003s	133.570	1m52.413s	3
15	E Gutiérrez	Sauber-Ferrari C33	44	1h26m07.381s	133.354	1m54.000s	2
16	M Chilton	Marussia-Ferrari MR03	43	1h25m38.307s	131.059	1m55.247s	2
17	M Ericsson	Caterham-Renault CT05	43	1h25m38.973s	131.042	1m55.900s	2
18	J Bianchi	Marussia-Ferrari MR03	39	Gearbox	-	1m56.347s	2
R	L Hamilton	Mercedes F1 W05	38	Crash damage	-	1m53.707s	2
R	R Grosjean	Lotus-Renault E22	33	Crash damage	-	1m55.649s	3
R	P Maldonado	Lotus-Renault E22	1	Exhaust	-	-	0
R	A Lotterer	Caterham-Renault CT05	1	Power unit	-	-	0

Fastest lap
N Rosberg 1m50.511s
(141.772mph) on lap 36

Fastest speed trap
N Rosberg 195.172mph
Slowest speed trap
P Maldonado 147.451mph

Fastest pit stop
1 K Magnussen 22.414s
2 J Button 22.588s
3 D Ricciardo 22.675s

CHAMPIONSHIP

	Driver	Pts
1	N Rosberg	220
2	L Hamilton	191
3	D Ricciardo	156
4	F Alonso	121
5	V Bottas	110
6	S Vettel	98
7	N Hülkenberg	70
8	J Button	68
9	F Massa	40
10	K Räikkönen	39
11	K Magnussen	37
12	S Pérez	33
13	J-É Vergne	11
14	R Grosjean	8
15	D Kvyat	8
16	J Bianchi	2

CONSTRUCTORS

	Team	Pts
1	Mercedes	411
2	Red Bull-Renault	254
3	Ferrari	160
4	Williams-Mercedes	150
5	McLaren-Mercedes	105
6	Force India-Mercedes	103
7	Toro Rosso-Renault	19
8	Lotus-Renault	8
9	Marussia-Ferrari	2

Esteban Gutiérrez

"The race strategy was to attack from the start, but it didn't work out as expected as I struggled with the medium tyres and my pace was too slow to finish in the points."

Jean-Éric Vergne

"My start wasn't great and cars were already passing me before La Source. It was then frustrating to sit in traffic, with my tyres going off and suffering a lack of performance."

Felipe Massa

"I had tyre debris stuck in the floor that came from Hamilton's car, costing me 2s per lap. This wasn't removed until my second stop and after that I was the fastest car on track."

Max Chilton

"It's great to end the weekend having gained three places and finished ahead of the Caterham. I'm pleased with how the race panned out, especially taking Ericsson right at the end."

Marcus Ericsson

"On the first lap, I got a good run after Eau Rouge and got by Chilton at Turn 5. After that, it was a long race fighting him, but he overtook me with two laps to go, which was frustrating."

Adrian Sutil

"Unfortunately, I got stuck behind Felipe. As I came in for my pit stop, he also pitted. In some sectors, I was faster, but on the straights his engine was simply too strong."

Daniil Kvyat

"It was good at the end when I was defending my position against Hülkenberg who was on new options. It was thrilling, as I had to look after my tyres while fighting to keep 10th place."

Valtteri Bottas

"I was stuck behind slower cars early on which made the first stint difficult, but I managed to make my way past cars when it was needed and that was important for my race."

Jules Bianchi

"There's not much to say beyond this was a race that wasn't meant to be. My race was lonely. Then it was a shame that I was unable to take the flag due to a gearbox problem."

André Lotterer

"I didn't even get the chance to sweat. I was really looking forward to a good race and had a good start, but then went a bit wide at Turn 17 and there was a sudden loss of power."

ROUND 13
GRAN PREMIO D'ITALIA

ITALY

LEWIS HAMILTON WAS IN
UNSTOPPABLE FORM AT THE
ITALIAN GP AND THERE WAS
NOTHING THAT MERCEDES
TEAMMATE NICO ROSBERG
COULD DO TO STOP HIM CUTTING
HIS CHAMPIONSHIP LEAD

ewis Hamilton got his World Championship campaign back on track with a faultless drive at Monza on a day when his teammate Nico Rosberg twice made mistakes, first going down the chicane escape road, then allowing his rival to claim the lead.

Or were they mistakes? The Italian GP came on the heels of the Spa controversy, which had led to a summit meeting between Mercedes' drivers and management in Brackley and an agreement that they could still race, as long as they behaved themselves. Inevitably, sceptics viewed the result as a handy "correction" by Rosberg after the collision that had caused so much grief at Spa, while others simply couldn't believe that the German could have engineered such a thing.

Whatever the truth of the matter, Hamilton was back on winning form and in so doing he cut the points margin from 29 to 22, heading into the run of six flyaway races to end the season.

Hamilton first delivered a statement of intent by beating Rosberg to pole position. He had lost track time with a problem on Friday and then Rosberg's Saturday started badly when an electronic gearbox issue meant that he didn't get a flying lap in FP3 and went into qualifying on the back foot.

Hamilton beat Rosberg in Q1, and again in Q2. On the first runs in Q2, Rosberg went top with 1m24.552s but, seconds later, when Hamilton crossed the line to deliver a stunning lap of 1m24.109s, Rosberg knew he had a huge task on his hands. Despite setting the fastest first sector on his second run, the German couldn't improve by enough and crossed the line in 1m24.383s, so Hamilton didn't have to go any faster on his final

> **"HAMILTON FIRST DELIVERED A STATEMENT OF INTENT BY BEATING ROSBERG TO POLE POSITION"**

Nico Rosberg leads through the first chicane, with Lewis Hamilton's slow start dropping him behind Kevin Magnussen and Felipe Massa. **Above left:** The top three qualifiers, Rosberg, Hamilton and Valtteri Bottas

attempt. It was Hamilton's first pole since the Spanish GP in May after a run of bad luck in qualifying.

As expected, Williams was strong at Monza, allowing Valtteri Bottas and Felipe Massa to qualify third and fourth, ensuring that they were in a good position should either Silver Arrow hit trouble. The value of Mercedes' power was ably demonstrated by the fact that the McLarens shared the third row, with Kevin Magnussen pipping Jenson Button right at the end to make it a 1-2-3-4-5-6 for Stuttgart. That hadn't been achieved by an engine since the days of Ford and Cosworth in 1980...

Fernando Alonso could qualify only seventh on Ferrari's home turf, sharing the fourth row with fellow former World Champion Sebastian Vettel. Daniel Ricciardo and Sergio Pérez completed the top 10.

Significantly, Toro Rosso's Daniil Kvyat became the first driver to pick up a 10-place grid penalty for using a sixth power unit element – the V6 engine – so he dropped from 11th to 21st on the grid and that

INSIDE LINE

MARCO MATTIACCI
FERRARI

I f you start lower on the grid, it's going to
be difficult if you don't have a strong power
unit. But I think we had the same pace as
Red Bull and some of the others, and could
have done better. So far, we have been good
in terms of reliability, but statistically we had
to face something. Fernando had an issue with
the ERS. We never had this issue before, but
it happened. Everybody was having reliability
issues this year except Ferrari.

"For me, it was important to experience
the impressive love and passion that there is
around Ferrari and to understand that Ferrari
is much more than just
a racing company. It's
an institution and we
have an obligation to
fans. This gives me a lot
of motivation towards
the team, to make sure
that this frustration
is going to end. I still
believe that we had
good pace, the car
confirmed an improvement, but definitely we
had a deficit in qualifying.

> "FERRARI IS AN
> INSTITUTION AND
> THIS GIVES ME A LOT
> OF MOTIVATION TO
> MAKE SURE THAT
> THIS FRUSTRATION IS
> GOING TO END"

"We have a clear picture about where
the deficit is and about the assets. We have
a lot of talented people, but it's evident in
which areas we are lagging behind and we've
already been working for a few months to
address those issues. I'm definitely not going
to make public where the weaknesses are, to
give our competitors an advantage. As I keep
saying, this is a medium- to long-term project,
because we are talking about engineering
investments, so it takes a while.

"There are many, many assets to start from,
and there is the tradition of winning. We know
how to win and are obsessed to go back to the
top. There is a huge motivation and hunger to
go back to the top, because we belong there."

Hamilton homes in
on Rosberg before
pressuring him into
making a second
mistake at the first
chicane. **Far left:**
Sebastian Vettel
gathers his
thoughts on
the grid

moved a frustrated Kimi Räikkönen
up a position from 12th.

The speculation about what
might happen at the first corner
between the Mercedes drivers came
to an end when Hamilton got away
badly due to an electronics glitch.
In an instant, he was passed by
Rosberg and then by Magnussen
and Massa. He managed to limit
the damage by slotting into fourth.

"At the start," explained
Hamilton, "there's a button that
you press which engages the launch
sequence and for the formation
lap it didn't work. I thought 'no
problem, I'll just put it on for
the race', and then when I got
to the grid I put it on and again
it didn't work. It's really very
strange, I've never really had
that happen before.

DI MONTEZEMOLO DEPARTS FERRARI

They say there's no smoke without fire, and that proved to be true in the case of Luca di Montezemolo. Following weeks of speculation about his future, it was confirmed on the Wednesday that the Ferrari chairman would be leaving his job in October.

Over the Monza weekend, the flamboyant executive had denied suggestions that he'd be stepping down. However, things were moving quickly behind the scenes as Fiat/Chrysler boss Sergio Marchionne orchestrated di Montezemolo's departure and nominated himself as replacement. How long he planned to keep the role, alongside those he already had, remained to be seen.

Di Montezemolo's second stint at Ferrari had lasted 23 years and he had presided over the hugely successful Michael Schumacher era. Bernie Ecclestone was moved to say that the departure of his sometime adversary was as significant as the death of Enzo Ferrari back in 1988.

> "THINGS WERE MOVING QUICKLY BEHIND THE SCENES AS BOSS SERGIO MARCHIONNE ORCHESTRATED DI MONTEZEMOLO'S DEPARTURE

In a statement, di Montezemolo said: "Ferrari will have an important role to play within the FCA Group in the upcoming flotation on Wall Street. This will open up a new phase that I feel should be spearheaded by the CEO of the group.

"This is the end of an era, so I have decided to leave my position as chairman after 23 marvellous and unforgettable years, in addition to those spent at Enzo's side in the 1970s.

"A warm farewell and my thanks also to all of our technical and commercial partners, our dealers and the clients and collectors whose passion I wholeheartedly share.

"Ferrari is the most wonderful company in the world. It has been a great privilege and honour to have been its leader. I devoted all of my enthusiasm and commitment to it. Together with my family, it was, and continues to be, the most important thing in my life."

With former team principal Stefano Domenicali having departed in April, and engine boss Luca Marmorini having carried the can for the poor form of the new power unit, these were interesting times at Maranello. The focus turned to whether Fernando Alonso would still be around in 2015.

The action behind Kamui Kobayashi is fast and furious as Daniil Kvyat, Jules Bianchi and Max Chilton get up close and personal

"Anyway, I tried to pull away as fast as possible. The revs were all over the place and luckily I managed not to lose too many places. I had no idea what I was supposed to do, so I just floored it and hoped for the best..."

As Rosberg made his escape, Hamilton found himself stuck behind Massa. On the fifth lap, the Brazilian passed Magnussen, and Hamilton followed him through to claim third. However, it took the Briton until lap 10 to finally find a way past the Williams and get into second place. Fortunately for him, Rosberg had run straight on at the first chicane a couple of laps earlier, and by doing so he lost some of the 3.6s gap he'd built up. He'd apparently just adjusted his brake balance.

That loss of time gave Hamilton a welcome bonus and, once in clean air, he sat 2s behind, before closing to within around 1.2-4s of his teammate as the first (and only) pit stops approached. The gap stayed roughly the same for several laps, until Rosberg made the first pit call on lap 24 and Hamilton followed him in just a lap later.

Hamilton was then advised by his race engineer to hang back by 2-2.5s and save his tyres for a push at the end of the race, but instead he took the initiative and closed in on Rosberg, hoping to take advantage of his new rubber.

It worked and just three laps later, on lap 29 with the gap down to 0.7s as they crossed the start/finish line, Rosberg again ran straight on at the first chicane. By the time

Above: Daniel Ricciardo found great speed to advance from 12th to fifth. **Left:** it wasn't a great event for Ferrari, with Fernando Alonso's run of points in every race brought to an end by ERS failure

he'd zigzagged through the escape road barriers, Hamilton was ahead.

"It was just Lewis was quick, coming from behind," said Rosberg of his mistake. "I needed to up my pace and then, as a result, just made the mistake. That was very bad and that lost me the lead in the end. Definitely, it was very disappointing from that point of view.

"Monza is one of the most difficult tracks for braking because of low downforce and the highest speed of the year. That isn't any excuse or anything, that's just the way it is. It's one of the challenges of this weekend here. Unfortunately, I got it wrong. Twice."

Was it stage-managed, or a genuine mistake? Whichever, it proved to be the end of any contest between the two, as Hamilton

gradually edged ahead. The gap stabilised at a little over 4s for most of the second half of the grand prix, and the final margin at the flag was 3.1s. Remarkably, it was the first Mercedes one-two finish since the Austrian GP back in June.

"I didn't ignore the team's orders," said Hamilton. "I have a great relationship with my engineer, and he's constantly in touch with me throughout the race and really guiding me. If I'm losing a bit of time here or there, he's telling me so that I know how to correct it.

"The engineers want to win just as much as I do, so they're just trying to guide me to what they think. But, at the end of the day, I am the one out there and had to decide 'OK, I can back off here and keep the tyres, but it might be better

> **"IT WAS JUST LEWIS WAS QUICK, COMING FROM BEHIND,' SAID ROSBERG OF HIS MISTAKE"**

the other way'. I knew that if I applied the pressure, an opportunity would eventually come."

After his strong early run, Massa held on to take his first podium of the season for Williams, a result that proved popular with the *tifosi*. It was a fairly lonely run for the Brazilian, but behind him there was some fabulous and sometimes mind-boggling action.

Massa's teammate Bottas had started in third, but got away badly and dropped to 11th on the first lap. However, the Finn had the pace with which to overtake and was able to gradually pick his way up to fourth. He even survived a wheel-banging incident with Magnussen as the pair battled for position.

Ricciardo was another to drop back with a bad start and a trip across the first chicane run-off on lap 1. Red Bull gave him a long opening stint and late pit stop just to try something different. It worked and, on fresher tyres than his rivals, he charged up to fifth. Along the way, he picked off teammate Vettel after a brief and entertaining scrap between the pair. Having stopped first, the German's tyres were eight laps older, so he was always going to lose out and had to settle for sixth place.

Magnussen finished seventh on the road after another feisty drive. However, he received a 5s stop-and-go penalty for his contact with Bottas. Because he had no more stops to make, it was added at the end of the race. Pérez was aware of the penalty, so happily sat behind the McLaren until the flag, knowing that he'd inherit seventh place. The Mexican had earlier enjoyed a great battle with former McLaren teammate Button, who finished behind him, while Räikkönen was also promoted a spot to ninth, with Magnussen classified 10th.

Alonso should have finished ahead of most of these drivers and perhaps in the mix with the Red Bulls but, having run solidly early on, he pulled off at the end of the pit straight with ERS gremlins on lap 29. It was the first time that he'd not made the points all season, and his first retirement since Malaysia 2013 when his front wing fell off after early contact with Vettel. So, these were turbulent times for Ferrari, both on and off the track.

> "PÉREZ WAS AWARE OF THE PENALTY, SO HAPPILY SAT BEHIND THE McLAREN UNTIL THE FLAG"

Above: Felipe Massa's first podium for Williams proved to be a popular result.
Left: Jenson Button finished two places behind teammate Magnussen on the track but was classified three places ahead

SNAPSHOT FROM ITALY

CLOCKWISE FROM ABOVE: a scene that never fades, a Ferrari at Monza; Alonso gets signing, but not on a Ferrari contract; Roberto Mehri was busy for Caterham; Nico Hülkenberg presses on; Lotus F1 chairman Gérard Lopez asks why the team's E22s aren't any faster; Adrian Sutil gets it wrong in his Sauber; the sixth-gear sweep through Curva Biassono; Kevin Magnussen continued to impress for McLaren; a Caterham at speed; Nico Rosberg visualises a quick lap

ITALY
MONZA
ROUND 13

RACE DATE 7 September
CIRCUIT LENGTH 3.600 miles
NO. OF LAPS 53
RACE DISTANCE 190.800 miles
WEATHER Sunny, 25ºC
TRACK TEMP 44ºC
LAP RECORD Rubens Barrichello, 1m21.046s, 159.909mph, 2004

PRACTICE 1				PRACTICE 2				PRACTICE 3				QUALIFYING 1			QUALIFYING 2	
	Driver	Time	Laps		Driver	Time	Laps		Driver	Time	Laps		Driver	Time		Driver	Time
1	L Hamilton	1m26.187s	25	1	N Rosberg	1m26.225s	41	1	L Hamilton	1m25.519s	23	1	L Hamilton	1m25.363s	1	L Hamilton	1m24.560s
2	J Button	1m26.810s	27	2	L Hamilton	1m26.286s	16	2	F Alonso	1m25.931s	13	2	N Rosberg	1m25.493s	2	N Rosberg	1m24.600s
3	N Rosberg	1m26.995s	26	3	K Räikkönen	1m26.331s	31	3	V Bottas	1m26.090s	19	3	F Massa	1m25.528s	3	V Bottas	1m24.858s
4	F Alonso	1m27.169s	23	4	F Alonso	1m26.565s	26	4	F Massa	1m26.114s	18	4	V Bottas	1m26.012s	4	F Massa	1m25.046s
5	K Magnussen	1m27.228s	30	5	V Bottas	1m26.758s	34	5	J Button	1m26.242s	21	5	J-É Vergne	1m26.140s	5	F Alonso	1m25.525s
6	S Vettel	1m27.271s	27	6	J Button	1m26.762s	34	6	S Vettel	1m26.290s	17	6	D Kvyat	1m26.261s	6	J Button	1m25.630s
7	K Räikkönen	1m27.493s	27	7	S Vettel	1m26.762s	27	7	K Räikkönen	1m26.327s	15	7	J Button	1m26.328s	7	S Vettel	1m25.769s
8	S Pérez	1m27.687s	13	8	K Magnussen	1m26.881s	44	8	D Kvyat	1m26.437s	21	8	K Magnussen	1m26.337s	8	S Pérez	1m25.863s
9	D Kvyat	1m27.741s	33	9	F Massa	1m26.935s	33	9	D Ricciardo	1m26.482s	16	9	N Hülkenberg	1m26.371s	9	D Ricciardo	1m25.946s
10	N Hülkenberg	1m28.112s	23	10	D Ricciardo	1m26.992s	37	10	N Hülkenberg	1m26.608s	17	10	F Alonso	1m26.514s	10	K Magnussen	1m25.973s
11	E Gutiérrez	1m28.114s	21	11	S Pérez	1m27.079s	42	11	K Magnussen	1m26.829s	20	11	S Pérez	1m26.569s	11	D Kvyat	1m26.070s
12	V Bottas	1m28.148s	20	12	N Hülkenberg	1m27.227s	39	12	E Gutiérrez	1m27.207s	18	12	S Vettel	1m26.631s	12	K Räikkönen	1m26.110s
13	F Massa	1m28.150s	21	13	D Kvyat	1m27.476s	37	13	S Pérez	1m27.312s	10	13	K Räikkönen	1m26.689s	13	J-É Vergne	1m26.157s
14	J-É Vergne	1m28.300s	30	14	E Gutiérrez	1m27.840s	33	14	J-É Vergne	1m27.479s	22	14	D Ricciardo	1m26.721s	14	N Hülkenberg	1m26.279s
15	G Van der Garde	1m28.429s	19	15	J-É Vergne	1m27.929s	33	15	A Sutil	1m27.498s	12	15	E Gutiérrez	1m26.999s	15	A Sutil	1m26.588s
16	D Ricciardo	1m28.487s	12	16	A Sutil	1m28.029s	35	16	J Bianchi	1m28.025s	19	16	A Sutil	1m27.034s	16	E Gutiérrez	1m26.692s
17	D Juncadella	1m29.192s	10	17	J Bianchi	1m28.659s	34	17	P Maldonado	1m28.137s	20	17	P Maldonado	1m27.520s			
18	P Maldonado	1m29.512s	24	18	P Maldonado	1m28.700s	42	18	K Kobayashi	1m28.265s	21	18	R Grosjean	1m27.632s			
19	M Chilton	1m30.017s	25	19	M Chilton	1m28.786s	29	19	R Grosjean	1m28.459s	14	19	K Kobayashi	1m27.671s			
20	J Bianchi	1m30.081s	27	20	R Grosjean	1m29.085s	29	20	M Chilton	1m28.579s	19	20	J Bianchi	1m27.738s			
21	C Pic	1m30.125s	23	21	K Kobayashi	1m29.178s	32	21	M Ericsson	1m29.251s	22	21	M Chilton	1m28.247s			
22	R Mehri	1m30.704s	29	22	M Ericsson	1m29.275s	37	22	N Rosberg	no time	3	22	M Ericsson	1m28.562s			

Best sectors – Practice		
Sec 1	J Button	27.614s
Sec 2	L Hamilton	29.082s
Sec 3	L Hamilton	28.604s

Speed trap – Practice		
1	L Hamilton	219.157mph
2	N Hülkenberg	216.734mph
3	J Button	216.610mph

Best sectors – Qualifying		
Sec 1	N Rosberg	27.162s
Sec 2	L Hamilton	28.562s
Sec 3	L Hamilton	28.229s

Speed trap – Qualifying		
1	N Rosberg	219.903mph
2	V Bottas	219.344mph
3	S Pérez	218.163mph

 **Sebastian Vettel**

"We wanted to get the McLarens so we went aggressive with my early stop, but the tyres started going off at the end and so that was the maximum we could do today."

 Nico Rosberg / Fernando Alonso

"I had a lock up in Turn 1 and I decided to go straight to avoid a flat spotted tyre. That cost me the lead. But Lewis was very quick behind me, so I had to push all the time."

"After my pit stop, I was at the back of a train of cars and we decided that I should drop back to conserve the tyres and try and attack at the end. Then came the ERS problem."

 Pastor Maldonado / Jenson Button

"I had a good start and a strong first lap, passing the Saubers. From there, I tried to attack the Toro Rosso, but their pace on the straights was too much to overcome."

"I had an amazing battle with Checo – we took Lesmo 1 side by side, which doesn't happen often. It's a pity I couldn't get by him, but he was so strong under braking."

 Sergio Pérez

"The best part of the race was the fight I had with Jenson, which reminded me of the old days. I know he's a driver you can fight really hard and it's always clean."

 Daniel Ricciardo / Lewis Hamilton

"Fifth place, even if I had made a good start, would have been the best I could do. The strategy helped as it kept my tyres fresh enough for those extra few laps at the end."

"My launch sequence didn't engage, so I just floored it. When I caught Nico, I didn't want to hold back as I knew my only chance would be when the tyres were fresh."

 Kimi Räikkönen / Romain Grosjean

"We knew this would be a tricky weekend. I was happy with the handling and the balance was good, but we lacked speed on the straight and I didn't have much grip."

"I had a dreadful start and was last by the first corner. I'm not sure what happened with Esteban. He was passing me, but then under braking he moved over on to me."

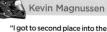 Kevin Magnussen / Nico Hülkenberg

"I got to second place into the first corner, but then inevitably fell back. It's frustrating to get another penalty and so it's unfortunate to come away with only a single point."

"I had a very good start, but soon lost contact with the cars ahead of me, so I was racing alone most of the time, neither being towed around nor benefiting from DRS."

POSITIONS LAP BY LAP

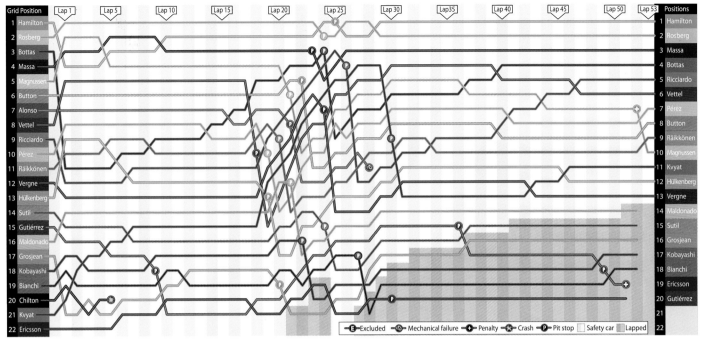

Grid Position													Positions
1 Hamilton	Lap 1	Lap 5	Lap 10	Lap 15	Lap 20	Lap 25	Lap 30	Lap35	Lap 40	Lap 45	Lap 50	Lap 53	1 Hamilton
2 Rosberg													2 Rosberg
3 Bottas													3 Massa
4 Massa													4 Bottas
5 Magnussen													5 Ricciardo
6 Button													6 Vettel
7 Alonso													7 Pérez
8 Vettel													8 Button
9 Ricciardo													9 Räikkönen
10 Pérez													10 Magnussen
11 Räikkönen													11 Kvyat
12 Vergne													12 Hülkenberg
13 Hülkenberg													13 Vergne
14 Sutil													14 Maldonado
15 Gutiérrez													15 Sutil
16 Maldonado													16 Grosjean
17 Grosjean													17 Kobayashi
18 Kobayashi													18 Bianchi
19 Bianchi													19 Ericsson
20 Chilton													20 Gutiérrez
21 Kvyat													21
22 Ericsson													22

E – Excluded **N** – Mechanical failure **+** – Penalty **K** – Crash **P** – Pit stop ☐ Safety car ▨ Lapped

QUALIFYING 3

	Driver	Time
1	L Hamilton	1m24.109s
2	N Rosberg	1m24.383s
3	V Bottas	1m24.697s
4	F Massa	1m24.865s
5	K Magnussen	1m25.314s
6	J Button	1m25.379s
7	F Alonso	1m25.430s
8	S Vettel	1m25.436s
9	D Ricciardo	1m25.709s
10	S Pérez	1m25.944s

GRID

	Driver	Time
1	L Hamilton	1m24.109s
2	N Rosberg	1m24.383s
3	V Bottas	1m24.697s
4	F Massa	1m24.865s
5	K Magnussen	1m25.314s
6	J Button	1m25.379s
7	F Alonso	1m25.430s
8	S Vettel	1m25.436s
9	D Ricciardo	1m25.709s
10	S Pérez	1m25.944s
11	K Räikkönen	1m26.110s
12	J-É Vergne	1m26.157s
13	N Hülkenberg	1m26.279s
14	A Sutil	1m26.588s
15	E Gutiérrez	1m26.692s
16	P Maldonado	1m27.520s
17	R Grosjean	1m27.632s
18	K Kobayashi	1m27.671s
19	J Bianchi	1m27.738s
20	M Chilton	1m28.247s
21	D Kvyat	1m26.070s
22	M Ericsson	1m28.562s

Grid penalties

M Ericsson	Made to start at back for ignoring yellow flags
D Kvyat	10-place penalty for using a sixth engine

RACE

	Driver	Car	Laps	Time	Av mph	Fastest	Stops
1	L Hamilton	Mercedes F1 W05	53	1h19m10.236s	144.444	1m28.004s	1
2	N Rosberg	Mercedes F1 W05	53	1h19m13.411s	144.341	1m28.206s	1
3	F Massa	Williams-Mercedes FW36	53	1h19m35.262s	143.680	1m28.342s	1
4	V Bottas	Williams-Mercedes FW36	53	1h19m51.022s	143.208	1m28.559s	1
5	D Ricciardo	Red Bull-Renault RB10	53	1h20m00.545s	142.923	1m28.588s	1
6	S Vettel	Red Bull-Renault RB10	53	1h20m10.201s	142.637	1m29.141s	1
7	S Pérez	Force India-Mercedes VJM07	53	1h20m12.754s	142.561	1m29.107s	1
8	J Button	McLaren-Mercedes MP4-29	53	1h20m13.299s	142.545	1m29.245s	1
9	K Räikkönen	Ferrari F14 T	53	1h20m13.771s	142.530	1m28.942s	1
10	K Magnussen	McLaren-Mercedes MP4-29	53	1h20m16.407s	142.453	1m29.283s	1
11	D Kvyat	Toro Rosso-Renault STR9	53	1h20m21.420s	142.304	1m28.486s	1
12	N Hülkenberg	Force India-Mercedes VJM07	53	1h20m22.842s	142.263	1m29.366s	1
13	J-É Vergne	Toro Rosso-Renault STR9	53	1h20m23.329s	142.248	1m29.121s	1
14	P Maldonado	Lotus-Renault E22	52	1h19m12.764s	141.634	1m29.856s	1
15	A Sutil	Sauber-Ferrari C33	52	1h19m24.548s	141.283	1m29.375s	1
16	R Grosjean	Lotus-Renault E22	52	1h19m48.754s	140.569	1m30.083s	1
17	K Kobayashi	Caterham-Renault CT05	52	1h20m19.283s	139.679	1m30.758s	1
18	J Bianchi	Marussia-Ferrari MR03	52	1h20m32.389s	139.300	1m30.521s	1
19	M Ericsson	Caterham-Renault CT05	51	1h19m25.655s	138.531	1m30.280s	1
20	E Gutiérrez	Sauber-Ferrari C33	51	1h19m34.772s	138.267	1m29.449s	3
R	F Alonso	Ferrari F14 T	28	ERS	-	1m29.680s	1
R	M Chilton	Marussia-Ferrari MR03	5	Spun off	-	1m32.569s	0

Fastest lap
L Hamilton 1m28.004s
(147.256mph) on lap 29

Fastest speed trap
D Ricciardo 224.998mph

Slowest speed trap
A Sutil 204.493mph

Fastest pit stop

1	K Magnussen	24.214s
2	P Maldonado	24.223s
3	F Massa	24.323s

CHAMPIONSHIP

	Driver	Pts
1	N Rosberg	238
2	L Hamilton	216
3	D Ricciardo	166
4	V Bottas	122
5	F Alonso	121
6	S Vettel	106
7	J Button	72
8	N Hülkenberg	70
9	F Massa	55
10	K Räikkönen	41
11	S Pérez	39
12	K Magnussen	38
13	J-É Vergne	11
14	R Grosjean	8
15	D Kvyat	8
16	J Bianchi	2

CONSTRUCTORS

	Team	Pts
1	Mercedes	454
2	Red Bull-Renault	272
3	Williams-Mercedes	177
4	Ferrari	162
5	McLaren-Mercedes	110
6	Force India-Mercedes	109
7	Toro Rosso-Renault	19
8	Lotus-Renault	8
9	Marussia-Ferrari	2

Esteban Gutiérrez
"From the start, I struggled on the hard tyres. We changed the strategy and I think that was a good decision. Back on track I was able to overtake a few cars, but that was it."

Jean-Éric Vergne
"Even though we've been working very hard, session after session, to improve the cars' handling, I found myself struggling throughout the race, making it very tough today."

Felipe Massa
"It was a great race. I had a good start and passed Magnussen. I had to work hard to establish that position. Sadly the Mercedes' were still too quick, so we did all we could."

Max Chilton
"It was a disappointing and premature end to my race. I braked slightly too late for Turn 4 and wasn't able to get around the corner. I hit the sausage kerbs, which launched me."

Marcus Ericsson
"Starting from the pit lane because of yesterday's penalty wasn't ideal, but in the end I think it was a decent race. I didn't do any mistakes and I was very consistent on the lap times."

Adrian Sutil
"It wasn't a spectacular race. We were easily able to run a one-stop strategy. The team worked well, but we were too slow, which is why I could not finish better than 15th."

Daniil Kvyat
"Starting from the back is never easy, but I got past a few cars and got close to a points finish. Then I had a brake disc failure, but managed to hang on and bring the car home in 11th."

Valtteri Bottas
"I had a few issues at the start that really affected how my race went. Once the tyres were up to temperature, it was fun to overtake so many people and we had some good pace too."

Jules Bianchi
"It was a really tough race for us, but I did everything that the team asked of me and nothing more was possible. In the end, we struggled a little with the speed on the straights."

Kamui Kobayashi
"I am pleased that I finished in front of Marussia, which is a good result for us. The new updates that were introduced in Spa are working well and we are definitely improving."

ROUND 14

SINGA

SINGAPORE AIRLINES SINGAPORE GRAND PRIX

AN IMPERIOUS DRIVE FROM LEWIS HAMILTON ENABLED THE MERCEDES
DRIVER TO TAKE THE WORLD CHAMPIONSHIP LEAD ON A NIGHT WHEN
BAD LUCK STRUCK HIS TEAMMATE NICO ROSBERG

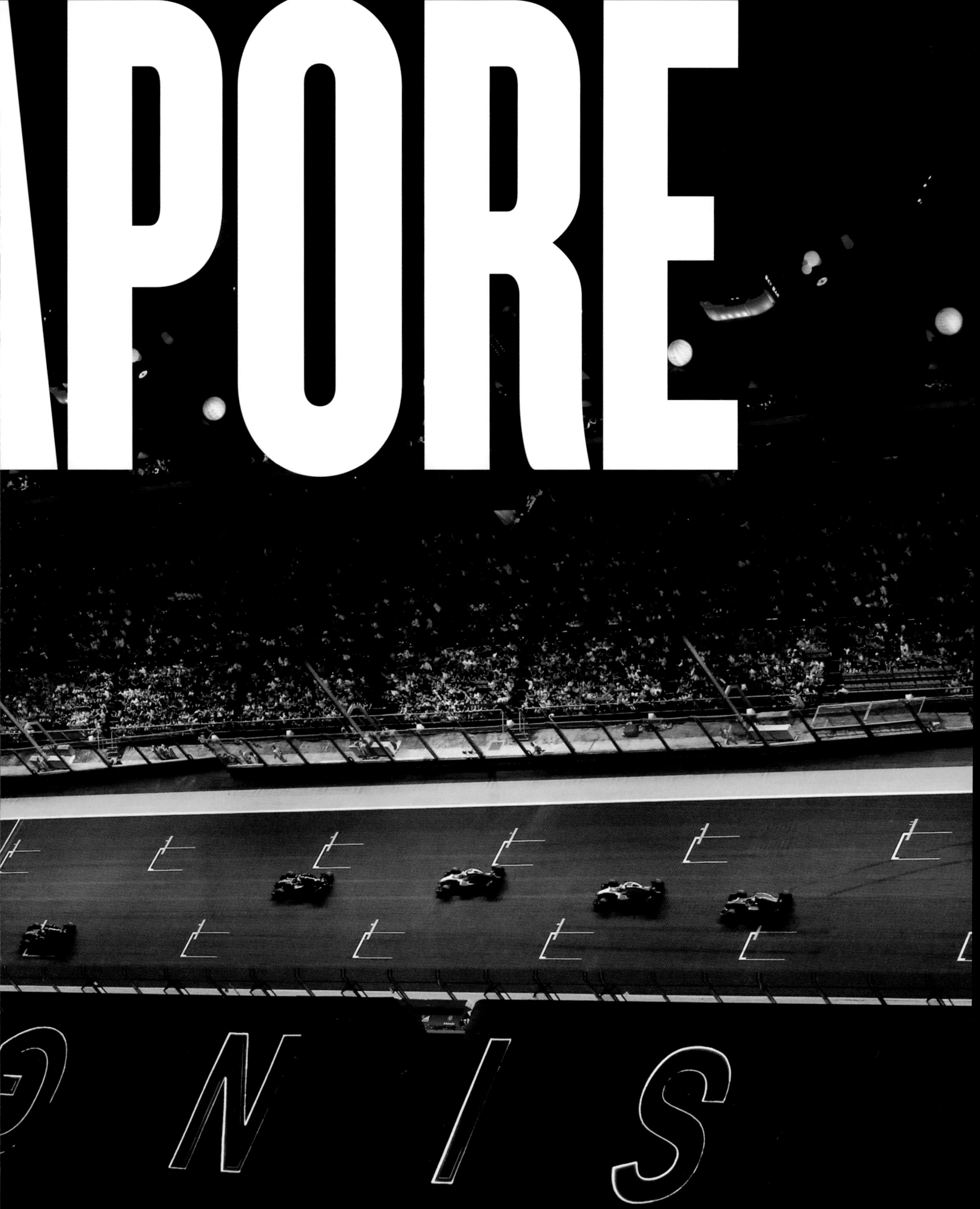
APORE

Hitherto, most misfortune at Mercedes had seemed to hit Lewis Hamilton, but this time a problem with an electrical loom connection meant that Nico Rosberg's steering wheel didn't communicate properly with the car. After starting from the pits, he retired at his first pit stop.

Meanwhile, what looked like a cruise to victory for Hamilton was made more complicated by a safety car period that compromised his strategy. Stirred into an unexpected fight to save his victory, he proved more than up to the task.

Things didn't appear to be going Mercedes' way in qualifying, although as ever it came together when it mattered. Kimi Räikkönen and Fernando Alonso were on top for Ferrari in Q1, with Hamilton and Rosberg only third and sixth. The last named even had to do a second run in order to guarantee his progress, while the other quick drivers stood on their times. In Q2, Rosberg and Hamilton were then first and second, but again Ferrari was fast, with Alonso and Räikkönen third and fourth.

The drama was building up nicely for Q3 and after the first runs it appeared that Mercedes was under pressure as Felipe Massa, Daniel Ricciardo and Alonso ensured that there were three different teams at the top, while Hamilton and Rosberg were fifth and sixth before they went out for their second and final runs when, as usual, both Mercedes drivers managed to find that little extra. Ricciardo initially went top, but he was beaten first by Rosberg and then by Hamilton. Despite locking up at the first turn and losing perhaps 0.1s, Hamilton went top by just 0.007s over Rosberg for the closest margin of the season. Hamilton reported that he hadn't got a clear run until that final set in Q3, while Rosberg said he'd been wrong-footed by the team changing his brakes after FP3.

Ricciardo retained third, beating Red Bull teammate Sebastian Vettel for the first time in four races, while Alonso had to be content with being fifth fastest. Nevertheless, the Spaniard reported himself happy to be so close to the front row with a gap of just 0.226s from pole.

Having been top after the first runs in Q3, Massa slipped back to sixth. Räikkönen was really unlucky as he was told to abandon his final run after the team detected a technical issue. Valtteri Bottas

Lewis Hamilton leads into Turn 3 as Fernando Alonso rejoins the track ahead of Sebastian Vettel and Daniel Ricciardo after straight-lining Turn 1

qualified eighth in the other Williams, ahead of Kevin Magnussen and Daniil Kvyat.

On Sunday evening, Rosberg's problems started as soon as he climbed aboard the car to go to the grid and, despite the team changing his steering wheel, the panic persisted. When the field moved away from the grid to start the formation lap, he was left stranded and had to be pushed into the pit lane. He joined the race when the rest of the cars had entered Turn 1.

With an empty space alongside, Hamilton led away from the start, while Vettel sneaked down the inside of Ricciardo as the Australian made a sluggish getaway due to a battery issue. Alonso then straight-lined the first corner by charging across the asphalt run-off area, cheekily jumping ahead of both Red Bulls. Mindful of a penalty for gaining an advantage, he soon let Vettel – but not Ricciardo – go back

Above: Anthony Hamilton wishes his son Lewis the best of luck before the start of the grand prix

Right: Mercedes was at a loss as to what to do when Nico Rosberg pitted with his failing steering wheel

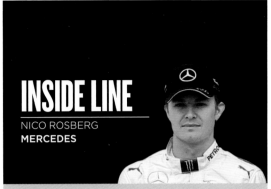

INSIDE LINE

NICO ROSBERG
MERCEDES

That was the toughest day for me this year, definitely the case, even worse than the British GP. It was probably a connection in the steering column between the steering wheel and car, but not at the steering wheel, so even changing the steering wheel didn't make a difference.

"It started as I got in the car in the garage. They'd sat in the car five times just before I got in, doing all sorts of checks and everything was OK. Then I got into the car and it didn't work any more, which is crazy.

"None of the steering wheel functions worked, I had no hybrid power, no DRS. The gear paddles sort of worked, which was strange, but they would always upshift two gears at a time, so I had no fourth gear and no sixth. It was just all over the place and that's why I was also very, very slow.

> **"THE GEAR PADDLES SORT OF WORKED, BUT THEY WOULD ALWAYS UPSHIFT TWO GEARS AT A TIME, SO I HAD NO FOURTH GEAR AND NO SIXTH"**

"My brake balance was completely in the wrong place, too, because I couldn't brake properly and I couldn't change that. Even coming into the pit stop I didn't have the pit limiter, so I couldn't go into neutral, I couldn't do anything. So they were going to jack me up, I'd have to go full revs and then they'd drop the car and I'd go. Then they decided it was too dangerous and so we called it a day.

"From a team perspective, reliability is our weakness and we need to get to the bottom of today and just keep on pushing and try and improve on that. That's the key thing for us. It's clear that that is the point that we need to focus on most because the performance is there and in the race today it was very strong. It's just reliability that needs to be improved."

McLAREN MERCEDES

CUTTING DOWN ON THE CHATTER

Shortly before the Singapore GP, Charlie Whiting told teams that the FIA would be introducing a radio traffic clampdown by invoking a rule stating that drivers should drive the car "alone and unaided".

The idea had emerged from the F1 Strategy Group, a body comprised of the FIA, Bernie Ecclestone and six major teams, namely Ferrari, Red Bull, Mercedes, McLaren, Williams and Lotus. The consensus was that drivers were being given too much help by engineers on the pit wall and that, in a phrase often repeated by departing Ferrari boss Luca di Montezemolo, they were being perceived as "taxi drivers".

> "A DRIVER SHOULDN'T BE TOLD THAT HE'S GOING A BIT TOO DEEP INTO THIS CORNER OR SHOULD TAKE A TIGHTER APEX ON THAT CORNER"

When Whiting clarified what couldn't be discussed on the radio, it appeared that drivers would be forced to take complete responsibility for the many complex functions and settings involved in operating their cars, with no help at all from the pit wall. Chat would be restricted to safety and strategy.

A meeting between team managers and the FIA in Singapore resulted in a U-turn. The FIA accepted that it would be harder for some teams than others to adapt because two types of dashboards are in use – one with a much larger screen that can convey more information. Thus the immediate restrictions were focused on driver coaching.

"We believe a driver should drive the car alone and unaided," said Whiting. "He shouldn't be told that he's going a bit too deep into this corner or should take a tighter apex on that corner. It's for him to decide, not for his team.

"We felt that this should extend to both car performance and driver performance related parameters, but when one looks into it in more detail it becomes clear that some teams will be at a disadvantage compared with the others."

The sport's decision-makers were trying to do the right thing by putting a greater focus on to driver skill. However, the whole on/off saga came across badly, with some fans feeling that they were being deprived of an element that adds much to the TV show. However, there was still plenty of scope for colourful radio chatter.

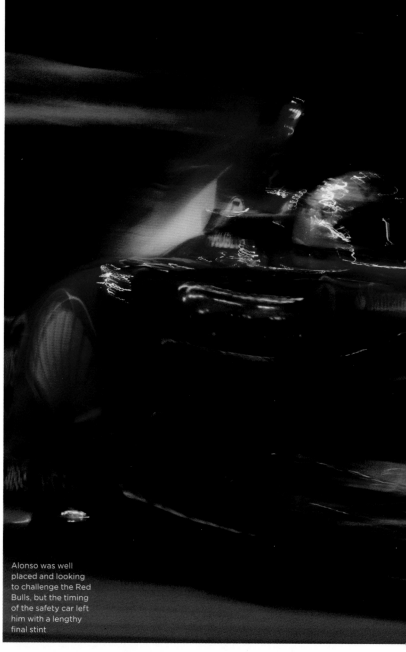

Alonso was well placed and looking to challenge the Red Bulls, but the timing of the safety car left him with a lengthy final stint

past. Race director Charlie Whiting was satisfied with that concession and thus there was no penalty, to the surprise of some observers.

Out front, Hamilton soon began opening up a gap on Vettel and, as usual, the Mercedes driver was the last frontrunner to pit, coming in for a second set of supersoft tyres on lap 13.

All eyes were on Rosberg's progress, but he still had gear selection problems and a lack of hybrid power and struggled to pass the backmarkers. The team knew that it would be hard to get him going in the pits – the only option appeared to be dropping him from the jacks with the wheels already spinning – so when he came in and the problems couldn't be resolved, it was decided to retire the car. A later

investigation revealed that the steering column had been compromised by materials used in routine servicing, namely a gel to facilitate ultrasonic testing and the substance then used to clean it.

Hamilton pitted from the lead for a second time on lap 26 for more supersofts and he continued to hold a handy lead. Meanwhile, at the second round of stops, Alonso pitted early and got ahead of Vettel to claim second. Crucially, Alonso stuck with supersofts for the third stint, while Vettel changed to softs.

The complexion of the race changed completely when the safety car was called for on lap 31 after Sergio Pérez made contact with Adrian Sutil and the Force India driver's front wing then came adrift and left debris on the track.

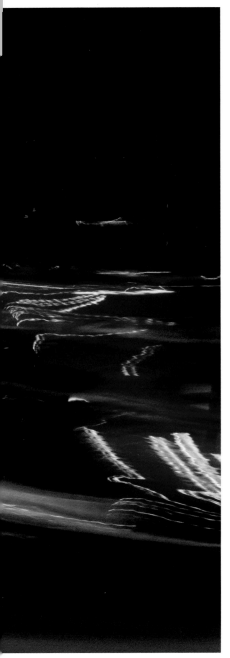

Right: Ricciardo raced to his seventh podium of 2014. **Below:** Kamui Kobayashi didn't get to start, having to jump out of his Caterham when its oil pressure fell on the parade lap. **Below right:** Valtteri Bottas leads Kimi Räikkönen and Nico Hülkenberg in the closing laps but would drop behind them when his tyres went off at the end

At this stage, some cars had already used both the supersoft and the soft tyres and so could run to the finish without pitting again. However, others had only used supersofts and were still obliged to use softs at some point. That group included both Hamilton and Alonso.

When the full-course yellows came out, Ferrari immediately pitted Alonso, dropping him to fourth in the queue, behind the Red Bulls. However, Mercedes kept Hamilton out, knowing that he would have to stop for softs at some point after the restart.

The safety car withdrew and the green flags were flown on lap 37. The extended yellow period had made it easier for anyone trying to make their tyres last to the finish, and there were only 23 laps to go.

Hamilton now had to build up enough of a lead to ensure that he would emerge from his stop in front. Even if he didn't, he'd have fresh tyres for the last few laps and would have the pace to pass anyone who'd jumped ahead of him. It seemed straightforward given the W05's performance advantage, but he still had to get the job done without making any mistakes.

The target Hamilton was aiming at was a lead of around 27-28s. He was 3.2s ahead of Vettel after the first flying lap and then continued to build up a lead by 2s a lap. However, as he got close to the target his tyres were almost shot. When the British driver finally came in on lap 52, he was around 26s ahead. He thus came out of the pits in second, behind Vettel.

"ROSBERG'S PROBLEMS STARTED AS SOON AS HE CLIMBED ABOARD THE CAR TO GO TO THE GRID"

"I extended that second-to-last stint as long as I could," explained Hamilton. "Then they said 'We need 27s'. And that was still 6s more that I needed to find and my tyres were dropping off, so I didn't really understand why. I was also nervous that, if the safety car came out, it might cause me big problems. Fortunately, I got to where I needed to go and pitted."

Now equipped with new tyres, Hamilton had eight laps in which to tackle Vettel. He didn't need them, though, as he blasted past his rival to take the lead on only the second and continued to pull away as Vettel massaged his ageing tyres to the flag. By the finish, Hamilton was 13.5s ahead of Vettel, who crossed the line with Ricciardo and Alonso right on his tail.

"I came out and saw Sebastian going past," said Hamilton. "But straight away I knew that they were obviously doing a two-stop and that I'd have good pace. So, I took it easy for the first lap. It was actually a bit of a tight gap I went for. Maybe I should have overtaken him somewhere else, but fortunately Sebastian was very fair and I got by."

"I wasn't quite sure what he was doing," said Vettel. "I thought that I would give him all the space to pass me on the inside for the next corner, but it seemed like he couldn't wait to get back in the lead. It was quite tight but I saw him, so I had to back off and let him through. There was no point fighting him at that stage, because I didn't have the tyres."

Ricciardo survived ongoing battery issues to take third, while the safety car cost Alonso a podium, although he was content with fourth. Massa had a lonely race as he claimed fifth place for Williams, despite having to keep his tyres alive for a marathon 38-lap final stint to the flag.

There was a lot of action behind as tyre strategy determined who was hot and who was not over the closing laps. Jean-Éric Vergne did a great job to claim sixth for Toro Rosso, the Frenchman picking up two 5s penalties for gaining an advantage by exceeding track limits, with one taken in the pits and the other added to his final race time. However, he still hung on to his position after fresh tyres allowed him to charge at the end.

In contrast, sticking with old tyres cost Bottas dearly and on the very last lap the Finn found himself tumbling down the order until he was eventually squeezed down to 11th. Despite the earlier incident that created the safety car period, Pérez charged up to seventh, another to benefit from fresh tyres.

Räikkönen, Nico Hülkenberg and Magnussen completed the top 10, the last-named overcoming problems with an overheating cockpit.

The safety car and Hamilton's subsequent charge had enlivened what might have otherwise have been a dull race. The key thing was that Hamilton now appeared to have momentum on his side. What could Rosberg do by way of response?

> "MASSA HAD A LONELY RACE BUT HAD TO KEEP HIS TYRES ALIVE FOR A MARATHON 38-LAP FINAL STINT"

Top: Jean-Éric Vergne powers across the Anderson Bridge en route to sixth place. **Left:** Lewis Hamilton had every reason to celebrate after arriving on the podium, as his seventh win moved him into the points lead ahead of teammate Rosberg, who left Singapore with nothing when his steering wheel failed and he retired after 13 laps. **Above:** Pastor Maldonado's Lotus flashes past the painted surface between the first and second corners en route to 12th place as the Renault-powered team continued to be short of speed. This matched his finishes in Austria and Germany

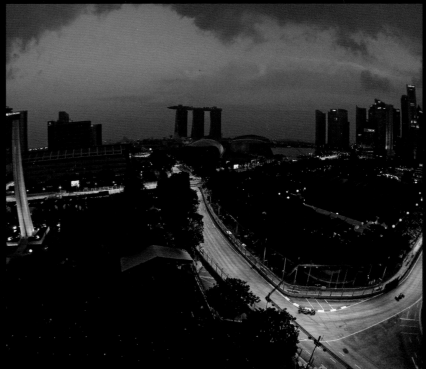

SNAPSHOT FROM SINGAPORE

CLOCKWISE FROM ABOVE: a Toro Rosso at night; Maldonado contemplates what he needs to do to get beyond Q1; city racing at its best; Bottas and Massa keep out of the rain; smiles all around as Sir Frank Williams shares a joke with Paddy Lowe and the Wolffs, Susie and Toto; Singapore Ferris wheel; Red Bull Racing chief Christian Horner grabs a word with the head man, Bernie Ecclestone; Bottas talks to the media; Niki Lauda explains the restriction of radio chatter

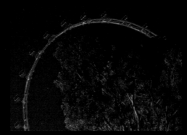

SINGAPORE
MARINA BAY
ROUND 14

Official Results © [2014]
Formula One World
Championship Limited, 6
Princes Gate, London, SW7
1QJ. No reproduction without
permission. All copyright and
database rights reserved.

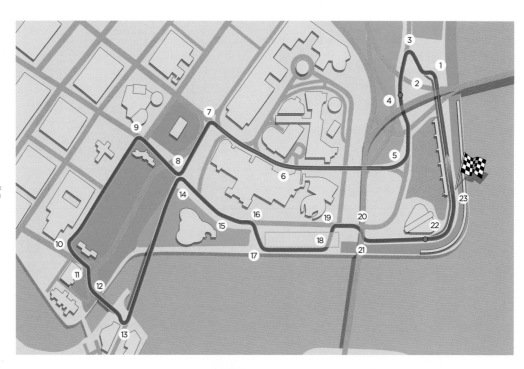

RACE DATE 21 September

CIRCUIT LENGTH 3.152 miles

NO. OF LAPS 60

RACE DISTANCE 189.120 miles

WEATHER Dark, 30ºC

TRACK TEMP 37ºC

LAP RECORD Kimi Räikkönen,
1m45.599s, 107.358mph, 2008

PRACTICE 1

	Driver	Time	Laps
1	F Alonso	1m49.056s	16
2	L Hamilton	1m49.178s	23
3	N Rosberg	1m49.205s	24
4	S Vettel	1m49.874s	27
5	D Ricciardo	1m50.122s	21
6	J-É Vergne	1m50.539s	11
7	K Räikkönen	1m50.783s	19
8	J Button	1m50.922s	21
9	D Kvyat	1m50.990s	26
10	S Pérez	1m51.131s	23
11	K Magnussen	1m51.217s	24
12	N Hülkenberg	1m51.604s	23
13	F Massa	1m51.953s	20
14	P Maldonado	1m52.125s	25
15	V Bottas	1m52.146s	19
16	E Gutiérrez	1m52.171s	15
17	A Sutil	1m52.237s	22
18	R Grosjean	1m52.906s	26
19	J Bianchi	1m54.113s	15
20	M Ericsson	1m54.475s	26
21	K Kobayashi	1m54.607s	21
22	M Chilton	1m55.170s	17

PRACTICE 2

	Driver	Time	Laps
1	L Hamilton	1m47.490s	25
2	F Alonso	1m47.623s	28
3	D Ricciardo	1m47.790s	28
4	K Räikkönen	1m48.031s	29
5	S Vettel	1m48.041s	5
6	K Magnussen	1m48.358s	33
7	J Button	1m48.435s	30
8	S Pérez	1m48.653s	30
9	N Hülkenberg	1m48.751s	31
10	D Kvyat	1m48.770s	31
11	J-É Vergne	1m48.800s	33
12	R Grosjean	1m49.062s	33
13	N Rosberg	1m49.075s	30
14	P Maldonado	1m49.139s	13
15	A Sutil	1m49.170s	34
16	E Gutiérrez	1m49.290s	37
17	F Massa	1m49.361s	29
18	V Bottas	1m49.971s	28
19	J Bianchi	1m50.612s	24
20	M Chilton	1m51.558s	21
21	K Kobayashi	1m52.075s	33
22	M Ericsson	1m52.936s	31

PRACTICE 3

	Driver	Time	Laps
1	F Alonso	1m47.299s	12
2	D Ricciardo	1m47.350s	15
3	N Rosberg	1m47.488s	15
4	J-É Vergne	1m47.693s	17
5	S Vettel	1m47.711s	17
6	L Hamilton	1m47.738s	12
7	F Massa	1m47.909s	15
8	V Bottas	1m48.205s	15
9	K Räikkönen	1m48.226s	16
10	E Gutiérrez	1m48.422s	20
11	N Hülkenberg	1m48.450s	11
12	K Magnussen	1m48.577s	9
13	J Button	1m48.599s	16
14	D Kvyat	1m48.637s	18
15	S Pérez	1m49.078s	15
16	A Sutil	1m49.115s	19
17	R Grosjean	1m49.485s	17
18	P Maldonado	1m50.149s	15
19	J Bianchi	1m50.376s	17
20	K Kobayashi	1m50.939s	17
21	M Chilton	1m51.221s	16
22	M Ericsson	1m51.598s	17

QUALIFYING 1

	Driver	Time
1	K Räikkönen	1m46.685s
2	F Alonso	1m46.889s
3	L Hamilton	1m46.921s
4	J Button	1m47.161s
5	V Bottas	1m47.196s
6	N Rosberg	1m47.244s
7	N Hülkenberg	1m47.370s
8	J-É Vergne	1m47.407s
9	S Vettel	1m47.476s
10	D Ricciardo	1m47.488s
11	F Massa	1m47.615s
12	D Kvyat	1m47.656s
13	R Grosjean	1m47.862s
14	E Gutiérrez	1m47.970s
15	K Magnussen	1m47.976s
16	S Pérez	1m48.143s
17	A Sutil	1m48.324s
18	P Maldonado	1m49.063s
19	J Bianchi	1m49.440s
20	K Kobayashi	1m50.405s
21	M Chilton	1m50.473s
22	M Ericsson	1m52.287s

QUALIFYING 2

	Driver	Time
1	N Rosberg	1m45.825s
2	L Hamilton	1m46.287s
3	F Alonso	1m46.328s
4	K Räikkönen	1m46.359s
5	F Massa	1m46.472s
6	D Ricciardo	1m46.493s
7	S Vettel	1m46.586s
8	V Bottas	1m46.622s
9	K Magnussen	1m46.700s
10	D Kvyat	1m46.926s
11	J Button	1m46.943s
12	J-É Vergne	1m46.989s
13	N Hülkenberg	1m47.308s
14	E Gutiérrez	1m47.333s
15	S Pérez	1m47.575s
16	R Grosjean	1m47.812s

Best sectors – Practice

Sec 1	F Alonso	28.595s
Sec 2	F Alonso	40.841s
Sec 3	D Ricciardo	37.346s

Speed trap – Practice

1	F Massa	187.964mph
2	L Hamilton	187.902mph
3	V Bottas	187.654mph

Best sectors – Qualifying

Sec 1	L Hamilton	28.207s
Sec 2	D Ricciardo	40.349s
Sec 3	N Rosberg	36.880s

Speed trap – Qualifying

1	F Massa	191.693mph
2	V Bottas	190.326mph
3	N Rosberg	189.456mph

Sebastian Vettel
"I had a good start and got past Daniel. I got undercut by Alonso. The safety car came at the worst time for us, but we made the tyres work at the end, which was tough."

Nico Rosberg
"My steering wheel problems began pre race. I was only able to change gear – there was no radio, no DRS and reduced hybrid power, and it never came back to life."

Fernando Alonso
"It's easy to ask how things would have gone if I hadn't made a mistake at the start and the safety car hadn't come out, but I'm pleased, as we were competitive."

Pastor Maldonado
"I'm happy about maximising our performance after our earlier issues. I pitted once more than the others during the safety car period, but it didn't affect my position."

Jenson Button
"I was cueing things up for the end: I'd been looking after my tyres and knew the last five laps were when things were going to get tricky for Valtteri. Then my car died."

Sergio Pérez
"Those in front of me had big degradation at the end, but this affected me too. When I caught the train ahead, I didn't have much grip and this made each pass tricky."

Daniel Ricciardo
"I wasn't fast enough in the first stint and had a few issues, with brakes and some power issues that were coming and going, but in terms of points we still got a good handful."

Lewis Hamilton
"My tyres went off. I wasn't sure whether to keep pushing. So I pitted and came out behind Seb, but he was on a two-stopper so I went for it on the straight."

Kimi Räikkönen
"After my first stop, I lost a place to Felipe, then was stuck behind a Williams. Every time I got close, I lost rear aero performance and degradation was very high."

Romain Grosjean
"Things were OK until the safety car, as I attacked too hard on the restart. With cold tyres it was just too much at one corner. From then on, I couldn't get back again."

Kevin Magnussen
"My seat started getting very hot, which made things extremely uncomfortable. Without that, I think I could have done better than 10th, but at least we got a point."

Nico Hülkenberg
"After the safety car, I had to do a 30-lap stint on the softs and was running out of grip near the end. With hindsight, it would have been better to pit again for fresh tyres."

POSITIONS LAP BY LAP

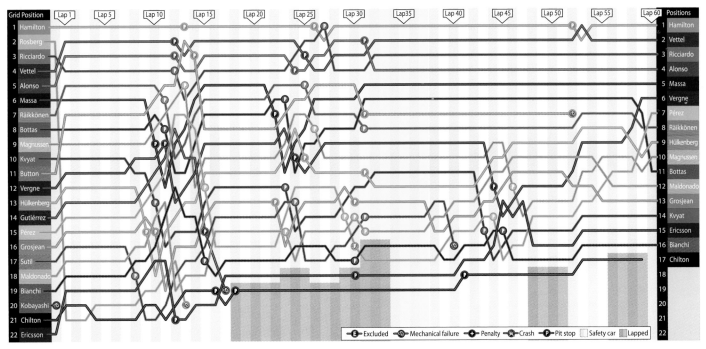

Grid Position	Lap 1	Lap 5	Lap 10	Lap 15	Lap 20	Lap 25	Lap 30	Lap35	Lap 40	Lap 45	Lap 50	Lap 55	Lap 60	Positions
1 Hamilton														1 Hamilton
2 Rosberg														2 Vettel
3 Ricciardo														3 Ricciardo
4 Vettel														4 Alonso
5 Alonso														5 Massa
6 Massa														6 Vergne
7 Räikkönen														7 Pérez
8 Bottas														8 Räikkönen
9 Magnussen														9 Hülkenberg
10 Kvyat														10 Magnussen
11 Button														11 Bottas
12 Vergne														12 Maldonado
13 Hülkenberg														13 Grosjean
14 Gutiérrez														14 Kvyat
15 Pérez														15 Ericsson
16 Grosjean														16 Bianchi
17 Sutil														17 Chilton
18 Maldonado														18
19 Bianchi														19
20 Kobayashi														20
21 Chilton														21
22 Ericsson														22

—E— Excluded —S— Mechanical failure —+— Penalty —X— Crash —P— Pit stop ▢ Safety car ▨ Lapped

QUALIFYING 3

	Driver	Time
1	L Hamilton	1m45.681s
2	N Rosberg	1m45.688s
3	D Ricciardo	1m45.854s
4	S Vettel	1m45.902s
5	F Alonso	1m45.907s
6	F Massa	1m46.000s
7	K Räikkönen	1m46.170s
8	V Bottas	1m46.187s
9	K Magnussen	1m46.250s
10	D Kvyat	1m47.362s

Grid penalties

GRID

	Driver	Time
1	L Hamilton	1m45.681s
2	N Rosberg	1m45.688s
3	D Ricciardo	1m45.854s
4	S Vettel	1m45.902s
5	F Alonso	1m45.907s
6	F Massa	1m46.000s
7	K Räikkönen	1m46.170s
8	V Bottas	1m46.187s
9	K Magnussen	1m46.250s
10	D Kvyat	1m47.362s
11	J Button	1m46.943s
12	J-É Vergne	1m46.989s
13	N Hülkenberg	1m47.308s
14	E Gutiérrez	1m47.333s
15	S Pérez	1m47.575s
16	R Grosjean	1m47.812s
17	A Sutil	1m48.324s
18	P Maldonado	1m49.063s
19	J Bianchi	1m49.440s
20	K Kobayashi	1m50.405s
21	M Chilton	1m50.473s
22	M Ericsson	1m52.287s

RACE

	Driver	Car	Laps	Time	Av mph	Fastest	Stops
1	L Hamilton	Mercedes F1 W05	60	2h00m04.795s	94.316	1m50.417s	3
2	S Vettel	Red Bull-Renault RB10	60	2h00m18.329s	94.134	1m52.519s	2
3	D Ricciardo	Red Bull-Renult RB10	60	2h00m19.068s	94.125	1m52.569s	2
4	F Alonso	Ferrari F14 T	60	2h00m20.184s	94.110	1m52.115s	3
5	F Massa	Williams-Mercedes FW36	60	2h00m46.956s	93.763	1m53.283s	2
6	J-É Vergne	Toro Rosso-Renault STR9	60	2h01m01.596s	93.574	1m51.937s	3
7	S Pérez	Force India-Mercedes VJM07	60	2h01m03.833s	93.545	1m52.007s	4
8	K Räikkönen	Ferrari F14 T	60	2h01m05.436s	93.524	1m52.872s	3
9	N Hülkenberg	Force India-Mercedes VJM07	60	2h01m06.456s	93.511	1m52.762s	3
10	K Magnussen	McLaren-Mercedes MP4-29	60	2h01m07.025s	93.504	1m51.639s	3
11	V Bottas	Williams-Mercedes FW36	60	2h01m09.860s	93.467	1m52.515s	2
12	P Maldonado	Lotus-Renault E22	60	2h01m11.710s	93.443	1m53.213s	4
13	R Grosjean	Lotus-Renault E22	60	2h01m12.824s	93.429	1m53.543s	3
14	D Kvyat	Toro Rosso-Renault STR9	60	2h01m16.803s	93.378	1m51.761s	3
15	M Ericsson	Caterham-Renault CT05	60	2h01m38.983s	93.094	1m55.416s	3
16	J Bianchi	Marussia-Ferrari MR03	60	2h01m39.338s	93.090	1m53.538s	3
17	M Chilton	Marussia-Ferrari MR03	60	2h00m26.131s	92.465	1m53.807s	3
R	J Button	McLaren-Mercedes MP4-29	52	Power box	-	1m53.707s	2
R	A Sutil	Sauber-Ferrari C33	40	Water leak	-	1m53.948s	3
R	E Gutiérrez	Sauber-Ferrari C33	17	Electrical	-	1m55.684s	1
R	N Rosberg	Mercedes F1 W05	13	Wiring loom	-	1m56.769s	0
NS	K Kobayashi	Caterham-Renault CT05	0	Power unit	-	-	-

Fastest lap
L Hamilton 1m50.417s
(102.616mph) on lap 39

Fastest speed trap
F Massa 190.263mph
Slowest speed trap
N Rosberg 168.764mph

Fastest pit stop
1 J Button 28.627s
2 J Button 28.641s
3 K Magnussen 28.684s

CHAMPIONSHIP

	Driver	Pts
1	N Rosberg	241
2	L Hamilton	238
3	D Ricciardo	181
4	F Alonso	133
5	S Vettel	124
6	V Bottas	122
7	J Button	72
8	N Hülkenberg	72
9	F Massa	65
10	S Pérez	45
11	K Räikkönen	45
12	K Magnussen	39
13	J-É Vergne	19
14	R Grosjean	8
15	D Kvyat	8
16	J Bianchi	2

CONSTRUCTORS

	Team	Pts
1	Mercedes	479
2	Red Bull-Renault	305
3	Williams-Mercedes	187
4	Ferrari	178
5	Force India-Mercedes	117
6	McLaren-Mercedes	111
7	Toro Rosso-Renault	27
8	Lotus-Renault	8
9	Marussia-Ferrari	2

Esteban Gutiérrez
"We have to extract 120% from what we have, but with the issues we're having it makes things complicated. There's nothing I can do to guard against the problems."

Jean-Éric Vergne
"It was a fantastic race and I'm extremely happy, especially considering my two penalties. I had to push in the closing laps. I had a lot of fun overtaking the ones in front of me."

Felipe Massa
"We changed the strategy from a three-stop to a two-stop after the safety car period and the final stint was pushing the tyre to the absolute limit, but I managed to make it work."

Max Chilton
"I almost got Ericsson at the start, then lost time to him when Rosberg got between us. I made my first pit stop, then soon after had to come in again when I suffered a puncture."

Marcus Ericsson
"We followed a great strategy as we decided to stay out on the primes and I knew that Bianchi was going to catch me, so I prepared myself for the final four laps and kept him behind."

Adrian Sutil
"I was in position to score, but had an engine problem. We were able to continue. Regarding the contact with Sergio, he simply drove into the back of the car."

Daniil Kvyat
"I had to fight more with myself than with the cars as my car was sliding a lot. Unfortunately, I also had a problem with my drink system, so I was without water for the whole race."

Valtteri Bottas
"I moved to a two-stop strategy, but the tyres just weren't able to hold on. On the final lap, I had a big lock up in the rear tyres and after that I had no grip and cars could easily sweep past."

Jules Bianchi
"We were closer to Maldonado and Sutil, so we're back to a more typical delta on this type of circuit. It's disappointing that we were unable to pass Ericsson due to brake-wear issues."

Kamui Kobayashi
"What a frustrating way to end the race weekend. During the formation lap, I felt no power and then it smelt as if something was burning. Then I suddenly lost the brakes so I decided to stop."

ROUND 15
JAPAN
JAPANESE GRAND PRIX

SADLY, THE 2014 JAPANESE GP WILL BE REMEMBERED NOT
FOR THE SUPERB VICTORY ACHIEVED IN THE WET BY LEWIS
HAMILTON, BUT FOR THE TERRIBLE ACCIDENT THAT BEFELL
MARUSSIA'S JULES BIANCHI, WHICH BROUGHT IT TO A CLOSE

After aborting the first start behind the safety car, the cars waited for 20 minutes in the pits before trying again. **Right:** conditions were still wet at the second start, as shown by Nico Rosberg leaving Lewis Hamilton and Valtteri Bottas in his spray. **Below right:** Jenson Button was again the driver who read the conditions best

A s evening descended on Suzuka, the sport was reeling after popular Frenchman Jules Bianchi suffered a serious head injury when he lost control in the wet and struck a tractor crane that was recovering Adrian Sutil's crashed Sauber.

As this was the most serious incident to hit the sport since the traumatic 1994 season, it overshadowed a hard-earned success for Lewis Hamilton that saw the Briton further extend his World Championship lead. Understandably, neither the driver nor his Mercedes team were in the mood to celebrate.

A typhoon was predicted to hit Japan and it became clear through Saturday that there would be heavy rain on race day. The FIA offered Suzuka owners Honda the option of starting the race a few hours early – the scheduled 3pm start allowed a window of daylight of little over two hours – but there was no change.

The other major talking point was the driver market and the Suzuka paddock was stunned on Saturday morning when Red Bull Racing announced that its lead driver Sebastian Vettel would be leaving the team. Red Bull quickly ended any speculation about its own future plans by confirming that Daniil Kvyat would be promoted from its junior team, Scuderia Toro Rosso. Although there was no confirmation from Ferrari, it was evident that Vettel was bound for Maranello and that Fernando Alonso would be allowed to leave.

On the track, Hamilton's chances of securing pole position were made more difficult when he had a heavy crash at Turn 1 at the end of Saturday morning practice. Fortunately, his chassis wasn't damaged and the car was repaired in time for qualifying. He was fastest in Q1, but teammate Nico Rosberg was quickest on both runs in Q2 and then again in Q3.

"I did the best I could," said Hamilton. "My guys did a fantastic job to rebuild the car after I binned it, so a big thank you for their hard work. I wasn't really feeling on top of things today. It was still fast, but Nico was fantastically fast."

The Mercedes duo were well ahead of the pursuing pack, which was led by Williams, with Valtteri Bottas qualifying third and Felipe Massa fourth. Alonso was fifth fastest, while once again Daniel Ricciardo beat his teammate Vettel to be sixth, with the German driver

> **"THE FIA OFFERED SUZUKA OWNERS HONDA THE POSSIBILITY OF STARTING THE RACE A FEW HOURS EARLY"**

back in ninth. The Red Bulls were split by the McLarens of Kevin Magnussen and Jenson Button.

Rain fell throughout Sunday, although conditions improved sufficiently to allow two support races to be completed. Heavier rain had been predicted for the afternoon and it returned as the cars were heading out to grid, before turning into a downpour in the minutes before the start.

A start behind the safety car was now inevitable, but even that slow running proved to be a bit too much and, after just two laps, the race was red-flagged. Conditions were so difficult that Caterham's Marcus Ericsson spun at the exit of the chicane and had to rejoin the queue in 22nd and last.

All the drivers filed into the pit lane and lined up at the exit. Teams were allowed to work on the cars and, after a 20-minute wait and with the rain easing off, the field was sent off again. There was then drama when, after just a few corners, Alonso's car switched itself off and the Spaniard coasted to a halt for his second retirement in three races.

After a few cautious laps behind the safety car, the drivers began to report that conditions were fit for racing, some of them sounding a little impatient. At the end of lap 9,

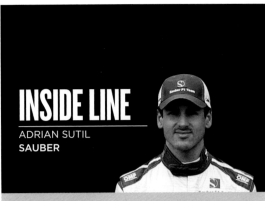

INSIDE LINE

ADRIAN SUTIL
SAUBER

At the time of the race, we'd had almost an hour without rain. The risk came at the end when the light came down, and then the drizzle started to fall more steadily.

"I struggled to stay on the circuit. Then it started to rain more and got really dark, so it was hard to see the patches on the track. I was following Jules very closely when I lost the car in Turn 7 with aquaplaning, I had a big snap and went into the wall. Luckily, nothing happened to me and I climbed out.

"One lap later, that whole incident happened with Jules; the same kind of mistake as I did, or at least the same aquaplaning. He lost the car — I saw him coming without control of the car.

"It was getting worse on those couple of laps. Of course, our tyres were closer to the end, so the resistance to aquaplaning wasn't so good any more. When I was standing there after the accident I saw quite a few cars shaking around, even when the safety car came out, so there must have been quite a river developing. That caused the two accidents, really. The rain came up, the tyres were at the end of their life, people were struggling and it was really difficult to drive.

"There's a big problem in our cars when it gets dark. You can still see, but we have very bright, irritating lights on the steering wheel. We have a very limited view from the helmet, and then there is this bright light, which is usually set up for maximum brightness in sunny conditions. In dark conditions it affects the eyesight a lot. In those last laps, with all the spray and the drops on the visor, it was really hard to see."

> "I LOST THE CAR IN TURN 7 WITH AQUAPLANING, I HAD A BIG SNAP AND WENT INTO THE WALL. LUCKILY, NOTHING HAPPENED"

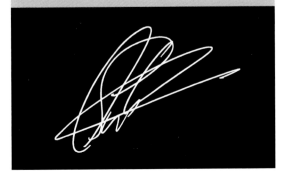

the green flag flew and Rosberg and Hamilton took off in front. Further back, Button, always good at making calls in tricky conditions, dived into the pits for intermediates.

It was a gamble, but it soon became apparent that it was a good one. At the end of lap 11, the second flying lap, half the field came in, led by Bottas, Ricciardo and Magnussen. Massa and Vettel followed on lap 12, and leader Rosberg came in on lap 13, along with Bianchi, who had boldly stayed out and briefly risen to third.

Hamilton led for a lap before pitting on lap 14, as the last driver to do so. A slight mistake at Spoon Curve on that lap cost him any chance of jumping Rosberg for the lead, and he emerged 2.1s behind. Meanwhile, Button's early pit stop had bounced him up to third place, ahead of Williams and the Red Bulls.

Hamilton soon began to close the gap to his teammate. Other

TALKING POINT
LOOKING FOR A SAFER SOLUTION

Jules Bianchi's accident was a reminder that racing at the highest level is still dangerous, despite all the safety improvements that followed the 1994 season. FIA President Jean Todt was quick to announce the creation of an Accident Panel, chaired by Peter Wright, to investigate the circumstances of the accident.

Of course, it's not easy to legislate for flying wheels or the possibility of cars taking off and striking solid objects, such as posts that support debris fences. What made Suzuka so frustrating is that a collision between a competing car and a recovery vehicle seemed so unnecessary.

Inevitably, the FIA came under scrutiny for not using the safety car to control the field after Adrian Sutil went off and a tractor crane was dispatched to recover his Sauber. However, race director Charlie Whiting was adamant that race control followed the usual protocol given that the stricken car was well off the circuit and that the marshals were protected by double-waved yellows, which mean slow down and "be prepared to stop".

> **"WITH THE FULL SUPPORT OF TEAMS AND DRIVERS, THE FIA'S IMMEDIATE RESPONSE WAS TO FOCUS ON CONTROLLING THE PACE OF DRIVERS"**

With the full support of teams and drivers, the FIA's immediate response was to focus on the thorny issue of controlling the pace of drivers through yellow flag zones. Nobody wants to lose time relative to rivals and so judging how much to back off has always been a problem. The FIA opted to address that by finding a way to effect a mandatory speed limit.

"There are some things to learn," Whiting explained a week after the accident, "and we want to engage with the teams and drivers to make sure that we come up with well-thought-through ideas. One of the most important things we learned is that it's probably better to take the decision to slow down away from the drivers... to put in place a system where it's much clearer to everybody how much cars should slow under similar circumstances. It won't be a speed limit as such, but we want drivers to slow down to a given and well-known speed in the relevant place. You need to give drivers warning of what's going to come, and then they need time to make the adjustments."

drivers on the move were Vettel and Ricciardo as the RB10 proved well suited to the conditions. Both made some good moves, Vettel overtaking Massa and then Bottas at the hairpin and Ricciardo doing the same at the Esses.

At the front, Hamilton maintained pressure on Rosberg, who began to struggle for rear grip as his intermediate tyres got older. The silver cars ran nose-to-tail for several laps, the drivers taking different lines as they sought grip. This was edge-of-the-seat stuff and something we had seen only a few times this year, due to one or the other hitting problems.

At the start of lap 27, Hamilton lost a few car lengths when he got a little squirrelly and ran wide at Turn 1, although he soon closed the gap again after he regained balance. Then, after Rosberg lost momentum out of the chicane, he swept past in a dramatic move around the outside at the same corner to claim the lead at the start of lap 29.

"I had a lot more pace than Nico," said Hamilton. "This isn't a very easy circuit on which to follow, but fortunately I was able to get quite close, and particularly in the last corner. I think, perhaps, he had a small oversteer moment out and I didn't. Obviously, the DRS enabled me to get alongside. I was fairly confident with the balance of the car, so I put it there and stuck it out."

Thereafter, he continued to pull away. Looking for grip, Rosberg pitted for fresh intermediates on lap 33, and Hamilton came in two laps after that. Ricciardo was close enough to take the lead for a lap before he too pitted on lap 36.

It was at around this time that the rain began to return and, with the light fading fast, conditions

> "THE RAIN BEGAN TO RETURN AND, WITH THE LIGHT FADING FAST, CONDITIONS WERE BECOMING EXTREMELY DIFFICULT"

were becoming extremely difficult. Indeed, Vettel lost 6s when he went grasstracking at the Esses. On lap 40, Hamilton passed the 75% distance mark – enough to guarantee full points – and at the same time several drivers down the field decided it was time to switch back to full wets.

Others preferred to maintain track position and push on with rapidly wearing intermediates. And yet, despite the conditions, everyone stayed on the road until Sutil spun into the tyre wall at the high-speed Dunlop left-hander on lap 42. It was a hefty impact, but the German hopped out and walked away. A tractor crane was dispatched to move the stricken Sauber and, while there was no safety car deployed, the marshals were protected by double-waved yellows.

It was under these conditions that Bianchi, coincidentally the

After Jules Bianchi's crash, joy was far from the minds of Nico Rosberg, Lewis Hamilton and Sebastian Vettel on the podium

driver Sutil had been chasing, went off. Video from track cameras showed that the Marussia driver had got sideways, overcorrected and then speared straight off the track towards the tractor crane, which was edging slowly backwards.

He hit the rear of the vehicle with a sickening force, pushing it upwards, before the Marussia came to an abrupt stop. The car's roll structure was torn off and the driver knocked unconscious.

It took a while for both race control and the pit lane to realise what had happened, as the live TV feed didn't show the accident. The safety car and the medical car both emerged as the leaders were on lap 44 and, as the seriousness of the situation became fully apparent, the red flag flew as the queue was about to complete the 46th of the 53 scheduled laps. With no question of resumption, the results were declared as of lap 44, with Hamilton's official margin over his teammate 9.1s.

A pit stop for wets under the safety car at the start of lap 45 had dropped Vettel behind Ricciardo just before the red flag came out. However, on the countback to lap 44, the positions were reversed, Vettel thus reclaiming the final podium spot.

Button's stop for intermediate tyres at the restart had bounced him up to third place and for a long time he looked set to keep it. However, both Red Bulls got past late in the race – Vettel at the second round of pit stops and Ricciardo on track – to demote him to fifth. Button also lost a few seconds in the pits when a new steering wheel was fitted, something that had already delayed his teammate Magnussen who had to make an extra pit visit for that to be carried out.

From the start of the race, it became apparent that the Williams drivers didn't have sufficient pace in the wet, but they hung on to finish sixth and seventh, with Bottas beating Massa. The top 10 was completed by Nico Hülkenberg, Jean-Éric Vergne and Sergio Pérez.

After the cars pulled off the circuit, it became apparent that Bianchi was in a critical condition. In the circumstances, the results of the race were of little consequence and, as the teams began to pack up for the trip to Russia, all thoughts were with the Marussia driver.

"BOTH RED BULLS GOT PAST BUTTON LATE IN THE RACE TO DEMOTE HIM TO FIFTH"

It was both wet and dark when the cars were brought in to the pits after the first start

CLOCKWISE FROM ABOVE: Roberto Mehri had another Friday run for Caterham; Valtteri Bottas flashes past the funfair; Felipe Massa was pleased with his form at Suzuka; Ferrari F1 boss Marco Mattiacci looks for progress; Max Verstappen tries the STR9 before his run; then checks his times; Ron Dennis looks on; Red Bull Racing power talk; Williams' Head of Performance Engineering Rob Smedley

SNAPSHOT FROM JAPAN

JAPAN
SUZUKA
ROUND 15

Official Results © [2014]
Formula One World
Championship Limited,
6 Princes Gate, London, SW7
1QJ. No reproduction without
permission. All copyright and
database rights reserved.

RACE DATE 5 October
CIRCUIT LENGTH 3.608 miles
NO. OF LAPS 44
RACE DISTANCE 158.579 miles
WEATHER Raining, 16°C
TRACK TEMP 23°C
LAP RECORD Kimi Räikkönen,
1m31.540s, 141.904mph, 2005

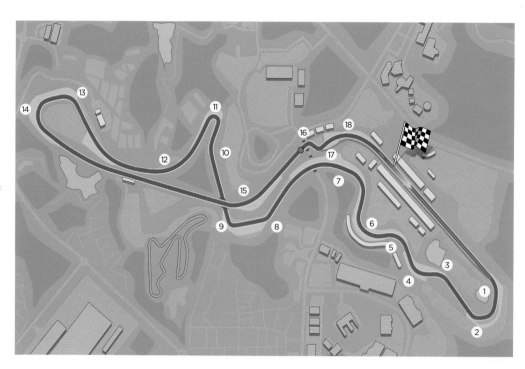

PRACTICE 1

	Driver	Time	Laps
1	N Rosberg	1m35.461s	27
2	L Hamilton	1m35.612s	26
3	F Alonso	1m36.037s	19
4	V Bottas	1m36.576s	25
5	K Räikkönen	1m37.187s	19
6	K Magnussen	1m37.327s	24
7	D Ricciardo	1m37.466s	27
8	J Button	1m37.649s	24
9	S Vettel	1m37.686s	26
10	D Kvyat	1m37.714s	26
11	F Massa	1m38.012s	22
12	M Verstappen	1m38.157s	22
13	S Pérez	1m38.324s	10
14	N Hülkenberg	1m38.582s	9
15	R Grosjean	1m38.851s	21
16	A Sutil	1m39.046s	19
17	P Maldonado	1m39.097s	26
18	E Gutiérrez	1m39.318s	18
19	M Ericsson	1m40.031s	18
20	R Mehri	1m41.472s	24
21	J Bianchi	1m41.580s	10
22	M Chilton	1m41.757s	15

PRACTICE 2

	Driver	Time	Laps
1	L Hamilton	1m35.078s	28
2	N Rosberg	1m35.318s	27
3	V Bottas	1m36.279s	24
4	J Button	1m36.409s	28
5	S Vettel	1m36.436s	24
6	K Räikkönen	1m36.529s	19
7	F Alonso	1m36.637s	26
8	K Magnussen	1m36.714s	31
9	D Kvyat	1m36.943s	27
10	D Ricciardo	1m37.186s	3
11	J-É Vergne	1m37.219s	19
12	N Hülkenberg	1m37.504s	16
13	R Grosjean	1m37.563s	31
14	F Massa	1m37.700s	18
15	S Pérez	1m37.786s	8
16	P Maldonado	1m37.798s	27
17	A Sutil	1m38.010s	25
18	E Gutiérrez	1m38.365s	9
19	M Ericsson	1m39.069s	22
20	J Bianchi	1m39.306s	20
21	M Chilton	1m39.333s	24
22	K Kobayashi	1m42.760s	3

PRACTICE 3

	Driver	Time	Laps
1	N Rosberg	1m33.228s	14
2	L Hamilton	1m34.210s	10
3	F Alonso	1m34.439s	12
4	F Massa	1m34.564s	12
5	V Bottas	1m35.061s	16
6	D Ricciardo	1m35.086s	13
7	K Magnussen	1m35.251s	16
8	J-É Vergne	1m35.494s	8
9	D Kvyat	1m35.538s	17
10	J Button	1m35.549s	16
11	N Hülkenberg	1m35.732s	15
12	K Räikkönen	1m35.995s	5
13	S Pérez	1m36.365s	8
14	E Gutiérrez	1m36.407s	22
15	S Vettel	1m36.460s	6
16	R Grosjean	1m36.558s	19
17	P Maldonado	1m36.617s	12
18	A Sutil	1m36.626s	20
19	M Ericsson	1m37.367s	12
20	M Chilton	1m37.883s	17
21	J Bianchi	1m38.102s	15
22	K Kobayashi	1m38.784s	12

QUALIFYING 1

	Driver	Time
1	L Hamilton	1m33.611s
2	N Rosberg	1m33.671s
3	V Bottas	1m34.301s
4	F Massa	1m34.483s
5	F Alonso	1m34.497s
6	K Magnussen	1m34.930s
7	K Räikkönen	1m34.984s
8	N Hülkenberg	1m35.000s
9	J Button	1m35.150s
10	J-É Vergne	1m35.155s
11	D Kvyat	1m35.210s
12	E Gutiérrez	1m35.308s
13	S Pérez	1m35.439s
14	S Vettel	1m35.517s
15	D Ricciardo	1m35.593s
16	A Sutil	1m35.736s
17	P Maldonado	1m35.917s
18	R Grosjean	1m35.984s
19	M Ericsson	1m36.813s
20	J Bianchi	1m36.943s
21	K Kobayashi	1m37.015s
22	M Chilton	1m37.481s

QUALIFYING 2

	Driver	Time
1	N Rosberg	1m32.950s
2	L Hamilton	1m32.982s
3	V Bottas	1m33.443s
4	F Massa	1m33.551s
5	F Alonso	1m33.675s
6	K Magnussen	1m34.229s
7	D Ricciardo	1m34.466s
8	J Button	1m34.648s
9	K Räikkönen	1m34.771s
10	S Vettel	1m34.784s
11	J-É Vergne	1m34.984s
12	S Pérez	1m35.089s
13	D Kvyat	1m35.092s
14	N Hülkenberg	1m35.099s
15	A Sutil	1m35.364s
16	E Gutiérrez	1m35.681s

Best sectors – Practice

Sec 1	N Rosberg	33.143s
Sec 2	N Rosberg	41.976s
Sec 3	N Rosberg	18.109s

Speed trap – Practice

1	V Bottas	193.992mph
2	L Hamilton	193.060mph
3	N Rosberg	192.935mph

Best sectors – Qualifying

Sec 1	N Rosberg	32.914s
Sec 2	N Rosberg	41.484s
Sec 3	N Rosberg	18.038s

Speed trap – Qualifying

1	V Bottas	195.794mph
2	F Massa	194.427mph
3	N Rosberg	194.178mph

Sebastian Vettel

"Everything that happened
with the racing is secondary
today. One of us is in a bad
shape and we don't yet know
how he is. We hope to have
some very good news soon."

Nico Rosberg

"I struggled for balance on
the intermediates, so I had
to push hard to keep Lewis
behind me. I had a lot of
oversteer which is why the
rear of my car was nervous."

Fernando Alonso

"I still don't know what caused
the unfortunate technical
problem, only that suddenly
the car lost all of its electrics,
perhaps down to a short
circuit caused by the rain."

Pastor Maldonado

"We were trying to anticipate
what others would do and
regained some places. I was
able to make some good
moves, but you had to be
careful about where to push."

Jenson Button

"The race doesn't really
matter today. I haven't seen
Jules' accident, but the most
important thing is that all our
thoughts are with him, his
family and his team."

Sergio Pérez

"To begin with, it was about
trying to keep the car on the
track. Our strategy was going
well, but we were unlucky to
make our final stop, which
lost me a few positions."

Daniel Ricciardo

"The race was tricky, but
it wasn't going too badly
and the set-up we had for
yesterday paid off. We tried
a different strategy, but
Bianchi is my main concern."

Lewis Hamilton

"The conditions were tricky
throughout, but I had more
pace than Nico. This isn't an
easy circuit for overtaking,
but he made a mistake out of
the last corner and I got by."

Kimi Räikkönen

"After the start behind the
safety car, conditions were
atrocious, but my handling
was OK. When the rain
eased, I fitted inters, but
after a few laps I had to slow."

Romain Grosjean

"After the restart, conditions
were better, but the rain
returned and it was difficult
to be on the right tyres and
find the grip we wanted. We
also soon used up our tyres."

Kevin Magnussen

"I had a problem with the
steering wheel, which dropped
me out of the race. I tried my
best to come back and get
some points, but unfortunately
it just wasn't possible."

Nico Hülkenberg

"Until the final laps, my race
was going well. I pitted late
and jumped a few cars. When
the final safety car came out
we decided to pit again as I
needed new rubber to finish."

POSITIONS LAP BY LAP

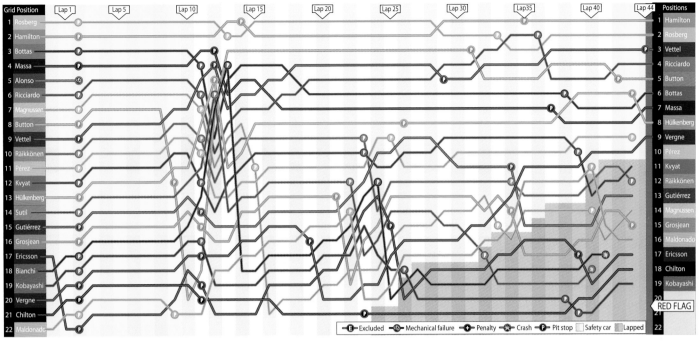

Grid Position | Lap 1 | Lap 5 | Lap 10 | Lap 15 | Lap 20 | Lap 25 | Lap 30 | Lap35 | Lap 40 | Lap 44 | Positions

Grid (left): 1 Rosberg, 2 Hamilton, 3 Bottas, 4 Massa, 5 Alonso, 6 Ricciardo, 7 Magnussen, 8 Button, 9 Vettel, 10 Räikkönen, 11 Pérez, 12 Kvyat, 13 Hülkenberg, 14 Sutil, 15 Gutiérrez, 16 Grosjean, 17 Ericsson, 18 Bianchi, 19 Kobayashi, 20 Vergne, 21 Chilton, 22 Maldonado

Positions (right): 1 Hamilton, 2 Rosberg, 3 Vettel, 4 Ricciardo, 5 Button, 6 Bottas, 7 Massa, 8 Hülkenberg, 9 Vergne, 10 Pérez, 11 Kvyat, 12 Räikkönen, 13 Gutiérrez, 14 Magnussen, 15 Grosjean, 16 Maldonado, 17 Ericsson, 18 Chilton, 19 Kobayashi, 20, 21, 22

RED FLAG

Legend: E Excluded — S Mechanical failure — + Penalty — X Crash — P Pit stop — Safety car — Lapped

QUALIFYING 3

	Driver	Time
1	N Rosberg	1m32.506s
2	L Hamilton	1m32.703s
3	V Bottas	1m33.128s
4	F Massa	1m33.527s
5	F Alonso	1m33.740s
6	D Ricciardo	1m34.075s
7	K Magnussen	1m34.242s
8	J Button	1m34.317s
9	S Vettel	1m34.432s
10	K Räikkönen	1m34.548s

GRID

	Driver	Time
1	N Rosberg	1m32.506s
2	L Hamilton	1m32.703s
3	V Bottas	1m33.128s
4	F Massa	1m33.527s
5	F Alonso	1m33.740s
6	D Ricciardo	1m34.075s
7	K Magnussen	1m34.242s
8	J Button	1m34.317s
9	S Vettel	1m34.432s
10	K Räikkönen	1m34.548s
11	S Pérez	1m35.089s
12	D Kvyat	1m35.092s
13	N Hülkenberg	1m35.099s
14	A Sutil	1m35.364s
15	E Gutiérrez	1m35.681s
16	R Grosjean	1m35.984s
17	M Ericsson	1m36.813s
18	J Bianchi	1m36.943s
19	K Kobayashi	1m37.015s
20	J-É Vergne	1m34.984s
21	M Chilton	1m37.481s
22	P Maldonado	1m35.917s

Grid penalties
P Maldonado — 10-place penalty for using sixth engine of 2014
J-É Vergne — 10-place penalty for using sixth engine of 2014

RACE

	Driver	Car	Laps	Time	Av mph	Fastest	Stops
1	L Hamilton	Mercedes F1 W05	44	1h51m43.021s	85.172	1m51.600s	3
2	N Rosberg	Mercedes F1 W05	44	1h51m52.201s	85.051	1m52.551s	3
3	S Vettel	Red Bull-Renault RB10	44	1h52m12.143s	84.799	1m51.915s	3
4	D Ricciardo	Red Bull-Renault RB10	44	1h52m21.389s	84.677	1m52.231s	3
5	J Button	McLaren-Mercedes MP4-29	44	1h52m50.571s	84.318	1m51.721s	4
6	V Bottas	Williams-Mercedes FW36	44	1h53m36.794s	83.746	1m54.103s	3
7	F Massa	Williams-Mercedes FW36	44	1h53m38.147s	83.730	1m53.450s	3
8	N Hülkenberg	Force India-Mercedes VJM07	44	1h53m38.969s	83.720	1m52.814s	4
9	J-É Vergne	Toro Rosso-Renault STR9	44	1h53m50.659s	83.576	1m53.562s	3
10	S Pérez	Force India-Mercedes VJM07	43	1h51m22.646s	83.484	1m53.556s	4
11	D Kvyat	Toro Rosso-Renault STR9	43	1h51m48.409s	83.163	1m54.021s	4
12	K Räikkönen	Ferrari F14 T	43	1h51m49.838s	83.146	1m52.426s	5
13	E Gutiérrez	Sauber-Ferrari C33	43	1h52m14.678s	82.839	1m55.372s	3
14	K Magnussen	McLaren-Mercedes MP4-29	43	1h52m22.070s	82.748	1m53.510s	5
15	R Grosjean	Lotus-Renault E22	43	1h52m22.780s	82.739	1m55.302s	5
16	P Maldonado	Lotus-Renault E22	43	1h52m42.898s	82.493	1m54.702s	4
17	M Ericsson	Caterham-Renault CT05	43	1h52m50.427s	82.401	1m54.669s	4
18	M Chilton	Marussia-Ferrari MR03	43	1h53m36.282s	81.847	1m56.472s	3
19	K Kobayashi	Caterham-Renault CT05	43	1h53m59.121s	81.573	1m55.641s	5
20	J Bianchi	Marussia-Ferrari MR03	41	Accident	-	1m55.985s	3
21	A Sutil	Sauber-Ferrari C33	40	Accident	-	1m55.753s	4
R	F Alonso	Ferrari F14 T	2	Electrical	-	-	0

Fastest lap
L Hamilton 1m51.600s
(116.402mph) on lap 39

Fastest speed trap
N Rosberg 170.007mph

Slowest speed trap
F Alonso 103.334mph

Fastest pit stop
1 S Vettel 23.443s
2 R Grosjean 23.656s
3 L Hamilton 23.677s

CHAMPIONSHIP

	Driver	Pts
1	L Hamilton	266
2	N Rosberg	256
3	D Ricciardo	193
4	S Vettel	139
5	F Alonso	133
6	V Bottas	130
7	J Button	82
8	N Hülkenberg	76
9	F Massa	71
10	S Pérez	46
11	K Räikkönen	45
12	K Magnussen	39
13	J-É Vergne	21
14	R Grosjean	8
15	D Kvyat	8
16	J Bianchi	2

CONSTRUCTORS

	Team	Pts
1	Mercedes	522
2	Red Bull-Renault	332
3	Williams-Mercedes	201
4	Ferrari	178
5	Force India-Mercedes	122
6	McLaren-Mercedes	121
7	Toro Rosso-Renault	29
8	Lotus-Renault	8
9	Marussia-Ferrari	2

Esteban Gutiérrez
"It was the right decision to stop the race. I fought all the way from the beginning to the end. The conditions were very challenging and it was difficult to get into the rhythm."

Jean-Éric Vergne
"Starting from the back and ending up in the points is a great achievement. In today's conditions, it was really difficult not to make mistakes while driving as fast as possible."

Felipe Massa
"I suffered at the start with aquaplaning and towards the end it started to get dark as rain fell again. The Red Bulls were too fast for us today, especially on the intermediates."

Max Chilton
No post-race comments were released by the team in the wake of Jules Bianchi's accident.

Marcus Ericsson
"The track was undriveable at the beginning behind the safety car. Unfortunately, I spun and lost all my advantage from yesterday. After that, I think I drove a fantastic race."

Adrian Sutil
"My thoughts are with Jules who went off where I did. Everything else is irrelevant. Everybody in the paddock should think of him and I hope that he is in good hands."

Daniil Kvyat
"The performance of the car was good, but our strategy didn't quite work out and with the safety car and red flag towards the end, my chances for a points finish were gone."

Valtteri Bottas
"The car wasn't particularly great in the wet, but we made the most of the strategy and extracted what we could. We're missing pace in the corners and so conceded a lot of time."

Jules Bianchi

Kamui Kobayashi
"My home race didn't really work out as I would've liked it to, but today was OK and it was amazing to see all the fans in the grandstands even though it hasn't stopped raining all day."

ROUND 16 RUSS

RUSSIAN GRAND PRIX

MERCEDES SCORED ITS NINTH
ONE-TWO OF 2014. BUT FOR A
LOCK-UP, THOUGH, IT COULD
HAVE BEEN NICO ROSBERG
WHO ENDED UP AS THE WINNER
RATHER THAN LEWIS HAMILTON

ercedes achieved its first aim for the season by securing the Constructors' World Championship title in Russia. It came from Lewis Hamilton and Nico Rosberg logging the team's ninth one-two finish of 2014, with a first-lap mistake by the German having determined the outcome.

Like other semi-street courses, notably the now-defunct one in Valencia, Sochi didn't produce great racing and it was an afternoon largely devoid of wheel-to-wheel action. It was a safe race, though, and above all that's what F1 needed just one week after Jules Bianchi's accident at Suzuka.

The Frenchman's name dominated conversations and he was acknowledged by stickers on helmets and cars, as well as by a tribute from his fellow drivers on the grid. Marussia's newly built-up

spare chassis sat in the garage carrying number 17 for the duration of the weekend.

After trying for more than 30 years and following various false starts in other potential venues, Bernie Ecclestone had finally achieved his dream of taking F1 to Russia. In so doing, he had opened up the doors to a huge market for the sport and, by a quirk of timing, he'd done it just as the country's young hero Daniil Kvyat had been nominated for a high-profile seat at Red Bull Racing for 2015. Even Ecclestone couldn't have predicted that when he set the wheels in motion for the creation of the Sochi Autodrom.

The plan to make use of the otherwise now superfluous Winter Olympics site proved to be inspired. Compromised by the space available, track designer Hermann Tilke did his best with a layout that snaked between buildings used for figure skating, hockey and curling. With echoes of Valencia, Korea and

Abu Dhabi, it was a very flat and artificial track and on TV it was hard to tell one concrete barrier-lined section from another.

However, it made for good live viewing and the drivers found the track more challenging than expected. It wasn't easy either to hone the car set-up or complete a perfect lap and throughout practice we saw cars locking up or taking to run-off areas. In Q3, when the top drivers have everything "turned up to 11", even some of the big names found themselves overdriving and running out of grip by the last few corners of the lap.

Rosberg was fastest in Q1, but Hamilton beat him in Q2 and on both runs in Q3, with a final margin of exactly 0.200s. Intriguingly, both Mercedes drivers were slower in the final session than in Q2.

Valtteri Bottas was third fastest in Q1 and Q2 and on his final run in Q3 he was on target to beat one if not both Mercedes drivers, but he made a mistake in the penultimate

> "ON HIS FINAL RUN IN Q3, BOTTAS WAS ON TARGET TO BEAT ONE IF NOT BOTH MERCEDES DRIVERS"

The moment Nico Rosberg locks up... **Below:** ...then runs wide out of Turn 2. **Below left:** Lewis Hamilton leads away from Rosberg, Valtteri Bottas and Jenson Button

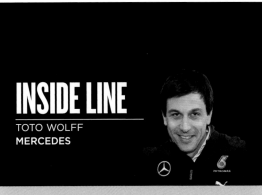

INSIDE LINE

TOTO WOLFF
MERCEDES

It's incredible – I have to pinch myself. We are part of the Mercedes-Benz history. We won the first constructors' title for Mercedes-Benz and I feel honoured to be part of that team. Part of a team whose foundations were built by Ross [Brawn], who played such an important role with the steps that were taken in 2012 and the people who joined us then.

"We constantly ramped our game up, we made the right decisions, we got the right resources. The big boys back in Stuttgart understood what it needed and, since then, we were on an upwards slope and this the result.

"Of course, Lewis Hamilton's advantage of 92 points means that Daniel [Ricciardo] would need to win all three remaining races and Lewis not to score eight points. Even though I'm a pessimist that would be a black swan event!

"WE WON THE FIRST CONSTRUCTORS' TITLE FOR MERCEDES-BENZ AND I FEEL HONOURED TO BE PART OF THAT TEAM"

"I don't think we're going to change anything in our approach because we want them to race each other respectfully and we saw that today. Probably that was Nico's corner and he missed the braking on the dirty line. Lewis was cold-blooded and good. So winning the title won't change the approach – we don't want it to end in some kind of event on the track.

"Somebody said yesterday's home runs don't win tomorrow's games. You can't rely on history, but I think we have all it needs. We have the right resources and two great drivers, and these are the ingredients you need to be on top. You must be realistic in terms of what we can expect in the following years. Of course, our target is to continue in the way we are going now, but we've also seen that things end sometimes. Hopefully, we're far away from that."

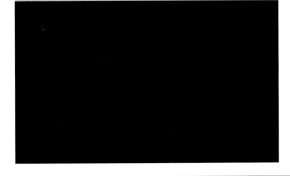

corner, then ran wide in the final turn and only just kept his Williams away from the barrier.

McLaren looked good from the start of the weekend and that paid off as Jenson Button qualified in a solid fourth place. Meanwhile, local hero Kvyat did an amazing job to qualify fifth for Toro Rosso. Kevin Magnussen was sixth fastest, but the Dane had a five-place grid penalty for a gearbox change and his misfortune gifted places to Daniel Ricciardo, Fernando Alonso, Kimi Räikkönen and Jean-Éric Vergne, after what proved to be a disappointing session for both Ferrari and Red Bull.

The biggest surprise in Q2 was that Sebastian Vettel failed to get in a quick, clean lap and ended the session in 11th – off the pace not just of teammate Ricciardo, but

both STR drivers. He did at least gain a place from Magnussen. It was worse for Felipe Massa who was stranded down in 18th after suffering a loss of power in Q1.

With tyre degradation low on the smooth surface, teams were aiming at a one-stop race and it was a question of the timing of that single stop. Any discussion about how strategy might impact the Hamilton v Rosberg battle was ended on the first lap as, convinced that the long run down to the first braking area at Turn 2 was his big chance, Rosberg threw everything into a bold move down the inside of his rival. However, committed to the dirty line, he locked up both front wheels and, with clouds of white smoke filling the air, skated wide across the run-off area on the outside. He emerged in front, but

TALKING POINT

TEAMS ASK FOR DEVELOPMENT LEEWAY

There had been much debate from early in the season about the possibility of an engine "unfreeze" for 2015 and in Russia tensions between Mercedes and its rivals became all too apparent.

It had long ago been agreed that under the turbo rules there would be no in-season development by the power-unit suppliers. However, it was clear during 2014 that the lack of upgrades did nothing to help the show, in that there was little that Renault and Ferrari could do to catch Mercedes. Everyone knew that the advantage that the manufacturer from Stuttgart had in Australia would still be there in Abu Dhabi.

> "RED BULL WAS KEEN TO SEE MORE LEEWAY, GIVEN THAT IT WAS PUSHING AHEAD WITH POWER UNIT DEVELOPMENT IN PARALLEL WITH RENAULT"

Updates had to wait for the winter "window" that had been built into the rules. While there was significant scope for changes to be made before the 2015 homologation deadline, the feeling at Renault and Ferrari was that in-season upgrades should be allowed. After 30 June, unanimity was required for such a rule change and in Singapore all parties agreed that it was the way forward. However, Mercedes later changed its stance, citing spiralling costs, to the obvious frustration of rivals.

"We're a company that produces the pinnacle of engineering, so I think it's important that innovation is at the centre of this F1," said Ferrari's Marco Mattiacci. "I can't go back to our fans and say we can't perform better with the engine, we need to wait one year. We absolutely stick to the principles of these new regulations. We're not asking to change, we're asking for a fine tuning, applying the same principle."

Red Bull was particularly keen to see more leeway introduced, given that the team was pushing ahead with power unit development in parallel to what Renault was doing – and it would take time for the results to come through.

"The immaturity of this technology is still quite raw and I think Mercedes shouldn't be afraid of competition," said Red Bull's Christian Horner. "They are doing a super job, but I think it's healthy for F1 that Ferrari, Honda and Renault should have that ability to close that gap. It's about what's right for the sport, what's right for the fans."

Daniil Kvyat holds off Red Bull's Sebastian Vettel and Daniel Ricciardo plus Kimi Räikkönen early on. **Top right:** Jenson Button keeps Fernando Alonso at bay as they fight over third. **Middle right:** Button would go on to finish fourth. **Bottom right:** Romain Grosjean was hit with a 5s penalty

was immediately warned by his team to give the lead back to Hamilton, as he had clearly cut the corner and gained an advantage.

"It was definitely do-able and I just messed up, very simple, no explanation," Rosberg admitted. "I just braked too late and too hard."

However, he had a bigger problem – his front tyres were so badly flatspotted that he had no choice but to come in at the end of the first lap and take on a new set of primes. The team then told him that his only chance of recovering something from the afternoon was to get to the chequered flag on that set of tyres. Even with everyone expecting low degradation, it was a big ask, but Rosberg got his head down and – from the very back of the field – went for it.

Hamilton's main opposition now came from Bottas, and the Finn was within 4-5s of his Mercedes after 15 laps. Then Hamilton seemed to find another gear and pulled away before making his single pit stop for the prime tyre at half distance.

At the same time, Rosberg had worked his way up the field, gaining places as others made their single stops, before eventually relieving Bottas of second place at the start of lap 31, at the very spot where he'd locked up on the opening lap.

Hamilton was of course well out of reach at the front and was controlling the pace. The gap stayed at 19-20s for a while before Hamilton eased off and, when the chequered flag fell on lap 53, he was 13.6s clear. Rosberg did a great job to make his set of primes last for 52 of those laps and the fact that he could still go so fast and for so long said a lot about the pace that Mercedes could draw upon when it was needed.

"ROSBERG LOCKED UP BOTH FRONT WHEELS AND SKATED WIDE ACROSS THE RUN-OFF AREA ON THE OUTSIDE"

"It was a good, good day and an amazing weekend," said Hamilton. "Firstly, I'm just so proud to have worked with this great team, to get the first Constructors' Championship for Mercedes-Benz. I could have only dreamed of that when I joined this team.

"Today, once I was out in the lead, I was really just having to look after the tyres and managing the fuel was quite straightforward. Then, towards the end of the race, the car felt great so I could push or not push. I wasn't really having to push much and, even when I was having to pick up the pace a little bit when I eventually found Nico was behind, it was easy to match the times. The car's been amazing this weekend and I really, really enjoyed the track."

Bottas again impressed as he logged his fifth podium of the season and moved ahead of both

Vettel and Alonso into fourth place in the World Championship.

It was also a good day for McLaren. Button ran third until dropping behind the recovering Rosberg after his stop on lap 22 and thereafter he ran fourth until the flag. Magnussen had a great first lap and was up to fifth by lap 3, but any chance to progress from there was spoiled by the need to save fuel in the latter part of the race.

Alonso jumped up to fourth at the start and chased Button hard in the opening stint. A slow pit stop due to a front jack issue helped

Magnussen to get ahead and thereafter Alonso ran sixth, pushed hard by Ricciardo in the latter stages. The Australian didn't have a great start and Vettel got ahead of him. The Red Bull pair ran together in the opening laps until Ricciardo made an early pit stop for tyres as he was starting to struggle and that led to them trading places.

Räikkönen found himself stuck behind other cars and didn't have the speed with which to pass and, like his teammate, had to keep an eye on saving fuel. He finished ninth, ahead of Sergio Pérez. The

Mexican put in a feisty performance and worked hard to keep Massa's Williams behind for much of the race, eventually claiming the final point, despite having to save fuel. Massa tried to recover with a first lap change from medium to soft tyres, but his attempt to run to the chequered flag was frustrated by the need to make a second stop and by his struggles to get past Pérez. To the disappointment of local fans, Kvyat faded to 14th after starting from fifth on the grid.

Bulletproof tyres, unexpectedly high fuel consumption that forced many drivers to ease off and a lack of incidents or safety car interventions meant there was little race action. To be fair to Tilke, the supporting GP2 and GP3 races were more eventful and it was that perfect storm of factors that made for one of the least exciting grands prix of the season.

Nevertheless, a good-sized crowd turned up, everything ran on schedule and F1 folk were pleasantly surprised by both the good weather and an unexpectedly appealing location, sandwiched between mountains and the sea.

Meanwhile, plans were already in hand to make Sochi a night race in the future, so the Russian GP is definitely here to stay.

"TO THE DISAPPOINTMENT OF LOCAL FANS, DANIIL KVYAT FADED TO 14TH AFTER STARTING FIFTH"

Lewis Hamilton had reason to celebrate as his win moved him 27 points clear

Paddy Lowe, Nico Rosberg, Hamilton, Niki Lauda et al celebrate Mercedes' first Constructors' Championship title

CLOCKWISE FROM RIGHT:
Sochi at night; Daniel
Ricciardo in his RB10;
photographers arrange the
Mercedes celebration shot;
fans in the sunset; Sochi's
mountainous backdrop;
Bernie Ecclestone chats to
President Putin; Max Chilton
was understandably pensive
a week on from his teammate
Jules Bianchi's accident; grid
girl elegance; Felipe Massa
waits in the pit lane; Fernando
Alonso and Jenson Button
discuss the possibility of
being teammates in 2015

SNAPSHOT FROM RUSSIA

RUSSIA
SOCHI
ROUND 16

Official Results © [2014]
Formula One World
Championship Limited,
6 Princes Gate, London, SW7
1QJ. No reproduction without
permission. All copyright and
database rights reserved.

RACE DATE 12 October

CIRCUIT LENGTH 3.634 miles

NO. OF LAPS 53

RACE DISTANCE 192.466 miles

WEATHER Sunny, 24ºC

TRACK TEMP 32ºC

LAP RECORD Valtteri Bottas,
1m40.896s, 129.654mph, 2014

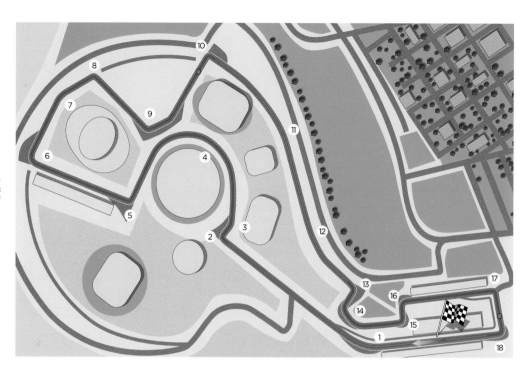

PRACTICE 1				PRACTICE 2				PRACTICE 3				QUALIFYING 1			QUALIFYING 2	
	Driver	Time	Laps		Driver	Time	Laps		Driver	Time	Laps		Driver	Time		Driver	Time
1	N Rosberg	1m42.311s	29	1	L Hamilton	1m39.360s	27	1	L Hamilton	1m38.726s	15	1	L Hamilton	1m38.759s	1	L Hamilton	1m38.338s
2	L Hamilton	1m42.376s	25	2	K Magnussen	1m40.494s	32	2	N Rosberg	1m39.016s	25	2	N Rosberg	1m39.076s	2	N Rosberg	1m38.606s
3	J Button	1m42.507s	28	3	F Alonso	1m40.504s	32	3	V Bottas	1m39.097s	20	3	V Bottas	1m39.125s	3	V Bottas	1m38.971s
4	F Alonso	1m42.720s	27	4	N Rosberg	1m40.542s	30	4	D Ricciardo	1m39.755s	16	4	J Button	1m39.560s	4	K Magnussen	1m39.022s
5	K Magnussen	1m43.026s	28	5	V Bottas	1m40.573s	33	5	F Massa	1m39.954s	22	5	K Magnussen	1m39.735s	5	D Kvyat	1m39.296s
6	S Pérez	1m43.129s	26	6	J Button	1m40.718s	32	6	D Kvyat	1m40.009s	27	6	D Kvyat	1m40.074s	6	J Button	1m39.381s
7	D Kvyat	1m43.164s	29	7	F Massa	1m40.731s	30	7	K Räikkönen	1m40.011s	20	7	K Räikkönen	1m40.098s	7	D Ricciardo	1m39.666s
8	K Räikkönen	1m43.212s	23	8	D Kvyat	1m41.108s	32	8	F Alonso	1m40.151s	15	8	F Alonso	1m40.255s	8	F Alonso	1m39.786s
9	J-É Vergne	1m43.327s	24	9	S Vettel	1m41.396s	30	9	J-É Vergne	1m40.205s	26	9	N Hülkenberg	1m40.273s	9	K Räikkönen	1m39.838s
10	V Bottas	1m43.542s	9	10	J-É Vergne	1m41.531s	33	10	S Vettel	1m40.338s	21	10	J-É Vergne	1m40.354s	10	J-É Vergne	1m39.929s
11	F Massa	1m43.741s	22	11	K Räikkönen	1m41.630s	24	11	J Button	1m40.355s	19	11	S Vettel	1m40.382s	11	S Vettel	1m40.052s
12	D Ricciardo	1m43.821s	25	12	N Hülkenberg	1m41.677s	27	12	N Hülkenberg	1m40.669s	23	12	D Ricciardo	1m40.519s	12	N Hülkenberg	1m40.058s
13	N Hülkenberg	1m43.976s	21	13	D Ricciardo	1m42.061s	25	13	S Pérez	1m40.699s	26	13	S Pérez	1m40.723s	13	S Pérez	1m40.163s
14	S Vettel	1m44.506s	30	14	S Pérez	1m42.090s	29	14	A Sutil	1m41.146s	21	14	A Sutil	1m40.766s	14	E Gutiérrez	1m40.536s
15	A Sutil	1m44.625s	26	15	A Sutil	1m42.233s	31	15	E Gutiérrez	1m41.520s	20	15	E Gutiérrez	1m41.159s	15	A Sutil	1m40.984s
16	P Maldonado	1m44.876s	26	16	R Grosjean	1m42.892s	30	16	R Grosjean	1m41.915s	22	16	R Grosjean	1m42.526s	16	R Grosjean	1m41.397s
17	S Sirotkin	1m45.032s	22	17	P Maldonado	1m42.905s	33	17	K Magnussen	1m42.436s	4	17	M Ericsson	1m42.648s			
18	R Grosjean	1m45.190s	25	18	E Gutiérrez	1m43.055s	33	18	M Ericsson	1m43.109s	11	18	F Massa	1m43.064s			
19	R Mehri	1m46.782s	18	19	M Ericsson	1m44.135s	22	19	K Kobayashi	1m43.975s	12	19	K Kobayashi	1m43.166s			
20	M Ericsson	1m46.922s	18	20	M Chilton	1m44.530s	29	20	M Chilton	1m44.737s	9	20	P Maldonado	1m43.205s			
21	M Chilton	1m47.284s	26	21	K Kobayashi	1m44.952s	27	21	P Maldonado	no time		21	M Chilton	1m43.649s			

Best sectors – Practice

Sec 1	L Hamilton	34.878s
Sec 2	V Bottas	34.132s
Sec 3	L Hamilton	29.328s

Speed trap – Practice

1	V Bottas	204.244mph
2	N Rosberg	204.058mph
3	F Massa	203.934mph

Best sectors – Qualifying

Sec 1	V Bottas	34.885s
Sec 2	L Hamilton	33.992s
Sec 3	N Rosberg	29.353s

Speed trap – Qualifying

1	V Bottas	206.668mph
2	K Magnussen	203.996mph
3	N Hülkenberg	203.623mph

Sebastian Vettel

"I had a good start and then a tough battle with Daniel, but from then onwards the speed was nothing special and we had the same issues as we had in qualifying."

Nico Rosberg

"I braked too late for the first corner. So I flatspotted my front tyres and had to pit. I thought the degradation would increase, but soon it was stable and I could push."

Fernando Alonso

"My front jack didn't work but, even without this problem, I would have finished in the same position because the McLarens were faster. At the end I had to save fuel."

Pastor Maldonado

"I struggled for balance and it made for a very tough race. I moved from the medium to the soft compound, but even late in the race it was a real struggle to find grip."

Jenson Button

"Well, that wasn't a bad day at all. I had a little scare at Turn 3 on lap 1, when Alonso and I got very close, but apart from that it was a pretty straightforward race."

Sergio Pérez

"It was a hard-earned point. I tried to push all race, but the fuel strategy was marginal. When I was on the softs, it was hard to save fuel as I had to defend from Felipe."

Daniel Ricciardo

"A tyre was blistered from qualifying and the first stint made it worse, so I had to pit early. Then, on the prime, I had good pace and could match Alonso, but couldn't get past."

Lewis Hamilton

"I had to manage the tyres throughout the race, but managing the fuel wasn't too bad. At the end, when Nico was behind, I needed to match his times, which I did."

Kimi Räikkönen

"I started well, but a Toro Rosso squeezed me towards the wall. Because I had to brake hard, a few cars passed me and from then on I was always stuck behind others."

Romain Grosjean

"It was so hard to get the tyres up to temperature in the first few laps, I thought I had a puncture. After that, it was straightforward, aside from the incident with Sutil."

Kevin Magnussen

"I decided to go flat-out to make up as many places as possible from my P11 grid slot and I moved up to P5 very quickly. After that, though, I had to do a lot of fuel-saving."

Nico Hülkenberg

"It was a difficult race for me. I started pretty far back and struggled for straightline speed compared to the cars with which I was battling, which made it hard to pass."

POSITIONS LAP BY LAP

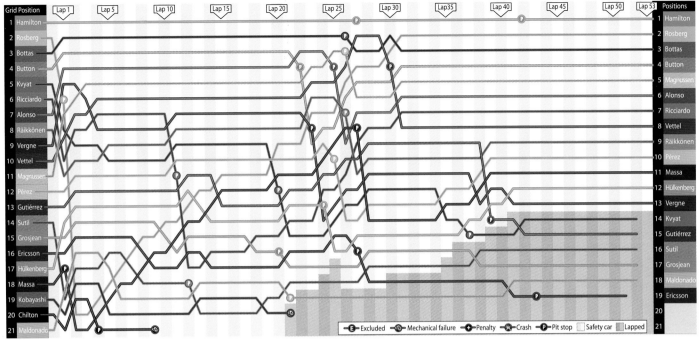

QUALIFYING 3

	Driver	Time
1	L Hamilton	1m38.513s
2	N Rosberg	1m38.713s
3	V Bottas	1m38.920s
4	J Button	1m39.121s
5	D Kvyat	1m39.277s
6	K Magnussen	1m39.629s
7	D Ricciardo	1m39.635s
8	F Alonso	1m39.709s
9	K Räikkönen	1m39.771s
10	J-É Vergne	1m40.020s

GRID

	Driver	Time
1	L Hamilton	1m38.513s
2	N Rosberg	1m38.713s
3	V Bottas	1m38.920s
4	J Button	1m39.121s
5	D Kvyat	1m39.277s
6	D Ricciardo	1m39.635s
7	F Alonso	1m39.709s
8	K Räikkönen	1m39.771s
9	J-É Vergne	1m40.020s
10	S Vettel	1m40.052s
11	K Magnussen	1m39.629s
12	S Pérez	1m40.163s
13	E Gutiérrez	1m40.536s
14	A Sutil	1m40.984s
15	R Grosjean	1m41.397s
16	M Ericsson	1m42.648s
17	N Hülkenberg	1m40.058s
18	F Massa	1m43.064s
19	K Kobayashi	1m43.166s
20	M Chilton	1m43.649s
21	P Maldonado	1m43.205s

RACE

	Driver	Car	Laps	Time	Av mph	Fastest	Stops
1	L Hamilton	Mercedes F1 W05	53	1h31m50.744s	125.732	1m41.606s	1
2	N Rosberg	Mercedes F1 W05	53	1h32m04.401s	125.421	1m41.360s	1
3	V Bottas	Williams-Mercedes FW36	53	1h32m08.169s	125.336	1m40.896s	1
4	J Button	McLaren-Mercedes MP4-29	53	1h32m20.978s	125.046	1m41.964s	1
5	K Magnussen	McLaren-Mercedes MP4-29	53	1h32m44.360s	124.521	1m43.076s	1
6	F Alonso	Ferrari F14 T	53	1h32m50.760s	124.377	1m42.179s	1
7	D Ricciardo	Red Bull-Renault RB10	53	1h32m52.556s	124.337	1m43.050s	1
8	S Vettel	Red Bull-Renault RB10	53	1h32m56.929s	124.240	1m42.630s	1
9	K Räikkönen	Ferrari F14 T	53	1h33m09.621s	123.958	1m42.919s	1
10	S Pérez	Force India-Mercedes VJM07	53	1h33m10.811s	123.932	1m42.924s	1
11	F Massa	Williams-Mercedes FW36	53	1h33m11.621s	123.914	1m42.879s	2
12	N Hülkenberg	Force India-Mercedes VJM07	53	1h33m12.053s	123.904	1m42.685s	1
13	J-É Vergne	Toro Rosso-Renault STR9	53	1h33m28.039s	123.551	1m42.550s	1
14	D Kvyat	Toro Rosso-Renault STR9	52	1h31m52.658s	123.315	1m42.022s	2
15	E Gutiérrez	Sauber-Ferrari C33	52	1h32m18.536s	122.739	1m44.075s	1
16	A Sutil	Sauber-Ferrari C33	52	1h32m35.037s	122.374	1m43.822s	1
17	R Grosjean	Lotus-Renault E22	52	1h32m43.112s	122.197	1m44.461s	1
18	P Maldonado	Lotus-Renault E22	52	1h33m05.788s	121.701	1m44.030s	1
19	M Ericsson	Caterham-Renault CT05	51	1h31m55.857s	120.872	1m43.979s	2
R	K Kobayashi	Caterham-Renault CT05	21	Brakes	-	1m47.407s	0
R	M Chilton	Marussia-Ferrari MR03	9	Suspension	-	1m48.268s	1

CHAMPIONSHIP

	Driver	Pts
1	L Hamilton	291
2	N Rosberg	274
3	D Ricciardo	199
4	V Bottas	145
5	S Vettel	143
6	F Alonso	141
7	J Button	94
8	N Hülkenberg	76
9	F Massa	71
10	K Magnussen	49
11	S Pérez	47
12	K Räikkönen	47
13	J-É Vergne	21
14	R Grosjean	8
15	D Kvyat	8
16	J Bianchi	2

Grid penalties

Magnussen, Hülkenberg, Maldonado & Chilton 5-place penalty for changing the gearbox

P Maldonado Rest of penalty for using a sixth engine

Fastest lap V Bottas 1m40.896s (129.654mph) on lap 53

Fastest speed trap D Ricciardo 203.996mph

Slowest speed trap M Chilton 178.644mph

Fastest pit stop

1	K Magnussen	29.736s
2	S Pérez	29.876s
3	F Massa	29.912s

CONSTRUCTORS

	Team	Pts
1	Mercedes	565
2	Red Bull-Renault	342
3	Williams-Mercedes	216
4	Ferrari	188
5	McLaren-Mercedes	143
6	Force India-Mercedes	123
7	Toro Rosso-Renault	29
8	Lotus-Renault	8
9	Marussia-Ferrari	2

Esteban Gutiérrez

"We were betting on having a safety-car period in the first stint and so extended this run. It wasn't ideal for the strategy and, in the end, the safety car didn't come out."

Jean-Éric Vergne

"We have to understand why we had to save so much fuel. It's a shame as the start was very positive. We were attacking as much as possible, but then I had to stop doing it."

Felipe Massa

"I stopped on lap 1 and then had good pace so made up places until I came up to Pérez who had strong straightline speed. After my second stop, I found myself behind him again."

Max Chilton

"I switched to the soft, but on lap 9 started to feel a vibration from the front left, so I pitted for the team to investigate. It turned out to be something we couldn't fix quickly."

Marcus Ericsson

"My start was a good one and then I was able to pull away from the Sauber and the Lotus. But the second stint on the prime tyres wasn't that good, as I just couldn't get them to work."

Adrian Sutil

"The start on the medium tyres was tricky. So we opted to go for an early stop and change to the soft tyres. After that, I was able to continue the race without major incidents."

Daniil Kvyat

"Apart from the fact that I couldn't find the right grip, we had to care too much about our fuel consumption compared with the others. I'd have liked to do much better here in Russia."

Valtteri Bottas

"We went into the race with the mentality that we were going to fight Mercedes for the win, but their pace surprised us a bit and in the end we need to be satisfied with taking third place."

Kamui Kobayashi

"When I heard over the radio that I needed to pit, I thought it was just a normal pit stop. However, I was then told that I needed to retire as my brakes were overheating."

ROUND 17
USA
UNITED STATES GRAND PRIX

LEWIS HAMILTON SECURED HIS FIFTH STRAIGHT
WIN AND EXTENDED HIS POINTS LEAD OVER
NICO ROSBERG IN AUSTIN, EARNING HIS WIN
WITH A PASS RATHER THAN CLEVER STRATEGY

L ewis Hamilton's win in Austin was a hugely popular one as the crowd here has always supported him. It also guaranteed that the 2014 title would be won by a Mercedes driver as Daniel Ricciardo's mathematical chance to overhaul Hamilton and Nico Rosberg finally faded away. It meant that the battle would go down to the wire in Abu Dhabi, where double points would be on offer, as Hamilton would now not be able to secure the title in Brazil.

Now in its third year, the event continued to attract a good crowd and, after the slim pickings of Sochi, members of the F1 travelling circus were pleased to be in a city that has so much to offer and which has rapidly become one of the favoured destinations for team personnel.

Not among them this year, alas, were the folk from Caterham and Marussia after financial realities hit home and both teams failed to make the trip. With only 18 cars in the field, the qualifying format was tweaked so that four cars were eliminated in both Q1 and Q2.

Rosberg underlined his determination to keep the title battle alive by taking pole position, leaving a frustrated Hamilton in second place. Having been fastest in all three practice sessions, Hamilton had a problem with the left front brake running cooler than the right, which led to locking issues. Although he was fastest in Q1, he lost out to Rosberg on both runs in Q2 and again on both runs when it mattered in Q3.

"The track was changing all the time and it wasn't easy to get everything right," said Rosberg. "I finally got there on set-up, together with my team. I felt comfortable and was able to push."

Hamilton responded: "I really struggled with braking. The left brake was always cooler than the right and it kept catching. If I can't fix the locking, it will be an issue throughout the race."

Valtteri Bottas continued his run of being the closest challenger to Mercedes by taking a solid third on the grid for Williams, ahead of teammate Felipe Massa after the Brazilian had been faster in both Q1 and Q2.

Daniel Ricciardo qualified fifth for Red Bull, ahead of Fernando Alonso and Jenson Button, but the Briton had a five-place grid penalty for a gearbox change and tumbled down to 12th place. The slowest in Q3 were Kevin Magnussen, Kimi

> "ALTHOUGH HE WAS FASTEST IN Q1, HAMILTON LOST OUT TO ROSBERG IN BOTH Q2 AND Q3"

Räikkönen and Adrian Sutil, the latter giving Sauber its best qualifying result of the season.

Sebastian Vettel, meanwhile, was committed to a pit lane start after he took a complete new power unit for Saturday, becoming the first driver to pick up the mandatory penalty. The German made only a token attempt in qualifying, just to fulfil the 107% requirement. He set the 17th best time, although it meant nothing.

At the start, poleman Rosberg led into the first corner, while Hamilton, despite being on the dirty side of the grid, managed to stay ahead of Bottas. Indeed, the Finn had clutch issues off the line and actually lost out to Massa. At the same time, Ricciardo got away badly, dropping behind Alonso and Magnussen, although he soon re-passed the Dane.

Further around the first lap, Sergio Pérez tried an ambitious

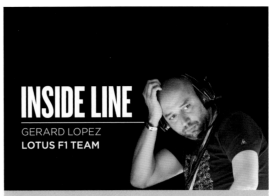

INSIDE LINE

GERARD LOPEZ
LOTUS F1 TEAM

I n the context of this season, ninth place for Pastor Maldonado in Austin was good. We had a host of small improvements, with a bit more power from the engine on the new fuel and some aero work, including a new floor. Soft tyres have always been good for us so, putting all the things together, at least we were back racing. It was a good feeling.

"This season has been a catastrophe. We haven't built the best car we've ever had. We took a bit of a gamble with a number of choices and we got the short end of the stick on the engine side. Renault has struggled and once it figured it was struggling it had to focus on the two teams with which it has developed everything. We found ourselves out of the driving seat there.

"So, a lot of things haven't really been good. We've had a season like this before, in 2011, when we did the forward-facing exhausts. The good thing about that season was that we learned a lot going into the next one. This time, we've learned a lot and we're also going to have a Mercedes engine.

"We know that Williams has taken a step forward and a lot of that comes from the engine. You don't feel blindly comfortable, but you feel a bit better, knowing that it should be a step in the right direction. We have the same people who designed good cars previously. Assuming this was a one-off, we shouldn't go too crazy about changing the way we do things.

"We take it on the chin, learn from it and should be back next year. I don't know if we're going to be fighting for podiums, but we should be in a different position for sure."

> "WE TOOK A BIT OF A GAMBLE WITH A NUMBER OF CHOICES AND WE GOT THE SHORT END OF THE STICK ON THE ENGINE SIDE"

Nico Rosberg leads Lewis Hamilton and the rest of the field at the start. **Below left:** Rosberg waves after taking pole. **Below:** Romain Grosjean crests a hill in his Lotus E22 Renault

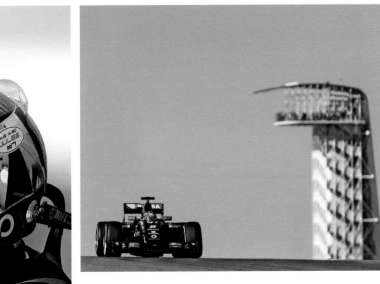

TALKING POINT
CATERHAM AND MARUSSIA STAY AWAY

The state of F1's finances was the main topic of conversation through the US GP weekend after both Marussia and Caterham failed to make the trip. The two teams, which had been inextricably linked since their 2010 debuts, both reached the point of no return at the same time as debts caught up with them.

Caterham was the more contentious situation. The team was sold by the Malaysian-based 1MRT on 29 June to the Swiss-based Engavest consortium fronted by Colin Kolles. Yet it was an associated company and supplier of services to the team, Caterham Sports Ltd, that went into administration in October.

Meanwhile, it became apparent that Tony Fernandes had not released the shares to Engavest and was still the de facto owner. The Caterham Sports administrator then took over the management of 1MRT as Kolles and his colleagues, who had kept the team alive, were forced to take a step back.

> "TWO TEAMS THAT HAD BEEN LINKED INEXTRICABLY SINCE THEIR DEBUTS IN 2010 BOTH REACHED THE POINT OF NO RETURN AT THE SAME TIME"

After consulting Bernie Ecclestone, the administrator decided to skip two races, permitted under F1's commercial agreements, and attempt to return for Abu Dhabi.

Marussia's financial problems, meanwhile, had been mounting over the years and the numbers simply became too big. On 27 October, Manor Grand Prix – the company behind the team – went into administration. CEO Graeme Lowdon met Ferrari boss Marco Mattiacci in Austin to discuss unpaid engine bills, but time ran out and on 7 November it was confirmed that the company had ceased trading.

Sauber, Lotus and Force India all made it clear that they were facing serious financial pressures too, lobbying for changes in the way F1's income was distributed. There was even talk of teams boycotting the race in order to make a point, but that was never a realistic possibility for teams desperately chasing championship points.

Ecclestone said he would do what he could to find some extra funds, while stressing that he was hamstrung by the long-term contracts signed with the big players who, inevitably, showed little sympathy for the plight of their rivals.

Clockwise from top left: Force India driver Nico Hülkenburg; Lewis Hamilton challenges Nico Rosberg for the lead; Adrian Sutil walks away from his Sauber; Jenson Button leaves a pit stop; Sebastian Vettel in full flow

move and bounced off Räikkönen into Sutil, putting both himself and the frustrated German out of the race, while also earning a seven-place grid penalty for Brazil. The safety car was immediately dispatched and it took four laps to clear up the mess.

At the restart, the order at the front remained the same, but further back Ricciardo passed Alonso in an aggressive but clean move at Turn 1 to secure fifth place. The Australian was clearly in determined mood.

Out front, Hamilton remained close to Rosberg throughout the first stint. Rosberg came in on lap 15 and Hamilton followed a lap later, having lost time by having to stay out longer on old rubber. Both changed to the medium tyre.

Meanwhile, by pitting a lap earlier than Bottas, Ricciardo managed to jump the Williams man for fourth, leaving himself with Massa as his next target.

Hamilton took off some front wing at his stop, putting himself more in line with Rosberg's starting set-up, and he seemed to find more pace on the medium tyre. He chased his teammate down and kept him under pressure, finally getting by with an impressive move at Turn 12 on lap 24. Rosberg admitted that, in attempting to defend by calling for extra ERS boost at the end of the straight, he used the wrong procedure and thus didn't get it.

"I made a mistake. I used the wrong things to give me KERS," he said after the race. "I thought I was

doing the right thing, but there's a delay with the switch. If I do it with a button it's immediate. So I never got the extra KERS. That's why he got a jump on me in the last metres. I went for extra boost, but the way I did it it only comes on the next straight, or it comes with a delay, so I didn't get it."

Asked if his error had made a difference he said: "I don't know. In that situation it would have helped, of course. I think he was pretty committed anyway. I'm sure I could have done better. It's a judgement thing. If I defend a lot, then he's going to brake late on the outside and try to get me on the next one. I thought to indicate that I'm closing the door would be enough to stop him from trying, but it wasn't. I was part way over already

and I thought that was enough to make it clear for him that he shouldn't try, but it wasn't."

Hamilton meanwhile was well aware what a psychological blow the move had dealt to his rival.

"It's obviously a very good circuit to be able to follow," he said. "But it was very hard through the middle sector to stay as close to him as possible – and get as close as I could to the DRS zone. I was quite a bit back, but I felt very confident. There was a big headwind into Turn 12 and I just felt like I was waiting for the moment to be just close enough to throw it up the inside. And that's what I did.

"You have to decide how much of a risk you're willing to take. Nico wasn't defending there really,

"PÉREZ TRIED AN AMBITIOUS MOVE ON LAP 1 AND BOUNCED OFF RÄIKKÖNEN INTO SUTIL"

so I almost caught him unaware. After that, I was just trying to maintain it."

As the leader, Hamilton now had the first call on pit stops at Mercedes and he came in for the final time on lap 33, with Rosberg following a lap later. The German stayed in touch for the rest of the race, but Hamilton had the situation under control, remaining 2-3s clear for the duration.

"Nico was very quick in qualifying yesterday," said Hamilton. "As I mentioned, I had a couple of problems and I corrected them today. You never know how the race is going to go, but I pushed as hard as I could, particularly in the first stint. Then I seemed to be even quicker in the second stint.

Lewis Hamilton puts on a show for the photographers. **Below:** champagne showers and Mercedes cheers for the Hamilton victory

"Once I got past Nico, it was about controlling the race. Coming here today, it was just having that same determination and hunger to get that win. And there's not a better crowd to do that in front of."

Ricciardo's superb charge continued when he repeated what he did to Bottas by jumping Massa at the second pit stop. Although most expected that Williams had the pace with which to fight back, the Red Bull man did a superb job to stay ahead and secure another podium result, leaving Bottas and Massa to finish fourth and fifth.

"I couldn't really hang with the Williams at first, but it seemed like the longer the stint went, the more pace we had," said Ricciardo. "As we know, Mercedes are a bit out of reach, so I think third was the best we could do today."

The best action was further down the order and there were some great battles as, for once in 2014, tyres played a role in determining who was hot and who was not. From his pit lane start on the medium tyre, Vettel switched to softs for one lap before pitting again to remove them, without losing any ground before the restart.

The plan was then to run mediums to the end with one stop, and this enabled him to move up the order. He was seventh, behind Alonso, when the team decided that the tyres wouldn't make it to the flag and he would come under pressure from behind.

So, with just eight laps to go, he pitted for new softs. This dropped him to 14th place, but the new rubber allowed him to pull off a spectacular charge back to seventh as he weaved his way through the pack, just failing to dislodge Alonso.

There was much swapping of places in the group that he threaded his way through. From the mayhem, Magnussen emerged eighth ahead of Pastor Maldonado, who had two 5s penalties, and yet still earned his first points of the season. Jean-Éric Vergne, who collected a 5s penalty for leaning on Romain Grosjean in an aggressive passing move, took 10th.

Among those who slipped out of the points in the late scramble were Grosjean, who finished 11th, and Button, who ultimately couldn't make up for his grid penalty and finished 12th.

> "WITH JUST EIGHT LAPS TO GO, VETTEL PITTED FOR NEW SOFTS. THIS DROPPED HIM TO 14TH"

SNAPSHOT FROM USA

CLOCKWISE FROM ABOVE:
Jenson Button sports the Texan
look in the riders' parade; patriotic
track markings; brass band
reflections; cowboy boots and
stetsons; the pit lane at sunset;
flags of the nations; Austin
sends out a message; a Red
Bull passes the tower in a blur

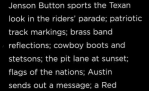

UNITED STATES
AUSTIN
ROUND 17

RACE DATE 2 November
CIRCUIT LENGTH 3.427 miles
NO. OF LAPS 56
RACE DISTANCE 191.912 miles
WEATHER Sunny and dry, 24ºC
TRACK TEMP 33ºC
LAP RECORD Sebastian Vettel,
1m39.347s, 124.132mph, 2012

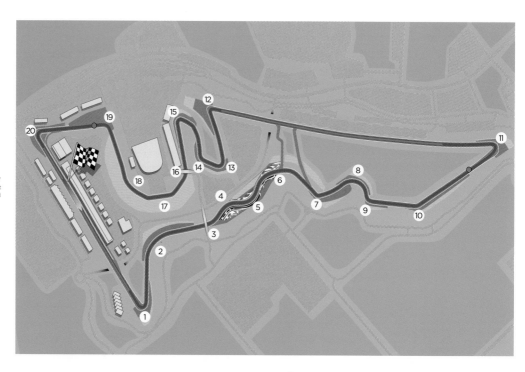

PRACTICE 1

	Driver	Time	Laps
1	L Hamilton	1m39.941s	28
2	N Rosberg	1m40.233s	32
3	J Button	1m40.319s	27
4	D Kvyat	1m40.887s	33
5	K Magnussen	1m40.987s	29
6	F Alonso	1m41.065s	27
7	S Vettel	1m41.463s	20
8	F Nasr	1m41.545s	19
9	N Hülkenberg	1m41.722s	24
10	M Verstappen	1m41.785s	32
11	F Massa	1m41.907s	21
12	K Räikkönen	1m41.965s	23
13	P Maldonado	1m42.329s	28
14	A Sutil	1m42.333s	23
15	S Pérez	1m42.359s	23
16	E Gutiérrez	1m42.516s	24
17	D Ricciardo	1m42.598s	5
18	R Grosjean	1m43.229s	26

PRACTICE 2

	Driver	Time	Laps
1	L Hamilton	1m39.085s	18
2	N Rosberg	1m39.088s	34
3	F Alonso	1m40.189s	29
4	D Ricciardo	1m40.390s	30
5	F Massa	1m40.457s	36
6	K Räikkönen	1m40.543s	32
7	D Kvyat	1m40.631s	34
8	K Magnussen	1m40.641s	38
9	J Button	1m40.698s	36
10	N Hülkenberg	1m40.800s	25
11	V Bottas	1m40.828s	37
12	R Grosjean	1m41.054s	31
13	J-É Vergne	1m41.110s	36
14	S Pérez	1m41.123s	35
15	P Maldonado	1m41.158s	37
16	A Sutil	1m41.332s	33
17	E Gutiérrez	1m41.420s	34
18	S Vettel	1m43.980s	19

PRACTICE 3

	Driver	Time	Laps
1	L Hamilton	1m37.107s	13
2	N Rosberg	1m37.990s	15
3	F Massa	1m38.214s	19
4	V Bottas	1m38.437s	20
5	F Alonso	1m38.727s	13
6	D Ricciardo	1m38.927s	16
7	N Hülkenberg	1m38.960s	20
8	A Sutil	1m39.000s	22
9	K Räikkönen	1m39.143s	17
10	J Button	1m39.241s	22
11	K Magnussen	1m39.335s	19
12	P Maldonado	1m39.448s	18
13	R Grosjean	1m39.561s	21
14	S Pérez	1m39.582s	21
15	D Kvyat	1m39.688s	19
16	E Gutiérrez	1m40.208s	22
17	J-É Vergne	1m41.443s	12
18	S Vettel	1m43.765s	25

QUALIFYING 1

	Driver	Time
1	L Hamilton	1m37.196s
2	F Massa	1m37.877s
3	V Bottas	1m38.249s
4	N Rosberg	1m38.303s
5	F Alonso	1m38.349s
6	K Magnussen	1m38.557s
7	J Button	1m38.574s
8	P Maldonado	1m38.608s
9	K Räikkönen	1m38.669s
10	D Ricciardo	1m38.814s
11	A Sutil	1m38.855s
12	N Hülkenberg	1m38.931s
13	D Kvyat	1m38.936s
14	S Pérez	1m39.200s
15	J-É Vergne	1m39.250s
16	E Gutiérrez	1m39.555s
17	S Vettel	1m39.621s
18	R Grosjean	1m39.679s

QUALIFYING 2

	Driver	Time
1	N Rosberg	1m36.290s
2	L Hamilton	1m37.287s
3	F Massa	1m37.347s
4	V Bottas	1m37.499s
5	D Ricciardo	1m37.873s
6	F Alonso	1m38.010s
7	J Button	1m38.024s
8	K Magnussen	1m38.047s
9	K Räikkönen	1m38.263s
10	A Sutil	1m38.378s
11	P Maldonado	1m38.467s
12	S Pérez	1m38.554s
13	N Hülkenberg	1m38.598s
14	D Kvyat	1m38.699s

Best sectors – Practice

Sec 1	L Hamilton	26.100s
Sec 2	L Hamilton	38.701s
Sec 3	L Hamilton	32.306s

Speed trap – Practice

1	V Bottas	208.407mph
2	N Rosberg	207.413mph
3	F Massa	206.978mph

Best sectors – Qualifying

Sec 1	N Rosberg	25.662s
Sec 2	N Rosberg	38.252s
Sec 3	L Hamilton	32.138s

Speed trap – Qualifying

1	F Massa	209.340mph
2	V Bottas	208.532mph
3	N Rosberg	208.097mph

 **Sebastian Vettel** Nico Rosberg Fernando Alonso Pastor Maldonado Jenson Button Sergio Pérez

"I made up ground in the second half with a stop near the end. We decided to go for fresh tyres, so were in a stronger position compared with others on older tyres."

"It feels horrible to finish second after starting from pole. It took me too long to find my rhythm. In F1, it's all about adapting quickly, but it just took me too long."

"Today went pretty much as expected, with the cars ahead of us clearing off. After a good start, I tried to manage sixth place, with a view to the constructors' championship."

"We lost out in the low-speed corners, but were competitive in the medium- and high-speed turns, which meant I could recover the time lost in the slow ones."

"I went backwards today. The only fun bit of the afternoon was my fight with Fernando. It's unusual for our car to suffer tyre degradation as damaging as we did today."

"I made a move on Adrian at Turn 15. Then he closed the door and I had to brake later than him. By doing so, I was unable to miss Kimi, which caused me to hit Adrian too."

 Daniel Ricciardo  Lewis Hamilton Kimi Räikkönen Romain Grosjean Kevin Magnussen Nico Hülkenberg

"My start wasn't good, but the recovery was good so I didn't really lose out. The stops were really good, Red Bull is known for being awesome in the pits and showed it today."

"I stayed as close as possible to Nico and waited for the moment to throw it up the inside. Once I got past, it was just about controlling the race."

"After fitting the mediums at the first stop things got tricky, with more degradation than expected and after a few laps I began to have problems with the front end."

"Fighting with Jenson was fun. It was less amusing with Jean-Éric as he broke my front wing and my rear floor, which made the car pretty difficult to drive afterwards."

"Eighth isn't a fantastic result, but I don't think we could have got much more out of the car. I was fortunate enough to be able to keep ahead of the cars that were chasing me down."

"I lost drive, so the team told me to stop the car. Even before that, it hadn't been easy as I was behind Sergio and Adrian when they crashed and I ran over Sergio's front wing."

POSITIONS LAP BY LAP

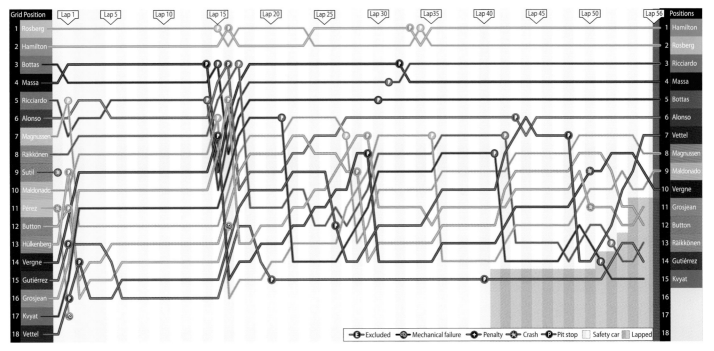

Legend: —E— Excluded —M— Mechanical failure —P— Penalty —X— Crash —P— Pit stop ☐ Safety car ▨ Lapped

QUALIFYING 3

	Driver	Time
1	N Rosberg	1m36.067s
2	L Hamilton	1m36.443s
3	V Bottas	1m36.906s
4	F Massa	1m37.205s
5	D Ricciardo	1m37.244s
6	F Alonso	1m37.610s
7	J Button	1m37.655s
8	K Magnussen	1m37.706s
9	K Räikkönen	1m37.804s
10	A Sutil	1m38.810s

GRID

	Driver	Time
1	N Rosberg	1m36.067s
2	L Hamilton	1m36.443s
3	V Bottas	1m36.906s
4	F Massa	1m37.205s
5	D Ricciardo	1m37.244s
6	F Alonso	1m37.610s
7	K Magnussen	1m37.706s
8	K Räikkönen	1m37.804s
9	A Sutil	1m38.810s
10	P Maldonado	1m38.467s
11	S Pérez	1m38.554s
12	J Button	1m37.655s
13	N Hülkenberg	1m38.598s
14	J-É Vergne	1m39.250s
15	E Gutiérrez	1m39.555s
16	R Grosjean	1m39.679s
17	D Kvyat	1m38.699s
PL	S Vettel	1m39.621s

RACE

	Driver	Car	Laps	Time	Av mph	Fastest	Stops
1	L Hamilton	Mercedes F1 W05	56	1h40m04.785s	114.888	1m41.929s	2
2	N Rosberg	Mercedes F1 W05	56	1h40m09.099s	114.814	1m41.932s	2
3	D Ricciardo	Red Bull-Renault RB10	56	1h40m30.345s	114.401	1m42.831s	2
4	F Massa	Williams-Mercedes FW36	56	1h40m31.709s	114.376	1m42.971s	2
5	V Bottas	Williams-Mercedes FW36	56	1h40m35.777s	114.299	1m42.505s	2
6	F Alonso	Ferrari F14 T	56	1h41m40.016s	113.095	1m41.474s	2
7	S Vettel	Red Bull-Renault RB10	56	1h41m40.519s	113.086	1m41.379s	4
8	K Magnussen	McLaren-Mercedes MP4-29	56	1h41m45.467s	112.994	1m44.287s	2
9	P Maldonado	Lotus-Renault E22	56	1h41m52.655s	112.861	1m43.808s	2
10	J-É Vergne	Toro Rosso-Renault STR9	56	1h41m53.648s	112.843	1m44.180s	2
11	R Grosjean	Lotus-Renault E22	55	1h40m09.963s	112.737	1m44.440s	2
12	J Button	McLaren-Mercedes MP4-29	55	1h40m11.110s	112.716	1m44.255s	2
13	K Räikkönen	Ferrari F14 T	55	1h40m24.599s	112.464	1m42.888s	3
14	E Gutiérrez	Sauber-Ferrari C33	55	1h40m25.672s	112.443	1m43.006s	3
15	S Kvyat	Toro Rosso-Renault STR9	55	1h40m32.052s	112.324	1m41.689s	3
R	N Hülkenberg	Force India-Mercedes VJM07	16	Power unit	-	1m46.226s	1
R	S Pérez	Force India-Mercedes VJM07	1	Accident	-	-	0
R	A Sutil	Sauber-Ferrari C33	0	Accident	-	-	0

CHAMPIONSHIP

	Driver	Pts
1	L Hamilton	316
2	N Rosberg	292
3	D Ricciardo	214
4	V Bottas	155
5	S Vettel	149
6	F Alonso	149
7	J Button	94
8	F Massa	83
9	N Hülkenberg	76
10	K Magnussen	53
11	S Pérez	47
12	K Räikkönen	47
13	J-É Vergne	22
14	R Grosjean	8
15	D Kvyat	8
16	P Maldonado	2
17	J Bianchi	2

Grid penalties

S Vettel	Had to start from pit lane for changing power unit
J Button	5-place penalty for changing the gearbox
D Kvyat	10-place penalty for using seventh power unit

Fastest lap
S Vettel 1m41.379s
(121.644mph) on lap 50

Fastest speed trap
S Vettel 209.402mph
Slowest speed trap
A Sutil 191.133mph

Fastest pit stop
1 J Button 23.546s
2 S Vettel 23.799s
3 R Grosjean 23.802s

CONSTRUCTORS

	Team	Pts
1	Mercedes	608
2	Red Bull-Renault	363
3	Williams-Mercedes	238
4	Ferrari	196
5	McLaren-Mercedes	147
6	Force India-Mercedes	123
7	Toro Rosso-Renault	30
8	Lotus-Renault	10
9	Marussia-Ferrari	2

Esteban Gutiérrez
"It was challenging to get the tyres to work after the safety car period. Not being able to manage the tyres as other drivers do put us in a really critical situation."

Jean-Éric Vergne
"It was an exciting race, but difficult too. In the final stages, I saw the opportunity to overtake Romain and decided to go for it. When he closed the door, it was just too late."

Felipe Massa
"I had a very good start to get up to third place, but unfortunately a slower than normal pit stop allowed Ricciardo to jump me and it cost us a podium finish."

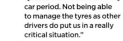

Adrian Sutil
"I was in a promising position. Sadly, Sergio crashed into my car, which was totally needless. It's disappointing that we missed our biggest chance of points."

Daniil Kvyat
"We had fantastic pace until the last part of the grand prix when I managed to pass Räikkönen, but unfortunately I damaged my front left tyre during the fight and had to pit again."

Valtteri Bottas
"I had a bit of clutch slip, which allowed Ricciardo to jump me in the first corner. The Red Bulls also had better tyre management than us and so were able to run at a better pace for longer."

BRAZIL

PRÊMIO PETROBRAS DO BRASIL 2014

NICO ROSBERG PUT IN A FAULTLESS
PERFORMANCE TO WIN THE BRAZILIAN
GP AFTER HIS MERCEDES TEAMMATE
LEWIS HAMILTON HAD A SPIN AND SO
BLEW HIS CHANCE TO TAKE THE LEAD

Nico Rosberg leads Lewis Hamilton, Felipe Massa and Valtteri Bottas at the start. **Top right:** Hamilton congratulates Rosberg on pole. **Right:** Sebastian Vettel had to fight back after a mistake on lap 1. **Bottom right:** São Paulo acts as a backdrop as the drivers negotiate their formation lap

A lthough championship leader Lewis Hamilton was able to claw back the time he lost after an error, working his way back on to Nico Rosberg's tail he didn't have the momentum with which to pass and so had to settle for runner-up and a reduction in his points lead.

It was a tense, nail-biting contest between the pair and, even if we didn't actually see a pass for the lead, it was one of the key races of the season. Rosberg's fifth victory meant that he was still very much in the frame as they left Brazil to head for the double points finale in Abu Dhabi, although he now knew that even a win, if Hamilton finished second again, wouldn't be quite enough to take the title.

In the build-up to the race weekend, it seemed likely that

"A JOINT APPEARANCE ON THE GRID BY NELSON PIQUET AND EMERSON FITTIPALDI WENT DOWN WELL"

Interlagos would be hit by rain on both afternoons, but conditions remained good for qualifying. An inspired Rosberg beat Hamilton to pole by the tiniest of margins and, in so doing, he secured the FIA trophy for the highest number of pole positions through the season, newly introduced for 2014.

Rosberg had been faster than his teammate all through practice and he repeated the feat in Q1 and Q2. On the first runs in Q3, he beat Hamilton by 0.029s and on the second run, when Hamilton had a very obvious locking-up moment, the margin was 0.033s. It was as close as that.

Nevertheless, Hamilton was unperturbed and remained confident that he could turn things around come the race, especially with rain still predicted. "I lost a bit of time in Turn 10 and perhaps a little bit in Turn 1," he said. "Pole position is the best place to start

here, but it's a long race and it should be quite exciting with the weather and the pit stops."

After the first runs in Q3, it appeared that local hero Felipe Massa might be quick enough to split the Mercedes duo. Alas, the Brazilian's final qualifying run started late due to engine issues in the garage and traffic led to him abandoning the lap. Third on the grid was still a great effort by the resurgent veteran, who kept Williams teammate Valtteri Bottas back in fourth place.

McLaren struggled on Friday, but the team turned things around successfully for qualifying as Jenson Button took a solid fifth and circuit newcomer Kevin Magnussen backed him up in seventh. They were split by Sebastian Vettel, who earned sixth after problems in the morning. The top 10 was completed by Fernando Alonso, Daniel Ricciardo and Kimi Räikkönen.

INSIDE LINE

JENSON BUTTON
McLAREN

It was a fun race. I had a great battle with Kimi, and I enjoyed that very much. I had to balance the brakes as well, which were getting eaten up pretty quickly. I ended up fourth, but it was a shame that I couldn't quite hang on to Massa. You always want more, to challenge for that podium. We felt that we were sort of playing with the Williams at one point, but it wasn't the case. To beat both Ferraris, both Red Bulls and a Williams, though, that's not a bad day's work.

"It was all pretty smooth up until the last pit stop. There was just a bit of miscommunication about coming into the pits, as the call wasn't entirely made to come in. It was talked about what would happen if I did stop, so it was just a bit of a miscommunication. I think we were talking over each other at the time. I did one extra lap, which could have cost us a place, but I think we would have got it back anyway.

"I FEEL I'M DOING A GOOD JOB AT THE MOMENT. I'VE GOT NOTHING TO PROVE. THIS IS WHAT I DO; THIS IS WHAT I'VE DONE FOR 15 YEARS"

"Judging the race was so tricky with the tyres, but I think that we did a good job. I pushed really hard on the first stint on the primes when I was up behind Bottas.

"I destroyed my rear tyres trying to stay with him, but I thought that if I could stay in DRS range I could gap the guys behind. It was worth it and it worked in the end, but I had to back off on the next stint to really conserve the tyres.

"I feel I'm doing a good job at the moment. I've got nothing to prove. This is what I do; this is what I've done for 15 years. I'll always do my best. Sometimes it obviously isn't enough, but today it definitely was."

TEAMS SEEK WAYS FOR SURVIVAL

It was no surprise that paddock talk in Brazil was dominated by the financial health of the teams. One week on from their failure to show at the United States GP, Marussia and Caterham were still in the headlines. It was announced on Friday that the former had ceased trading but, despite that seemingly damning news, CEO Graeme Lowdon later said that he had not yet given up.

On the same day, Caterham's administrators unveiled a crowdfunding scheme with a view to raising £2.35m to make it to the final race in Abu Dhabi. The idea of a team asking fans to pay its way didn't sit well with Bernie Ecclestone.

The 2015 driver situation at Sauber provided another sign of the squeeze some teams were facing. Adrian Sutil (above) had an ongoing two-year contract, with no requirement to bring sponsorship, while Giedo van der Garde — after paying to spend a year as third driver — also had a race deal for 2015. However, after announcing that Caterham refugee Marcus Ericsson would be joining for 2015, the Swiss team then revealed in Brazil that Williams' third driver Felipe Nasr would also be coming on board, with funding from Banco do Brasil. Thus, four race drivers were seemingly now under contract.

> "THE IDEA OF A TEAM ASKING FANS TO PAY ITS WAY DIDN'T SIT WELL WITH BERNIE ECCLESTONE"

It was a simple matter of financial survival — two candidates with substantial budgets had trumped the pair already signed. Sutil and van der Garde, who heard the Nasr news only when the press release came out, were stunned — and now had to negotiate some form of compensation.

Meanwhile, Sauber, Lotus and Force India mulled over their future prospects. One area of concern was the huge rise in power-unit costs associated with the new rules and that was linked to ongoing discussions about an engine unfreeze. All manufacturers had a window during which to update their engines for homologation by 28 February 2015, but Renault, Ferrari and Honda wanted a second bite of the cherry in the summer. Unanimity was required, but Mercedes held out, claiming that it could only lead to further expense. Talk of a return to the cheaper V8 — along with filling the grid with "Super GP2 cars" — indicated that the direction of the sport was a little unclear.

Hamilton recovers from the spin that might have cost him victory. **Above right:** Massa finds the right pit crew. **Right:** McLaren discovered form as the meeting went on and Jenson Button came home fifth

Against expectations, the rain again stayed away on Sunday and, indeed, the sun shone brightly all morning. As usual at Interlagos, the atmosphere built steadily during the day, with the presence of Massa on the second row giving the crowd something to cheer about. A joint appearance on the grid by Nelson Piquet and Emerson Fittipaldi also went down well.

Heading into the race, the big question was how long the leaders would remain on the less-favoured soft tyres – blistering was an issue all weekend – before abandoning them. Three pit stops, with a short run on the soft tyres followed by three stints on mediums, was the most obvious strategy.

It was a clean start as Rosberg led Hamilton, Massa and Bottas away. Further back, Vettel ran wide at Turn 4, allowing Magnussen and Alonso to pass him. The leader soon opened up a 1.2s advantage on his teammate and Hamilton was

content to hold it there as he kept his tyres alive. The first stops came early: Massa came in from third at lap 5. Rosberg pitted on lap 7, with Hamilton following a lap later.

Four drivers outside the top 10 had started on the medium compound and were thus in no hurry to come in, so from 12th on the grid Nico Hülkenberg moved into the lead ahead of Daniil Kvyat, who had been relegated to the back row thanks to a power-unit penalty carried over from the United States GP. Rosberg ran third for a while, but soon found his way past Toro Rosso and Force India, not before Force India's Hülkenberg had enjoyed five laps of glory in front.

Rosberg reclaimed the lead on lap 14 and for a while Hamilton was right with him, until he dropped around 2s back. As the next round of pit stops approached, he closed the gap again and appeared to be ready to pounce. Rosberg came in on lap 26 and

Hamilton expected to come in a lap later. As is usual practice, he used his tyres hard on what he thought was his in-lap, but his first two sectors were so fast that his engineer then told him to stay out for one more lap. He duly set what was then the fastest lap as he crossed the line, but unfortunately he'd taken too much out of the Pirellis and they were shot. At Turn 4 on that extra lap he spun, losing some 7s before he was back up to speed. Had he not done so, he was on course to pit and come out in the lead.

"I think ultimately it cost me the win," he explained later. "I mean, I was much quicker up until that point and on that lap I'd gone a second quicker while Nico pitted, and I thought I was going to pit at the end of that lap, so I used everything of the tyres. The next lap, I had nothing left. Either way, at the end of the day, I made a mistake. I locked the rears into Turn 4 and, with the under-rotation, this

just spun me around. So, it was no-one's fault but mine."

Hamilton now had a lot of work to do to make up the lost ground. By the time Rosberg pitted for the third and final time on lap 50, he had brought the margin down from 7.4s after the spin, to around 2s. This time he stayed out for just the one extra lap, before emerging right on his rival's tail. He had a 20-lap final stint to find a way past Rosberg but, despite often sitting 0.5s behind – and benefiting from DRS – he couldn't quite do so, as Rosberg withstood the pressure in style. On the last lap, Hamilton backed off to finish 1.4s behind.

"It was a great weekend, all in all," said a delighted and relieved Rosberg. "It proved to be a tough day for me on Sunday at Austin, so it was important for me just to improve because I simply didn't do a good enough job in the race in Austin. Today, though, I managed to do that, so I'm happy about that.

"AT TURN 4 ON THAT EXTRA LAP, HAMILTON SPUN, LOSING SOME 7S"

I learned from Austin and did better, so that's a big step in the right direction. One race too late, perhaps, but there's still all to play for.

"I was confident, definitely, because already in the first stint I could see that I could control the gap and could just make sure that Lewis didn't come into the region where he could launch an attack. From that point of view, once I saw that, I was very confident that I could keep on controlling the gap for the whole race.

"Also, when Lewis had the spin and was further behind, I saved my tyres more than I normally would have done and so I could just make sure that I had enough tyre life at the end of the stint because it was so critical on tyres today. And that worked out really well, too."

Hamilton was frustrated not to win, but the championship permutations provided some consolation. "Overall, I'm really happy," he said. "I came back, I clearly had a lot more pace than Nico today. I know that he would have seen that, obviously, by closing down the 7s [gap], but he did a good job to not make any mistakes while I was there, so I'm looking forward to the final grand prix."

Massa delighted the home crowd by taking third place for Williams, despite landing a 5s stop-and-go penalty for speeding in the pit lane. He also tried to stop in the McLaren pits – both crews wear white overalls – and had to be waved through to his own garage. He put in a good performance, though, to take the final podium spot, albeit some way behind the leaders.

Button had a solid race to fourth place, enjoying battles with Räikkönen and others. He finished in front of three fellow World Champions as Vettel recovered from his disappointing first lap to claim fifth position, ahead of Alonso and Räikkönen. The two Ferrari drivers enjoyed an intriguing battle late in the race. Adopting a two-stop strategy rather than the three stops that everyone else was planning, Räikkönen held off his teammate for several laps, despite being on older tyres.

Unusually for a season during which youngsters had made such a big impression, the top seven places were filled by the seven most experienced drivers – including the five World Champions.

Hülkenberg's strategy of starting on the mediums and finishing with an 11-lap sprint on fresh softs at the end earned him eighth place and he was right with the Ferraris at the flag. Had he made that tyre change a lap or two earlier, he could have passed them. Magnussen and Bottas completed the top 10, the last named having lost time when his belts had to be secured at his first pit stop, and later with tyre issues.

The race's most significant retirement was that of Ricciardo, the Australian driver suffering a front suspension failure when heading for more points. Nevertheless, the result confirmed him in third place in the World Championship, as teammate Vettel could now no longer beat him.

On Sunday evening, attention turned to the finale and the prospects of the two main protagonists. The big question was whether double points would play a role...

"MASSA DELIGHTED THE HOME CROWD TO TAKE THIRD FOR WILLIAMS, DESPITE LANDING A STOP-AND-GO PENALTY"

Massa acknowledges the fans after coming third. **Top right:** Grosjean heads Maldonado. **Above right:** Rosberg parks up after winning

SNAPSHOT FROM BRAZIL

CLOCKWISE FROM ABOVE: Nico Rosberg shows his delight after taking pole position and the season's FIA trophy for poles; Force India's reserve driver Daniel Juncadella ended his FP1 run like this; the view from Cotovelo; Lewis Hamilton finds himself the focus of the media scrum; Daniil Kvyat seeks advice from Helmut Marko; former Spice Girl Geri Halliwell with her fiancé Christian Horner; Jenson Button tackled questions about his F1 future; pit reflection

BRAZIL
INTERLAGOS
ROUND 18

Official Results © [2014]
Formula One World
Championship Limited,
6 Princes Gate, London, SW7
1QJ. No reproduction without
permission. All copyright and
database rights reserved.

RACE DATE 9 November
CIRCUIT LENGTH 2.667 miles
NO. OF LAPS 71
RACE DISTANCE 190.067 miles
WEATHER Sunny & dry, 25°C
TRACK TEMP 55°C
LAP RECORD Juan Pablo Montoya,
1m11.473s, 134.837mph, 2004

	PRACTICE 1				PRACTICE 2				PRACTICE 3				QUALIFYING 1			QUALIFYING 2	
	Driver	Time	Laps		Driver	Time	Laps		Driver	Time	Laps		Driver	Time		Driver	Time
1	N Rosberg	1m12.764s	30	1	N Rosberg	1m12.123s	36	1	N Rosberg	1m10.446s	28	1	N Rosberg	1m10.347s	1	N Rosberg	1m10.303s
2	L Hamilton	1m12.985s	32	2	L Hamilton	1m12.336s	36	2	L Hamilton	1m10.560s	20	2	L Hamilton	1m10.457s	2	F Massa	1m10.343s
3	D Kvyat	1m13.723s	39	3	K Räikkönen	1m12.696s	32	3	F Massa	1m10.875s	21	3	F Massa	1m10.602s	3	V Bottas	1m10.421s
4	F Alonso	1m13.742s	30	4	D Ricciardo	1m12.956s	24	4	V Bottas	1m11.054s	23	4	V Bottas	1m10.832s	4	L Hamilton	1m10.712s
5	F Massa	1m13.811s	28	5	V Bottas	1m13.035s	31	5	D Ricciardo	1m11.188s	11	5	J Button	1m11.097s	5	J Button	1m11.127s
6	M Verstappen	1m13.827s	26	6	F Massa	1m13.099s	27	6	J Button	1m11.210s	19	6	K Magnussen	1m11.134s	6	S Vettel	1m11.129s
7	P Maldonado	1m14.034s	31	7	F Alonso	1m13.122s	20	7	K Räikkönen	1m11.316s	15	7	K Räikkönen	1m11.193s	7	K Räikkönen	1m11.188s
8	K Räikkönen	1m14.114s	32	8	D Kvyat	1m13.254s	35	8	F Alonso	1m11.399s	8	8	D Kvyat	1m11.423s	8	D Ricciardo	1m11.208s
9	K Magnussen	1m14.136s	30	9	S Vettel	1m13.333s	28	9	K Magnussen	1m11.499s	19	9	E Gutiérrez	1m11.520s	9	K Magnussen	1m11.211s
10	D Ricciardo	1m14.197s	27	10	K Magnussen	1m13.479s	33	10	D Kvyat	1m11.834s	26	10	F Alonso	1m11.558s	10	F Alonso	1m11.215s
11	A Sutil	1m14.434s	31	11	P Maldonado	1m13.497s	33	11	S Vettel	1m11.967s	21	11	D Ricciardo	1m11.593s	11	E Gutiérrez	1m11.591s
12	F Nasr	1m14.522s	22	12	R Grosjean	1m13.714s	37	12	P Maldonado	1m12.069s	29	12	N Hülkenberg	1m11.848s	12	N Hülkenberg	1m11.976s
13	N Hülkenberg	1m14.678s	33	13	N Hülkenberg	1m13.882s	32	13	A Sutil	1m12.184s	27	13	S Vettel	1m11.880s	13	A Sutil	1m12.099s
14	S Vettel	1m14.902s	24	14	E Gutiérrez	1m13.902s	25	14	R Grosjean	1m12.235s	30	14	A Sutil	1m11.943s	14	D Kvyat	no time
15	R Grosjean	1m15.109s	23	15	A Sutil	1m14.204s	36	15	J-É Vergne	1m12.235s	29	15	R Grosjean	1m12.037s			
16	D Juncadella	1m16.030s	17	16	J Button	1m14.209s	31	16	E Gutiérrez	1m12.286s	24	16	J-É Vergne	1m12.040s			
17	E Gutiérrez	no time	6	17	J-É Vergne	1m17.171s	5	17	N Hülkenberg	1m12.324s	17	17	S Pérez	1m12.076s			
18	J Button	no time	1	18	S Pérez	no time	0	18	S Pérez	1m12.942s	25	18	P Maldonado	1m12.233s			

Best sectors – Practice

Sec 1	L Hamilton	17.814s
Sec 2	N Rosberg	35.983s
Sec 3	N Rosberg	16.468s

Speed trap – Practice

1	N Rosberg	208.718mph
2	V Bottas	208.656mph
3	L Hamilton	208.470mph

Best sectors – Qualifying

Sec 1	N Rosberg	17.565s
Sec 2	N Rosberg	35.821s
Sec 3	F Massa	16.388s

Speed trap – Qualifying

1	F Massa	213.068mph
2	V Bottas	210.023mph
3	N Rosberg	208.470mph

Sebastian Vettel
"Into Turn 4, I didn't know how aggressive Kevin was going to be and left too much space. I went wide and lost two places. Then I had to fight hard to get the places back."

Nico Rosberg
"I learned from Austin so was able to control the pace better and didn't let Lewis get too close. When he spun, I was able to relax and so saved some life in the tyres."

Fernando Alonso
"Degradation was really high, especially on the softs. When I passed Kimi, my tyres were newer, but I was having to save fuel. From then on, there was nothing more I could do."

Pastor Maldonado
"My start wasn't great, but we became more competitive towards the end and were aiming to score points. I was hoping to overtake Bottas, but it wasn't possible."

Jenson Button
"It all went smoothly until my final pit stop. There was a bit of miscommunication, which meant I ended up doing an extra lap and that could have cost me a podium finish."

Sergio Pérez
"With the track time lost on Friday and the grid penalty, it was going to be hard to make up ground and I lost a lot of track position following the 5s penalty."

Daniel Ricciardo
"When I went into Turn 1, the car went right and I knew there was a problem. I came into the pits and the team told me that it was suspension failure and we retired the car."

Lewis Hamilton
"When I'm told to push, it means the team is bringing me in that lap. But they left me out and by the time I came round to do the second lap, my rear tyres were gone."

Kimi Räikkönen
"During the second stint, we realised that if we went for a two-stop strategy, we could make up ground, but at my second stop, I lost time and that cost me some places."

Romain Grosjean
"The start was good and I was able to run high up the field. I had to switch from a two-stop to a three-stop run mid-race, though, and that came with some challenges."

Kevin Magnussen
"That wasn't a great race for me, as I had a lot of degradation. I tried to keep people from getting past me, but Fernando and Nico simply had more pace than I did."

Nico Hülkenberg
"With a three-stop race, you're always pushing, but the team made the right calls and we maximised our performance. Maybe with one or two more laps, I could've come sixth."

POSITIONS LAP BY LAP

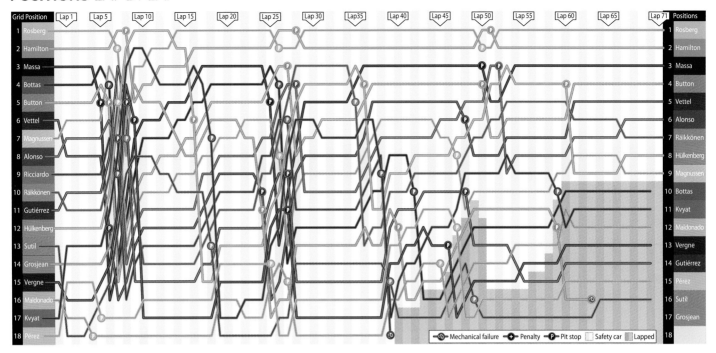

QUALIFYING 3

	Driver	Time
1	N Rosberg	1m10.023s
2	L Hamilton	1m10.056s
3	F Massa	1m10.247s
4	V Bottas	1m10.305s
5	J Button	1m10.930s
6	S Vettel	1m10.938s
7	K Magnussen	1m10.969s
8	F Alonso	1m10.977s
9	D Ricciardo	1m11.075s
10	K Räikkönen	1m11.099s

GRID

	Driver	Time
1	N Rosberg	1m10.023s
2	L Hamilton	1m10.056s
3	F Massa	1m10.247s
4	V Bottas	1m10.305s
5	J Button	1m10.930s
6	S Vettel	1m10.938s
7	K Magnussen	1m10.969s
8	F Alonso	1m10.977s
9	D Ricciardo	1m11.075s
10	K Räikkönen	1m11.099s
11	E Gutiérrez	1m11.591s
12	N Hülkenberg	1m11.976s
13	A Sutil	1m12.099s
14	R Grosjean	1m12.037s
15	J-É Vergne	1m12.040s
16	P Maldonado	1m12.233s
17	D Kvyat	no time
18	S Pérez	1m12.076s

Grid penalties

D Kvyat	7-place penalty for using sixth engine
S Pérez	7-place penalty for reckless driving in the US GP

RACE

	Driver	Car	Laps	Time	Av mph	Fastest	Stops
1	N Rosberg	Mercedes F1 W05	71	1h30m02.555s	126.661	1m13.619s	3
2	L Hamilton	Mercedes F1 W05	71	1h30m04.012s	126.627	1m13.555s	3
3	F Massa	Williams-Mercedes FW36	71	1h30m43.586s	125.707	1m14.101s	3
4	J Button	McLaren-Mercedes MP4-29	71	1h30m51.213s	125.531	1m13.999s	3
5	S Vettel	Red Bull-Renault RB10	71	1h30m53.975s	125.468	1m14.018s	3
6	F Alonso	Ferrari F14 T	71	1h31m04.461s	125.227	1m14.313s	3
7	K Räikkönen	Ferrari F14 T	71	1h31m06.285s	125.185	1m14.963s	2
8	N Hülkenberg	Force India-Mercedes VJM07	71	1h31m06.489s	125.180	1m13.728s	3
9	K Magnussen	McLaren-Mercedes MP4-29	71	1h31m12.640s	125.040	1m14.544s	3
10	V Bottas	Williams-Mercedes FW36	70	1h30m13.622s	124.622	1m14.229s	3
11	D Kvyat	Toro Rosso-Renault STR9	70	1h30m14.317s	124.606	1m14.144s	3
12	P Maldonado	Lotus-Renault E22	70	1h30m20.337s	124.468	1m14.810s	3
13	J-É Vergne	Toro Rosso-Renault STR9	70	1h30m21.377s	124.444	1m14.774s	3
14	E Gutiérrez	Sauber-Ferrari C33	70	1h30m25.706s	124.345	1m14.875s	3
15	S Pérez	Force India-Mercedes VJM07	70	1h30m29.316s	124.262	1m14.550s	3
16	A Sutil	Sauber-Ferrari C33	70	1h30m41.360s	123.987	1m14.834s	3
17	R Grosjean	Lotus-Renault E22	63	Power unit	-	1m14.070s	3
R	D Ricciardo	Red Bull-Renault RB10	39	Suspension	-	1m15.387s	2

Fastest lap

L Hamilton 1m13.555s
(131.044mph) on lap 62

Fastest speed trap

D Kvyat	207.786mph

Slowest speed trap

A Sutil	193.619mph

Fastest pit stop

1	J Button	22.620s
2	S Vettel	22.746s
3	P Maldonado	22.865s

CHAMPIONSHIP

	Driver	Pts
1	L Hamilton	334
2	N Rosberg	317
3	D Ricciardo	214
4	S Vettel	159
5	F Alonso	157
6	V Bottas	156
7	J Button	106
8	F Massa	98
9	N Hülkenberg	80
10	K Magnussen	55
11	K Räikkönen	53
12	S Pérez	47
13	J-É Vergne	22
14	R Grosjean	8
15	D Kvyat	8
16	P Maldonado	2
17	J Bianchi	2

CONSTRUCTORS

	Team	Pts
1	Mercedes	651
2	Red Bull-Renault	373
3	Williams-Mercedes	254
4	Ferrari	210
5	McLaren-Mercedes	161
6	Force India-Mercedes	127
7	Toro Rosso-Renault	30
8	Lotus-Renault	10
9	Marussia-Ferrari	2

Esteban Gutiérrez

"It was looking good until half distance. When I tried to fight with a car in front, I lost grip and the tyres soon overheated. It was very hard to cope with the loss of grip."

Jean-Éric Vergne

"I spent almost the whole race behind Pérez and I was slower than him, so even with the DRS open on the straight it wasn't possible to overtake him. From then on, my race was over."

Felipe Massa

"The car had strong, consistent pace and this let me stay third despite issues in my pit stops, firstly incurring a stop-and-go penalty for speeding, then stopping in the wrong box."

Adrian Sutil

"It was an uneventful race. I had to start from the pit lane due to a problem with the cooling configuration. Then there was an incident at my first stop that cost me time."

Daniil Kvyat

"Starting from the 17th on the grid, 11th was the best result I could achieve today. I did my best, but unfortunately the Mercedes-powered cars were a lot quicker on the straights."

Valtteri Bottas

"I had an issue with my seatbelts that we resolved at the first pit stop and I then also lost time in the second pit stop. Today's conditions were very challenging as tyre wear was really high."

ROUND 19

ABU

ETIHAD AIRWAYS ABU DHABI GRAND PRIX

DHABI

DESPITE NEEDING ONLY SECOND BEHIND NICO ROSBERG TO BECOME
CHAMPION, LEWIS HAMILTON SHOT INTO THE LEAD. THEN ROSBERG'S
CAR HIT TROUBLE AND HAMILTON SECURED THE DRIVERS' TITLE AGAIN

T here was much debate in the build-up to the Abu Dhabi GP about the possibility of Nico Rosberg snatching the title from Lewis Hamilton with the help of the double points on offer at this season finale, and what that might mean for the image of the sport.

In the end, Hamilton secured his second drivers' title in the best possible manner by logging his 11th victory of 2014 as bad luck left Rosberg struggling to the finish with a crippled car. The consensus was that this was the just result and a good one for the health of F1. Had it been Hamilton's car that failed, the post-race ambience might have been a little different.

Rosberg came to the Middle East in confident mood and he beat Hamilton to pole position to give himself the best possible chance of winning the title. Although second place in the race would still be enough to clinch the title for Hamilton – he had to slip to third with Rosberg winning for the title to go to the German – the pressure was now on the Briton's shoulders, as any problem for him could hand the honours to his teammate.

Hamilton was fastest by 0.101s in Q1 and by 0.224s in Q2. However, the balance of power edged towards Rosberg in the final session when Hamilton ran wide and off the track on his first run, and then locked up as he tried to get the car turned into the last corner.

Rosberg was thus comfortably quicker after those first runs and then he improved his time further on the second. Pushing hard and overdriving a touch, Hamilton couldn't match him – and was left 0.386s behind, a huge margin by the duo's 2014 standards. It was Rosberg's 11th pole of the season, and he took the opportunity to remind his teammate, and the world, who might have the psychological advantage.

"Of course pressure is one of the hopes that I have," he said. "If Lewis feels the pressure and then makes a mistake as a result of it, a bit like he did today and a bit like in Brazil, that's the sort of opportunities I'm looking for. I push flat-out all the time to try and keep the level extremely high and that's all I can do really and try to go for the win and keep the pressure on."

After a difficult Friday, Williams made a big step forward come qualifying. Indeed, Valtteri Bottas set sector times on his final run that

"THERE WAS A BOMBSHELL AFTER THE SESSION WHEN BOTH RED BULLS WERE REPORTED TO THE FIA STEWARDS"

were quick enough to suggest that he could make the front row, but in the end he just missed out. His teammate Felipe Massa backed him up by being fourth fastest.

Daniel Ricciardo again outqualified Sebastian Vettel – officially announced on the Thursday as a Ferrari driver for 2015 – as the pair took fifth and sixth at their last race as Red Bull teammates. However, there was a bombshell after the session when both cars were reported to the FIA stewards for a front-wing flap flexing offence. A spring device had been uncovered by technical delegate Jo Bauer and the team was found guilty as charged, so both drivers were sent to the back of the grid. They then had to change the wings to a legal specification under parc fermé conditions – and that meant that they had to start from the pit lane.

The first man to benefit was

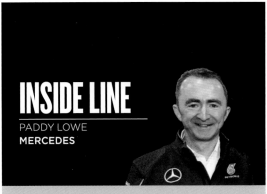

INSIDE LINE

PADDY LOWE
MERCEDES

It wasn't the ideal race for us. We came into the race with a target of a one-two finish and we told Nico that, even if it had meant Lewis had won the championship anyway.

"It wasn't a perfect result. There was a failure in the cooling system for the hybrid systems and that was the thing that caused everything to fall apart around it. That was the core of the problem and it cascaded into a number of other issues. Everything is linked together, the turbo isn't working very well, and so on. Different things were coming in and out.

"If we analyse the whole season, we weren't as reliable as we should have been, but the unreliability fell quite equitably in the end. Overall, though, it was great to win the race itself, as it takes us to 16 wins, and it was great for Lewis.

"I think it has been the most fantastic season. We wanted to finish it in a nice way and that's what's been done. Of course, Nico won't particularly feel like that, but he's been an absolutely fantastic sport, very respectful to Lewis and the team. Great credit to him for that. I think it must be quite difficult for him, but he won the inaugural pole position trophy, and that's no mean feat.

"They have both driven exceptionally well in this last part of the season. It's the closing part, where you're under pressure, that really counts and it's most difficult to keep it together. Both have shown themselves to be capable World Champions and that gives promise to Nico for the future.

"You can't take anything for granted over the winter in F1. We just have to do our best and see where we turn up next year."

> "ANALYSING THE WHOLE SEASON, WE WEREN'T AS RELIABLE AS WE SHOULD HAVE BEEN, BUT THE UNRELIABILITY FELL QUITE EQUITABLY IN THE END"

Clockwise from above: Nico Rosberg had greater reason to be pleased after qualifying when he took his 11th pole of the season, leaving Lewis Hamilton feeling the pressure; tension mounts both in the grandstands and on the grid in the final countdown to the last race of the year; Hamilton made a remarkable start and is already ahead of title rival Rosberg before they reach the first corner, with Bottas being swamped

TALKING POINT
CATERHAM MAKES IT TO ABU DHABI

Against all the odds, Caterham reappeared in Abu Dhabi after the team had skipped the US and Brazilian races. Having taken control of the operation – split confusingly between two companies, 1MRT and Caterham Sports – administrator Finbarr O'Connell had launched a crowdfunding scheme, which allowed fans to make personal contributions to a fighting fund. The intended target of £2.35m wasn't met, but nevertheless the team committed to the trip. Employees who were made redundant the previous week were signed up as contractors.

Kamui Kobayashi agreed to drive, but Marcus Ericsson – recently signed to Sauber for 2015 – opted out, despite his sponsors having already fulfilled their commitments for the whole season. Various drivers were mooted as replacements before the job went to Formula Renault 3.5 race winner Will Stevens, who had tested for Caterham in the past. There was a question mark over the Briton's superlicence eligibility, but the required paperwork came through late on Thursday.

Irishman O'Connell declared himself team principal and quickly became something of a celebrity in the paddock; he was even invited to participate in Friday's FIA press conference, alongside Toto Wolff and Christian Horner. Remarkably, it was his first visit to a motor race.

Meanwhile, the buzz in the Abu Dhabi paddock on Wednesday was that Marussia would also make a last-minute trip, despite the earlier announcement that the company had ceased trading. An empty garage was waiting and the Ferrari engineers assigned to the team were present and wearing their Marussia shirts. But, at the last moment, plans were cancelled when the funding didn't come through.

"Anyone who knows us knows we only want to do things properly and it just couldn't be done in the end," said CEO Graeme Lowdon. "There are various scenarios for the team, but to race it is very important to have a car ready for 2015. That is what potential investors are interested in – ensuring that work on the 2015 programme can be resumed quickly. Don't count us out yet."

> **"THE CATERHAM TEAM'S INTENDED TARGET OF £2.35M WASN'T MET, BUT NEVERTHELESS THE TEAM COMMITTED TO THE TRIP TO THE ABU DHABI GP"**

Clockwise from main picture: Massa rounded out his season with a fighting second; Maldonado's engine blew; Pérez raced to seventh; Bottas locks up during his run to third place

Daniil Kvyat, who had done a great job to qualify seventh for Toro Rosso and thus advanced to fifth. After a troubled Friday, Jenson Button, still not aware of what his future held, would start sixth for McLaren. Kimi Räikkönen and Fernando Alonso rounded out Q3, the Spaniard having run very few laps in FP3 prior to a power unit change, and the pair moved up to seventh and eighth on the final grid.

The race got underway with the unusual sight of both Red Bulls waiting in the pit lane. Vettel and Ricciardo opted for the prime tyre, as did Kevin Magnussen, Sergio Pérez, Nico Hülkenberg and Jean-Éric Vergne. All went into the race knowing that they could run a long opening stint and stay out when those on the supersoft pitted early.

The complexion of the championship battle changed completely when Hamilton made a brilliant getaway and comfortably charged into the lead, slotting ahead of his teammate well before Turn 1. From that moment on, Rosberg knew he was on the back foot.

At the same time, Bottas had a bad start from third place, and Massa, Button, Räikkönen, Alonso and Kvyat all charged past the Finn, who had looked like being the main challenger to the Mercedes duo. The first corner proved uneventful, but exiting Turn 7 Adrian Sutil and Magnussen collided, although both were able to continue.

Rosberg ran a couple of seconds behind Hamilton until the Briton made his first stop on lap 10 and offloaded the supersoft tyre, leaving Rosberg to lead for a lap before he too came in. The Williams could go further on the tyre and Massa was able to lead for a couple of laps until pitting on lap 13, allowing Hamilton back into the lead. By staying out, Bottas regained some spots, and slotted into fourth.

Rosberg continued to circulate around 2s behind Hamilton until he ran into trouble on lap 24. He ran wide and lost 1.2s, but that was just the tip of the iceberg as it soon emerged via radio traffic that he had lost ERS, a result of a cooling failure. As at the Canadian GP, he instantly lost 160bhp and hence a huge chunk of lap time. Some

desperate radio messages followed as Rosberg asked the team for help and tried to adjust his driving.

There was little that the team could do to help its driver, who soon began to drop back into the clutches of third-placed Massa, who got by on lap 27. For a while, Hamilton's times also dropped as there was a concern that the same problem might occur with him, but he soon picked up his pace again.

"I was asking the team whether I could turn the power down," he said. "When the gap started to increase between me and Nico, I was thinking: 'Alright, I've got to back off, got to look after the tyres, look after the car'. I started avoiding kerbs, all those kind of things.

"A couple of times on the straight, I was rubbing the cockpit, saying: 'Come on baby, we can make it. Stick with me.' I really did. You won't see it, but I did."

Rosberg knew by now that his only hope was for Hamilton to retire and his fear was that he would fall lower than fifth – the position he had to secure to win the title should Hamilton drop out. It soon

became apparent that it would be a struggle. Meanwhile, Hamilton made his second stop on lap 31 and dropped behind Massa. The Brazilian was going well on the prime tyre and he was able to lead until he pitted on lap 43. Williams made an aggressive move by putting him on the supersoft, giving extra pace for the 12-lap sprint to the flag. Hamilton was ahead 10s up the road on his older primes.

By now, Rosberg was tumbling down the top 10 and it had become obvious that he wouldn't be able to achieve the fifth place he required. That allowed Hamilton to focus on trying to win, as it no longer mattered if he retired – indeed the pit told him: "Nico isn't a threat any more, we can fight this."

It then looked as though we were in for a grandstand finish. While Massa tried hard, Hamilton had just enough pace in reserve. He crossed the line with 2.5s to spare to secure the title in the best way possible. It was clear to see what it meant to him as he alighted from the car and celebrated with his girlfriend, family and friends, but

"ROSBERG RAN WIDE AND LOST 1.2s, BUT THAT WAS JUST THE TIP OF THE ICEBERG"

what was really telling was the TV image of the moments that he spent alone, gathering his thoughts, prior to the podium ceremony.

"Going into the race, I had a couple of different options of how to approach it," he said. "If I was behind, then we'd see how it goes until the first stop. But, if I was ahead, I knew that I had to really race all the way. The car was fantastic. We really got it spot-on for the race. Qualifying wasn't perfect, but we got it ready for the race and that is what's most important."

Rosberg crossed the line 14th after politely refusing a request from the team to park the car in the closing laps. He made the effort to go to the podium backstage area and congratulate Hamilton even

before he got his trophy. It was a sporting gesture.

Second was a great end to the season for Massa, coming on the heels of his third in Brazil, while Bottas added to his podiums with a good run to third. Having started from the pit lane, Ricciardo managed to charge his way to fourth after his strategy of running the prime tyre for a long opening stint paid off. It was telling that, despite following the same strategy, Vettel couldn't pass so successfully and ended up four places and 35s behind his teammate.

Button did his usual solid job to claim fifth after showing feisty form while battling with Alonso. Force India's strategy of starting on the prime worked well as Hülkenberg and Pérez took sixth and seventh, the German having taken a 5s penalty after an incident with Magnussen. Behind Vettel, Alonso and Räikkönen finished ninth and 10th as Ferrari's season, and the Spaniard's career at Maranello, ended on a low note. It was unusual to see three World Champions floundering at the bottom of the top 10, but for two of them at least, a new challenge awaited.

> "IT WAS UNUSUAL TO SEE THREE WORLD CHAMPIONS FLOUNDERING AT THE BOTTOM OF THE TOP 10"

SNAPSHOT FROM ABU DHABI

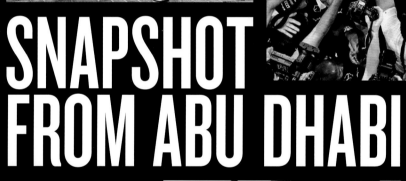

CLOCKWISE FROM ABOVE: Nico Rosberg and wife Vivian arrive at the circuit; Prince Harry enjoyed his visit to the race; Hamilton is carried aloft into the media frenzy; Bernie Ecclestone offers Hamilton a word of encouragement; singer Pharrell Williams was one of many people wishing Hamilton luck before the race; Felipe Massa seems pensive before the start of the race; the fans got their message across; Toto Wolff with Mercedes boss Dieter Zetsche

ABU DHABI
YAS MARINA
ROUND 19

RACE DATE 23 November

CIRCUIT LENGTH 3.451 miles

NO. OF LAPS 55

RACE DISTANCE 189.805 miles

WEATHER Warm and dry, 26ºC

TRACK TEMP 33ºC

LAP RECORD Sebastian Vettel, 1m40.279s, 131.387mph, 2009

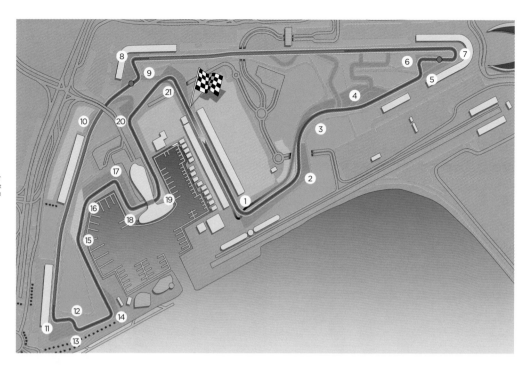

PRACTICE 1

	Driver	Time	Laps
1	L Hamilton	1m43.476s	32
2	N Rosberg	1m43.609s	31
3	F Alonso	1m45.184s	22
4	S Vettel	1m45.334s	30
5	D Ricciardo	1m45.361s	23
6	J-É Vergne	1m45.718s	17
7	D Kvyat	1m45.835s	32
8	V Bottas	1m45.913s	8
9	S Pérez	1m45.983s	23
10	N Hülkenberg	1m46.030s	24
11	K Magnussen	1m46.049s	23
12	K Räikkönen	1m46.131s	23
13	F Massa	1m46.549s	7
14	E Gutiérrez	1m46.556s	28
15	P Maldonado	1m46.711s	31
16	E Ocon	1m47.066s	29
17	J Button	1m47.235s	8
18	K Kobayashi	1m47.971s	24
19	A Fong	1m48.269s	25
20	W Stevens	1m50.684s	14

PRACTICE 2

	Driver	Time	Laps
1	L Hamilton	1m42.113s	35
2	N Rosberg	1m42.196s	37
3	K Magnussen	1m42.895s	37
4	S Vettel	1m42.959s	33
5	V Bottas	1m43.070s	34
6	D Ricciardo	1m43.183s	32
7	K Räikkönen	1m43.489s	33
8	J Button	1m43.503s	23
9	D Kvyat	1m43.546s	38
10	F Massa	1m43.558s	34
11	S Pérez	1m43.746s	37
12	P Maldonado	1m44.005s	38
13	N Hülkenberg	1m44.068s	32
14	J-É Vergne	1m44.157s	39
15	E Gutiérrez	1m44.316s	38
16	A Sutil	1m44.763s	37
17	R Grosjean	1m44.986s	35
18	K Kobayashi	1m45.505s	38
19	W Stevens	1m47.057s	34
20	F Alonso	no time	2

PRACTICE 3

	Driver	Time	Laps
1	N Rosberg	1m41.424s	19
2	L Hamilton	1m41.793s	17
3	F Massa	1m42.429s	18
4	F Alonso	1m42.653s	8
5	S Vettel	1m42.679s	19
6	J Button	1m42.768s	20
7	D Ricciardo	1m42.773s	14
8	V Bottas	1m42.794s	19
9	D Kvyat	1m42.809s	20
10	K Räikkönen	1m43.038s	14
11	K Magnussen	1m43.112s	13
12	J-É Vergne	1m43.352s	20
13	S Pérez	1m43.360s	19
14	N Hülkenberg	1m43.501s	18
15	E Gutiérrez	1m43.643s	24
16	P Maldonado	1m43.718s	17
17	R Grosjean	1m43.788s	18
18	A Sutil	1m44.022s	22
19	K Kobayashi	1m45.044s	16
20	W Stevens	1m45.959s	21

QUALIFYING 1

	Driver	Time
1	L Hamilton	1m41.207s
2	N Rosberg	1m41.308s
3	F Massa	1m41.475s
4	K Magnussen	1m42.104s
5	J Button	1m42.137s
6	D Ricciardo	1m42.204s
7	D Kvyat	1m42.302s
8	V Bottas	1m42.346s
9	J-É Vergne	1m42.413s
10	K Räikkönen	1m42.439s
11	N Hülkenberg	1m42.444s
12	F Alonso	1m42.467s
13	S Vettel	1m42.495s
14	S Pérez	1m42.654s
15	A Sutil	1m42.746s
16	R Grosjean	1m42.768s
17	E Gutiérrez	1m42.819s
18	P Maldonado	1m42.860s
19	K Kobayashi	1m44.540s
20	W Stevens	1m45.095s

QUALIFYING 2

	Driver	Time
1	L Hamilton	1m40.920s
2	F Massa	1m41.144s
3	V Bottas	1m41.376s
4	N Rosberg	1m41.459s
5	D Ricciardo	1m41.692s
6	J Button	1m41.875s
7	F Alonso	1m41.940s
8	D Kvyat	1m42.082s
9	S Vettel	1m42.147s
10	K Räikkönen	1m42.168s
11	K Magnussen	1m42.198s
12	J-É Vergne	1m42.207s
13	S Pérez	1m42.239s
14	N Hülkenberg	1m42.384s
15	A Sutil	1m43.074s

Best sectors – Practice

Sec 1	L Hamilton	17.649s
Sec 2	N Rosberg	42.530s
Sec 3	N Rosberg	40.994s

Speed trap – Practice

1	J Button	208.842mph
2	L Hamilton	208.221mph
3	N Rosberg	207.351mph

Best sectors – Qualifying

Sec 1	V Bottas	17.562s
Sec 2	N Rosberg	42.000s
Sec 3	N Rosberg	40.856s

Speed trap – Qualifying

1	V Bottas	212.384mph
2	F Massa	211.328mph
3	J Button	208.718mph

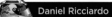

Sebastian Vettel

"I felt there was more, but once I got stuck behind Kevin it was quite tough, so I can't be completely happy with today as I think that we had the pace to finish higher up."

Nico Rosberg

"It was disappointing for me when the car developed its problem, losing its ERS, as I really wanted to give it a fight to the very last lap. But it was taken from me."

Fernando Alonso

"My time with Ferrari comes to an end, as does a very tricky season. Even if we were unable to do much against the technical dominance of our rivals, we fought all the way to the end."

Pastor Maldonado

"Our race pace was pretty good and I was able to fight the Ferraris. Unfortunately, my race had to end early. The flames showed the engine wasn't working too well."

Jenson Button

"We made the best of what we had. We did the right thing with strategy, but never had enough pace to attack the cars in front. So, fifth was as good as it was going to be."

Sergio Pérez

"I think I could've been even higher up, but we came in too late for the final stop. If we'd been on the supersofts earlier, maybe we could've been closer to Button."

Daniel Ricciardo

"It was pretty much a faultless race. I had fun passing, so it was pretty much what I asked for. One spot better would have been nice, but fourth is really cool from the pit lane."

Lewis Hamilton

"It was probably the best start I ever had. I knew that if I was in front, I had to really, really race, but the car was fantastic and we got it spot-on for the race."

Kimi Räikkönen

"We knew from the start that this track would be tough. The start was good but then, at the first stop, I already lost a few places and from then on I couldn't advance."

Romain Grosjean

"My race wasn't that eventful, so I think that we're all glad that the season is over. We thought about doing a three-stop strategy early on, but swapped back to two stops."

Kevin Magnussen

"I had contact with Adrian on the first lap and, after that, the front of the car never felt right. Once I'd pitted and changed to the Option tyre, though, the race slipped away from us."

Nico Hülkenberg

"I'm very happy with this result. After struggling with the car on Friday and in qualifying, we can be proud of this race and our performance is a good sign for next year."

POSITIONS LAP BY LAP

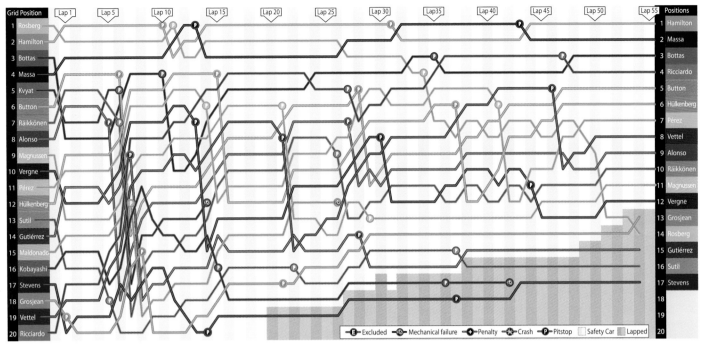

Grid Position		Lap 1	Lap 5	Lap 10	Lap 15	Lap 20	Lap 25	Lap 30	Lap 35	Lap 40	Lap 45	Lap 50	Lap 55	Positions	
1	Rosberg													1	Hamilton
2	Hamilton													2	Massa
3	Bottas													3	Bottas
4	Massa													4	Ricciardo
5	Kvyat													5	Button
6	Button													6	Hülkenberg
7	Räikkönen													7	Pérez
8	Alonso													8	Vettel
9	Magnussen													9	Alonso
10	Vergne													10	Räikkönen
11	Pérez													11	Magnussen
12	Hülkenberg													12	Vergne
13	Sutil													13	Grosjean
14	Gutiérrez													14	Rosberg
15	Maldonado													15	Gutiérrez
16	Kobayashi													16	Sutil
17	Stevens													17	Stevens
18	Grosjean													18	
19	Vettel													19	
20	Ricciardo													20	

-E- Excluded **-S-** Mechanical failure **-+-** Penalty **-K-** Crash **-P-** Pitstop ▢ Safety Car ▨ Lapped

QUALIFYING 3

	Driver	Time
1	N Rosberg	1m40.480s
2	L Hamilton	1m40.866s
3	V Bottas	1m41.025s
4	F Massa	1m41.119s
5	D Ricciardo	1m41.267s
6	S Vettel	1m41.893s
7	D Kvyat	1m41.908s
8	J Button	1m41.964s
9	K Räikkönen	1m42.236s
10	F Alonso	1m42.866s

GRID

	Driver	Time
1	N Rosberg	1m40.480s
2	L Hamilton	1m40.866s
3	V Bottas	1m41.025s
4	F Massa	1m41.119s
5	D Kvyat	1m41.908s
6	J Button	1m41.964s
7	K Räikkönen	1m42.236s
8	F Alonso	1m42.866s
9	K Magnussen	1m42.198s
10	J-É Vergne	1m42.207s
11	S Pérez	1m42.239s
12	N Hülkenberg	1m42.384s
13	A Sutil	1m43.074s
14	E Gutiérrez	1m42.819s
15	P Maldonado	1m42.860s
16	K Kobayashi	1m44.540s
17	W Stevens	1m45.095s
18	R Grosjean	1m42.768s
19	S Vettel	-
20	D Ricciardo	-

RACE

	Driver	Car	Laps	Time	Ave. mph	Fastest	Stops
1	L Hamilton	Mercedes F1 W05	55	1h39m02.619s	114.942	1m45.599s	2
2	F Massa	Williams-Mercedes FW36	55	1h39m05.195s	114.892	1m44.826s	2
3	V Bottas	Williams-Mercedes FW36	55	1h39m31.499s	114.386	1m45.727s	2
4	D Ricciardo	Red Bull-Renault RB10	55	1h39m39.856s	114.226	1m44.496s	2
5	J Button	McLaren-Mercedes MP4-29	55	1h40m02.953s	113.787	1m46.739s	2
6	N Hülkenberg	Force India-Mercedes VJM07	55	1h40m04.767s	113.752	1m45.777s	2
7	S Pérez	Force India-Mercedes VJM07	55	1h40m13.679s	113.584	1m45.808s	2
8	S Vettel	Red Bull-Renault RB10	55	1h40m14.664s	113.565	1m45.552s	2
9	F Alonso	Ferrari F14 T	55	1h40m28.432s	113.306	1m47.424s	2
10	K Räikkönen	Ferrari F14 T	55	1h40m30.439s	113.268	1m47.736s	2
11	K Magnussen	McLaren-Mercedes MP4-29	55	1h40m32.995s	113.220	1m46.824s	2
12	J-É Vergne	Toro Rosso-Renault STR9	55	1h40m34.566s	113.191	1m45.686s	3
13	R Grosjean	Lotus-Renault E22	54	1h39m12.427s	112.666	1m47.897s	3
14	N Rosberg	Mercedes F1 W05	54	1h39m14.344s	112.629	1m46.869s	2
15	E Gutiérrez	Sauber-Ferrari C33	54	1h39m15.948s	112.599	1m47.698s	2
16	A Sutil	Sauber-Ferrari C33	54	1h39m32.663s	112.283	1m47.508s	3
17	W Stevens	Caterham-Renault CT05	54	1h40m49.632s	110.855	1m48.398s	2
R	K Kobayashi	Caterham-Renault CT05	42	Vibration	-	1m47.431s	2
R	P Maldonado	Lotus-Renault E22	26	Engine	-	1m48.933s	1
R	D Kvyat	Toro Rosso-Renault STR9	14	Engine	-	1m48.748s	1

CHAMPIONSHIP

	Driver	Pts
1	L Hamilton	384
2	N Rosberg	317
3	D Ricciardo	238
4	V Bottas	186
5	S Vettel	167
6	F Alonso	161
7	F Massa	134
8	J Button	126
9	N Hülkenberg	96
10	S Pérez	59
11	K Magnussen	55
12	K Räikkönen	55
13	J-É Vergne	22
14	R Grosjean	8
15	D Kvyat	8
16	P Maldonado	2
17	J Bianchi	2

Grid penalties

R Grosjean	20-place grid penalty for using a sixth power unit
S Vettel	Excluded for excess front-wing deflection
D Ricciardo	Excluded for excess front-wing deflection

Fastest lap
D Ricciardo 1m44.496s
(118.894mph) on lap 50

Fastest speed trap
V Bottas 209.837mph

Slowest speed trap
K Räikkönen 193.370mph

Fastest pit stop
1	K Räikkönen	21.546s
2	R Grosjean	21.574s
3	D Ricciardo	21.582s

CONSTRUCTORS

	Team	Pts
1	Mercedes	701
2	Red Bull-Renault	405
3	Williams-Mercedes	320
4	Ferrari	216
5	McLaren-Mercedes	181
6	Force India-Mercedes	155
7	Toro Rosso-Renault	30
8	Lotus-Renault	10
9	Marussia-Ferrari	2

Esteban Gutiérrez
"We managed to keep our planned two-stop-strategy, but on my last stint I had to drive as many laps as possible on this set of tyres, which worked out for us."

Jean-Éric Vergne
"Today, I gave my maximum to catch the ones in front, but the pace just wasn't good enough. It's a shame as our starting position made us think we could have finished in the top 10."

Felipe Massa
"I didn't think the win was there, but it was so close. It was good to be pushing Mercedes. I hope this is a strong building block to go on for next year. The team has progressed so much."

Will Stevens

"I completed my objective, to finish. I struggled on the Options, getting graining on the front. But the middle stint wasn't bad and I got into a rhythm. It's great to have finished my first F1 race!"

Adrian Sutil
"On lap 1, Kevin drove into me and I lost many places. I can't say if my car was damaged. After this, I tried to get back into the race, but had to switch to a three-stop strategy."

Daniil Kvyat
"This is one of those races in which we just weren't able to show our full potential. We were expecting a much better final race, but an engine-related problem forced me to retire."

Valtteri Bottas
"We were very competitive. I got a bad start and the race was compromised after I was stuck behind a few cars, so to walk away with a podium is incredible. It was a good race; I could really push."

Kamui Kobayashi
"It's a real shame to finish 2014 with a retirement, but I started to feel a strange vibration and a couple of laps later it began to be undriveable, so the team decided to retire the car as a precaution."

2014 CHAMPIO

DRIVER RESULTS

	Driver	Nationality	Car	Round 1 AUS	Round 2 MAL	Round 3 BAH	Round 4 CHI	Round 5 SPN	Round 6 MON	Round 7 CAN
1	L Hamilton	British	Mercedes F1 W05	RF	1PF	1	1P	1P	2	R
2	N Rosberg	German	Mercedes F1 W05	1F	2	2PF	2F	2	1P	2P
3	D Ricciardo	Australian	Red Bull-Renault RB10	D2	R	4	4	3	3	1
4	V Bottas	Finnish	Williams-Mercedes FW36	5	8	8	7	5	R	7
5	S Vettel	German	Red Bull-Renault RB10	R	3	6	5	4F	R	3
6	F Alonso	Spanish	Ferrari F14 T	4	4	9	3	6	4	6
7	F Massa	Brazilian	Williams-Mercedes FW36	R	7	7	15	13	7	12F
8	J Button	British	McLaren-Mercedes MP4-29	3	6	17	11	11	6	4
9	N Hülkenberg	German	Force India-Mercedes VJM07	6	5	5	6	10	5	5
10	S Pérez	Mexican	Force India-Mercedes VJM07	10	NS	3	9	9	R	11
11	K Magnussen	Danish	McLaren-Mercedes MP4-29	2	9	R	13	12	10	9
12	K Räikkönen	Finnish	Ferrari F14 T	7	12	10	8	7	12F	10
13	J-É Vergne	French	Toro Rosso-Renault STR9	8	R	R	12	R	R	8
14	R Grosjean	French	Lotus-Renault E22	R	11	12	R	8	8	R
15	D Kvyat	Russian	Toro Rosso-Renault STR9	9	10	11	10	14	R	R
16	P Maldonado	Venezuelan	Lotus-Renault E22	R	R	14	14	15	R	R
17	J Bianchi	French	Marussia-Ferrari MR03	R	R	16	17	18	9	R
18	A Sutil	German	Sauber-Ferrari C33	11	R	R	R	17	R	13
19	M Ericsson	Swedish	Caterham-Renault CT05	R	14	R	20	20	11	R
20	E Gutiérrez	Mexican	Sauber-Ferrari C33	12	R	R	16	16	R	14
21	M Chilton	British	Marussia-Ferrari MR03	13	15	13	19	19	14	R
22	K Kobayashi	Japanese	Caterham-Renault CT05	R	13	15	18	R	13	R
23	W Stevens	British	Caterham-Renault CT05	-	-	-	-	-	-	-
24	A Lotterer	German	Caterham-Renault CT05	-	-	-	-	-	-	-

CONSTRUCTOR RESULTS

1	Mercedes	1/R	1/2	1/2	1/2	1/2	1/2	2/R
2	Red Bull-Renault	D/R	3/R	4/6	4/5	3/4	3/R	1/3
3	Williams-Mercedes	5/R	7/8	7/8	7/15	5/13	7/R	7/12
4	Ferrari	4/7	4/12	9/10	3/8	6/7	4/12	6/10
5	McLaren-Mercedes	2/3	6/9	17/R	11/13	11/12	6/10	4/9
6	Force India-Mercedes	6/10	5/NS	3/5	6/9	9/10	5/R	5/11
7	Toro Rosso-Renault	8/9	10/R	11/R	10/12	14/R	R/R	8/R
8	Lotus-Renault	R/R	11/R	12/14	14/R	8/15	8/R	R/R
9	Marussia-Ferrari	13/R	15/R	13/16	17/19	18/19	9/14	R/R
10	Sauber-Ferrari	11/12	R/R	R/R	16/R	16/17	R/R	13/14
11	Caterham-Renault	R/R	13/14	15/R	18/20	20/R	11/13	R/R

RACE SCORING | **1ST=25**PTS **2ND=18**PTS **3RD=15**PTS **4TH=12**PTS **5TH=10**PTS **6TH=8**PTS **7TH=6**PTS **8TH=4**PTS **9TH=2**PTS **10TH=1**PTS · DOUBLE AT FINAL ROUND

SHIP RESULTS

Round 9 GB	Round 10 GER	Round 11 HUN	Round 12 BEL	Round 13 ITA	Round 14 SNG	Round 15 JAP	Round 16 RUS	Round 17 USA	Round 18 BRA	Round 19 ABU*	TOTAL
1F	3F	3	R	1PF	1PF	1F	1P	1	2F	1	384
RP	1P	4PF	2PF	2	R	2P	2	2P	1P	14P	317
3	6	1	1	5	3	4	7	3	R	4F	238
2	2	8	3	4	11	6	3F	5	10	3	186
5	4	7	5	6	2	3	8	7F	5	8	167
6	5	2	7	R	4	R	6	6	6	9	161
R	R	5	13	3	5	7	11	4	3	2	134
4	8	10	6	8	R	5	4	12	4	5v	126
8	7	R	10	12	9	8	12	R	8	6	96
11	10	R	8	7	7	10	10	R	15	7	59
7	9	12	12	10	10	14	5	8	9	11	55
R	11	6	4	9	8	12	9	13	7	10	55
10	13	9	11	13	6	9	13	10	13	12	22
12	R	R	R	16	13	15	17	11	17	13	8
9	R	14	9	11	14	11	14	15	11	R	8
17	12	13	R	14	12	16	18	9	12	R	2
14	15	15	18	18	16	20	-	-	-	-	2
13	R	11	14	15	R	21	16	R	16	16	0
R	18	R	17	20	15	17	19	-	-	-	0
R	14	R	15	19	R	13	15	14	14	15	0
16	17	16	16	R	17	18	R	-	-	-	0
15	16	R	-	17	R	19	R	-	-	R	0
-	-	-	-	-	-	-	-	-	-	17	0
-	-	-	R	-	-	-	-	-	-	-	0
1/R	1/3	3/4	2/R	1/2	1/R	1/2	1/2	1/2	1/2	1/14	701
3/5	4/6	1/7	1/5	5/6	2/3	3/4	7/8	3/7	5/R	4/8	405
2/R	2/R	5/8	3/13	3/4	5/11	6/7	3/11	4/5	3/10	2/3	320
6/R	5/11	2/6	4/7	9/R	4/8	12/R	6/9	6/13	6/7	9/10	216
4/7	8/9	10/12	6/12	8/10	10/R	5/14	4/5	8/12	4/9	5/11	181
8/11	7/10	R/R	8/10	7/12	7/9	8/10	10/12	R/R	8/15	6/7	155
9/10	13/R	9/14	9/11	11/13	6/14	9/11	13/14	10/15	11/13	12/R	30
12/17	12/R	13/R	R/R	14/16	12/13	15/16	17/18	9/11	12/17	13/R	10
14/16	15/17	15/16	16/18	18/R	16/17	18/20	R/-	-/-	-/-	-/-	2
13/R	14/R	11/R	14/15	15/19	R/R	13/21	15/16	14/R	14/16	15/16	0
15/R	16/18	R/R	17/R	17/20	15/R	17/19	19/R	-/-	-/-	17/R	0

DATA KEY | D DISQUALIFIED **F** FASTEST LAP **NC** NON-CLASSIFIED **NS** NON-STARTER **NQ** NON-QUALIFIER **P** POLE POSITION **R** RETIRED **W** WITHDRAWN

2014 FASTEST SPEED TRAPS

	Track	Driver	Speed
1	Monza	Daniel Ricciardo	224.998mph
2	Montreal	Felipe Massa	215.678mph
3	Hockenheim	Lewis Hamilton	214.497mph
4	Barcelona	Felipe Massa	212.695mph
5	Yas Marina	Valtteri Bottas	209.837mph
6	Circuit of the Americas	Sebastian Vettel	209.402mph
7	Shanghai	Nico Rosberg	209.277mph
8	Sakhir	Felipe Massa	208.594mph
9	Interlagos	Daniil Kvyat	207.786mph
10	Silverstone	Valtteri Bottas	204.741mph
11	Sochi	Daniel Ricciardo	203.996mph
12	Sepang	Felipe Massa	201.635mph
13	Red Bull Ring	Felipe Massa	199.708mph
14	Melbourne	Kevin Magnussen	196.912mph
15	Hungaroring	Valtteri Bottas	196.104mph
16	Spa-Francorchamps	Nico Rosberg	195.172mph
17	Marina Bay	Felipe Massa	190.263mph
18	Monaco	Lewis Hamilton	180.197mph
19	Suzuka	Nico Rosberg	170.007mph

2014 HEAD TO HEA

	Contructors	No 1 Drive
1	Red Bull-Renault	Sebastian Vet
2	Mercedes	Nico Rosberg
3	Ferrari	Fernando Alc
4	Lotus-Renault	Romain Grosj
5	McLaren-Mercedes	Jenson Butto
6	Force India-Mercedes	Sergio Pérez
7	Sauber-Ferrari	Esteban Gutié
8	Toro Rosso-Renault	Jean-Éric Ver
9	Williams-Mercedes	Felipe Massa
10	Marussia-Ferrari	Jules Bianchi
11	Caterham-Renault	Marcus Ericss

F1 HISTORY: MOST STARTS

	Driver	Starts	Date		Driver	Starts	Years		Contructors	Starts	Years
1	Rubens Barrichello	325	1993-2011	21	Graham Hill	176	1958-1975	1	Ferrari	889	1950-2014
2	Michael Schumacher	308	1991-2012	22	Jacques Laffite	175	1974-1986	2	McLaren	762	1966-2014
3	Jenson Button	266	2000-2014	23	Niki Lauda	171	1971-1985	3	Williams	681	1972-2014
4	Riccardo Patrese	256	1977-1993	24	Nico Rosberg	166	2006-2014	4	Lotus	492	1958-1994
	Jarno Trulli	256	1997-2011	25	Jacques Villeneuve	165	1996-2006	5	Tyrrell	418	1970-1998
6	David Coulthard	247	1994-2008	26	Thierry Boutsen	163	1983-1993	6	Brabham	394	1962-1992
7	Fernando Alonso	236	2001-2014	27	Mika Häkkinen	162	1991-2001	7	Arrows	383	1978-2002
8	Giancarlo Fisichella	230	1996-2009		Johnny Herbert	162	1989-2000		Sauber	383	1993-2014
9	Mark Webber	216	2002-2013	29	Ayrton Senna	161	1984-1994	9	Minardi	341	1985-2005
10	Kimi Räikkönen	213	2001-2014	30	Heinz-Harald Frentzen	159	1994-2003	10	Ligier	326	1976-1996
11	Felipe Massa	211	2002-2014	31	Martin Brundle	158	1984-1996	11	Benetton	260	1986-2001
12	Gerhard Berger	210	1984-1997		Olivier Panis	158	1994-2005	12	Jordan	250	1991-2004
13	Andrea de Cesaris	208	1980-1994	33	John Watson	152	1973-1985	13	March	230	1970-1992
14	Nelson Piquet	204	1978-1991	34	René Arnoux	149	1978-1989	14	BRM	197	1951-1977
15	Jean Alesi	201	1989-2001	35	Lewis Hamilton	148	2007-2014	15	Red Bull	184	2005-2014
16	Alain Prost	199	1980-1993	36	Eddie Irvine	147	1993-2002	16	Renault*	177	2002-2011
17	Michele Alboreto	194	1981-1994		Derek Warwick	147	1981-1993	17	Toro Rosso	166	2006-2014
18	Nigel Mansell	187	1980-1995	38	Carlos Reutemann	146	1972-1982	18	Toyota	139	2008-2014
19	Nick Heidfeld	185	2000-2011	39	Emerson Fittipaldi	144	1970-1980	19	Osella	132	1980-1990
20	Ralf Schumacher	180	1997-2007	40	Sebastian Vettel	139	2007-2014	20	Force India	131	2008-2014

The Lotus stats are for the original Lotus team that ran from 1958-1994, whereas those listed as Lotus are for the third team to use the Lotus name, taking it over in 2012 from the team that became Caterham. This team based at Enstone started life as Toleman in 1981 before becoming Benetton and later being the second coming of Renault. All of their stats are listed separately, with this latter-day Renault outfit that ran from 2002 to 2011 listed as Renault* to differentiate it from the original Renault team that ran from 1977-1985. Likewise, Mercedes GP's stats are separate from those of the teams that begat it, namely BAR, Honda Racing and Brawn GP. Thus Red Bull Racing's stats are kept apart from those of i progenitors Stewart GP and Jaguar Racing, while Force India's are listed alongside those of the teams that led to its formation – Jordan, Midland and Spyker – and Scuderia Toro Rosso's those of Minardi from which it was formed in 2006.

QUALIFYING/RACES

2 Driver	Qualifying	Races
el Ricciardo	7-12	6-13
s Hamilton	12-7	7-12
Räikkönen	16-3	16-3
or Maldonado	15-4	8-8
n Magnussen	10-9	15-4
Hülkenberg	7-12	7-10
an Sutil	9-10	8-7
l Kvyat	7-12	9-8
eri Bottas	6-13	9-10
Chilton	12-3	9-5
ayashi/Lotterer	4-12	6-7

2014 LAPS COVERED

	Driver	Team	Laps
1	Jenson Button	McLaren	1118
2	Kevin Magnussen	McLaren	1111
3	Valtteri Bottas	Williams	1110
4	Daniel Ricciardo	Red Bull	1095
5	Kimi Räikkönen	Ferrari	1076
6	Fernando Alonso	Ferrari	1067
7	Nico Rosberg	Mercedes	1062
8	Lewis Hamilton	Mercedes	1049
9	Nico Hülkenberg	Force India	1036
10	Jean-Éric Vergne	Toro Rosso	971
11	Sebastian Vettel	Red Bull	970
12	Felipe Massa	Williams	954
13	Romain Grosjean	Lotus	953
14	Esteban Gutiérrez	Sauber	933
15	Daniil Kvyat	Toro Rosso	924
16	Sergio Pérez	Force India	887
17	Adrian Sutil	Sauber	867
18	Pastor Maldonado	Lotus	847
19	Max Chilton	Marussia	769
20	Jules Bianchi	Marussia	754

MOST USED CIRCUITS

Track	No.	Country
Monza	64	Italy
Monaco	61	Monaco
Silverstone	48	Great Britain
Spa-Francorchamps	47	Belgium
Nürburgring	40	Germany
Montreal	35	Canada
Hockenheim	34	Germany
Interlagos	32	Brazil
Zandvoort	30	Holland
Hungaroring	29	Hungary

MOST CIRCUIT WINS

Track	No.	Team
Monza	18	Ferrari
Monaco	15	McLaren
Nürburgring	14	Ferrari
Silverstone	13	Ferrari
Spa-Francorchamps	12	Ferrari
Silverstone	12	McLaren
Hockenheim	11	Ferrari
Hungaroring	11	McLaren

F1 HISTORY: MOST WINS IN A SEASON

	Driver	Wins	Year		Contructor	Wins	Year
1	Michael Schumacher	13	2004	1	Mercedes GP	16	2014
	Sebastian Vettel	13	2013	2	Ferrari	15	2002
3	Michael Schumacher	11	2002		Ferrari	15	2004
	Sebastian Vettel	11	2011		McLaren	15	1998
	Lewis Hamilton	11	2014	5	Red Bull	13	2013
6	Nigel Mansell	9	1992	6	McLaren	12	1984
	Michael Schumacher	9	1995		Red Bull	12	2011
	Michael Schumacher	9	2000		Williams	12	1996
	Michael Schumacher	9	2001	9	Benetton	11	1995
10	Mika Häkkinen	8	1998	10	Ferrari	10	2000
	Damon Hill	8	1996		McLaren	10	1989
	Michael Schumacher	8	1994		McLaren	10	2005
	Ayrton Senna	8	1988		Williams	10	1992
14	Fernando Alonso	7	2005		Williams	10	1993
	Fernando Alonso	7	2006	15	Ferrari	9	2001
	Jim Clark	7	1963		Ferrari	9	2006
	Alain Prost	7	1984		Ferrari	9	2007
	Alain Prost	7	1988		McLaren	9	1998
	Alain Prost	7	1993		Red Bull	9	2010
	Kimi Räikkönen	7	2005		Williams	9	1986
	Ayrton Senna	7	1991		Williams	9	1987
	Jacques Villeneuve	7	1997				

F1 HISTORY: MOST RACE WINS

	Driver	Wins	Years	Teams		Constructors	Wins	Years
1	Michael Schumacher	91	1992-06	Benetton & Ferrari	1	Ferrari	221	1950-2013
2	Alain Prost	51	1981-1993	Renault, McLaren, Ferrari & Williams	2	McLaren	181	1968-2012
3	Ayrton Senna	41	1985-193	Lotus & McLaren	3	Williams	114	1979-2012
4	Sebastian Vettel	39	2007-13	Toro Rosso & Red Bull	4	Lotus	79	1960-1987
5	Lewis Hamilton	33	2007-14	McLaren & Mercedes GP	5	Red Bull	50	2008-2014
6	Fernando Alonso	32	2003-13	Renault, McLaren & Ferrari	6	Brabham	35	1964-1985
7	Nigel Mansell	31	1985-94	Williams & Ferrari	7	Benetton	27	1986-1997
8	Jackie Stewart	27	1965-73	BRM, Matra & Tyrrell	8	Tyrrell	23	1971-1983
9	Jim Clark	25	1962-68	Lotus	9	Mercedes GP	20	2012-2014
	Niki Lauda	25	1974-85	Ferrari, Brabham & McLaren		Renault*	20	2003-2008
11	Juan Manuel Fangio	24	1950-57	Alfa Romeo, Maserati, Mercedes & Ferrari	11	BRM	17	1959-1972
12	Nelson Piquet	23	1980-91	Brabham, Williams & Benetton	12	Cooper	16	1958-1967
13	Damon Hill	22	1993-98	Williams & Jordan	13	Renault	15	1979-1983
14	Mika Häkkinen	20	1997-01	McLaren	14	Alfa Romeo	10	1950-1951
	Kimi Räikkönen	20	2003-13	McLaren, Ferrari & Lotus*	15	Ligier	9	1977-1996
16	Stirling Moss	16	1955-61	Mercedes, Maserati, Vanwall & Rob Walker Racing		Maserati	9	1953-1957
17	Jenson Button	15	2006-12	Honda, Brawn & McLaren		Matra	9	1968-1969
18	Jack Brabham	14	1959-70	Cooper & Brabham		Mercedes	9	1954-1955
	Emerson Fittipaldi	14	1970-75	Lotus & McLaren		Vanwall	9	1955-1958
	Graham Hill	14	1962-69	BRM & Lotus	20	Brawn GP	8	2009
21	Alberto Ascari	13	1951-53	Ferrari	21	Jordan	4	1998-2003
	David Coulthard	13	1997-03	Williams & McLaren	22	March	3	1970-1976
23	Mario Andretti	12	1971-78	Ferrari & Lotus		Wolf	3	1977
	Alan Jones	12	1977-81	Shadow & Williams	24	Honda	2	1965-1967
	Carlos Reutemann	12	1974-81	Brabham, Ferrari & Williams		Lotus*	2	2012-2013
26	Rubens Barrichello	11	2000-09	Ferrari & Brawn	26	BMW Sauber	1	2008
	Felipe Massa	11	2006-08	Ferrari		Eagle	1	1962
	Jacques Villeneuve	11	1996-97	Williams		Hesketh	1	1975
29	Gerhard Berger	10	1986-97	Benetton, Ferrari & McLaren		Honda Racing	1	2006
	James Hunt	10	1975-77	Hesketh & McLaren		Penske	1	1976
	Ronnie Peterson	10	1973-78	Lotus & March		Porsche	1	1962
	Jody Scheckter	10	1974-79	Tyrrell, Wolf & Ferrari		Shadow	1	1977
33	Mark Webber	9	2008-12	Red Bull		Stewart	1	1999
34	Denny Hulme	8	1967-74	Brabham & McLaren		Toro Rosso	1	2007
	Jacky Ickx	8	1968-72	Ferrari & Brabham				
	Nico Rosberg	8	2012-14	Mercedes GP				

F1 HISTORY: MOST POLE POSITIONS

Driver	Poles	Years	Teams		Constructors	Poles	Years
Michael Schumacher	68	1994-06	Benetton & Ferrari	1	Ferrari	207	1951-2012
Ayrton Senna	65	1985-94	Lotus , McLaren & Williams	2	McLaren	154	1972-2012
Sebastian Vettel	45	2008-13	Toro Rosso & Red Bull	3	Williams	128	1979-2014
Lewis Hamilton	38	2007-14	McLaren & Mercedes GP	4	Lotus	107	1960-1987
Jim Clark	33	1962-68	Lotus	5	Red Bull	57	2009-2013
Alain Prost	33	1981-93	Renault, McLaren, Ferrari & Williams	6	Brabham	39	1964-1985
Nigel Mansell	32	1984-94	Lotus, Williams & Ferrari	7	Renault	31	1979-1984
Juan Manuel Fangio	29	1950-58	Alfa Romeo, Maserati, Mercedes & Ferrari	8	Mercedes GP	27	2012-2014
Mika Häkkinen	26	1997-00	McLaren	9	Renault*	18	2003-2009
Niki Lauda	24	1974-78	Ferrari & Brabham	10	Benetton	15	1986-1998
Nelson Piquet	24	1980-87	Brabham & Williams	11	Tyrrell	14	1970-1976
Fernando Alonso	22	2003-12	Renault, McLaren & Ferrari	12	Alfa Romeo	12	1950-1982
Damon Hill	20	1993-96	Williams	13	BRM	11	1959-1973
Mario Andretti	18	1968-82	Ferrari & Lotus		Cooper	11	1959-1966
René Arnoux	18	1979-83	Renault & Ferrari	15	Maserati	10	1953-1958
Jackie Stewart	17	1969-72	Matra & Tyrrell	16	Ligier	9	1976-1981
Felipe Massa	16	2006-14	Ferrari & Williams	17	Mercedes	8	1954-1955
Stirling Moss	16	1955-61	Mercedes, Maserati, Vanwall & Rob Walker Racing	18	Vanwall	7	1957-1958
Kimi Räikkönen	16	2003-08	McLaren & Ferrari	19	Brawn GP	5	2009
Nico Rosberg	15	2012-14	Mercedes GP		March	5	1970-1989

F1 HISTORY: MOST FASTEST LAPS

Driver	Fastest laps	Date	Teams		Constructors	Fastest laps	Years
Michael Schumacher	76	1992-12	Benetton, Ferrari & Mercedes GP	1	Ferrari	229	1952-2014
Alain Prost	41	1981-93	Renault, McLaren, Ferrari & Williams	2	McLaren	152	1970-2013
Kimi Räikkönen	40	2002-14	McLaren, Lotus & Ferrari	3	Williams	133	1978-2014
Nigel Mansell	30	1983-12	Lotus, Williams & Ferrari	4	Lotus	71	1960-1989
Jim Clark	28	1961-68	Lotus	5	Red Bull	43	2009-2014
Mika Häkkinen	25	1997-01	McLaren	6	Brabham	40	1963-1984
Niki Lauda	24	1974-85	Ferrari, Brabham & McLaren	7	Benetton	36	1986-1998
Sebastian Vettel	24	2009-14	Red Bull	8	Tyrrell	22	1971-1989
Juan Manuel Fangio	23	1950-85	Alfa Romeo, Maserati, Mercedes & Ferrari	9	Mercedes GP	21	2012-2014
Nelson Piquet	23	1979-87	Brabham & Williams	10	Renault	18	1979-1984
Fernando Alonso	21	2003-13	Renault, McLaren & Ferrari	11	BRM	15	1959-1972
Gerhard Berger	21	1986-97	Benetton, Ferrari & McLaren		Maserati	15	1952-1958
Lewis Hamilton	20	2007-14	McLaren & Mercedes GP	13	Alfa Romeo	14	1950-1983
Damon Hill	19	1993-96	Williams	14	Cooper	13	1959-1966
Stirling Moss	19	1954-61	Moss, Mercedes, Maserati, Vanwall & Rob Walker	15	Matra	12	1968-1972
Ayrton Senna	19	1984-93	Toleman, Lotus & McLaren		Renault*	12	2003-2010
Mark Webber	19	2009-13	Red Bull	17	Ligier	9	1977-1985
David Coulthard	18	1994-02	Williams & McLaren		Mercedes	9	1954-1955
Rubens Barrichello	17	2000-09	Ferrari & Brawn GP	19	March	7	1970-1989
Felipe Massa	15	2006-14	Ferrari & Williams	20	Vanwall	6	1957-1958
Clay Regazzoni	15	1970-79	Ferrari & Williams	21	Brawn GP	4	2009
Jackie Stewart	15	1968-73	Matra & Stewart				

F1 HISTORY: MOST POINTS

	Driver	Points	Years	Teams		Constructors	Pts	Years
1	Fernando Alonso	1767	2003-14	Renault, McLaren & Ferrari	1	Ferrari	5816.5	1958-2014
2	Sebastian Vettel	1618	2007-14	BMW Sauber, Toro Rosso & Red Bull	2	McLaren	4990.5	1966-2014
3	Michael Schumacher	1566	1991-12	Benetton, Ferrari & Mercedes GP	3	Williams	3081	1974-2014
4	Lewis Hamilton	1486	2007-14	McLaren & Mercedes GP	4	Red Bull	2865.5	2005-2014
5	Jenson Button	1198	2000-14	Williams, Benetton, Renault, BAR, Honda, Brawn & McLaren	5	Mercedes GP	1582	2010-
6	Mark Webber	1047.5	2002-13	Minardi, Jaguar, Williams & Red Bull	6	Lotus	1514	1958-1993
7	Kimi Räikkönen	1024	2001-14	Sauber, McLaren, Ferrari & Lotus*	7	Renault*	952	2002-2011
8	Felipe Massa	950	2002-14	Sauber, Ferrari & Williams	8	Benetton	861.5	1986-2001
9	Nico Rosberg	887.5	2006-14	Williams & Mercedes GP	9	Brabham	854	1962-1991
10	Alain Prost	798.5	1980-93	McLaren, Renault, Ferrari & Williams	10	Sauber	767	1993-2013
11	Rubens Barrichello	658	1993-11	Jordan, Stewart, Ferrari, Honda, Brawn & Williams	11	Lotus*	626	2012-2014
12	Ayrton Senna	614	1984-93	Toleman, Lotus & McLaren	12	Tyrrell	617	1971-1997
13	David Coulthard	535	1994-08	Williams, McLaren & Red Bull	13	Force India	491	2009-2014
14	Nelson Piquet	485.5	1979-91	Brabham, Williams, Lotus & Benetton	14	BRM	439	1958-1974
15	Nigel Mansell	482	1981-94	Lotus, Williams & Ferrari	15	Ligier	388	1976-1996
16	Niki Lauda	420.5	1973-85	BRM, Ferrari, Brabham & McLaren	16	Cooper	333	1958-1968
17	Mika Häkkinen	420	1991-01	Lotus & McLaren	17	Renault	312	1978-1985
18	Gerhard Berger	385	1985-97	Arrows, Benetton, Ferrari & McLaren	18	Jordan	291	1991-2004
19	Damon Hill	360	1993-99	Williams, Arrows & Jordan	19	Toyota	278.5	2002-2009
20	Jackie Stewart	360	1965-73	BRM, Matra & Tyrrell	20	BAR	227	1999-2005
21	Ralf Schumacher	329	1997-07	Jordan, Williams & Toyota	21	Toro Rosso	199	2006-2014
22	Carlos Reutemann	310	1972-82	Brabham, Ferrari, Lotus & Williams	22	Brawn GP	172	2009
23	Juan Pablo Montoya	307	2001-06	Williams & McLaren	23	March	171.5	1970-1992
24	Graham Hill	289	1960-74	BRM, Lotus, Rob Walker, Brabham & Embassy	24	Arrows	167	1978-2002
25	Emerson Fittipaldi	281	1970-80	Lotus, McLaren & Fittipaldi	25	Matra	155	1968-1972
	Riccardo Patrese	281	1977-93	Shadow, Arrows, Brabham, Alfa Romeo, Williams & Benetton	26	Honda Racing	106	2006-2008

F1 HISTORY: MOST CHAMPIONSHIPS

	Driver	Titles	Years		Constructors	Wins
1	Michael Schumacher	7	1994, '95, '00, '01, '02, '03, '04	1	Ferrari	16
2	Juan Manuel Fangio	5	1951, 1954, 1955, 1956, 1957	2	McLaren	9
3	Alain Prost	4	1985, 1986, 1989, 1993	3	Williams	8
	Sebastian Vettel	4	2010, 2011, 2012, 2013	4	Lotus	7
5	Jack Brabham	3	1959, 1960, 1966	5	Red Bull	4
	Niki Lauda	3	1975, 1977, 1984	6	Brabham	2
	Nelson Piquet	3	1981, '83, '87		Cooper	2
	Ayrton Senna	3	1988, '90, '91		Renault*	2
	Jackie Stewart	3	1969, '71, '73	9	Benetton	1
10	Fernando Alonso	2	2005, 2006		Brawn	1
	Alberto Ascari	2	1952, 1953		BRM	1
	Jim Clark	2	1963, 1965		Matra	1
	Emerson Fittipaldi	2	1972, 1974		Mercedes GP	1
	Mika Häkkinen	2	1998, 1999		Tyrrell	1
	Lewis Hamilton	2	2008, 2014		Vanwall	1
	Graham Hill	2	1962, 1968			

F1 HISTORY: RACES LED

Drivers	Races led		Constructors	Races led
Michael Schumacher	142	1	Ferrari	410
Ayrton Senna	86	2	McLaren	322
Fernando Alonso	84	3	Williams	223
Alain Prost	84	4	Lotus	150
Lewis Hamilton	67	5	Brabham	91
Sebastian Vettel	66	6	Red Bull	81
David Coulthard	62	7	Benetton	55
Kimi Räikkönen	62	8	Renault*	49
Nelson Piquet	58	9	BRM	40
Nigel Mansell	55	10	Tyrrell	38
Rubens Barrichello	51	11	Renault	36
Jackie Stewart	51	12	Mercedes GP	32
Mika Häkkinen	48	13	Cooper	23
Damon Hill	45		Matra	23
Jim Clark	43	15	Maserati	21
Jenson Button	42	16	Ligier	18
Niki Lauda	41	17	Alfa Romeo	16
Felipe Massa	41		March	16
Juan Manuel Fangio	38	19	Sauber	13
Gerhard Berger	32	20	Vanwall & Jordan	12

F1 HISTORY: LAPS LED

	Drivers	Laps led		Constructors	Laps led
1	Michael Schumacher	5111	1	Ferrari	13672
2	Ayrton Senna	2987	2	McLaren	10578
3	Alain Prost	2684	3	Williams	7568
4	Sebastian Vettel	2438	4	Lotus	5498
5	Nigel Mansell	2089	5	Red Bull	3068
6	Jim Clark	1943	6	Brabham	2717
7	Jackie Stewart	1921	7	Benetton	1544
8	Lewis Hamilton	1837	8	Tyrrell	1493
9	Fernando Alonso	1767	9	BRM	1347
10	Nelson Piquet	1600	10	Renault*	1329
11	Niki Lauda	1592	11	Renault	1183
12	Mika Häkkinen	1488	12	Mercedes GP	11545
13	Damon Hill	1358	13	Cooper	829
14	Juan Manuel Fangio	1348	14	Maserati	826
15	Stirling Moss	1181	15	Alfa Romeo	701
16	Kimi Räikkönen	1156	16	Matra	668
17	Graham Hill	1102	17	Mercedes	589
18	Alberto Ascari	926	18	Ligier	537
19	Felipe Massa	917	19	Brawn GP	405
20	David Coulthard	897	20	Vanwall	371

FASTEST LAP RECORDS

Track	Year	Speed
Monza	2004	159.909mph
Silverstone	1987	153.053mph
Spa-Francorchamps	1970	152.049mph
Österreichring	1987	150.509mph
Hockenheim	1992	150.059mph
Avus	1959	149.129mph
Suzuka	2005	141.904mph
Red Bull Ring	2003	141.606mph
Reims	1966	141.439mph
Melbourne	2004	141.009mph

RACES BEFORE TITLE

Driver	Races	Nationality
Nigel Mansell	180	British
Jenson Button	170	British
Kimi Räikkönen	121	Finnish
Mika Häkkinen	112	Finnish
Jody Scheckter	97	South African
Alain Prost	87	French
Mario Andretti	80	American
Alan Jones	80	Australian

MOST TYRE BRAND WINS

	Brand	Wins	Years
1	Goodyear	325	1965-1998
2	Bridgestone	175	1998-2010
3	Pirelli	121	1950-2014
4	Michelin	102	1978-2006
5	Dunlop	83	1958-1970
6	Firestone	38	1966-1972
7	Continental	10	1955-1958
8	Englebert	8	1952-1958

WINS WITHOUT TITLE

	Track	Wins	Nationality
1	Stirling Moss	16	British
2	David Coulthard	13	British
3	Carlos Reutemann	12	Argentinian
4	Rubens Barrichello	11	Brazilian
	Felipe Massa	11	Brazilian
6	Gerhard Berger	10	Austrian
	Ronnie Peterson	10	Swedish
8	Mark Webber	9	Australian
9	Jacky Ickx	8	Belgian
	Nico Rosberg	8	German

COUNTRIES' WINS

	Country	Wins
1	Great Britain	238
2	Germany	150
3	Brazil	101
4	France	79
5	Finland	46
6	Italy	43
7	Austria	41
8	Argentina	38

ONE-TWO FINISHES

	Constructors	1-2s
1	Ferrari	78
2	McLaren	47
3	Williams	32
4	Mercedes GP	18
5	Red Bull	15
6	Brabham	8
	Tyrrell	8
8	Lotus	7
9	BRM	5
	Mercedes	5

SEE YOU NEXT YEAR

FIRST RACE: 15 MARCH MELBOURNE